# CHRISTOLOGY OF THE
# LATER FATHERS

THE LIBRARY OF CHRISTIAN CLASSICS

ICHTHUS EDITION

# CHRISTOLOGY OF THE LATER FATHERS

*Edited by*

EDWARD ROCHIE HARDY, Ph.D.

Professor of Church History in the Berkeley Divinity School,
New Haven, Connecticut

*In collaboration with*

CYRIL C. RICHARDSON, Th.D., D.D.

Washburn Professor of Church History in the Union Theological Seminary,
New York

*PHILADELPHIA*
THE WESTMINSTER PRESS

Published simultaneously in Great Britain and the United States of America
by the S.C.M. Press, Ltd., London, and The Westminster Press, Philadelphia

*First published MCMLIV*

Library of Congress Catalog Card No.: 54-9949

9  8  7  6  5  4  3  2  1

*Printed in the United States of America*

# GENERAL EDITORS' PREFACE

The Christian Church possesses in its literature an abundant and incomparable treasure. But it is an inheritance that must be reclaimed by each generation. THE LIBRARY OF CHRISTIAN CLASSICS is designed to present in the English language, and in twenty-six volumes of convenient size, a selection of the most indispensable Christian treatises written prior to the end of the sixteenth century.

The practice of giving circulation to writings selected for superior worth or special interest was adopted at the beginning of Christian history. The canonical Scriptures were themselves a selection from a much wider literature. In the Patristic era there began to appear a class of works of compilation (often designed for ready reference in controversy) of the opinions of well-reputed predecessors, and in the Middle Ages many such works were produced. These medieval anthologies actually preserve some noteworthy materials from works otherwise lost.

In modern times, with the increasing inability even of those trained in universities and theological colleges to read Latin and Greek texts with ease and familiarity, the translation of selected portions of earlier Christian literature into modern languages has become more necessary than ever; while the wide range of distinguished books written in vernaculars such as English makes selection there also needful. The efforts that have been made to meet this need are too numerous to be noted here, but none of these collections serves the purpose of the reader who desires a library of representative treatises spanning the Christian centuries as a whole. Most of them embrace only the age of the Church Fathers, and some of them have iong been out of print. A fresh translation of a work already translated may shed much new light upon its meaning. This is true even of Bible translations despite the work of many experts through the centuries. In some instances old translations have been adopted in this series, but wherever necessary or desirable, new ones have been made. Notes have been supplied where these were needed to explain the author's meaning. The introductions provided for the several treatises and extracts will, we believe, furnish welcome guidance.

JOHN BAILLIE
JOHN T. McNEILL
HENRY P. VAN DUSEN

# CONTENTS

# PREFACE

The material included in this volume represents the formulation of historic Christian convictions on the Person of Christ in the period of the Ecumenical Councils. Major works are included by three authors who are important as well for their central position in the stream of tradition as for the significance of their own contributions. The Introduction and series of Documents will, it is hoped, be sufficient to indicate the questions which the ancient Church at large faced in this field, as it saw them, and the answers which it gave, in its own terms. For Athanasius, Gregory of Nazianzus, and Leo it has seemed best to reprint, with new notes and some slight corrections, careful translations of the last century. The works of Gregory of Nyssa, and most of the Documents, appear in new versions; the combination of reprints and new translation produces some variations in method, but this may in part correspond to the various influences (Biblical, learned, and popular) which give a certain variety to patristic Greek.

I am deeply indebted to Dr. Richardson for his contribution to this volume, and to the General Editors for their guidance and suggestions.

*Berkeley Divinity School.*  EDWARD ROCHIE HARDY.

# General Introduction:
## Faith in Christ, Theology and Creeds

### I

"GOD WAS IN CHRIST RECONCILING THE WORLD unto himself" (II Cor. 5:19). In these simple words Paul expressed the central Christian conviction which Christian theology ever since has labored to preserve, to defend, and as far as possible to understand. Ever since the fifth century we have been accustomed to consider that the central problem of Christology is how to maintain the true humanity of the Saviour without obscuring the affirmation that God was indeed acting in Christ. The first four Christian centuries faced rather a different problem in the intellectual definition of the faith— to assert the true deity of the God who acted in Christ without obscuring the ancient faith of Israel that "the Lord our God, the Lord is one" (Deut. 6:4, R. S. V., margin). By the end of the second century the possible alternative solutions had been explored. Holding firm to the unity of God, or, as that age would have said, to the divine monarchy, one might say that Father and Son are merely two appearances of the same subject—two parts (*prosōpa, personae,* as in *dramatis personae*) assumed by the same simple being. This is modalism, commonly known from the name of one of its conspicuous representatives as Sabellianism. Or one could adopt the opposite course and say that God the Father, and he only, is God in the true sense. Then the Word who was known on earth was another, a second and subordinate, divine entity—*theos kai kurios heteros*—as Justin Martyr[1] rather carelessly says, although that phrase would not mean for him quite what it does for us. Arius later formalized this subordinationism. But this is dangerously close to polytheism, and it might be safer to say that the

---

[1] Dialogue with Trypho, 56.

eternal Word is simply an attribute of God, or an aspect of his working, and that in these last days he spoke supremely through Jesus as he had in old times spoken through prophets and sages. This was the view that was attributed to Paul of Samosata, bishop of Antioch.

None of these positions was formally excluded by the Church's "rule of faith" as it existed in the third century, in various local forms of creeds taught to catechumens in preparation for their baptism in the threefold name. The Old Roman Symbol, known to us in a later form as the Apostles' Creed, is an excellent case in point. In the late second century converts at Rome were asked in the baptismal rite, "Do you believe in God the Father Almighty?" and "Do you believe in Christ Jesus, the Son of God . . .?"[2] By the end of the third century the second phrase probably read as we now know it, "his only Son our Lord," thus excluding any tendency to reduce Jesus to the rank of one among many. By general agreement the Church seems thus to have rejected the extreme positions that had been explored by some Christian teachers at Rome—modalism on the one hand, and the treatment of Jesus as a mere man on the other. But further definition there was none, nor in this Creed, still commonly used by the Churches of the West, is there to this day.

In the East, forms of Christian profession were likely to dwell somewhat more on God the Word as well as on Jesus the Son of God. So Origen tells us that the common rule of faith as he understood it included the confession that Jesus Christ was born of the Father before all creatures, and served God in the making of the world before he himself came into the world that he had made, becoming man while he yet remained divine. When formally expounding his own understanding of the doctrine he stays close to Biblical titles—the Word and Wisdom of God, and the image of his being (*hypostasis*, Heb. 1:3). But he introduces one principle, philosophical though not technical, which is of great importance in the later discussion. As God is eternal, so his Word and Wisdom is equally eternal, as also his Spirit—in other words, Son and Spirit belong on the divine side of the infinite division between deity and all that is not God. Equally Origen asserts that, as man, Christ was a real man, with no element lacking in his humanity that is necessary to man. But in him whom we know as both God and man, dying and returning victor over death,

[2] Hippolytus Apostolic Tradition, 21.

godhead and manhood coexist, like fire and metal in red-hot iron. Yet Origen sometimes seems to speak of Son and Spirit as coeternal, and yet not quite divine; he certainly accepts the suggestion that they might be the seraphim who cried, "Holy, holy, holy."[3]

The history of theology can be written in large part by the explanation of a series of technical terms, the understanding, misunderstanding, and final definition of which make up the development of doctrine. Such terms were already available for trinitarian and Christological thought in the time of Origen, and the third century use of them was to cause some confusion when some were, for more precise clarification, given different meanings in the fourth century. Behind appearances is the permanent being which underlies them—that which, as it were, stands under, *hypo-stasis*. The cognate Latin *substantia* was already in use in the West since the time of Tertullian for the essential being which is common to Father, Son, and Holy Ghost. The Greek term had the advantage of being a Biblical one, since the New Testament tells us that Christ is the image of the Father's *hypostasis* (Heb. 1:3). Greek also had a more abstract term for being or essence, *ousia*; if one wished to affirm the closest unity of Father and Son one could describe them as being of the same essence, *homoousios*. But this term had unfortunate associations in the Eastern Church. Origen's pupil, Dionysius of Alexandria, had rejected it as being non-Scriptural and as suggestive of Sabellianism, against which he was writing in A.D. 259–260. His namesake of Rome called him to task for this, and in further correspondence the Alexandrian admitted the propriety of the term, in the sense that the divine Father and Son are, like any father and son, of the same essence, though he still didn't like it. But a few years afterwards the leaders of the Eastern Church generally took part in the condemnation of Paul of Samosata, who was supposed to have used *homoousios* to express his idea of the eternal Word which is merely one form of divine action. In this sense the Councils of Antioch which condemned Paul seem also to have branded *homoousios* as a term of, at least, heretical tendency.

[3] On First Principles, Preface; i, 2, 3; ii, 6; the standard later interpretation is of course that the seraphim sing, "Holy, holy, holy," to Father, Son, and Spirit (cf. Athanasius, On "All Things Were Delivered to Me," 4).

## II

Clarity in general principles but uncertainty in details—such was the state of Christian thought on these important matters when the last great persecution suspended theological discussion. When toleration came in 313, the leadership of the Church was divided between older men who had survived the persecution, and were sometimes only too glad to welcome the sunshine of imperial and popular favor that followed it, and younger men whose position was not yet firmly established. Eusebius of Caesarea is an example of the former class, and Athanasius of Alexandria of the latter. To this moment of pause between persecution and controversy belong the two essays of Athanasius, Against the Heathen and On the Incarnation. The latter remains to this day a classic statement of the ancient Church's faith in the re-creation of a fallen world by the divine Word who made it in the beginning, and so stands as the first major work reprinted in this volume. At this moment of apparent triumph Athanasius sets out the central theme of the Alexandrian Christology at its best. His chief concern is with the power of the new life in Christ which we share; his divinity makes his life mighty and his humanity makes it ours. The discussion is not yet forced into making the technical distinctions which were to be found necessary later. Athanasius can say simply of the incarnate Word that "he was made man," and certainly does not mean to imply that his was a reduced humanity; but his only formal terms for the humanity of Christ are his "flesh" or "body." Conversely the distinctness of the Father and the Word is implied rather than clearly stated. Such lack of strict definition would have been impossible later, but at the moment was neither surprising nor harmful. On the Incarnation is one of those great books which develop one great theme supremely.

In contrast to the caution of the bright young deacon stood the rashness of the respected presbyter of the Baucalis church in the Greek section of Alexandria. If Athanasius at this stage does not define as much as he might, Arius seems to have defined too brightly and too soon. His teacher, Lucian, was probably a well-known presbyter and martyr of Antioch, though he may have been another of the same name. The serious interest of the Lucianists, however, was not in the historical considerations which are customarily connected with Antiochene Christology, but in others of a philosophical order.

They were engaged in the always delicate and sometimes dangerous process of commending the gospel to the best thought of the age, and may well have felt that the new opportunities offered to the Christian preacher demanded a statement of Christian truths in terms the age could understand. Now for the Neo-Platonist mind the ultimate Being was too remote to be incarnate, and man was too low in the scale of existence to be capable of receiving deity. But the idea of intermediate beings who could connect God and man while themselves being neither was quite congenial to them. And such a being, thought Arius, developing one side of Origen's speculations and ignoring others, was the Son of God who appeared on earth in the body of Jesus.

A modern writer has spoken of Arianism as "one of those 'sensible' synthetic religions which are so strongly recommended today and which, then as now, included among their devotees many highly cultivated clergymen." [4] A certain bumptiousness is not unknown among cultured theologians—one may think of such later examples as Erasmus and Dean Inge —and Arius seems to have possessed it to a high degree. Certainly the early statements of Arian ideas treat Bishop Alexander's theology with a superciliousness that doubtless reflects local and personal tensions—as between the parish priest of the metropolitan parish, one of those whom the bishop properly addressed as "fellow presbyters," [5] and the bishop, who already had almost patriarchal authority among the simpler Egyptian Christians of the countryside—as well as the clash of ideas. But the latter is real. Arius' Christ is a demigod, "made, or created or established" (Documents I and II) in time, and Alexander's is at least coeternal with the Father. In spite of Arius' claim that he, and he only, avoided all heresies, the proper criticism of Arianism in its early crude form is that it is not really a form of Christianity.

One can understand the vigorous reaction that led the church of Egypt, still struggling to re-establish its unity after the stresses of the persecution, to condemn and expel the intransigent presbyter—and also Arius' perfectly natural attempt to secure support from the "fellow Lucianists" and other friends of his who were scattered through the Eastern churches. It is at this point that the verses of his *Thalia* made an attempt to

[4] C. S. Lewis, in his Introduction to *The Incarnation of the Word of God, Being the Treatise of St. Athanasius*, newly translated, London, 1944, p. 11.
[5] Cf. Dionysius in Eusebius, Ecclesiastical History, vii, 11, 3.

appeal to the populace of Alexandria. This was never, I think, very successful, but there was a persistent Arian minority at Alexandria for some fifty years. The fragments that Athanasius quotes do not sound much like popular songs, but such they apparently were. As Miss Dorothy Sayers has neatly paraphrased the general effect of Arius' verse,

"If you want the Logos doctrine, I can serve it hot and hot: God begat him and before he was begotten he was not." [6]

The emperor Constantine was naturally annoyed when, after having decided that the unity and welfare of his Empire demanded his support of the Christian Church, he found that the new religion was itself plagued with divisions. Typically, a problem of discipline was most conspicuous in the West (Donatism), and a division about the faith in the East. The Arian controversy had probably been in progress for some years when Constantine defeated his last rival and became sole emperor in A.D. 324. The need for a united Church as a unifying force in the Empire was presumably from his point of view the main reason for the summoning of a General Council at Nicaea in 325. Arianism was not the only problem discussed, but certainly had the main place on the agenda.

Two things are clear in our rather fragmentary accounts of what happened at Nicaea: first, that out-and-out Arians were in a hopeless minority; secondly, that the means adopted to exclude Arianism, the introduction of the disputed word *homoousios* into the Creed, was a startling proposal, somewhat unwelcome to many of those who accepted it. No theologian quite liked it, and some professed, more or less disingenuously, that what it suggested to them was the idea of Godhead broken into fragments. Though obviously a theological term, it was in a way a layman's term for those who wanted to say undeniably that Christ is divine—something like the phrase of our modern Faith and Order Conference, "Jesus Christ as God and Saviour," which is a reasonably clear statement but not precisely the way a theologian would want to put things. The method, moreover, of stating the common faith in a conciliar creed was new. The original use of creeds is to provide, by expansion of the three-fold formula of baptism, a brief statement of the faith which the convert accepts as the living tradition of the Body of Christ. Harmony among the leaders of the Church had already, since the days of the Gnostic controversies in the second century,

[6] Dorothy Sayers, *The Emperor Constantine*, Harper & Brothers, 1951, p. 119.

been expressed by the assertion that they had learned, believed, and transmitted to their converts one common rule of faith. But the expression of this in a brief formula specially set forth by a council of bishops was a new idea. As a basis of their operations the Fathers of Nicaea seem to have taken one (or possibly more) of the creeds in use in the Eastern Church— probably not, as a first reading of Eusebius of Caesarea's letter to his church would suggest, the Creed of Caesarea in particular.[7] Into this they inserted various phrases intended to exclude Arius' particular line of interpretation. "If you do that kind of thing, you might as well say *homoousios*," said a letter of Eusebius of Nicomedia, the prelate friend of Arius who had secured his transfer from the church of Beyrout to the imperial residence. and was later to move again to the new imperial city of Constantinople.[8] Whether or not in response to this challenge, the Council decided to do just that, and with encouragement from the highest quarters added the disputed term to its creed, which all except Arius and his closest band of followers proceeded to accept.

The text of the original Nicene Creed is best preserved in the apologetic letter which Eusebius of Caesarea wrote to his church (Document III). Only with explanations, some of which sound a little disingenuous, was he prepared to accept it, and such was doubtless the position of many another prelate besides the learned guardian of the great library. Though it may be held, I think correctly, that the Nicene Creed presented the solid basis of the common faith, it introduced a sharpness of definition which was new, and in the process raised new and rather puzzling questions. If the Father and Son were clearly defined as of one substance, how were they distinct—and how, now that the point is raised, are we to think of the eternal Son as really "made man"?

## III

The details of the post-Nicene controversy, though a fascinating episode in general Church history, are of no great importance for specifically doctrinal history until the issues in the confused battle were gradually clarified. The detailed maneuvers exhibit the close connection of religion and politics

---

[7] Cf. discussion in J. N. D. Kelly, *Early Christian Creeds*, Ch. vii.
[8] Ambrose, *De fide*, iii, 15 (and in H. G. Opitz, "Urkunden zur Geschichte des Arianischen Streites," in *Athanasius Werke*, Vol. iii, no. 21, p. 42).

which was generally accepted from the time of Constantine to the eighteenth century. The history can be understood almost as well if for "Arian" we read "imperialist," and for "orthodox" "ecclesiastical." In the first stage of reaction prominent Nicenes were attacked personally. Eustathius of Antioch, Paul of Constantinople, and Athanasius of Alexandria were exiled from their sees, the first two permanently. Then a series of credal statements appeared which ignored Nicaea rather than contradicting it. The Nicene cause suffered in the minds of conservatives from its extreme representative, Marcellus of Ancyra, for whom the Son was, it appears, but a temporary manifestation of the Father. Only after 350, when Constantius became sole emperor, were lines clearly drawn. Constantius favored, naturally enough, the party in the Church that looked to the imperial alliance for support. Credally this was expressed in a variety of statements which avoided the crudities of early Arianism and said great and lofty things about the Son of God, but fell short of declaring that his divinity was as the Father's. It does seem possible to see an inner connection between theological and political positions. Those for whom Christ was Lord and God defended the "crown rights of the Lord Jesus" over his Church, while those for whom he was a lesser being, however close to God, were more prepared to bow to the will of the emperor, as also God's vicegerent on earth.[9]

In the broader sense, the positions supported under Constantius can be called "Semi-Arian," saying in one way or another that the Son was like the Father. The last of these creeds, for further confusion given its final touches at the little town of Nice in Thrace, was nominally at least accepted by all the bishops in possession of their sees in either East or West, including the delegates of the Western Church assembled at Ariminum (Rimini) in 360 (Document IV). It is this specific moment to which Jerome refers in his famous phrase, "The whole world groaned and was astonished to find itself Arian."[10] The Creed of Ariminum was taken to the Goths by their apostle, Ulfilas, and so became the formal confession of Germanic Arianism for three centuries more. In the Greek East, however, a further split followed almost immediately. The

[9] Cf. George H. Williams, "Christology and Church–State Relations in the Fourth Century," *Church History*, Vol. xx, 1951, no. 3, pp. 3–33; no. 4, pp. 3–26.
[10] *Dialogus adversus Luciferianos*, 19.

Arians of Constantinople and its neighborhood swung to the more extreme position of original Arianism, or something very much like it, and Semi-Arians like Macedonius of Constantinople were now expelled from their positions. Others of similar sentiments began to find their way into the ranks of the Nicene party, which (apart from its own intransigents) was ready to receive them.

It was in these years that the minds of men who were to lead the next generation were being formed. The two noble Cappadocians Basil of Caesarea and Gregory of Nazianzus were students at Athens through most of the last decade of Constantius. The brief pagan reaction under Julian the Apostate at least removed imperial pressure in favor of one form of Christianity against another, and at its end what may be called a Neo-Nicene party was prepared to take the lead in the Eastern Church. The years from 361 to 381, from the death of Constantius to the First Council of Constantinople, are of great importance in the history of Christian doctrine. At Alexandria the old lion Athanasius was prepared to make the necessary explanations to unite those who accepted generally the Nicene position. His works of this period also deal with the related questions which the long-continued discussion had brought up. The Letters to Serapion defend the place of the Holy Spirit in the sphere of deity, which Arianism had rather incidentally challenged, and the Letter to Epictetus, bishop of Corinth, asserts clearly the completeness of the humanity of Christ. Basil's theological work moved along similar lines, Against Eunomius attacking out-and-out Arianism, and On the Holy Spirit asserting the deity of the Holy Ghost.

An important shift in technical terminology is the use of ousia, essence, for the being of godhead, and hypostasis, subsistence, for its particular expression in Father, Son, and Spirit. The anathemas attached to the Nicene Creed had used the two words as synonyms, which seems on the whole to have been the usage that Athanasius preferred. But in his conciliatory Letter to the Bishops of Africa he agreed that hypostasis might be used either way, and the general usage has become, as Basil defines it, that ousia indicates the universal and hypostasis the particular.[11] "One ousia and three hypostaseis" is therefore in Trinitarian theology recognized as the equivalent of the Latin phrase, "Three persons in one substance." It is necessary to remember that Greek hypostasis corresponds in etymology but

11 Epistle 236.

not in meaning to the Latin (and English) substance, which confused the young Jerome when he came to Antioch and found those whom he supposed to be orthodox talking, as it seemed to him, of three divine substances. Ancient Latin being chary of abstract terms, *substantia* with its concreteness had to serve for the general idea of being until medieval philosophers felt more at home with *esse* and *essentia*.[12]

Political Arianism was again supported by the emperor Valens, ruler of the Roman East from 364 to 378. This delay in the victory of the Neo-Nicene party was probably helpful in the long run, since it gave time for the clearer statement of its ideas and consolidation of its forces. In 379, Theodosius came from the West, where, except in certain parts of the Balkans, Arianism had never had any real foothold in the Latin Church. His recognition of the doctrine of the coequal Trinity as the creed of the Empire, and of its supporters as the officially recognized leaders of the Church, put the seal on the Church's own development. The Nicene formula, not wholly welcome even to its proponents in 325, had now become the palladium of orthodoxy, as it has ever since remained. Men had suffered for it, and welcomed its return as something simple and straightforward after the various complex substitutes offered for it.

But as the phrase "coequal Trinity" indicates, the faith now accepted was Nicene with some difference and further development. Out of the storm and tempest of the Arian struggle had come the classical orthodox doctrine of God and Christ— worked out in the later writings of Athanasius, and those of his assistant in the School of Alexandria, Didymus the Blind, and from a somewhat different standpoint by Basil and the other Cappadocians. It is this Neo-Nicene faith that Theodosius accepted and enforced, and whose supporters gathered at the Council of Constantinople in 381 to settle the affairs and state the faith of the sees of the two imperial cities, Antioch and Constantinople. Historians have commonly minimized the contemporary importance of the Council, considering it as a regional gathering which only in retrospect acquired the status of a General Council because it did in fact mark the end of Arianism. But more recent study seems to show that the Council was more important at the moment than has been usually

---

[12] Epistle 15; cf. the same confusion noted from the other side in Gregory Nazianzen's eulogy on Athanasius, Oration xxi, 35; on *essentia* and *substantia*, cf. Augustine, *De Trinitate*, v, 3, 10; vii, 7–11.

supposed. It was indeed not concerned with the affairs of the West or of Egypt, where Arianism was already defeated. Still the Egyptians did finally arrive at its sessions, and so did the bishop of Thessalonica, whose connections were as much Western as Eastern. It did issue a *tomos*, or compendious doctrinal statement (more than a creed and less than a treatise), which though now lost was evidently a document of some importance and authority. Alexandria and Rome were both rebuffed in its disciplinary decisions, which left the Egyptians a little sulky, and led to unsuccessful efforts to re-open these matters in Western Councils in the next few years. It may be for this reason that the acceptance of the practical decisions of Constantinople was not accompanied by stress on the authority of that particular gathering until it took its place in the list of Ecumenical Councils in the decrees of Chalcedon seventy years later.

The ambiguous position of the Council itself probably accounts for the obscurity which surrounds the early history of the creed known to most of the world as Nicene, but more precisely referred to as Constantinopolitan.[13] Apparently at this period any baptismal creed that incorporated the key phrases of Nicaea could be described as a statement of the Nicene faith; interest in the precise background of particular forms of the creed is relatively modern. So it does not seem at all impossible that the Council of Constantinople included in its *tomos* a local form of creed, Nicene in this broader sense, and in so doing felt that it was honestly decreeing that the Nicene faith should prevail. There are slight hints in the proceedings of Chalcedon that this creed may have been spread on the records as that used at the baptism of Nectarius, who, in the course of the Council, was chosen to succeed Gregory of Nazianzus as bishop of Constantinople. It was, and is, usable as a basis for general instruction in a way that the original Nicene formula, never so intended anyway, was not. It omits, or rather, probably, never included, some of the technical phrases referring to the details of Arianism. It amplifies the brief conclusion, "And in the Holy Spirit," with phrases about the life in the Spirit such as baptismal creeds commonly included long before Nicaea, and with a declaration of the lordship of the Spirit called forth by contemporary denials. It would seem to be well described by Gregory of Nazianzus' statement that his creed was that of the Fathers of Nicaea,

[13] Cf. Kelly, *Early Christian Creeds*, Ch. x.

"completing in detail that which was incompletely said by them concerning the Holy Ghost."[14]

May not the simplest explanation be that this was the baptismal creed used by Gregory as pastor of the orthodox remnant at Constantinople in 379–381? Its contacts with Syrian and Cilician forms could be accounted for by Cappadocia's contacts with the Southeast, and its acceptance by the Fathers of Constantinople by the fact that they found it in use where they were meeting. Like the Eucharistic prayer of the Liturgy of Saint Basil, it seems to reflect a natural line of influence at this particular period—from Syria to Constantinople by way of Cappadocia. As a working baptismal creed, which Nicaea was not, the Creed of Constantinople found its way into general use and was the creed later introduced into the Liturgy. Only the Armenians, when they adopted a creed for public use, went back to the original Nicene text (though expanded), and still proclaim before the altar that the Catholic Church anathematizes those who say that there was when he was not.

## IV

In 382 a second Council of Constantinople addressed a letter to the Western bishops in which the main decisions of the Council of 381 are summarized. Stating what the Nicene faith means, they seem in this letter to give the general sense of the lost *tomos* of 381 (Document V). The balanced statement of theology has gone somewhat beyond the threefold faith of the creed; its main points are belief in one God whose undivided substance exists in three *hypostases* and in the perfect incarnation of the Son. Here the solid structure of classical orthodox Christian theology now clearly appears, with its main doctrines of the Trinity and the incarnation. In adopting this formula the Council put the seal of its approval on the work of the three great Cappadocians, Basil and the two Gregorys.

The Cappadocian Fathers are represented in this volume by two of their great works in which the ideas hammered out by Basil were more systematically presented. Gregory of Nazianzus' Theological Orations belong to his ministry at Constantinople before the Council; Gregory of Nyssa's Address on Religious Instruction is a guide for Christian teachers written in the calmer years after it. Full discussion of Cappadocian teaching would be a theological treatise in itself, but some points about

[14] Epistle 102 (p. 225).

it call for historical observations. The first is the completion of Trinitarianism by the formal statement of the deity of the Holy Spirit. The baptismal formula and many New Testament references had always told Christians that they knew God as Father, Son, and Spirit, and theology was obliged to maintain that this experience was not deceptive. To be sure, it came more naturally to some to think of the Spirit as an impersonal working of God, or as the leader of the heavenly hosts.[15] Justin in a famous passage mentions Father, Son, and angels, as do the Gospels more than once, and then refers to the Spirit almost as an afterthought.[16] Indeed in all ages Christians have been tempted to neglect the Spirit, practically as well as theoretically, and this need not surprise us at any period. But to formalize his position on any less than the divine level is a slip backward rather than a stage of development. Nazianzen, one may note, was as well aware of this historical problem as we are and met it by a theory of development in doctrine—the Father was known in the Old Testament, the Son in the New, and the Spirit in the experience of the Church. If Christian worship is rarely formally directed to the Spirit, that is because our prayers are themselves an expression of the life of the Spirit in us (Fifth Theological Oration, 12).

Happily, the doctrine of the Holy Spirit was only briefly and occasionally of controversial interest. Tertullian's Montanist sympathies led him to stress the power of the Paraclete, and helped him perhaps to fix the term *trias* in theological terminology. But the ordinary Christian teacher before 325 felt no need to define in particular terms what his faith in the Holy Spirit meant. The fourth century difficulty is not so much, I think, a matter of gradual advance from this undefined faith as of temporary retrogression. If in Arian and Semi-Arian circles the being of the Son was defined as distinct from and inferior to that of the Father, obviously something similar was implied about the Holy Spirit. He could not be put on a higher level than the Son; he might be on a third level of deity—or merely a term for the Father and Son at work in our hearts— or another archangelic being of the same status as the Arian Son of God. Phrases implying this even found their way into liturgical usage—at least we may assume that some Arians actually said something like what the compiler of the *Apostolic Constitutions* wrote in the preface of his Eucharistic prayer:

[15] Cf. Gregory Nazianzen, Theological Orations, v, 5 (p. 196).
[16] First Apology, 6; cf. Mark 8:38.

"Thee every bodiless and holy rank worships, thee the Paraclete worships, before all thy holy child Jesus, the Christ, the
Lord, and our God, thine Angel and Commander of thy Host,
and eternal and everlasting High Priest, thee the well-ordered
armies of angels . . ." [17] adore, and so on. Once in circulation,
such ideas about the Spirit seem to have been more or less
accidentally taken up by some who were almost or quite
Nicene in their doctrine about the Son. But the refutation
undertaken by Athanasius and Basil was not really particularly
difficult, and the Constantinopolitan amplification of the creed
provided indeed a highly desirable balance. The formal statement was new, but the idea and attitude that it expressed was
an inheritance from the apostles. Here as elsewhere the true
Christian teacher was bringing out of his treasure things new
and old (Matt. 13:52).

The formal recognition of the deity of the Holy Spirit at
last made possible complete definition of the doctrine of the
Triune God. On this point the Cappadocians have, I think,
been somewhat unfairly treated by many modern interpreters.
They formally state that, since they use *ousia* for the general
and *hypostasis* for the particular, the three divine persons share
one common essence, as three human persons, such as Peter,
James, and John, share the common essence of humanity.
"Tritheism," or something very much like it, say Harnack and
various other writers. But the criticism seems to me to fail on
two points. First, we must remember that we are the heirs of
the nominalists, and find it hard to take the reality of general
entities seriously—for us Peter, James, and John are three
individuals possessing human qualities, while for the Cappadocians they were rather a threefold manifestation of manhood.
Secondly, in developing the Peter–James–John parallel they
were concerned with the use of language, showing the propriety
of speaking of three manifestations of a common essence. They
were perfectly well aware that there is no room in the realm
of being for three separate infinities, as there is for indefinite
multiplication of finite beings such as men. Thus, for instance,
as Gregory of Nyssa points out when writing on this topic in
That We Should Not Think of Saying There Are Three Gods,
the divine actions are all those of the Father acting through the

---

[17] *Apostolic Constitutions*, viii, 12, 27; text of Vat. Gr. 1506 (in *Didascalia et
constitutiones apostolorum*, ed. F. X. Funk, Paderborn, 1905, Vol. i, p. 505);
cf. C. H. Turner, "Notes on the Apostolic Constitutions," *The Journal of
Theological Studies*, Vol. 16, 1914–1915, pp. 54–61.

Son and by the Spirit. A few years later Augustine was to expound the doctrine of the Trinity as ascribing to God the fullness of personality rather than any multiplicity in the divine nature. The approach of the Cappadocians is different—they asserted the unity of the Three rather than the threefoldness of the One—but the final result is similar.

In their theology the Cappadocians speak both as philosophers and as Christian believers. For their kind of Platonism the ineffability of the Supreme Being was a central truth of religious thought. Even the Greek word *theos* refers to a divine act—swift motion, perhaps, says Nazianzen, after Plato, or supervision, says Nyssa [18]—rather than to God in himself. The goal and proper nature of religion is the glimpse of realities beyond human description. But the ineffable has manifested himself as Creator, Redeemer, and Sanctifier. Here the Cappadocians rest on solid Biblical grounds. Their Trinitarianism is primarily based on the fact that Christians have come to know God as Father, Son, and Spirit, knowing also that these three are one, and may be sure that this revelation does not deceive us as to ultimate reality, even though it may not wholly express it. Hence there is not even as much speculation as Augustine indulges in as to why there are precisely three divine hypostases, though there are slight hints that in this threefold motion being is complete. [19] But the main point is that the Christian revelation tells us of a godhead complete in the Son and Spirit and the Wisdom and Love of the Father, and the Christian theologian should rather adore God as he has manifested himself than speculate as to whether the nature of deity might conceivably have been different. The Son is begotten and the Spirit proceeds, one as the Image and the other as the Breath of God. The distinction is obviously important, since otherwise there is no distinction between the two [20]—but having noted this, as a Biblical fact, the Cappadocians do not seem concerned to note just why it is or what it is; we have many true things to say about God, but should not dream that our thought will mount to a complete understanding of him, which was indeed the specific central error of the Eumonians.

In writing of the incarnation the Cappadocians ring the changes on the idea that Christ is both true God and true man. Here they were met with an annoying heresy within the Nicene

[18] Theological Orations, iv, 18 (p. 189); Not Three Gods (p. 261).
[19] Cf. Gregory Nazianzen, Theological Orations, iii, 2 (p. 161).
[20] *Ibid.*, iii, 3 (pp. 161, 162); v, 9 (p. 199).

camp. The Apollinarians could claim to have developed ideas of Athanasius, much as, in a different way, Arius could claim to have developed the principles of Origen. Athanasius had commonly spoken of Christ's humanity as his "body" or "flesh," and had emphasized that God was indeed living and working in him. This might easily sound as if the divine Word took the place of the human mind or soul, leaving in the humanity of Christ only a body, though a living body with, if one wants to make the distinction, the animal soul that animals also possess. Curiously enough, this seems also to have been the Christology of Arianism. This becomes less surprising, however, when we consider that the finite and infinite are capable of union, as different kinds of being, while a being himself finite, however majestic, like the Arian Christ, could only enter into manhood by some kind of mixture. But the idea that God-made-man involves some kind of omission from humanity, to make room for godhead, as it were, has often commended itself to adherents of Nicene orthodoxy.

Such ideas were apparently in the air of the 360's—Athanasius' Letter to Epictetus deals with speculations of this sort, though not exactly along the lines of Apollinaris. The latter was an embarrassing heretic. Bishop of Laodicea, he was a pillar of the Nicene faith in Syria, famous for his piety and learning. When Julian forbade Christians to teach the pagan classics, he embarked on the ambitious project of constructing a whole Christian literature in appropriate classical forms. Such a background doubtless accounted for the facile Apollinarian composition of new psalms and scriptures that Nazianzen complains of, and apparently for a confusing Apollinarian habit of editing or even falsifying works of respected Fathers in their own interest. Nothing could be said against Apollinaris except that his ideas were wrong, and, after a time, that his Church politics were irresponsible. For Apollinarianism was a party as well as an opinion, and its history needs more study from that particular point of view. Apollinaris consecrated a competing bishop for Antioch, and his followers troubled the peace of the Cappadocian Church in the 380's.

It is only a convenience of textbooks that Apollinarianism is often listed as the main heresy condemned at the Second General Council in 381. It was included among several side issues of the Arian controversy which were being tidied up, and was at the moment probably of less importance than the Macedonian attack on the Holy Spirit. But it had considerable significance for the future. The classic reply to it came in Gregory Nazianzen's letters on the subject after his retirement to Cappadocia, which incidentally set the terms for coming discussion of Christology. "What was not assumed was not redeemed," is Gregory's keynote—the fullness of Christ's humanity is stressed in connection, not so much with the genuineness of his human example, as with the completeness of his mystical identification with our race. As in so many questions, the patristic approach is almost the reverse of ours. We are reasonably sure of the existence of the historic Jesus, but may find some difficulty in grasping the presence of God in that human life; Godhead is, as it were, added to humanity. Few of the Fathers had any difficulty in the idea of God the Word appearing on earth and taking to himself a human body. Their problem was rather in seeing how the divine manifestation, in which manhood was added to Godhead, could have taken place in a complete human nature. In this connection the term *theotokos*, "God bearer," is first formally employed with a reverse emphasis from that which it carries later. To say that Mary really bore the incarnate God is a way of saying that Christ was really divine. It is also a way of saying that God, in becoming man, really submitted to the experience of birth, and this seems to be Gregory's purpose in using in dogmatic statement a phrase that doubtless already had devotional associations.

## V

With the work of the Cappadocians the main lines of classical Christian theology were laid down, but its development was by no means over. In the later fourth century the Syrian church produced the school of historical interpreters who are likely to be in mind when we speak of the School of Antioch, though most of them did not work at Antioch, and theirs was by no means the only influence in the Antiochene Patriarchate. The straightforward preaching of John Chrysostom reflected their spirit. Others, most conspicuously Theodore of Mopsuestia, seem to have shared some of our modern difficulty in uniting the Jesus of history with the eternal Son, and met it by distinguishing carefully between the temple of the humanity and the indwelling Emmanuel. Nominally at least, it was in opposition to this that Cyril spoke for the Alexandrian School in defense of the unity of Christ.

Cyril was many things besides a theologian—national leader,

ecclesiastical politician, manager of mobs and courts—but he had a theological word to say, the emphasis on a real union in which God and Man are one Christ, united in one concrete being, *hypostasis*, and not simply in outward appearance, *prosōpon*. Latin and English confuse our understanding of this discussion by translating both terms as *persona*, person. Nestorius, the Antiochene bishop of Constantinople, seems to have fallen before his brother of Alexandria rather because of his muddle-headedness in thought and ineptness in politics than for the heresy he was supposed to hold. But Cyril did secure, by the general acceptance of his Ephesian Council of 431, the re-affirmation of the unity of Christ, God and man in one *hypostasis* (Document VI). He also insisted, perhaps as against the newer creed of Constantinople, on the original creed of Nicaea as the central statement of the faith. For a while after Ephesus, Alexandria and Antioch were in schism from each other. But in 433 union was restored, after due explanation. Cyril's letter to John of Antioch is in effect a concordat of the two sees—it accepts as orthodox a statement prepared by the Antiochenes that the union in Christ was a "union of natures," and clears Cyril from charges of Apollinarianism (Document VII).

Fifteen years later the Alexandrian attack on Constantinople was resumed, nominally in defense of the abbot Eutyches, who claimed that there were two natures in Christ before the union (i.e., in divine foreknowledge of the incarnation), but only one afterward. Again there was an Alexandrian victory at Ephesus, in the so-called Robber Council of 449. But this time Rome, the consistent friend of Alexandria since the days of Athanasius, was swinging to the other side. The dominance of the Eastern Church by Alexandria was intolerable, and on the doctrine in question Leo of Rome had already pronounced in his Tome addressed to the bishop of Constantinople, Flavian (Document VIII). The theology of the Tome is simple and, except for new terms, little beyond that of the previous century. But it is meant to be a dogmatic statement, and often the proper purpose of dogma is to call a halt to mere speculation. There are in Christ two natures and substances (*physes* and *ousiae*) united in one person (*prosōpon* and *hypostasis*). Under a new emperor the question was reopened in the East, and, in 451, Alexandrian politics were defeated and Alexandrian theology corrected at the Council of Chalcedon. Leo would doubtless have been glad if his Tome had been recognized as settling the question. The Council did not do this, however, although it did endorse the

Tome, along with other orthodox documents, and the later opponents of Chalcedon in the East often spoke as if the "impious Tome" was what they were rejecting. But the Council decided to produce its own *tomos* and after some difficulty accepted the draft produced by a committee (how modern is this particular procedure!) as the Chalcedonian Decree (Document IX). The time was over for drawing up new creeds, but the original Creed of Nicaea was again ratified, and the Creed of Constantinople again proclaimed, with a further interpretation in which the key phrase, "In two natures," appears in a carefully balanced statement.

## VI

Chalcedon, like Nicaea, had introduced a new phrase to affirm the ancient faith, and it was followed by a similar reaction. But the end of the controversy was less happy. Anti-Chalcedonians, or Monophysites, were a strong party in the Eastern Church for a century, and the final result of the struggle was a group of schisms which have endured to the present day. For two centuries the Byzantine emperors attempted a series of compromises which might maintain the unity of their Eastern and Western provinces—for "Chalcedonian" and "Monophysite" in this history one may equally well read "Western" and "Oriental," with Constantinople as the meeting point of the two parties. The failure of this policy is one of many proofs that the emperors were not so dominant in Church affairs as is often supposed. The total result is one of the tragedies of history, but even in this controversy some developments of theological interest took place, and one of some liturgical importance. Monophysites, to stress their loyalty to Nicaea as against innovations, began the custom of reciting the Nicene Creed in the Eucharistic Liturgy—meaning by this, in fact, the adapted Creed of Constantinople. The custom at once proved popular, and since then the rolling periods of Nicaea have had their place in public worship. This development has some importance in the history of the creed itself, since it puts Christian confession in its proper context of prayer and praise rather than in an atmosphere of debate.

Even the rather barren sixth century deserves more attention than it often receives in the history of Christian thought. The accession of Justin I in 518 restored Chalcedon at Constantinople, as the accession of Theodosius had restored Nicaea.

Monophysite exiles gathered at Alexandria, where the national patriarch was not interfered with for some twenty years more. Among them was the leading theologian of the party, Severus of Antioch, patriarch of that great see since 512. Factions developed among exiles, as often happens in such situations, and in this case took a theological form. Severus hated Chalcedon with a perfect hatred, and strongly repudiated the formula, "In two natures," but still insisted that in the one nature of Christ there is manhood consubstantial with ours just as there is deity consubstantial with the Father. This seems to be the faith of Leo, but with a different emphasis, and a confusing usage of *physis* as something more like *hypostasis* than *ousia*. Another exile, Julian of Halicarnassus, taught, it would seem more logically, that the one nature of Christ was not in itself capable of suffering and decay, as alien to the Godhead, though the cross and other moments of suffering were accepted for our sake. In particular, the body of Christ was not only preserved from corruption by the resurrection, but was in fact incorruptible. This point of discussion seems to have taken its departure from Athanasius' rather ambiguous references to this particular question.[21] Recondite though it seems to be, it is in fact the watershed between those for whom the Monophysite doctrine meant indeed a loss of human qualities by absorption into the Godhead, a more delicate form of Apollinarianism, and those who basically agreed with what Chalcedon was trying to say. Cyril had at least tended in the former direction, as when he wrote, for instance, of the tears of Jesus at Lazarus' tomb: "He permitted his own flesh to weep a little, although it was in its nature tearless and incapable of any grief."[22] The followers of Severus were known to their opponents as "worshipers of the corruptible," Phthartolatrae, and Julian's in turn as Phantasiasts or Aphthartodocetae, "supporters of the incorruptible and imaginary" humanity of Christ. Under these strange terms there lies the crucial question, Was Christ a real man?

On the other side many supporters of Chalcedon found it desirable to introduce into their system some ideas which the Monophysite emphasis on unity preserved, and which Leo's stress on the distinction of natures might obscure. As the

[21] On the Incarnation, 21–23, 26; cf. J. Lebon, "Une ancienne opinion sur la condition du corps du Christ dans la mort," *Revue d'histoire ecclésiastique,* Vol. 23, 1927, pp. 5–43.
[22] *Commentary on John,* vii (on John 11: 33–37).

theologian Leontius of Byzantium pointed out, the union of God and man is, in Origen's old metaphor, like the union of iron (or wood) and fire (Document X). Christ's whole personality finds its center in God, and the neat division of his actions between the divine and human must not obscure this. Others even more daringly accepted the conclusion of some Monophysites that, in the sufferings of Christ, God himself suffered, in his flesh, with and for us. So out of the tradition of Greek philosophical theology itself comes a repudiation of the philosophical assumption of the utterly impassible deity. Others even anticipated some modern Christology in teaching that God in Christ must somehow have shared our human experience of limited knowledge; but these "ignorantists," Agnoetae, were in their own time generally repudiated by all sides—the age was not accustomed to think in such historical terms.

Though the efforts at conciliation of parties failed, there was thus more exchange of ideas than is generally supposed. The emperor Justinian's efforts at political conciliation reached their climax in the condemnation of the so-called "Three Chapters"—the teachings of Theodore of Mopsuestia, thus posthumously branded as a heretic—and certain writings of Theodoret and Ibas, Antiochenes who had been cleared at the Council of Chalcedon. Politically the maneuver failed, in spite of the general acceptance of Justinian's demands by the Second Council of Constantinople (Fifth Ecumenical) in 553. But though no Monophysite persons were restored to the Church by this gesture, it did secure the acceptance into the orthodox tradition of a number of ideas and phrases dear to members of that party (Document XI), and was thus a more significant moment in the history of doctrine than is commonly supposed. With more good will and less politics in the background, such a confluence of Chalcedonian and Monophysite traditions might have been the basis of a general reconciliation. But under the conditions of the age such was not to be.

The last imperial effort of this sort was sponsored by Heraclius after he recovered the Oriental provinces from the Persians in 622–628. The formula now proposed, which won some apparent success—"a watery union," as a later historian calls it [23]—was that whatever we may say of natures, certainly God and man are united in Christ in one common energy or operation, or, in another form of this heresy, in one single will. Politics and theology were again deeply intertwined, and the Monothelete

[23] Theophanes, *Chronographia*, 6121.

controversy lingered on for some time after its political cause was removed by the Moslem conquest of the Orient. It has its own complexities, perhaps all the more because no great mind was brought to bear on it, apart from the heroic defender of orthodoxy, Maximus the Confessor, the monk of Carthage who died in exile in the Crimea, so far did the imperial power still extend. He is a neglected writer now receiving more attention, but his main interests were not in this particular field. Indeed there is a certain weariness about the whole controversy, and the proceedings of the Third Council of Constantinople (Sixth Ecumenical) which brought it to an end in 681 are correct, but unenthusiastic. Yet the doctrine proclaimed by the Council of 681 is of considerable importance. There are two genuine wills in Christ—not, as this is sometimes understood, in the sense of a split human personality, but in that of the fullness of the humanity as well as the deity of the Son of God (Document XII). When, in the key text of this controversy, Jesus said, "Not my will, but thine be done" (Luke 22:42), he was really saying something. [24] With the decisions of this Council the great debate of five centuries was at last ended, and the structure of classical Christology was complete.

## VII

Complex and technical as parts of this historic discussion are, it is sometimes obviously close to the heart of Biblical and practical Christianity, and never entirely removed from it—although, then as now, nontheological considerations were always present and often predominant in local and personal divisions. Somewhat less technically, the main principles of conciliar Christology may be put in a few brief statements. The first is the affirmation of Nicaea against Arianism, that it is God himself who is at work in Christ, and not some lesser being called honorifically the Son of God. With this goes the Trinitarian formula, that Son and Spirit are, as such, distinct from the Father, and yet in each we see equally the one eternal Deity—or, to put this in other words, the New Testament Christian meets God as Father, Son, and Spirit, yet knowing that these three are one, and in this experience he is not deceived. Moving in Biblical terms, for all their philosophical language, the

---

[24] Cf. on this Gregory Nazianzen (Theological Orations, iv, 12, p. 185), who asserts the distinction of wills by nature, but denies any difference in content.

Cappadocian Fathers proceeded from the three to the one, first asserting the Godhead of Son and Spirit and then the corollary of the union of the three. It was left for somewhat later Latins to move in the reverse direction, more logical but less concrete. So Augustine's *De Trinitate* builds up the three-foldness of God on the basis of his unity, and a somewhat later statement, the psalm *Quicunque*, commonly miscalled the Athanasian Creed, rings the changes on the equality of the three persons and their unity in the one substance—"For there is one Person of the Father, another of the Son, and another of the Holy Ghost: But the Godhead of the Father, of the Son, and of the Holy Ghost, is all one; the glory coequal, the majesty coeternal." [25]

A second pair of propositions are concerned with the relation of God and man in Christ. As Origen long ago put it, he is true God and true man; and so the Church rejected, whenever the question was raised, any suggestion that his manhood was incomplete, something being left out, as it were, to make room for deity. We are likely to think of the presence of God in Christ as the highest and unique form of God's presence in man, known to all his saints; and would say that in him as in us this is an addition to and a perfection of manhood, not something secured by a subtraction from it. More boldly, the Fathers thought of the incarnation in the reverse and logical order, as God's assumption of humanity, and asserted that it was a complete humanity that was assumed. Here the balancing proposition comes in, that God and Man are one Christ—this was not a man, once existing otherwise, on whom the Spirit came, but one whose whole life was lived from the beginning in personal union with God, and whose truly human experiences are in some way the experiences of God the Word. In other terms, here too a simple Biblical experience is asserted to be justified by ultimate reality—we have known Christ as our brother and worship him as our Lord, and yet know that he is one and not two.

The purpose of this introduction is historical and not strictly theological or apologetic, but one cannot forget that the questions faced by the Councils are still with us, in dogma, theology, and practical religion. The purpose of dogmatic definition is properly a strictly limited one. It aims on the one hand to keep the way open for faith, and on the other to provide both the right kind of encouragement and the right

[25] As translated in the (English) *Book of Common Prayer*.

kind of discouragement for speculation. Each of the great definitions has a certain air of paradox; the profession of a simple answer to all questions is indeed one of the best indications of a heresy. Chalcedon is an outstanding instance, since the Chalcedonian Decree states the apparently opposing truths of Christian faith in Christ and asserts their harmony without attempting to show the manner of that harmony.[26] It marks the beginning rather than the end of sound speculation on the subject, while indicating (as Nicaea did on the broader question) the lines within which Christian speculation should proceed. So after the series of Councils comes the formal summary of their teaching in the work of John of Damascus, and after that in turn, with new philosophical presuppositions, the work of Thomas Aquinas and the other scholastics, and further revival and development of Christological studies down to our own day. It may be that this is always a dangerous process, that the Middle Age tended to be Apollinarian and our modern historical studies have given us a tendency towards Nestorianism; the unity of God and man in Christ may be the commonly neglected side of Christology just now. The old truths must always be newly stated—even merely to repeat the old formulas involves some change in their meaning, as the details of their terms ("perfect man," for instance) have different senses for different ages. But in our life in Christ we should not depart from the ancient facts of the faith, which Fathers and Councils endeavored to state and understand—our knowledge of God as Maker, Redeemer, and Sanctifier, and these three all one Deity—and our conviction that in Jesus our brother the eternal Truth speaks.

26 "The formula did exactly what an authoritative formula ought to do: it stated the fact" (William Temple, *Christ the Truth*, London and New York, 1924 p. 159 n).

# GENERAL BIBLIOGRAPHY

Outstanding general works in this field are those of A. von Harnack, *A History of Dogma* (English trans. from 3d German edition, 7 vols., London, 1894–1899; 4th edition of *Lehrbuch der Dogmengeschichte*, 3 vols., Berlin, 1908–1909), a basic and classical work, even though the modern student is likely to differ from Harnack in detail, and may consider that his categories and judgments are too easily assumed; J. Tixeront, *History of Dogmas* (English trans., 3 vols., St. Louis, 1910–1916); and A. C. McGiffert, *A History of Christian Thought*, Vol. I, *Early and Eastern*, Charles Scribner's Sons, 1932. J. N. D. Kelly, *Early Christian Creeds*, Longmans, Green & Company, Inc., 1950, covers much of the history of ideas as well as of their formal statement. One of the most brilliant of many efforts at a brief summary is that of William Temple in *Christ the Truth*, London, 1924, Ch. VIII.

Among special studies relating to the period mainly represented in this volume are Charles E. Raven, *Apollinarianism, An Essay on the Christology of the Early Church*, Cambridge, 1923; R. V. Sellers, *Two Ancient Christologies, A Study in the Christological Thought of the Schools of Alexandria and Antioch*, London, S.P.C.K. (for the Church Historical Society), 1940; and *Nestorius, The Bazaar of Heracleides*, edited and translated by G. R. Driver and Leonard Hodgson, Oxford, 1925. In the *Bazaar*, so called by a confusion of Syriac translators (who probably rendered the Greek *pragmateia* literally, "business," instead of figuratively, "discussion" or "treatise"), one of the condemned theologians speaks for himself. An orthodox thinker often little appreciated in modern times is expounded in Herbert M. Relton, *A Study in Christology*, London, 1917, which follows a general survey with a discussion of the unity of the two natures of Christ along lines suggested by Leontius of Byzantium. Many of the original works of the Fathers still await scientific editing; happily the Acts of the Councils of Ephesus and Chalcedon are available in Eduard Schwartz, *Acta conciliorum oecumenicorum*, Berlin, 1922–    , and the more official dogmatic statements are conveniently gathered in T. H. Bindley, *The Oecumenical Documents of the Faith*, 4th ed., ed. F. W. Green, Methuen & Co., Ltd., London, 1950. The proceedings of Chalcedon and the discussion before and after the Council are treated in detail in R. V. Sellers, *The Council of Chalcedon, A Historical and Doctrinal Survey*, S.P.C.K., London, 1953.

# ATHANASIUS

# Introduction to Athanasius

## BACKGROUND AND IDEAS

FOR FORTY-FIVE YEARS BISHOP OF ALEXANDRIA, for fifty a central figure in the exposition and defense of orthodox theology, Athanasius is one of the dominating personalities in the history of the Church. Yet practically all his writings were produced in response to some immediate need, or as a blow for the faith in one of the crises of his long struggle with successive emperors. Even the Life of Antony, the preparation of which seems to have been a kind of recreation in his laborious days, serves the immediately practical purpose of depicting the pattern of life of the loyal and orthodox hermit. The writings that we think of as historical are in fact personal defenses. The Defense Against the Arians is Athanasius' vindication against the personal charges that had been the pretext for his first and second exiles under Constantine and Constantius (335–337 and 339–346). The third exile, which followed when Constantius finally had a free hand in ecclesiastical as well as civil affairs (356–361), is the occasion of the Defense to Constantius, Defense of His Flight, and History of the Arians. Shortly before this exile came the defense of Nicaea and its Creed in the treatise On the Decrees, and during it the attack on rival creeds and councils in the treatise On the Synods, and the more formally theological but still basically occasional Orations Against the Arians. The last exiles under Julian and Valens were pinpricks in comparison with what the old warrior had gone through, but by this time he was an old warrior. His final contributions to the clarification of orthodox thought were made in slighter though important documents such as the synodal Tome to the Antiochenes and the theological letters addressed to Serapion and Epictetus. In these writings

Athanasius gave his blessing to newer and more balanced formulas, the detailed exposition of which he left to others, such as his own assistant in the School at Alexandria, Didymus the Blind, and the rising Cappadocian group of theologians.

Only in the masterly two-volume work of his youth do we see Athanasius expressing himself apart from the attacks of heretics and politicians. What Jerome describes as *Adversus gentes libri duo* [1] are commonly treated as two separated though related works: Against the Heathen and On the Incarnation of the Word. As the references to current conditions in the latter show, they date from 316–318: persecution is ended, but still vividly remembered (28, 29; 48); the Arian heresy has not yet arisen to trouble the Church, although there is a hint at the schisms that were an aftermath of the Great Persecution (24). Most significant perhaps, and mournful reading for Christians of all later generations, are the passages where as in a continuous song of triumph Athanasius proclaims the visible victory of the cross, which is now bringing, not only holiness to individuals and destruction to idols, but peace to the world (51–55). From these works, says Athanasius, we may see the power of the Redeemer as from the harmony of the universe we see the wisdom of the Creator. Such assurance was possible only in the few years of confidence that followed the victory of Constantine. Later generations of believers can only sadly reflect that, though knowing in many ways the power of the same Lord, "we see not yet all things put under him" (Heb. 2:8).

The combination of the enthusiasm of a youthful mind with the wisdom of a great one has given the treatise On the Incarnation its place among those Christian classics which are read not only as documents in the history of Christian thought but as treatments of the subjects with which they deal. Historically it stands at the meeting point between the work of the Apologists and that of the theologians of the age of the councils. In Against the Heathen, Athanasius attacks, as Jews and Christians at Alexandria had for centuries, the absurdity of popular paganism, and defends on rational grounds the principle that a unified and orderly universe is the work of one Creator, who rules it by his Logos (Word, or Reason). The universe continues to move as the Word, conductor of the universal chorus, directs, but man has abused his privilege of freedom by turning away to his own irrational courses. The second treatise takes up the argument at this point, and shows

[1] *De viris illustribus*, 87.

how the Word through whom we were made is also the Redeemer by whom we are reclaimed. This is a threefold action: the life-giving power of the Word heals our illness of soul as well as of body, his teaching by word and deed restores to us the true knowledge of God, and his sacrifice pays the debt of justice which man could never pay (7, 19, 20). Indeed, nothing less can be said than that he became man so that we might become divine (54).

Like all Apologies, On the Incarnation is not so much an exercise in speculative reasoning as an appeal for personal decision. Macarius—and I think the person addressed at the beginning of each treatise is the prospective reader, whoever he may be, and not a particular person—is not treated as a neutral student, but as one drawn to the faith, yet needing to have his decision for it encouraged by assurance of its rationality and presentation of its power. At the end he is told that there is indeed more to learn, which he can find by reading the Scriptures and by associating with the saints—or, in other words, in the fellowship of the Church, although the secrecy made customary in the days of persecution prevents Athanasius from saying this in so many words. It is typically Alexandrian that he thinks of the Church as a successful rival of the schools of the philosophers (50), and speaks of the prophets as having been a school of the knowledge of God for the world (12). Macarius may be considered as a specimen of the kind of prospective convert with whom the Alexandrian Church was accustomed to deal, an educated pagan prepared to become an intelligent Christian. Not that Athanasius was unaware of the appeal of Christianity to the common man and the significance of the gospel preached to the poor and to what a Greek would call barbarous nations (29, 30, 50, 51), but he is at the moment writing immediately for the educated and even sophisticated world of Alexandria. He was probably already in touch with the Coptic monk Antony, whose life he was later to write —at least no later period can be found for the extensive contacts claimed in the preface to the Life of Antony. It was only, however, after the duties of his episcopate took him into all parts of Egypt that Athanasius developed fully his sympathies with the simple Coptic as well as with the more sophisticated Greek Christian.[2] An important point of contact was the common ground between the Greek philosophical ascetic, such as

2 Cf. the visitations listed in *Fetasl Index*, 2–6 (Post-Nicene Fathers, Vol. IV, p. 503).

Origen had been, and the straightforward Egyptian devotee. In On the Incarnation Athanasius points to the new virtue of voluntary continence as a sign of the triumph of the Word (51), and at his election to the episcopate in 328 he was himself to be hailed as "one of the ascetics." [3]

To some extent the treatise On the Incarnation is an educational exercise—Athanasius' B.D. thesis, so to speak—a brilliant restatement of what he had learned from martyr teachers (56) such as the bishop Peter who had passed from the teacher's chair to the bishop's seat, guided the Church of Alexandria through the persecution of Diocletian, and died himself as one of its last victims in 311. Here is the prospectus, as it were, of the young graduate who was now about to embark on his career as a Christian teacher himself. In an interesting way its illustrations reflect the interests of a young man whose native town was Alexandria, the cosmopolitan city which was also the capital of Greco-Roman Egypt. The world-city, the great *cosmopolis*, is a familiar figure of late Greek philosophy— Marcus Aurelius' "dear city of Zeus." [4] But Athanasius' use of the figure does seem to take on a special coloring from the scenes of his own city—the Word governs the universe like the conductor of a chorus, or a royal founder supervising the public and private life of a great town (Against the Heathen 43). Alas, the world-city has rebelled and nothing less than a personal visit from the true prince will be enough to bring it back to its true allegiance (On the Incarnation 10, 55). Athanasius must often have heard in his childhood of the rebellion of a Roman official who had been set up as a rival emperor about the time of his birth. In 297–298, Diocletian had come in person to reconquer the city, destroying it in part. So also, but in grace more than in vengeance, the Word of God has come to his own, bringing to nought the usurpation of the wicked spirits who have set themselves up as gods (55). Greco-Roman Egypt was used to the solemn visits of high officials to inspect the administration and render judicial decisions; such associations lie behind the use of *parousia* and *epidēmia* for the solemn visit of the Word to his own (13, 27). Or again, the Original has appeared so that the defaced portrait may be restored; the figure in Athanasius' mind is evidently the portrait on wood, such as Greco-Egyptians attached to their mummies of their dead, as we may see in our museums today (14).

[3] Defense Against the Arians, 6.
[4] *Meditations*, IV, 23; cf. Philo, *De opificio mundi*, 17–20, 24.

Intellectually Athanasius was certainly a Greek of Alexandria rather than an Egyptian—though he had enough Egyptian feeling to thrill at the thought that the infant Saviour had been brought into his own land and, as legend evidently already told, the idols of Egypt had fallen before him (36, 37). The philosophical ideas which he easily takes as common ground are those of eclectic Greek thought, partly Stoic, partly Platonic —the unity of the universe and the presence of an Orderer behind its order, whose status and relation to the world is the point of difference between the schools. On the doctrine of the Creator, Jew and Christian at Alexandria agreed. They could even go farther together, asserting the fact of a fall from the divine plan into idolatry and wickedness and the need of divine redemption. Here Athanasius was following a tradition of theistic apologetic which goes back to such Hellenistic Jewish works as the Wisdom of Solomon, which he was accustomed to read for edification, along with Scripture.[5] Against their pagan surroundings Jews and Christians at Alexandria were still in many ways sects of one religion. Athanasius' arguments against Judaism have a practical as well as historical character, and deal with texts in a manner that Christian teachers inherited from their rabbinical predecessors. Few Christian Apologists would now proceed in quite the same manner. But this section of On the Incarnation ought not to be skipped by the student, since the Old Testament is an important part of Athanasius' thought and devotion. Nor can the Christian ever forget safely this part of the claims of Christ, that in him we see the glory of Israel as well as the light of the Gentiles.

As the treatise On the Incarnation comes to terms with the Jewish and pagan background of Christianity, so it also lays down lines for the future development of Christian thought. This is all the more true because it is an apologetic and missionary appeal and not a systematic treatise on theology. It concentrates on its theme, the redemption of the world by the incarnate Word, to the exclusion of much else in which Athanasius certainly believed. There is nothing about the Spirit; nothing except incidentally about the Church; nothing about the life of prayer and sacrament which was certainly for Athanasius the means by which the new life brought to the world by Christ was shared by the individual Christian. Some of these things were omitted because Macarius could not be told them until he received his final instruction as a Christian

[5] Festal Epistles, 39.

neophyte; some because they were not in place in this particular book.

As Athanasius does not expound the whole faith, even less does he engage in speculation for its own sake, though he touches in passing on a number of matters of interest to theological experts. Man's original state, apparently, was one of natural perfection as the near image of God to which, had he not fallen, the gift of immortality would easily have been added—as in the book of Wisdom, it is by the envy of the devil that death came into the world (3–6; Wisdom 2:23, 24). We are not told how the old deceiver fell into his deception; he is not worth so much attention. The coming of the Word is a victory over the usurper and his angels. As part of it the Word, being man, pays for man and as man the sacrifice which fallen man could never pay, but there is no special statement as to why this is necessary. It is certainly not a price paid to the devil—probably a reparation due in justice to God (7, 20). But for Athanasius, cross and resurrection go together (as in his Church calendar there was probably no Good Friday apart from Easter), and the chief meaning of the cross is that there "the powers of death have done their worst" and have been defeated. So the cross is above all the trophy of victory, that victory which is first Christ's and then also ours as we live in him. As his own Christian name indicated, he was brought up in circles for which the gift of immortality was a main interest in religion—Athanasios, the man of immortality. For man this will be more than a restoration to the incorruption (moral and metaphysical) and immortality for which man was created; it is a state so high that in union with the divine Word we are indeed in some sense divine (54; cf. II Peter 1:4). As to what happens to those who do not enter the realm of redemption, Athanasius sees no need to be explicit. Sin and corruption is the loss of true being, and there seems to be a hint that its final terminus will be the complete loss of being, but the end of evil like its origin is not discussed in detail (6).

Athanasius would probably have agreed with the definition of our modern conferences that take the confession of Christ as God and Saviour as a convenient statement of the heart of the gospel—especially if we remember that *Sōtēr* in Greek means healer and life giver. He was also aware that much else was implied in this confession or required by it; in this sense On the Incarnation is the point of departure of later patristic thought. The Arians in their blatant early statements shortly challenged its central convictions by asserting that the Word was not God but only the greatest of God's creatures. It was, as it were, a viceroy and not the King who had come to earth after all. Against this reversion to the idea of great and lesser deities Athanasius stood, sometimes bitterly, always bravely, for the rest of his life. This is the central proclamation of the Nicene Creed, that one who was of the same stuff as God the Father became man for our salvation. In On the Incarnation and the early Nicene controversy Athanasius stood for the true deity of the divinity of Christ. In his later writings he develops the balancing truth, always present in his thought though in On the Incarnation not clearly defined, of the true humanity of his manhood. Around these terms the further discussion proceeded until the Church had clarified its faith in one Christ, perfect God and perfect Man.

## TEXT, STRUCTURE, AND TRANSLATION

The preservation and study of the writings of Athanasius is itself a long and not uninteresting story. The very success of his ideas led to their incorporation in more systematic works than he had himself produced, and for some centuries after his death his works seem to have been preserved mainly for the light that some of his phrases threw on matters currently in dispute. Two collections, of apologetic-historical and doctrinal treatises, seem to be the basis of the various selections found in Greek manuscripts. On the Incarnation falls into the latter class, and sometimes also appears separately in collections of miscellaneous edifying matter. The ideas of Athanasius entered into the general stock of Western theology, and one of his central thoughts inspired one of the loveliest of old Latin prayers:

"O God who didst wonderfully create and yet more wonderfully renew the dignity of human nature, grant that (by this mystery of water and wine) we may be partakers of his divinity who vouchsafed to share our humanity, Jesus Christ thy Son our Lord." [6]

But there was little interest in his writings until the Renaissance. On the Incarnation was translated into Latin in the fifteenth century and printed with some other works at Vicenza in 1482. The Greek was first printed by Commelin at Heidelberg in

---

[6] *Leonine Sacramentary*, Christmas (and at the blessing of the water in the Roman Mass).

1600 in an edition for which the manuscripts were studied, rather confusingly, by Felckmann. In 1698 appeared the edition by the great French Benedictine scholar Montfaucon, which marks the beginning of modern scientific study of both life and works of Athanasius. The Benedictine text is still the latest critical edition of On the Incarnation, since the Berlin edition by Opitz begun in 1935 has not reached this work.

In the nineteenth century the great importance of the writings of Athanasius for both general Church history and the history of Christian thought was increasingly recognized, and, then and since, new discoveries of documents have clarified our knowledge of his career. The prominent place given to On the Incarnation in the Honours School of Theology at Oxford since 1870 has been both a result and a cause of further study. The first English translation appeared in 1880. Robertson, who edited the volume of Athanasius in the Post-Nicene Fathers, also published two editions of the text of On the Incarnation; the first (1882) followed the Benedictine edition, while in the second (1893) he decided instead to follow a single outstanding manuscript, S (Codex Seguerianus). The same text has been used by Cross (1936), and as the basis of the textual studies of Ryan and Casey (1945–1946). At present the increasing knowledge of manuscripts seems rather to postpone than to bring nearer the day when a definitive edition can be produced.

However, these uncertainties of text do not affect the general sense of On the Incarnation. But in 1925, Professor Lebon of Louvain identified a "Short Recension" of the work, of which several manuscripts are now known. Apart from a number of slight variations it has several interesting substitutions, usually definitely shorter than the passages they replace. Though all possible views of the relation of the two recensions seem to have been suggested, comparison seems to show that the Short Recension is intelligible as a revision of the Long Recension and not vice versa, and that it comes from the later years of Athanasius, or at least from his circle.[7] The principal alterations are indicated in the notes below; they seem generally to replace the more speculative interpretations by a more theological interest, and show Athanasius (or his editor) a little

[7] Some of its special readings may reflect an Apollinarian edition of On the Incarnation, e.g., the addition at the end of Ch. 26: "When this took place there was no doubt that he who worked in the body and dwelt there was not man but God's Word. Faith in such demonstrations is not obscure but confident."

more careful and less exuberant. Both texts are probably Athanasian, but the first thoughts of the Long Recension are still the primary text.

The translation here reprinted is that of Robertson, 1885, as in the Library of Nicene and Post-Nicene Fathers, Vol. IV. However, the use of capitals has been reduced, the editor's chapter summaries are omitted, and the spelling of proper names is regularized, with Biblical names in their usual English forms. The chapter divisions (which apparently go back to Montfaucon) are retained for convenience, but the deceptive division into verses is not.

As Athanasius wrote it, On the Incarnation was one continuous discourse, in which, however, he fairly clearly indicated the main divisions, approximately as follows:

> I Prologue (1–3)
> II The Coming of the Word (4–19)
> III The Victory of the Cross (20–32)
> IV Reply to Criticisms of: A. Jews (33–40)
> B. Greeks (41–54)
> V Epilogue (55–57)

From a literary point of view this is crossed by another arrangement: the Prologue summarizes the discussion of Against the Heathen and leads naturally into the exposition of "II," based on general considerations; the sections I have listed as "III" and "IV. A." are primarily Biblical in their references, "IV. B." is again more general, and its closing sections, though formally a refutation of opponents, become more and more a paean of victory for Christ, picking up what was begun in "III," and leading into the quieter conclusion which directs the reader to prepare himself for further instruction. In an age in which literature was still thought of basically as prepared for oral presentation such an interlocking arrangement was more natural than the sharper divisions that we should expect in a written document.

# BIBLIOGRAPHY

## EDITIONS

*Complete Editions of Athanasius*:
Commelin, Heidelberg, 1600 (*De incarnatione*, Vol. I, pp. 37–81).
Montfaucon, Paris, 1698, reprinted in Migne, *Patrologia Graeca*,
Vols. XXV–XXVIII. Paris, 1857. (*De incarnatione*, Vol.
XXV, cols. 95–198.)

*Separate*:
Archibald Robertson, *St. Athanasius on the Incarnation*. London,
1882. 2d ed., 1893 (reprinted in Ryan and Casey, *The De
incarnatione*, Part II, pp. 1–86).
Frank L. Cross, *Athanasius De incarnatione, an Edition of the Greek
Text* (Texts for Students, 39). London, S.P.C.K., 1939.

## TRANSLATIONS

*English*:
A. Robertson, 1885, and in Select Library of Nicene and Post-
Nicene Fathers, Series II, Vol. IV, London, 1892, pp. 31–67.
(An excellent version, here reprinted; the general "Prolegom-
ena," pp. xi–xci, remain one of the best introductions to
Athanasius.)
T. H. Bindley, *Athanasius on the Incarnation* (Christian Classics
Series III). London, n.d. (but between 1885 and 1890, as
noted by Robertson, p. 34). (A good, unpretentious version,
unfortunately rare.)
Anon., *The Incarnation of the Word of God, Being the Treatise of
St. Athanasius De incarnatione verbi Dei*, newly translated into
English by a Religious of C.S.M.V., with an Introduction
by C. S. Lewis. London, Geoffrey Bles (New York, Macmillan),
1944. (An attractive modern version, but with a considerable
amount of unnoted paraphrase and abridgment.)

*French:*

Th. Camelot, O.P., *Athanase d'Alexandrie contre les païens et sur l'incarnation du verbe* (Sources chrétiennes 18). Paris, Éditions du Cerf, 1946 (with a valuable introduction, pp. 7–106).

*German:*

J. Fisch, *Ausgewählte Schriften des heiligen Athanasius*, Vol. I (Bibliothek der Kirchenväter, Vol. 15). Kempten, 1872 ("Ueber die Menschwerdung," pp. 117–195).

J. Stegmann in *Des heiligen Athanasius ausgewählte Schriften* (Bibliothek der Kirchenväter, new series, Vol. 31). Kempten, 1917 ("Ueber die Menschwerdung," pp. 602–676).

## SPECIAL STUDIES

Frank L. Cross, *The Study of St. Athanasius, an Inaugural Lecture Delivered Before the University of Oxford on 1 December, 1944.* Oxford, Clarendon Press, 1945. (A masterly survey.)

Karl Hoss, *Studien über das Schrifttum und die Theologie des Athanasius auf Grund einer Echtheitsuntersuchung von* Athanasius contra gentes *und* de incarnatione. Freiburg, 1899.

J. Lebon, "Pour une édition critique de Saint Athanase," *Revue d'histoire ecclésiastique*, Vol. 21, 1925, pp. 324–330.

H. G. Opitz, *Untersuchungen zur Überlieferung der Schriften des Athanasius* (*Arbeiten zur Kirchengeschichte*, 23). Berlin and Leipzig, de Gruyter, 1935.

George J. Ryan and Robert Pierce Casey, *The De incarnatione of Athanasius* (Studies and Documents, XIV): Part I, G. J. Ryan, "The Long Recension Manuscripts"; Part II, R. P. Casey, "The Short Recension." Philadelphia, University of Pennsylvania Press, 1945–1946.

## GENERAL

The life and ideas of Athanasius are treated in all works on Church history, history of doctrine, and Egyptian history covering the period; see General Bibliography. Two classic accounts always worth consulting are:

Gregory Nazianzen, Oration XXI, "On the Great Athanasius," delivered at Constantinople in 379 or 380 (translation in Post-Nicene Fathers, Series II, Vol. VII, pp. 269–280. London, 1894).

A. P. Stanley, *Lectures on the History of the Eastern Church*, Lecture VII. London, 1861.

*On Egypt and Its Church in This Period*:

H. I. Bell, *Jews and Christians in Egypt*, London, 1924 (side lights on Church history in papyri from monasteries).

E. R. Hardy, *Christian Egypt*: *Church and People*, Ch. 2, "The Two Worlds of Athanasius." New York, Oxford University Press, 1952.

J. G. Milne, *A History of Egypt Under Roman Rule*, 3d ed. London, 1924.

# On the Incarnation of the Word

## THE TEXT

### PROLOGUE

1. Whereas in what precedes we have drawn out—choosing a few points from among many—a sufficient account of the error of the heathen concerning idols, and of the worship of idols, and how they originally came to be invented; how, namely, out of wickedness men devised for themselves the worshiping of idols; and whereas we have by God's grace noted somewhat also of the divinity of the Word of the Father, and of his universal providence and power, and that the good Father through him orders all things, and all things are moved by him, and in him are quickened, come now, Macarius[1] (worthy of that name), and true lover of Christ, let us follow up the faith of our religion, and set forth also what relates to the Word's becoming man, and to his divine appearing amongst us, which Jews traduce and Greeks laugh to scorn, but we worship; in order that, all the more for the seeming low estate of the Word, your piety toward him may be increased and multiplied. For the more he is mocked among the unbelieving, the more witness does he give of his own Godhead; inasmuch as he not only himself demonstrates as possible what men mistake, thinking impossible, but what men deride as unseemly, this by his own goodness he clothes with seemliness, and what men, in their conceit of wisdom, laugh at as merely human, he by his own power demonstrates to be divine, subduing the pretensions of idols by his supposed humiliation—by the cross —and those who mock and disbelieve invisibly winning over to recognize his divinity and power. But to treat this subject it

---

[1] Macarius, "blessed"; probably not a particular person, although the name is, somewhat later, not uncommon among Egyptian Christians, but the "gentle reader"; perhaps suggested by Luke's Theophilus.

is necessary to recall what has been previously said; in order that you may neither fail to know the cause of the bodily appearing of the Word of the Father, so high and so great, nor think it a consequence of his own nature that the Saviour has worn a body; but that being incorporeal by nature, and Word from the beginning, he has yet of the loving-kindness and goodness of his own Father been manifested to us in a human body for our salvation. It is, then, proper for us to begin the treatment of this subject by speaking of the creation of the universe, and of God its Artificer, that so it may be duly perceived that the renewal of creation has been the work of the selfsame Word that made it at the beginning. For it will appear not inconsonant for the Father to have wrought its salvation in him by whose means he made it.

2. Of the making of the universe and the creation of all things many have taken different views, and each man has laid down the law just as he pleased. For some say that all things have come into being of themselves, and in a chance fashion; as, for example, the Epicureans, who tell us, in their self-contempt, that universal providence does not exist, speaking right in the face of obvious fact and experience. For if, as they say, everything has had its beginning of itself, and independently of purpose, it would follow that everything had come into mere being so as to be alike and not distinct. For it would follow in virtue of the unity of body that everything must be sun or moon, and in the case of men it would follow that the whole must be hand, or eye, or foot. But as it is this is not so. On the contrary, we see a distinction of sun, moon, and earth; and again, in the case of human bodies, of foot, hand, and head. Now, such separate arrangement as this tells us not of their having come into being of themselves, but shows that a cause preceded them; from which cause it is possible to apprehend God also as the maker and orderer of all. But others, including Plato, who is in such repute among the Greeks, argue that God has made the world out of matter previously existing and without beginning. For God could have made nothing had not the material existed already; just as the wood must exist ready at hand for the carpenter, to enable him to work at all. But in so saying they know not that they are investing God with weakness. For if he is not himself the cause of the material, but makes things only of previously existing material, he proves to be weak, because unable to produce anything he makes without the material; just as it is without doubt a weakness of the

carpenter not to be able to make anything required without his timber. For, *ex hypothesi*, had not the material existed, God would not have made anything. And how could he in that case be called maker and artificer, if he owes his ability to make to some other source—namely, to the material? So that if this be so, God will be on their theory a mechanic only, and not a creator out of nothing; if, that is, he works at existing material, but is not himself the cause of the material. For he could not in any sense be called creator unless he is creator of the material of which the things created have in their turn been made. But the sectaries imagine to themselves a different artificer of all things, other than the Father of our Lord Jesus Christ, in deep blindness even as to the words they use. For whereas the Lord says to the Jews, "Have ye not read that from the beginning he which created them made them male and female, and said, For this cause shall a man leave his father and mother, and shall cleave to his wife, and they twain shall become one flesh?" and then, referring to the Creator, says, "What, therefore, God hath joined together let not man put asunder" [2]: how come these men to assert that the creation is independent of the Father? Or if, in the words of John, who says, making no exception, "All things were made by him," and "Without him was not anything made," [3] how could the artificer be another, distinct from the Father of Christ?

3. Thus do they vainly speculate. But the godly teaching and the faith according to Christ brands their foolish language as godlessness. For it knows that it was not spontaneously, because forethought is not absent; nor of existing matter, because God is not weak; but that out of nothing, and without its having any previous existence, God made the universe to exist through his word, as he says firstly through Moses: "In the beginning God created the heaven and the earth" [4]; secondly, in the most edifying book of the Shepherd, "First of all believe that God is one, which created and framed all things, and made them to exist out of nothing." [5] To which also Paul refers when he says, "By faith we understand that the worlds have been framed by the Word of God, so that what is seen hath not been made out of things which do appear." [6]

---

[2] Matt. 19:4–6.                    [3] John 1:3.                    [4] Gen. 1:1.
[5] Shepherd of Hermas, Mandate 1; Athanasius was accustomed to list the Shepherd, along with the O.T. Apocrypha and the Didache, not as part of the Bible, but as a book read for instruction with it (Festal Epistles, 39).
[6] Heb. 11:3.

For God is good, or rather is essentially the source of goodness, nor could one that is good be niggardly of anything; whence, grudging existence to none, he has made all things out of nothing by his own Word, Jesus Christ our Lord. And among these, having taken especial pity, above all things on earth, upon the race of men, and having perceived its inability, by virtue of the condition of its origin, to continue in one stay, he gave them a further gift, and he did not barely create man, as he did all the irrational creatures on the earth, but made them after his own image, giving them a portion even of the power of his own Word; so that having as it were a kind of reflection of the Word, and being made rational, they might be able to abide ever in blessedness, living the true life which belongs to the saints in paradise.[7] But knowing once more how the will of man could sway to either side, in anticipation he secured the grace given them by a law and by the spot where he placed them. For he brought them into his own Garden, and gave them a law: so that, if they kept the grace and remained good, they might still keep the life in paradise without sorrow or pain or care, besides having the promise of incorruption in heaven; but that if they transgressed and turned back, and became evil, they might know that they were incurring that corruption in death which was theirs by nature, no longer to live in paradise, but cast out of it from that time forth to die and to abide in death and in corruption. Now this is that of which Holy Writ also gives warning, saying in the person of God: "Of every tree that is in the garden, eating thou shalt eat: but of the tree of knowledge of good and evil, ye shall not eat of it, but on the day that ye eat, dying ye shall die." [8] But by "dying ye shall die," what else could be meant than not dying merely, but also abiding ever in the corruption of death?

## The Coming of the Word

4. You are wondering, perhaps, for what possible reason, having proposed to speak of the incarnation of the Word, we are at present treating of the origin of mankind. But this too properly belongs to the aim of our treatise. For in speaking of the appearance of the Saviour amongst us, we must needs speak also of the origin of men, that you may know that the reason of

[7] The familiar play between *Logos* and *logikos*; by sharing in the divine Word, or Reason, men become truly rational.
[8] Gen. 2:16, 17.

his coming down was because of us, and that our transgression called forth the loving-kindness of the Word, that the Lord should both make haste to help us and appear among men. For of his becoming incarnate we were the object, and for our salvation he dealt so lovingly as to appear and be born even in a human body. Thus, then, God has made man, and willed that he should abide in incorruption; but men, having despised and rejected the contemplation of God, and devised and contrived evil for themselves (as was said in the former treatise), received the condemnation of death with which they had been threatened; and from thenceforth no longer remained as they were made, but were being corrupted according to their devices; and death had the mastery over them as king. For transgression of the commandment was turning them back to their natural state, so that just as they have had their being out of nothing, so also, as might be expected, they might look for corruption into nothing in the course of time. For if, out of a former normal state of nonexistence, they were called into being by the presence and loving-kindness of the Word, it followed naturally that when men were bereft of the knowledge of God and were turned back to what was not (for what is evil is not, but what is good is), they should, since they derive their being from God who is, be everlastingly bereft even of being; in other words, that they should be disintegrated and abide in death and corruption. For man is by nature mortal, inasmuch as he is made out of what is not; but by reason of his likeness to Him that is (and if he still preserved this likeness by keeping him in his knowledge) he would stay his natural corruption, and remain incorrupt; as Wisdom says: "The taking heed to his laws is the assurance of immortality" [9]; but being incorrupt, he would live henceforth as God, to which I suppose the divine Scripture refers, when it says: "I have said ye are gods; and ye are all sons of the Most High; but ye die like men, and fall as one of the princes." [10]

5. For God has not only made us out of nothing; but he gave us freely, by the grace of the Word, a life in correspondence with God. But men, having rejected things eternal, and, by counsel of the devil, turned to the things of corruption, became the cause of their own corruption in death, being, as I said before, by nature corruptible, but destined, by the grace following

[9] Wisdom 6:18 ("immortality," literally "incorruption"); cf. ch. 13:1, "him that is."
[10] Ps. 82:6, 7.

from partaking of the Word, to have escaped their natural state, had they remained good. For because of the Word dwelling with them, even their natural corruption did not come near them, as Wisdom also says: "God made man for incorruption, and as an image of his own eternity; but by envy of the devil death came into the world." [11] But when this was come to pass, men began to die, while corruption thenceforward prevailed against them, gaining even more than its natural power over the whole race, inasmuch as it had, owing to the transgression of the commandment, the threat of the Deity as a further advantage against them. For even in their misdeeds men had not stopped short at any set limits; but, gradually pressing forward, have passed on beyond all measure: having, to begin with, been inventors of wickedness and called down upon themselves death and corruption; while later on, having turned aside to wrong and exceeding all lawlessness, and stopping at no one evil but devising all manner of new evils in succession, they have become insatiable in sinning. For there were adulteries everywhere and thefts, and the whole earth was full of murders and plunderings. And as to corruption and wrong, no heed was paid to law, but all crimes were being practiced everywhere, both individually and jointly. Cities were at war with cities, and nations were rising up against nations; and the whole earth was rent with civil commotions and battles, each man vying with his fellows in lawless deeds. Nor were even crimes against nature far from them, but, as the apostle and witness of Christ says: "For their women changed the natural use into that which is against nature: and likewise also the men, leaving the natural use of the women, burned in their lust one toward another, men with men working unseemliness, and receiving in themselves that recompense of their error which was meet." [12]

6. For this cause, then, death having gained upon men, and corruption abiding upon them, the race of man was perishing; the rational man made in God's image was disappearing, and the handiwork of God was in process of dissolution. For death, as I said above, gained from that time forth a legal hold over us, and it was impossible to evade the law, since it had been laid down by God because of the transgression, and the result was in truth at once monstrous and unseemly. For it were monstrous, firstly, that God, having spoken, should prove false —that, when once he had ordained that man, if he transgressed

[11] Wisdom 2:23, 24.      [12] Rom. 1:26, 27.

the commandment, should die the death, after the transgression man should not die, but God's word should be broken. For God would not be true if, when he had said we should die, man died not. Again, it were unseemly that creatures once made rational, and having partaken of the Word, should go to ruin, and turn again toward nonexistence by the way of corruption. For it were not worthy of God's goodness that the things he had made should waste away, because of the deceit practiced on men by the devil. Especially it was unseemly to the last degree that God's handicraft among men should be done away, either because of their own carelessness, or because of the deceitfulness of evil spirits. So, as the rational creatures were wasting and such works in course of ruin, what was God in his goodness to do? Suffer corruption to prevail against them and death to hold them fast? And where were the profit of their having been made, to begin with? For better were they not made than, once made, left to neglect and ruin. For neglect reveals weakness, and not goodness on God's part—if, that is, he allows his own work to be ruined when once he had made it —more so than if he had never made man at all. For if he had not made them, none could impute weakness; but once he had made them, and created them out of nothing, it were most monstrous for the work to be ruined, and that before the eyes of the maker. It was, then, out of the question to leave men to the current of corruption; because this would be unseemly, and unworthy of God's goodness.

7. But just as this consequence must needs hold, so, too, on the other side the just claims of God lie against it: that God should appear true to the law he had laid down concerning death. For it were monstrous for God, the father of truth, to appear a liar for our profit and preservation. So here, once more, what possible course was God to take? To demand repentance of men for their transgression? For this one might pronounce worthy of God; as though, just as from transgression men have become set toward corruption, so from repentance they may once more be set in the way of incorruption. But repentance would, firstly, fail to guard the just claim of God. For he would still be none the more true, if men did not remain in the grasp of death; nor, secondly, does repentance call men back from what is their nature—it merely stays them from acts of sin. Now, if there were merely a misdemeanor in question, and not a consequent corruption, repentance were well enough. But if, when transgression had once gained a start, men became

involved in that corruption which was their nature, and were deprived of the grace which they had, being in the image of God, what further step was needed? or what was required for such grace and such recall, but the Word of God, which had also at the beginning made everything out of nought? For his it was once more both to bring the corruptible to incorruption, and to maintain intact the just claim of the Father upon all. For being Word of the Father, and above all, he alone of natural fitness was both able to re-create everything, and worthy to suffer on behalf of all and to be ambassador for all with the Father.

8. For this purpose, then, the incorporeal and incorruptible and immaterial Word of God comes to our realm, howbeit he was not far from us before. For no part of creation is left void of him: he has filled all things everywhere, remaining present with his own Father. But he comes in condescension to show loving-kindness upon us, and to visit us. And seeing the race of rational creatures in the way to perish, and death reigning over them by corruption; seeing, too, that the threat against transgression gave a firm hold to the corruption which was upon us, and that it was monstrous that before the law was fulfilled it should fall through; seeing, once more, the unseemliness of what was come to pass: that the things whereof he himself was artificer were passing away; seeing, further, the exceeding wickedness of men, and how by little and little they had increased it to an intolerable pitch against themselves; and seeing, lastly, how all men were under penalty of death, he took pity on our race, and had mercy on our infirmity, and condescended to our corruption, and, unable to bear that death should have the mastery—lest the creature should perish, and his Father's handiwork in men be spent for nought—he takes unto himself a body, and that of no different sort from ours. For he did not simply will to become embodied, or will merely to appear. For if he willed merely to appear, he was able to effect his divine appearance by some other and higher means as well. [13] But he takes a body of our kind, and not merely so, but from a spotless and stainless virgin, knowing not a man, a body clean and in very truth pure from intercourse of men. For being himself mighty, and artificer of everything, he prepares the body in the virgin as a temple unto himself, and makes it his very own as an instrument, in it manifested, and in it

[13] I.e., a mere appearance of the Word could as easily have been in more than human form.

dwelling. And thus taking from our bodies one of like nature, because all were under penalty of the corruption of death he gave it over to death in the stead of all, and offered it to the Father—doing this, moreover, of his loving-kindness, to the end that, firstly, all being held to have died in him, the law involving the ruin of men might be undone (inasmuch as its power was fully spent in the Lord's body, and had no longer holding ground against men, his peers), and that, secondly, whereas men had turned toward corruption, he might turn them again toward incorruption, and quicken them from death by the appropriation of his body and by the grace of the resurrection, banishing death from them like straw from the fire.

9. For the Word, perceiving that not otherwise could the corruption of men be undone save by death as a necessary condition, while it was impossible for the Word to suffer death, being immortal, and Son of the Father; to this end he takes to himself a body capable of death, that it, by partaking of the Word who is above all, might be worthy to die in the stead of all, and might, because of the Word which was come to dwell in it, remain incorruptible, and that thenceforth corruption might be stayed from all by the grace of the resurrection. Whence, by offering unto death the body he himself had taken, as an offering and sacrifice free from any stain, straightway he put away death from all his peers by the offering of an equivalent. For, being over all, the Word of God naturally by offering his own temple and corporeal instrument for the life of all satisfied the debt by his death. And thus he, the incorruptible Son of God, being conjoined with all by a like nature, naturally clothed all with incorruption, by the promise of the resurrection. For the actual corruption in death has no longer holding ground against men, by reason of the Word, which by his one body has come to dwell among them. And like as when a great king has entered into some large city and taken up his abode in one of the houses there, such city is at all events held worthy of high honor, nor does any enemy or bandit any longer descend upon it and subject it; but, on the contrary, it is thought entitled to all care, because of the king's having taken up his residence in a single house there; so, too, has it been with the monarch of all. For now that he has come to our realm, and taken up his abode in one body among his peers, henceforth the whole conspiracy of the enemy against mankind is checked, and the corruption of death which before was prevailing against them is done away. For the race of men had

gone to ruin, had not the Lord and Saviour of all, the Son of God, come among us to meet the end of death.

10. Now in truth this great work was peculiarly suited to God's goodness. For if a king, having founded a house or city, if it be beset by bandits from the carelessness of its inmates, does not by any means neglect it, but avenges and reclaims it as his own work, having regard, not to the carelessness of the inhabitants, but to what beseems himself; much more did God the Word of the all-good Father not neglect the race of men, his work, going to corruption: but, while he blotted out the death which had ensued by the offering of his own body, he corrected their neglect by his own teaching, restoring all that was man's by his own power. And of this one may be assured at the hands of the Saviour's own inspired writers, if one happen upon their writings, where they say: "For the love of Christ constraineth us; because we thus judge, that if one died for all, then all died, and he died for all that we should no longer live unto ourselves, but unto him who for our sakes died and rose again," [14] our Lord Jesus Christ. And, again: "But we behold him, who hath been made a little lower than the angels, even Jesus, because of the suffering of death crowned with glory and honor, that by the grace of God he should taste of death for every man." Then he also points out the reason why it was necessary for none other than God the Word himself to become incarnate, as follows: "For it became him, for whom are all things, and through whom are all things, in bringing many sons unto glory, to make the captain of their salvation perfect through suffering"; by which words he means that it belonged to none other to bring man back from the corruption which had begun than the Word of God, who had also made them from the beginning. And that it was in order to the sacrifice for bodies such as his own that the Word himself also assumed a body; to this, also, they refer in these words: "Forasmuch then as the children are the sharers in blood and flesh, he also himself in like manner partook of the same, that through death he might bring to nought him that had the power of death, that is, the devil; and might deliver them who, through fear of death, were all their lifetime subject to bondage." [15] For by the sacrifice of his own body, he both put an end to the law which was against us, and made a new beginning of life for us, by the hope of resurrection which he has given us. For since from man it was that death prevailed over men, for this cause con-

[14] II Cor. 5:14, 15.                    [15] Heb. 2:9, 10, 14, 15.

versely, by the Word of God being made man has come about
the destruction of death and the resurrection of life; as the man
which bore Christ says: "For since by man came death, by man
came also the resurrection of the dead. For as in Adam all die,
so also in Christ shall all be made alive" [16]; and so forth. For
no longer now do we die as subject to condemnation; but as
men who rise from the dead we await the general resurrection
of all, "which in its own times he shall show,"[17] even God, who
has also wrought it, and bestowed it upon us. This, then, is the
first cause of the Saviour's being made man. But one might see
from the following reasons also that his gracious coming amongst
us was fitting to have taken place.

11. God, who has the power over all things, when he was
making the race of men through his own Word, seeing the
weakness of their nature, that it was not sufficient of itself to
know its maker, nor to get any idea at all of God; because while
he was uncreate, the creatures had been made of nought, and
while he was incorporeal, men had been fashioned in a lower
way in the body, and because in every way the things made
fell far short of being able to comprehend and know their
maker—taking pity, I say, on the race of men, inasmuch as
he is good, he did not leave them destitute of the knowledge
of himself, lest they should find no profit in existing at all.
For what profit to the creatures if they knew not their maker?
or how could they be rational without knowing the Word [and
reason] of the Father, in whom they received their very being?
For there would be nothing to distinguish them even from brute
creatures if they had knowledge of nothing but earthly things.
Nay, why did God make them at all, as he did not wish to be
known by them? Whence, lest this should be so, being good,
he gives them a share in his own image, our Lord Jesus Christ,
and makes them after his own image and after his likeness: so
that by such grace perceiving the image, that is, the Word of
the Father, they may be able through him to get an idea of the
Father, and, knowing their maker, live the happy and truly
blessed life. But men once more in their perversity having set
at nought, in spite of all this, the grace given them, so wholly
rejected God, and so darkened their soul, as not merely to
forget their idea of God, but also to fashion for themselves one
invention after another. For not only did they grave idols for
themselves, instead of the truth, and honor things that were
not before the living God, "and serve the creature rather than

16 I Cor. 15:21, 22.                    17 I Tim. 6:15.

C.L.F.—5

the Creator," [18] but, worst of all, they transferred the honor of God even to stocks and stones and to every material object and to men, and went even further than this, as we have said in the former treatise. So far indeed did their impiety go, that they proceeded to worship devils, and proclaimed them as gods, fulfilling their own lusts. For they performed, as was said above, offerings of brute animals, and sacrifices of men, as was meet for them, binding themselves down all the faster under their maddening inspirations. For this reason it was also that magic arts were taught among them, and oracles in divers places led men astray, and all men ascribed the influences of their birth and existence to the stars and to all the heavenly bodies, having no thought of anything beyond what was visible. And, in a word, everything was full of irreligion and lawlessness, and God alone, and his Word, was unknown, albeit he had not hidden himself out of men's sight, nor given the knowledge of himself in one way only; but had, on the contrary, unfolded it to them in many forms and by many ways.

12. For whereas the grace of the divine image was in itself sufficient to make known God the Word, and through him the Father, still God, knowing the weakness of men, made provision even for their carelessness; so that if they cared not to know God of themselves, they might be enabled through the works of creation to avoid ignorance of the maker. But since men's carelessness, by little and little, descends to lower things, God made provision, once more, even for this weakness of theirs, by sending a law, and prophets, men such as they knew, so that even if they were not ready to look up to heaven and know their Creator, they might have their instruction from those near at hand. For men are able to learn from men more directly about higher things. So it was open to them, by looking into the height of heaven, and perceiving the harmony of creation, to know its ruler, the Word of the Father, who by his own providence over all things makes known the Father to all, and to this end moves all things, that through him all may know God. Or, if this were too much for them, it was possible for them to meet at least the holy men, and through them to learn of God, the maker of all things, the Father of Christ; and that the worship of idols is godlessness, and full of all impiety. Or it was open to them, by knowing the law even, to cease from all lawlessness and live a virtuous life. For neither was the law for the Jews alone, nor were the prophets sent for them only,

[18] Rom. 1:25.

but, though sent to the Jews and persecuted by the Jews, they were for all the world a holy school of the knowledge of God and the conduct of the soul. God's goodness then and loving-kindness being so great, men nevertheless, overcome by the pleasures of the moment and by the illusions and deceits sent by demons, did not raise their heads toward the truth, but loaded themselves the more with evils and sins, so as no longer to seem rational, but from their ways to be reckoned void of reason.

13. So, then, men having thus become brutalized, and demoniacal deceit thus clouding every place, and hiding the knowledge of the true God, what was God to do? To keep still silence at so great a thing, and suffer men to be led astray by demons and not to know God? And what was the use of man having been originally made in God's image? For it had been better for him to have been made simply like a brute animal, than, once made rational, for him to live the life of the brutes. Or where was any necessity at all for his receiving the idea of God to begin with? For if he be not fit to receive it even now, it were better it had not been given him at first. Or what profit to God who has made them, or what glory to him could it be, if men, made by him, do not worship him, but think that others are their makers? For God thus proves to have made these for others instead of for himself. Once again, a merely human king does not let the lands he has colonized pass to others to serve them, nor go over to other men; but he warns them by letters, and often sends to them by friends, or, if need be, he comes in person, to put them to rebuke in the last resort by his presence, only that they may not serve others and his own work be spent for nought. Shall not God much more spare his own creatures, that they be not led astray from him and serve things of nought? especially since such going astray proves the cause of their ruin and undoing, and since it was unfitting that they should perish which had once been partakers of God's image. What, then, was God to do? or what was to be done save the renewing of that which was in God's image, so that by it men might once more be able to know him? But how could this have come to pass save by the presence of the very image of God, our Lord Jesus Christ? For by men's means it was impossible, since they are but made after an image; nor by angels either, for not even they are [God's] images. Whence the Word of God came in his own person, that, as he was the image of the Father, he might be able to create afresh the man after the image. But, again,

it could not else have taken place had not death and corruption been done away. Whence he took, in natural fitness, a mortal body, that while death might in it be once for all done away, men made after his image might once more be renewed. None other, then, was sufficient for this need, save the image of the Father.

14. For as, when the likeness painted on a panel has been effaced by stains from without, he whose likeness it is must needs come once more to enable the portrait to be renewed on the same wood, for, for the sake of his picture, even the mere wood on which it is painted is not thrown away, but the outline is renewed upon it; in the same way also the most holy Son of the Father, being the image of the Father, came to our region to renew man once made in his likeness, and find him, as one lost, by the remission of sins; as he says himself in the Gospels, "I came to find and to save the lost." [19] Whence he said to the Jews also, "Except a man be born again," [20] not meaning, as they thought, birth from woman, but speaking of the soul born and created anew in the likeness of God's image. But since wild idolatry and godlessness occupied the world, and the knowledge of God was hid, whose part was it to teach the world concerning the Father? Man's, might one say? But it was not in man's power to penetrate everywhere beneath the sun; for neither had they the physical strength to run so far, nor would they be able to claim credence in this matter, nor were they sufficient by themselves to withstand the deceit and impositions of evil spirits. For where all were smitten and confused in soul from demoniacal deceit, and the vanity of idols, how was it possible for them to win over man's soul and man's mind—whereas they cannot even see them? Or how can a man convert what he does not see? But perhaps one might say creation was enough; but if creation were enough, these great evils would never have come to pass. For creation was there already, and, all the same, men were groveling in the same error concerning God. Who, then, was needed, save the Word of God, that sees both soul and mind, and that gives movement to all things in creation, and by them makes known the Father? For he who by his own providence and ordering of all things was teaching men concerning the Father, he it was that could renew this same teaching as well. How, then, could this have been done? Perhaps one might say that the same means were open as before, for him to show forth the truth about the Father once

[19] Luke 19:10.                    [20] John 3:3.

more by means of the work of creation. But this was no longer a sure means. Quite the contrary; for men missed seeing this before, and have turned their eyes no longer upward but downward. Whence, naturally, willing to profit men, he sojourns here as man, taking to himself a body like the others, and from things of earth, that is, by the works of his body [he teaches them], so that they who would not know him from his providence and rule over all things may even from the works done by his actual body know the Word of God which is in the body, and through him the Father.

15. For like a kind teacher who cares for his disciples, if some of them cannot profit by higher subjects, comes down to their level, and teaches them at any rate by simpler courses, so also did the Word of God. As Paul also says, "For seeing that in the wisdom of God the world through its wisdom knew not God, it was God's good pleasure through the foolishness of the [word] preached to save them that believe." 21 For seeing that men, having rejected the contemplation of God, and with their eyes downward, as though sunk in the deep, were seeking about for God in nature and in the world of sense, feigning gods for themselves of mortal men and demons; to this end the loving and general Saviour of all, the Word of God, takes to himself a body, and as man walks among men and meets the senses of all men halfway, to the end, I say, that they who think that God is corporeal may from what the Lord effects by his body perceive the truth, and through him recognize the Father. So, men as they were, and humans in all their thoughts, on whatever objects they fixed their senses, there they saw themselves met halfway, and taught the truth from every side. For if they looked with awe upon the creation, yet they saw how it confessed Christ as Lord; or if their mind was swayed toward men, so as to think them gods, yet from the Saviour's works, supposing they compared them, the Saviour alone among men appeared Son of God; for there were no such works done among the rest as have been done by the Word of God. Or if they were biased toward evil spirits, even, yet seeing them cast out by the Word, they were to know that he alone, the Word of God, was God, and that the spirits were none. Or if their mind had already sunk even to the dead, so as to worship heroes, and the gods spoken of in the poets, yet, seeing the Saviour's resurrection, they were to confess them to be false gods, and that the Lord alone is true, the Word of the

21 I Cor. 1:21.

Father, that was lord even of death. For this cause he was both born and appeared as man, and died, and rose again, dulling and casting into the shade the works of all former men by his own, that in whatever direction the bias of men might be, from thence he might recall them, and teach them of his own true Father, as he himself says, "I came to save and to find that which was lost." [22]

16. For, men's mind having finally fallen to things of sense, the Word disguised himself by appearing in a body, that he might, as man, transfer men to himself, and center their senses on himself, and, men seeing him thenceforth as man, persuade them by the works he did that he is not man only, but also God, and the Word and wisdom of the true God. This too is what Paul means to point out when he says: "That ye, being rooted and grounded in love, may be strong to apprehend with all the saints what is the breadth and length, and height and depth, and to know the love of Christ which passeth knowledge, that ye may be filled unto all the fullness of God." [23] For by the Word revealing himself everywhere, both above and beneath, and in the depth and in the breadth—above, in the creation; beneath, in becoming man; in the depth, in Hades; and in the breadth, in the world—all things have been filled with the knowledge of God. Now for this cause, also, he did not immediately upon his coming accomplish his sacrifice on behalf of all, by offering his body to death and raising it again, for by this means he would have made himself invisible. But he made himself visible enough by what he did, abiding in it, and doing such works, and showing such signs, as made him known no longer as man, but as God the Word. For by his becoming man, the Saviour was to accomplish both works of love: first, in putting away death from us and renewing us again; secondly, being unseen and invisible, in manifesting and making himself known by his works to be the Word of the Father, and the ruler and king of the universe.

17. For he was not, as might be imagined, circumscribed in the body, nor, while present in the body, was he absent elsewhere; nor, while he moved the body, was the universe left void of his working and providence; but, thing most marvelous, Word as he was, so far from being contained by anything, he rather contained all things himself; and just as while present in the whole of creation, he is at once distinct in being from the universe, and present in all things by his own power—

giving order to all things, and over all and in all revealing his
own providence, and giving life to each thing and all things,
including the whole without being included, but being in his
own Father alone wholly and in every respect [24]—thus, even
while present in a human body and himself quickening it, he
was, without inconsistency, quickening the universe as well,
and was in every process of nature, and was outside the whole,
and while known from the body by his works, he was none the
less manifest from the working of the universe as well. Now, it
is the function of the soul to behold even what is outside its own
body, by acts of thought, without, however, working outside its
own body, or moving by its presence things remote from the
body. Never, that is, does a man, by thinking of things at a
distance, by that fact either move or displace them; nor if a
man were to sit in his own house and reason about the heavenly
bodies, would he by that fact either move the sun or make the
heavens revolve. But he sees that they move and have their
being, without being actually able to influence them. Now, the
Word of God in his man's nature was not like that; for he was
not bound to his body, but was rather himself wielding it, so
that he was not only in it, but was actually in everything, and
while external to the universe, abode in his Father only. And
this was the wonderful thing that he was at once walking as
man, and as the Word was quickening all things, and as the
Son was dwelling with his Father. So that not even when the
Virgin bore him did he suffer any change, nor by being in the
body was [his glory] dulled: but, on the contrary, he sanctified
the body also. For not even by being in the universe does he
share in its nature, but all things, on the contrary, are quickened
and sustained by him. For if the sun too, which was made by
him, and which we see as it revolves in the heaven, is not defiled
by touching the bodies upon earth, nor is it put out by darkness, but on the contrary itself illuminates and cleanses them
also, much less was the all-holy Word of God, maker and lord
also of the sun, defiled by being made known in the body; on
the contrary, being incorruptible, he quickened and cleansed
the body also, which was in itself mortal: "who did," for so it
says, "no sin, neither was guile found in his mouth." [25]

18. Accordingly, when inspired writers on this matter speak
of him as eating and being born, understand that the body, as
body, was born, and sustained with food corresponding to its

[24] The Word is in the Father in his full being; elsewhere manifested in one
aspect or another.          [25] I Peter 2:22.

nature, while God the Word himself, who was united with the body, while ordering all things, also by the works he did in the body showed himself to be, not man, but God the Word. But[26] these things are said of him because the actual body which ate, was born, and suffered, belonged to none other but to the Lord: and because, having become man, it was proper for these things to be predicated of him as man, to show him to have a body in truth, and not in seeming. But just as from these things he was known to be bodily present, so from the works he did in the body he made himself known to be Son of God. Whence also he cried to the unbelieving Jews: "If I do not the works of my Father, believe me not. But if I do them, though ye believe not me, believe my works; that ye may know and understand that the Father is in me, and I in the Father."[27] For just as, though invisible, he is known through the works of creation; so, having become man, and being in the body unseen, it may be known from his works that he who can do these is not man, but the power and Word of God.[26] For his charging evil spirits, and their being driven forth, this deed is not of man, but of God. Or who that saw him healing the diseases to which the human race is subject, can still think him man and not God? For he cleansed lepers, made lame men to walk, opened the hearing of deaf men, made blind men to see again, and in a word drove away from men all diseases and infirmities: from which acts it was possible even for the most ordinary observer to see his Godhead. For who that saw him give back what was deficient to men born lacking, and open the eyes of the man blind from his birth, would have failed to perceive that the nature of men was subject to him, and that he was its artificer and maker? For he that gave back that which the man from his birth had not must be, it is surely evident, the Lord also of men's natural birth. Therefore, even to begin with, when he was descending to us, he fashioned his body for himself from a virgin, thus to afford to all no small proof of his Godhead, in that he who formed this is also maker of everything else as well. For who, seeing a body proceeding forth from a virgin alone without man, can fail to infer that he who appears in it

---

[26] For the passage, "But these things . . . Word of God," the Short Recension reads, "For being a lover of man and only-begotten Son of the good Father he left nothing void of himself, but was made known invisibly to the invisible [powers] through his forethought for his own creation, while to men he abundantly made the Father known through his own body, showing himself by his divine teaching and his works to be the Son of God."    [27] John 10:37, 38.

is maker and Lord of other bodies also? Or who, seeing the substance of water changed and transformed into wine, fails to perceive that he who did this is Lord and creator of the substance of all waters? For to this end he went upon the sea also as its master, and walked as on dry land, to afford evidence to them that saw it of his lordship over all things. And in feeding so vast a multitude on little, and of his own self yielding abundance where none was, so that from five loaves five thousand had enough, and left so much again over, did he show himself to be any other than the very Lord whose providence is over all things?

19. But all this it seemed well for the Saviour to do; that since men had failed to perceive his Godhead shown in creation, they might at any rate from the works of his body recover their sight, and through him receive an idea of the knowledge of the Father, inferring, as I said before, from particular cases his providence over the whole. For who that saw his power over evil spirits, or who that saw the evil spirits confess that he was their Lord, will hold his mind any longer in doubt whether this be the Son and wisdom and power of God? For he made even the creation break silence: in that even at his death, marvelous to relate, or rather at his actual trophy over death— the cross I mean—all creation was confessing that he that was made manifest and suffered in the body was not man merely, but the Son of God and Saviour of all. For the sun hid his face, and the earth quaked and the mountains were rent; all men were awed. Now these things showed that Christ on the cross was God, while all creation was his slave, and was witnessing by its fear to its master's presence. Thus, then, God the Word showed himself to men by his works. But our next step must be to recount and speak of the end of his bodily life and course, and of the nature of the death of his body, especially as this is the sum of our faith, and all men without exception are full of it;[28] so that you may know that no whit the less from this also Christ is known to be God and the Son of God.

## The Victory of the Cross

20. We have, then, now stated in part, as far as it was possible, and as ourselves had been able to understand, the reason of his bodily appearing; that it was in the power of none other to turn the corruptible to incorruption, except the Saviour

[28] Or, "chatter about it"—the cross, the central point of the faith, still to the Greeks foolishness.

himself, that had at the beginning also made all things out of nought; and that none other could create anew the likeness of God's image for men, save the image of the Father; and that none other could render the mortal immortal, save our Lord Jesus Christ, who is the very life; and that none other could teach men of the Father, and destroy the worship of idols, save the Word, that orders all things and is alone the true only-begotten Son of the Father. But since it was necessary also that the debt owing from all should be paid again, for, as I have already said, it was owing that all should die—for which especial cause, indeed, he came among us—to this intent, after the proofs of his Godhead from his works, he next offered up his sacrifice also on behalf of all, yielding his temple to death in the stead of all, in order firstly to make men quit and free of their old trespass, and further to show himself more powerful even than death, displaying his own body incorruptible as first fruits of the resurrection of all. And do not be surprised if we frequently repeat the same words on the same subject. For since we are speaking of the counsel of God, therefore we expound the same sense in more than one form, lest we should seem to be leaving anything out, and incur the charge of in-adequate treatment; for it is better to submit to the blame of repetition than to leave out anything that ought to be set down. The body, then, as sharing the same nature with all, for it was a human body, though by an unparalleled miracle it was formed of a virgin only, yet being mortal, was to die also, conformably to its peers. But by virtue of the union of the Word with it, it was no longer subject to corruption according to its own nature, but by reason of the Word that was come to dwell in it it was placed out of the reach of corruption. And so it was that two marvels came to pass at once, that the death of all was accomplished in the Lord's body, and that death and corruption were wholly done away by reason of the Word that was united with it. For there was need of death, and death must needs be suffered on behalf of all, that the debt owing from all might be paid. Whence, as I said before, the Word, since it was not possible for him to die, as he was immortal, took to himself a body such as could die, that he might offer it as his own in the stead of all, and as suffering, through his union with it, on behalf of all, "bring to nought him that had the power of death, that is, the devil; and might deliver them who through fear of death were all their lifetime subject to bondage." [29]

29 Heb. 2:14, 15.

21. Why, now that the common Saviour of all has died on our behalf, we, the faithful in Christ, no longer die the death as before, agreeably to the warning of the law; for this condemnation has ceased; but, corruption ceasing and being put away by the grace of the resurrection, henceforth we are only dissolved, agreeably to our bodies' mortal nature, at the time God has fixed for each, that we may be able to gain a better resurrection. For like the seeds which are cast into the earth, we do not perish by dissolution, but, sown in the earth, shall rise again, death having been brought to nought by the grace of the Saviour. Hence it is that blessed Paul, who was made a surety of the resurrection to all, says: "This corruptible must put on incorruption, and this mortal must put on immortality; but when this corruptible shall have put on incorruption, and this mortal shall have put on immortality, then shall be brought to pass the saying that is written, Death is swallowed up in victory. O death, where is thy sting? O grave, where is thy victory?" [30] Why, then, [31] one might say, if it were necessary for him to yield up his body to death in the stead of all, did he not lay it aside as man privately, instead of going as far as even to be crucified? For it were more fitting for him to have laid his body aside honorably, than ignominiously to endure a death like this. Now, see to it, I reply, whether such an objection be not merely human, whereas what the Saviour did is truly divine and for many reasons worthy of his Godhead. Firstly, because the death which befalls men comes to them agreeably to the weakness of their nature; for, unable to continue in one stay, they are dissolved with time. Hence, too, diseases befall them, and they fall sick and die. But the Lord is not weak, but is the power of God and Word of God and very life. If, then, he had laid aside his body somewhere in private, and upon a bed, after the manner of men, it would have been thought that he also did this agreeably to the weakness of his nature,

---

[30] I Cor. 15:53–55.

[31] For the passage, "Why, then ... counsel against him," the Short Recension reads: "Therefore he did not surrender his body to a death of its own, but to one inflicted by others. Why indeed did he not hide from the plotting of the Jews, that he might guard his temple wholly immortal? Because this too was unfitting the Lord, for it was not fitting for the Word of God, being Life, to inflict death of himself on his own body, nor to flee what came from others, and not rather to follow it up to destruction; for which reason he naturally neither laid aside his body of himself nor fled from the Jews when they took counsel against him. For being Life he did not allow his body to be injured by death, but rather brought it to nought in his body."

and because there was nothing in him more than in other men. But since he was, firstly, the life and the Word of God, and it was necessary, secondly, for the death on behalf of all to be accomplished, for this cause, on the one hand, because he was life and power, the body gained strength in him; while on the other, as death must needs come to pass, he did not himself take, but received at others' hands, the occasion of perfecting his sacrifice. Since it was not fit, either, that the Lord should fall sick, who healed the diseases of others; nor again was it right for that body to lose its strength, in which he gives strength to the weakness of others also. Why, then, did he not prevent death, as he did sickness? Because it was for this that he had the body, and it was unfitting to prevent it, lest the resurrection also should be hindered, while yet it was equally unfitting for sickness to precede his death, lest it should be thought weakness on the part of him that was in the body. Did he not then hunger? Yes; he hungered, agreeably to the properties of his body. But he did not perish of hunger, because of the Lord that wore it. Hence, even if he died to ransom all, yet he saw not corruption.[32] For [his body] rose again in perfect soundness, since the body belonged to none other, but to the very life.

22. But it were better, one might say, to have hidden from the designs of the Jews, that he might guard his body altogether from death. Now let such a one be told that this too was unbefitting the Lord. For as it was not fitting for the Word of God, being the life, to inflict death himself on his own body, so neither was it suitable to fly from death offered by others, but rather to follow it up unto destruction, for which reason he naturally neither laid aside his body of his own accord, nor, again, fled from the Jews when they took counsel against him.[31] But this did not show weakness on the Word's part, but, on the contrary, showed him to be Saviour and Life; in that he both awaited death to destroy it and hasted to accomplish the death offered him for the salvation of all. And besides, the Saviour came to accomplish not his own death, but the death of men; whence he did not lay aside his body by a death of his own— for he was life and had none—but received that death which came from men, in order perfectly to do away with this when it met him in his own body. Again, from the following also one might see the reasonableness of the Lord's body meeting this end. The Lord was especially concerned for the resurrection of

[31] See p. 75.     [32] Cf. Acts 2:31.

the body which he was set to accomplish. For what he was to do was to manifest it as a monument of victory over death, and to assure all of his having effected the blotting out of corruption, and of the incorruption of their bodies from thenceforward; as a gage of which and a proof of the resurrection in store for all, he has preserved his own body incorrupt. If, then, once more, his body had fallen sick, and the Word had been sundered from it in the sight of all, it would have been unbecoming that he who healed the diseases of others should suffer his own instrument to waste in sickness. For how could his driving out the diseases of others have been believed in if his own temple fell sick in him? For either he had been mocked as unable to drive away diseases, or if he could, but did not, he would be thought insensible toward others also.

23. But even if, without any disease and without any pain, he had hidden his body away privily and by himself "in a corner," [33] or in a desert place, or in a house, or anywhere, and afterwards suddenly appeared and said that he had been raised from the dead, he would have seemed on all hands to be telling idle tales, and what he said about the resurrection would have been all the more discredited, as there was no one at all to witness to his death. Now, death must precede resurrection, as it would be no resurrection did not death precede; so that if the death of his body had taken place anywhere in secret, the death not being apparent nor taking place before witnesses, his resurrection too had been hidden and without evidence. Or why, while when he had risen he proclaimed the resurrection, should he cause his death to take place in secret? or why, while he drove out evil spirits in the presence of all, and made the man blind from his birth recover his sight, and changed the water into wine, that by these means he might be believed to be the Word of God, should he not manifest his mortal nature as incorruptible in the presence of all, that he might be believed himself to be the Life? Or how were his disciples to have boldness in speaking of the resurrection, were they not able to say that he first died? Or how could they be believed, saying that death had first taken place and then the resurrection, had they not had as witnesses of his death the men before whom they spoke with boldness? For if, even as it was, when his death and resurrection had taken place in the sight of all, the Pharisees of that day would not believe, but compelled even those who had seen the resurrection to deny it, why, surely if

[33] Cf. Acts 26:26.

these things had happened in secret, how many pretexts for disbelief would they have devised? Or how could the end of death, and the victory over it, be proved, unless challenging it before the eyes of all he had shown it to be dead, annulled for the future by the incorruption of his body?

24. But what others also might have said, we must anticipate in reply. For perhaps a man might say even as follows: If it was necessary for his death to take place before all, and with witnesses, that the story of his resurrection also might be believed, it would have been better at any rate for him to have devised for himself a glorious death, if only to escape the ignominy of the cross. But had he done even this, he would have given ground for suspicion against himself, that he was not powerful against every death, but only against the death devised for him; and so again there would have been a pretext for disbelief about the resurrection all the same. So death came to his body, not from himself, but from hostile counsels, in order that whatever death they offered to the Saviour, this he might utterly do away. And just as a noble wrestler, great in skill and courage, does not pick out his antagonists for himself, lest he should raise a suspicion of his being afraid of some of them, but puts it in the choice of the onlookers, and especially so if they happen to be his enemies, so that against whomsoever they match him, him he may throw, and be believed superior to them all; so also the life of all, our Lord and Saviour, even Christ, did not devise a death for his own body, so as not to appear to be fearing some other death; but he accepted on the cross, and endured, a death inflicted by others, and above all by his enemies, which they thought dreadful and ignominious and not to be faced; so that, this also being destroyed, both he himself might be believed to be the life and [34] the power of

---

[34] The Short Recension omits the passage, "And the power . . . take place. For" (ch. 26), and substitutes: "And no one should doubt in the future whether [or not] death was completely brought to nought and life had prevailed over it. For though this death of the cross was fearful and dishonorable among men the Lord himself welcomed and accepted it voluntarily, so that in this he might bring death to nought, and that from then on the victory which he had achieved over death might be thoroughly believed in. For this reason he did not die by illness because it was unfitting, nor by a death that came from himself because [text defective], nor by a death which he himself devised, because of the reproaches of the unbelievers, but his body accepted death from the plotting of his enemies. And he was crucified on high and lifted up so that, as his death was manifest to all, his resurrection also, being manifest to all, might be acknowledged and believed in. For the body suffered and died according

death be brought utterly to nought. So something surprising and startling has happened; for the death, which they thought to inflict as a disgrace, was actually a monument of victory against death itself. Whence neither did he suffer the death of John, his head being severed, nor, as Isaiah, was he sawn in sunder; in order that even in death he might still keep his body undivided and in perfect soundness, and no pretext be afforded to those that would divide the Church.

25. And thus much in reply to those without who pile up arguments for themselves. But if any of our own people also inquire, not from love of debate but from love of learning, why he suffered death in none other way save on the cross, let him also be told that no other way than this was good for us, and that it was well that the Lord suffered this for our sakes. For if he came himself to bear the curse laid upon us, how else could he have "become a curse," unless he received the death set for a curse? and that is the cross. For this is exactly what is written: "Cursed is he that hangeth on a tree." [35] Again, if the Lord's death is the ransom of all, and by his death "the middle wall of partition" [36] is broken down, and the calling of the nations is brought about, how would he have called us to him, had he not been crucified? for it is only on the cross that a man dies with his hands spread out. Whence it was fitting for the Lord to bear this also and to spread out his hands, that with the one he might draw the ancient people, and with the other those from the Gentiles, and unite both in himself. For this is what he himself has said, signifying by what manner of death he was ransom to all: "I, when I am lifted up," he says, "shall draw all men unto me." [37] And once more, if the devil, the enemy of our race, having fallen from heaven, wanders about our lower atmosphere, and there bearing rule over his fellow spirits, as his peers in disobedience, not only works illusions by their means in them that are deceived, but tries

to the nature of bodies. But he had faith in his incorruptibility from the Word who dwelt in him. For when the body died the Word was not smitten with it. But he was impassible and incorruptible and immortal, as being God's Word, present with his body. Rather, he warded off from it that corruption which is according to the nature of bodies, as the Spirit also said to him, Thou shalt not suffer thy Holy One to see corruption" (Ps. 16:11; Acts 2:27). "So then the body, being a human body, as I said before, was smitten by separation from the Word, but he being the Power of God and Wisdom of God and Word and Life of all."

35 Gal. 3:13; Deut. 21:23.
36 Eph. 2:14.                          37 John 12:32; cf. Isa. 65:2.

to hinder them that are going up (and about this the apostle says: "According to the prince of the power of the air, of the spirit that now worketh in the sons of disobedience") [38]; while the Lord came to cast down the devil, and clear the air and prepare the way for us up into heaven, as said the apostle: "Through the veil, that is to say, his flesh" [39]—and this must needs be by death—well, by what other kind of death could this have come to pass than by one which took place in the air, I mean the cross? for only he that is perfected on the cross dies in the air. Whence it was quite fitting that the Lord suffered this death. For thus being lifted up he cleared the air of the malignity both of the devil and of demons of all kinds, as he says: "I beheld Satan as lightning fall from heaven" [40]; and made a new opening of the way up into heaven, as he says once more: "Lift up your gates, O ye princes, and be ye lift up, ye everlasting doors." [41] For it was not the Word himself that needed an opening of the gates, being Lord of all; nor were any of his works closed to their maker; but we it was that needed it, whom he carried up by his own body. For as he offered it to death on behalf of all, so by it he once more made ready the way up into the heavens.

26. The death on the cross, then, for us has proved seemly and fitting, and its cause has been shown to be reasonable in every respect; and it may justly be argued that in no other way than by the cross was it right for the salvation of all to take place. For not even thus—not even on the cross—did he leave himself concealed; but far otherwise, while he made creation witness to the presence of its maker, he suffered not the temple of his body to remain long, but having merely shown it to be dead, by the contact of death with it, he straightway raised it up on the third day, bearing away, as the mark of victory and the triumph over death, the incorruptibility and impassibility which resulted to his body. For he could, even immediately on death, have raised his body and shown it alive; but this also the Saviour, in wise foresight, did not do. For one might have said that he had not died at all, or that death had not come into perfect contact with him, if he had manifested the resurrection at once. Perhaps, again, had the interval of his dying and rising again been one of two days only, the glory of his incorrup-

---

[38] Eph. 2:2; cf. Antony's visions of souls impeded on their way to heaven by hostile powers (Athanasius, *Life of Antony*, 65, 66) and Apocalypse of Paul 14 (M. R. James, *Apocryphal New Testament*, Oxford, 1925, p. 531).
[39] Heb. 10:20.      [40] Luke 10:18.      [41] Ps. 24:7.

tion would have been obscure. So in order that the body might be proved to be dead, the Word tarried yet one intermediate day, and on the third showed it incorruptible to all. So then, that the death on the cross might be proved, he raised his body on the third day. But lest, by raising it up when it had remained a long time and been completely corrupted, he should be disbelieved, as though he had exchanged it for some other body —for a man might also from lapse of time distrust what he saw, and forget what had taken place—for this cause he waited not more than three days; nor did he keep long in suspense those whom he had told about the resurrection; but while the word was still echoing in their ears and their eyes were still expectant and their mind in suspense, and while those who had slain him were still living on earth, and were on the spot and could witness to the death of the Lord's body, the Son of God himself, after an interval of three days, showed his body, once dead, immortal and incorruptible; and it was made manifest to all that it was not from any natural weakness of the Word that dwelt in it that the body had died, but in order that in it death might be done away by the power of the Saviour.

27. For that death is destroyed, and that the cross is become the victory over it, and that it has no more power but is verily dead, this is no small proof, or rather an evident warrant, that it is despised by all Christ's disciples, and that they all take the aggressive against it and no longer fear it; but by the sign of the cross and by faith in Christ tread it down as dead. For of old, before the divine sojourn of the Saviour took place, even to the saints death was terrible,[42] and all wept for the dead as though they perished. But now that the Saviour has raised his body, death is no longer terrible; for all who believe in Christ tread him under as nought, and choose rather to die than to deny their faith in Christ. For they verily know that when they die they are not destroyed, but actually [begin to] live, and become incorruptible through the resurrection. And that devil that once maliciously exulted in death, now that its pains were loosed, remained the only one truly dead. And a proof of this is, that before men believe Christ, they see in death an object of terror, and play the coward before him. But when they are gone over to Christ's faith and teaching, their contempt for death is so great that they even eagerly rush upon it, and become witnesses for the resurrection the Saviour has accomplished against it. For while still tender in years they make haste

42 This clause ("even . . . terrible, and") is omitted in the Short Recension.

to die, and not men only, but women also, exercise themselves by bodily discipline against it. So weak has he become, that even women who were formerly deceived by him, now mock at him as dead and paralyzed. For as when a tyrant has been defeated by a real king, and bound hand and foot, then all that pass by laugh him to scorn, buffeting and reviling him, no longer fearing his fury and barbarity, because of the king who has conquered him; so also, death having been conquered and exposed by the Saviour on the cross, and bound hand and foot, all they who are in Christ, as they pass by, trample on him, and witnessing to Christ scoff at death, jesting at him, and saying what has been written against him of old: "O death, where is thy victory? O grave, where is thy sting?" [43]

28. Is this, then, a light proof of the weakness of death? or is it a slight demonstration of the victory won over him by the Saviour, when the youths and young maidens that are in Christ despise this life and practice to die? For man is by nature afraid of death and of the dissolution of the body; but there is this most startling fact, that he who has put on the faith of the cross despises even what is naturally fearful, and for Christ's sake is not afraid of death. And just as, whereas fire has the natural property of burning, if someone said there was a sub-stance which did not fear its burning, but on the contrary proved it weak—as the asbestos among the Indians is said to do—then one who did not believe the story, if he wished to put it to the test, is at any rate, after putting on the fireproof material and touching the fire, thereupon assured of the weak-ness attributed to the fire; or if anyone wished to see the tyrant bound, at any rate by going into the country and domain of his conqueror he may see the man, a terror to others, reduced to weakness; so if a man is incredulous even still, after so many proofs and after so many who have become martyrs in Christ, still, if his mind be even yet doubtful as to whether death has been brought to nought and had an end, he does well to wonder at so great a thing, only let him not prove obstinate in incredulity, nor case-hardened in the face of what is so plain. But just as he who has got the asbestos knows that fire has no burning power over it, and as he who would see the tyrant bound goes over to the empire of his conqueror, so too let him who is incredulous about the victory over death receive the faith of Christ, and pass over to his teaching, and he shall see the weakness of death, and the triumph over it. For many who

[43] I Cor. 15:55 (Hos. 13:14).

were formerly incredulous and scoffers have afterwards believed and so despised death as even to become martyrs for Christ himself.[44]

29. Now if by the sign of the cross, and by faith in Christ, death is trampled down, it must be evident before the tribunal of truth that it is none other than Christ himself that has displayed trophies and triumphs over death, and made him lose all his strength. And if, while previously death was strong, and for that reason terrible, now after the sojourn of the Saviour and the death and resurrection of his body it is despised, it must be evident that death has been brought to nought and conquered by the very Christ that ascended the cross. For as, if after nighttime the sun rises, and the whole region of earth is illumined by him, it is at any rate not open to doubt that it is the sun who has revealed his light everywhere, that has also driven away the dark and given light to all things; so, now that death has come into contempt, and been trodden underfoot, from the time when the Saviour's saving manifestation in the flesh and his death on the cross took place, it must be quite plain that it is the very Saviour that also appeared in the body who has brought death to nought, and who displays the signs of victory over him day by day in his own disciples. For when one sees men, weak by nature, leaping forward to death, and not fearing its corruption nor frightened of the descent into Hades, but with eager soul challenging it, and not flinching from torture, but on the contrary, for Christ's sake electing to rush upon death in preference to life upon earth; or even if one be an eyewitness of men and females and young children rushing and leaping upon death for the sake of Christ's religion; who is so silly, or who is so incredulous, or who so maimed in his mind, as not to see and infer that Christ, to whom the people witness, himself supplies and gives to each the victory over death, depriving him of all his power in each one of them that hold his faith and bear the sign of the cross. For he that sees the serpent trodden underfoot, especially knowing his former fierceness, no longer doubts that he is dead and has quite lost his strength, unless he is perverted in mind and has not even his bodily senses sound. For who that sees a lion, either, made sport of by children, fails to see that he is either dead or has lost all his power? Just as, then, it is possible to see with the eyes the truth of all this, so, now that death is made sport of and despised by believers in Christ, let none any

[44] Or better, "themselves" (*autous* for *autou* with better MSS.).

longer doubt, nor any prove incredulous, of death having been brought to nought by Christ, and the corruption of death destroyed and stayed.

30. What we have so far said, then, is no small proof that death has been brought to nought, and that the cross of the Lord is a sign of victory over him. But of the resurrection of the body to immortality thereupon accomplished by Christ, the common Saviour and true life of all, the demonstration by facts is clearer than arguments to those whose mental vision is sound. For if, as our argument showed, death has been brought to nought, and because of Christ all tread him under-foot, much more did he himself first tread him down with his own body, and bring him to nought. But supposing death slain by him, what could have happened save the rising again of his body, and its being displayed as a monument of victory against death? or how could death have been shown to be brought to nought unless the Lord's body had risen? But if this demonstra-tion of the resurrection seem to anyone insufficient, let him be assured of what is said even from what takes place before his eyes. For whereas on a man's decease he can put forth no power, but his influence lasts to the grave and thenceforth ceases; and actions, and power over men, belong to the living only; let him who will, see and be judge, confessing the truth from what appears to sight. For now that the Saviour works so great things among men, and day by day is invisibly per-suading so great a multitude from every side, from them that dwell both in Greece and in foreign lands, to come over to his faith, and all to obey his teaching, will anyone still hold his mind in doubt whether a resurrection has been accomplished by the Saviour, and whether Christ is alive, or rather is himself the Life? Or is it like a dead man to be pricking the consciences of men, so that they deny their hereditary laws and bow before the teaching of Christ? Or how, if he is no longer active (for this is proper to one dead), does he stay from their activity those who are active and alive, so that the adulterer no longer com-mits adultery, and the murderer murders no more, nor is the inflicter of wrong any longer grasping, and the profane is henceforth religious? Or how, if he be not risen but is dead, does he drive away, and pursue, and cast down those false gods said by the unbelievers to be alive, and the demons they worship? For where Christ is named, and his faith, there all idolatry is deposed and all imposture of evil spirits is exposed, and any spirit is unable to endure even the name, nay, even on

barely hearing it, flies and disappears. But this work is not that of one dead, but of one that lives—and especially of God. In particular, it would be ridiculous to say that while the spirits cast out by him and the idols brought to nought are alive, he who chases them away, and by his power prevents their even appearing, yea, and is being confessed by them all to be Son of God, is dead.

31. But they who disbelieve in the resurrection afford a strong proof against themselves, if instead of all the spirits and the gods worshiped by them casting out Christ, who, they say, is dead, Christ on the contrary proves them all to be dead. For if it be true that one dead can exert no power, while the Saviour does daily so many works, drawing men to religion, persuading to virtue, teaching of immortality, leading on to a desire for heavenly things, revealing the knowledge of the Father, inspiring strength to meet death, showing himself to each one, and displacing the godlessness of idolatry, and the gods and spirits of the unbelievers can do none of these things, but rather show themselves dead at the presence of Christ, their pomp being reduced to impotence and vanity—whereas by the sign of the cross all magic is stopped, and all witchcraft brought to nought, and all the idols are being deserted and left, and every unruly pleasure is checked, and everyone[45] is looking up from earth to heaven—whom is one to pronounce dead? Christ, that is doing so many works? But to work is not proper to one dead. Or him that exerts no power at all, but lies as it were without life? which is essentially proper to the idols and spirits, dead as they are. For the Son of God is "living and active," and works day by day, and brings about the salvation of all. But death is daily proved to have lost all his power, and idols and spirits are proved to be dead rather than Christ, so that henceforth no man can any longer doubt of the resurrection of his body. But he who is incredulous of the resurrection of the Lord's body would seem to be ignorant of the power of the Word and Wisdom of God. For if he took a body to himself at all, and—in reasonable consistency, as our argument showed— appropriated it as his own, what was the Lord to do with it? or what should be the end of the body when the Word had once descended upon it? For it could not but die, inasmuch as it was mortal, and to be offered unto death on behalf of all: for which purpose it was that the Saviour fashioned it for himself. But it

[45] Or "faith" (*pistis* for *pas tis*); but the other reading is probably better, and is supported by the Short Recension MSS.

was impossible for it to remain dead, because it had been made the temple of life. Whence, while it died as mortal, it came to life again by reason of the life in it; and of its resurrection the works are a sign.

32. But if, because he is not seen, his having risen at all is disbelieved, it is high time for those who refuse belief to deny the very course of nature. For it is God's peculiar property at once to be invisible and yet to be known from his works, as has been already stated above. If, then, the works are not there, they do well to disbelieve what does not appear. But if the works cry aloud and show it clearly, why do they choose to deny the life so manifestly due to the resurrection? For even if they be maimed in their intelligence, yet even with the external senses men may see the unimpeachable power and Godhead of Christ. For even a blind man, if he see not the sun, yet if he but take hold of the warmth the sun gives out, knows that there is a sun above the earth. Thus let our opponents also, if they do not yet believe, still being blinded to the truth, yet at least knowing his power by others who believe, not deny the Godhead of Christ and the resurrection accomplished by him. For it is plain that if Christ be dead, he could not be expelling demons and spoiling idols; for a dead man the spirits would not have obeyed. But if they be manifestly expelled by the naming of his name, it must be evident that he is not dead; especially as spirits, seeing even what is unseen by men, could tell if Christ were dead and refuse him any obedience at all. But as it is, what irreligious men believe not, the spirits see—that he is God— and hence they fly and fall at his feet, saying just what they uttered when he was in the body: "We know thee who thou art, the Holy One of God" [46]; and, "Ah, what have we to do with thee, thou Son of God? I pray thee, torment me not." [47] As, then, demons confess him, and his works bear him witness day by day, it must be evident—and let none brazen it out against the truth—both that the Saviour raised his own body and that he is the true Son of God, being from him, as from his Father, his own Word, and Wisdom, and Power, who in ages later took a body for the salvation of all, and taught the world concerning the Father, and brought death to nought, and bestowed incorruption upon all by the promise of the resurrection, having raised his own body as a first fruits of this, and having displayed it by the sign of the cross, as a monument of victory over death and its corruption.

[46] Mark 1:24 (Luke 4:34).         [47] Luke 8:28 (Mark 5:7).

## REPLY TO OBJECTIONS: JEWISH

33. These things being so, and the resurrection of his body and the victory gained over death by the Saviour being clearly proved, come now, let us put to rebuke both the disbelief of the Jews and the scoffing of the Gentiles. For these, perhaps, are the points where Jews express incredulity, while Gentiles laugh, finding fault with the unseemliness of the cross, and of the Word of God becoming man. But our argument shall not delay to grapple with both, especially as the proofs at our command against them are clear as day. For Jews in their incredulity may be refuted from the Scriptures, which even themselves read; for this text and that, and, in a word, the whole inspired Scripture, cries aloud concerning these things, as even its express words abundantly show. For prophets proclaimed beforehand concerning the wonder of the Virgin and the birth from her, saying: "Lo, the virgin shall be with child, and shall bring forth a son, and they shall call his name Emmanuel, which is, being interpreted, God with us." [48] But Moses, the truly great, and whom they believe to speak truth, with reference to the Saviour's becoming man, having estimated what was said as important, and assured of its truth, set it down in these words: "There shall rise a star out of Jacob, and a man out of Israel, and he shall break in pieces the captains of Moab." And again: "How lovely are thy habitations, O Jacob, thy tabernacles, O Israel, as shadowing gardens, and as parks by the rivers, and as tabernacles which the Lord hath fixed, as cedars by the waters. A man shall come forth out of his seed, and shall be Lord over many peoples." [49] And again, Isaiah: "Before the child know how to call father or mother, he shall take the power of Damascus and the spoils of Samaria before the king of Assyria." [50] That a man, then, shall appear is foretold in those words. But that he that is to come is Lord of all, they predict once more as follows: "Behold the Lord sitteth upon a light cloud, and shall come into Egypt, and the graven images of Egypt shall be shaken." [51] For from thence also it is that the Father calls him back, saying, "I called my Son out of Egypt." [52]

34. Nor is even his death passed over in silence; on the contrary it is referred to in the divine Scriptures, even exceeding clearly. For to the end that none should err for want of instruc-

---

[48] Matt. 1:23 (Isa. 7:14).      [49] Num. 24: 17, 5–7.
[50] Isa. 8:4.            [51] Isa. 19:1.            [52] Hos. 11:1.

tion in the actual events, they feared not to mention even the cause of his death—that he suffers it, not for his own sake, but for the immortality and salvation of all, and the counsels of the Jews against him and the indignities offered him at their hands. They say then: "A man in stripes, and knowing how to bear weakness, for his face is turned away; he was dishonored and held in no account. He beareth our sins, and is in pain on our account; and we reckoned him to be in labor, and in stripes, and in ill-usage; but he was wounded for our sins, and made weak for our wickedness. The chastisement of our peace was upon him, and by his stripes we were healed." O marvel at the loving-kindness of the Word, that for our sakes he is dishonored, that we may be brought to honor. "For all we," it says, "like sheep were gone astray; man had erred in his way; and the Lord delivered him for our sins; and he openeth not his mouth, because he hath been evilly intreated. As a sheep was he brought to the slaughter, and as a lamb dumb before his shearer, so openeth he not his mouth: in his abasement his judgment was taken away." Then lest any should from his suffering conceive him to be a common man, Holy Writ anticipates the surmises of man, and declares the power [which worked] for him, and the difference of his nature compared with ourselves, saying: "But who shall declare his generation? For his life is taken away from the earth. From the wickedness of the people was he brought to death. And I will give the wicked instead of his burial, and the rich instead of his death; for he did no wickedness, neither was guile found in his mouth. And the Lord will cleanse him from his stripes." [53]

35. But, perhaps, having heard the prophecy of his death, you ask to learn also what is set forth concerning the cross. For not even this is passed over: it is displayed by the holy men with great plainness. For first Moses predicts it, and that with a loud voice, when he says: "Ye shall see your Life hanging before your eyes, and shall not believe." [54] And next, the prophets after him witness of this, saying: "But I as an innocent lamb brought to be slain, knew it not; they counseled an evil counsel against me, saying, Hither and let us cast a tree upon his bread, and efface him from the land of the living." [55] And again: "They pierced my hands and my feet, they numbered all my bones, they parted my garments among them, and for my vesture they cast lots." [56] Now a death raised aloft, and that

[53] Isa. 53:3–10 (LXX).
[55] Jer. 11:19.
[54] Deut. 28:66.
[56] Ps. 22:16–18.

takes place on a tree, could be none other than the cross; and again, in no other death are the hands and feet pierced, save on the cross only. But since by the sojourn of the Saviour among men all nations also on every side began to know God; they did not leave this point, either, without a reference: but mention is made of this matter as well in the holy Scriptures. For "there shall be," he says, "the root of Jesse, and he that riseth to rule the nations, on him shall the nations hope." [57] This, then, is a little in proof of what has happened. But all Scripture teems with refutations of the disbelief of the Jews. For which of the righteous men and holy prophets, and patriarchs, recorded in the divine Scriptures, ever had his corporeal birth of a virgin only? Or what woman has sufficed without man for the conception of human kind? Was not Abel born of Adam, Enoch of Jared, Noah of Lamech, and Abraham of Terah, Isaac of Abraham, Jacob of Isaac? Was not Judah born of Jacob, and Moses and Aaron of Amram? Was not Samuel born of Elkanah, was not David of Jesse, was not Solomon of David, was not Hezekiah of Ahaz, was not Josiah of Amon, was not Isaiah of Amos, was not Jeremiah of Hilkiah, was not Ezekiel of Buzi? Had not each a father as author of his existence? Who, then, is he that is born of a virgin only? For the prophet made exceeding much of this sign. Or whose birth did a star in the skies forerun, to announce to the world him that was born? For when Moses was born, he was hid by his parents; David was not heard of, even by those of his neighborhood, inasmuch as even the great Samuel knew him not, but asked had Jesse yet another son? Abraham, again, became known to his neighbors as a great man only subsequently to his birth. But of Christ's birth the witness was not man, but a star in that heaven whence he was descending.

36. But what king that ever was, before he had strength to call father or mother, reigned and gained triumphs over his enemies? Did not David come to the throne at thirty years of age, and Solomon, when he had grown to be a young man? Did not Joash enter on the kingdom when seven years old, and Josiah, a still later king, receive the government about the seventh year of his age? And yet they at that age had strength to call father or mother. Who, then, is there that was reigning and spoiling his enemies almost before his birth? Or what king of this sort has ever been in Israel and in Judah—let the Jews, who have searched out the matter, tell us—in whom all the

[57] Isa. 11:10.

nations have placed their hopes and had peace, instead of being at enmity with them on every side? For as long as Jerusalem stood there was war without respite betwixt them, and they all fought with Israel; the Assyrians oppressed them, the Egyptians persecuted them, the Babylonians fell upon them; and, strange to say, they had even the Syrians their neighbors at war against them. Or did not David war against them of Moab, and smite the Syrians, Josiah guard against his neighbors, and Hezekiah quail at the boasting of Sennacherib, and Amalek make war against Moses, and the Amorites oppose him, and the inhabitants of Jericho array themselves against Joshua, son of Nun? And, in a word, treaties of friendship had no place between the nations and Israel. Who, then, it is on whom the nations are to set their hope, it is worth-while to see. For there must be such a one, as it is impossible for the prophet to have spoken falsely. But which of the holy prophets or of the early patriarchs has died on the cross for the salvation of all? Or who was wounded and destroyed for the healing of all? Or which of the righteous men, or kings, went down to Egypt, so that at his coming the idols of Egypt fell? For Abraham went thither, but idolatry prevailed universally all the same. Moses was born there, and the deluded worship of the people was there none the less.

37. Or who among those recorded in Scripture was pierced in the hands and feet, or hung at all upon a tree, and was sacrificed on a cross for the salvation of all? For Abraham died, ending his life on a bed; Isaac and Jacob also died with their feet raised on a bed; Moses and Aaron died on the mountain; David in his house, without being the object of any conspiracy at the hands of the people; true, he was pursued by Saul, but he was preserved unhurt. Isaiah was sawn asunder, but not hung on a tree. Jeremiah was shamefully treated, but did not die under condemnation; Ezekiel suffered, not however for the people, but to indicate what was to come upon the people. Again, these, even where they suffered, were men resembling all in their common nature; but he that is declared in Scripture to suffer on behalf of all is called not merely man, but the Life of all, albeit he was in fact like men in nature. For "ye shall see," it says, "your Life hanging before your eyes"; and "who shall declare his generation?" [58] For one can ascertain the genealogy of all the saints, and declare it from the beginning, and of whom each was born; but the generation of him that

[58] Deut. 28:66; Isa. 53:8.

is the Life the Scriptures refer to as not to be declared. Who, then, is he of whom the divine Scriptures say this? Or who is so great that even the prophets predict of him such great things? None else, now, is found in the Scriptures but the common Saviour of all, the Word of God, our Lord Jesus Christ. For he it is that proceeded from a virgin and appeared as man on the earth, and whose generation after the flesh cannot be declared. For there is none that can tell his father after the flesh, his body not being of a man, but of a virgin alone; so that no one can declare the corporeal generation of the Saviour from a man in the same way as one can draw up a genealogy of David and of Moses and of all the patriarchs. For he it is that caused the star also to mark the birth of his body; since it was fit that the Word, coming down from heaven, should have his constellation also from heaven, and it was fitting that the king of creation when he came forth should be openly recognized by all creation. Why, he was born in Judaea, and men from Persia came to worship him. He it is that even before his appearing in the body won the victory over his demon adversaries and a triumph over idolatry. All heathen at any rate from every region, abjuring their hereditary tradition and the impiety of idols, are now placing their hope in Christ, and enrolling themselves under him, the like of which you may see with your own eyes. For at no other time has the impiety of the Egyptians ceased, save when the Lord of all, riding as it were upon a cloud, came down there in the body and brought to nought the delusion of idols, and brought over all to himself, and through himself to the Father.[59] He it is that was crucified before the sun and all creation as witnesses, and before those who put him to death: and by his death has salvation come to all, and all creation been ransomed. He is the Life of all, and he it is that as a sheep yielded his body to death as a substitute, for the salvation of all, even though the Jews believe it not.

38. For if they do not think these proofs sufficient, let them be persuaded at any rate by other reasons, drawn from the oracles they themselves possess. For of whom do the prophets say: "I was made manifest to them that sought me not; I was found of them that asked not for me: I said, Behold, here am I, to the nation that had not called upon my name. I stretched

[59] Referring both to the visit of the holy family to Egypt, and legends of the fall of idols before them—cf. Gospel of Pseudo-Matthew 22–24 (M. R. James, *Apocryphal New Testament*, pp. 75, 76)—and the contemporary spread of the gospel in Egypt.

out my hands to a disobedient and gainsaying people" 60?
Who, then, one might say to the Jews, is he that was made
manifest? For if it is the prophet, let them say when he was
hid, afterward to appear again. And what manner of prophet
is this, that was not only made manifest from obscurity, but
also stretched out his hands on the cross? None surely of the
righteous, save the Word of God only, who, incorporeal by
nature, appeared for our sakes in the body and suffered for all.
Or if not even this is sufficient for them, let them at least be
silenced by another proof, seeing how clear its demonstrative
force is. For the Scripture says: "Be strong ye hands that hang
down, and feeble knees; comfort ye, ye of faint mind; be strong,
fear not. Behold, our God recompenseth judgment; he shall
come and save us. Then shall the eyes of the blind be opened,
and the ears of the deaf shall hear; then shall the lame man
leap as an hart, and the tongue of the stammerers shall be
plain." 61 Now what can they say to this, or how can they dare
to face this at all? For the prophecy not only indicates that God
is to sojourn here, but it announces the signs and the time of
his coming. For they connect the blind recovering their sight,
and the lame walking, and the deaf hearing, and the tongue of
the stammerers being made plain, with the divine coming
which is to take place. Let them say, then, when such signs
have come to pass in Israel, or where in Judah anything of the
sort has occurred. Naaman, a leper, was cleansed, but no deaf
man heard nor lame walked. Elijah raised a dead man; so did
Elisha; but none blind from birth regained his sight. For in
good truth, to raise a dead man is a great thing, but it is not
like the wonder wrought by the Saviour. Only, if Scripture
has not passed over the case of the leper, and of the dead son
of the widow, certainly, had it come to pass that a lame man
also had walked and a blind man recovered his sight, the
narrative would not have omitted to mention this also. Since,
then, nothing is said in the Scriptures, it is evident that these
things had never taken place before. When, then, have they
taken place, save when the Word of God himself came in the
body? Or when did he come, if not when lame men walked,
and stammerers were made to speak plain, and deaf men heard,
and men blind from birth regained their sight? For this was
the very thing the Jews said who then witnessed it, because
they had not heard of these things having taken place at any
other time: "Since the world began it was never heard that

60 Isa. 65:1, 2 (Rom. 10:20, 21).　　　　61 Isa. 35:3–6.

any one opened the eyes of a man born blind. If this man were not from God, he could do nothing." [62]

39. But perhaps, being unable, even they, to fight continually against plain facts, they will, without denying what is written, maintain that they are looking for these things, and that the Word of God is not yet come. For this it is on which they are forever harping, not blushing to brazen it out in the face of plain facts. But on this one point, above all, they shall be all the more refuted, not at our hands, but at those of the most wise Daniel, who marks both the actual date and the divine sojourn of the Saviour, saying: "Seventy weeks are cut short upon thy people, and upon the holy city, for a full end to be made of sin, and for sins to be sealed up, and to blot out iniquities, and to make atonement for iniquities, and to bring everlasting righteousness, and to seal vision and prophet, and to anoint a Holy of Holies; and thou shalt know and understand from the going forth of the word to restore and to build Jerusalem unto Christ the Prince." [63] Perhaps with regard to the other [prophecies] they may be able even to find excuses and to put off what is written to a future time. But what can they say to this, or can they face it at all? Where not only is the Christ referred to, but he that is to be anointed is declared to be not man simply, but Holy of Holies; and Jerusalem is to stand till his coming, and thenceforth prophet and vision cease in Israel. David was anointed of old, and Solomon and Hezekiah; but then, nevertheless, Jerusalem and the place stood, and prophets were prophesying: Gad and Asaph and Nathan; and, later, Isaiah and Hosea and Amos and others. And again, the actual men that were anointed were called holy, and not Holy of Holies. But if they shield themselves with the Captivity, and say that because of it Jerusalem was not, what can they say about the prophets too? For in fact when first the people went down to Babylon, Daniel and Jeremiah were there, and Ezekiel and Haggai and Zechariah were prophesying.

40. So the Jews are trifling, and the time in question, which they refer to the future, is actually come. For when did prophet and vision cease from Israel, save when Christ came, the Holy of Holies? For it is a sign, and an important proof, of the coming of the Word of God, that Jerusalem no longer stands, nor is any prophet raised up nor vision revealed to them—and that very naturally. For when he that was signified was come, what need was there any longer of any to signify him? When

[62] John 9:32, 33.　　　　　　　　　　[63] Dan. 9:24, 25.

the truth was there, what need any more of the shadow? For this was the reason of their prophesying at all—namely, till the true righteousness should come, and he that was to ransom the sins of all. And this was why Jerusalem stood till then— namely, that there they might be exercised in the types as a preparation for the reality. So when the Holy of Holies was come, naturally vision and prophecy were sealed and the king-dom of Jerusalem ceased. For kings were to be anointed among them only until the Holy of Holies should have been anointed; and Jacob prophesies that the kingdom of the Jews should be established until him, as follows: "The ruler shall not fail from Judah, nor the Prince from his loins, until that which is laid up for him shall come; and he is the expectation of the nations." [64] Whence the Saviour also himself cried aloud and said, "The law and the prophets prophesied until John." [65] If, then, there is now among the Jews king or prophet or vision, they do well to deny the Christ that is come. But if there is neither king nor vision, but from that time forth all prophecy is sealed and the city and temple taken, why are they so irreligious and so per-verse as to see what has happened, and yet to deny Christ, who has brought it all to pass? Or why, when they see even heathen deserting their idols, and placing their hope, through Christ, on the God of Israel, do they deny Christ, who was born of the root of Jesse after the flesh and henceforth is king? For if the nations were worshiping some other god, and not confessing the God of Abraham and Isaac and Jacob and Moses, then, once more, they would be doing well in alleging that God had not come. But if the Gentiles are honoring the same God that gave the law to Moses and made the promise to Abraham, and whose word the Jews dishonored—why are they ignorant, or rather why do they choose to ignore, that the Lord foretold by the Scriptures has shone forth upon the world, and appeared to it in bodily form, as the Scripture said: "The Lord God hath shined upon us" [66]; and again: "He sent his Word and healed them" [67]; and again: "Not a messenger, not an angel, but the Lord himself saved them" [68]? Their state may be compared to that of one out of his right mind, who sees the earth illumined by the sun but denies the sun that illumines it. For what more is there for him whom they expect to do when he is come? To call the heathen? But they are called already. To make prophecy, and king, and vision to cease? This too has already

[64] Gen. 49:10.                        [65] Matt. 11:13 (Luke 16:16).
[66] Ps. 118:27.            [67] Ps. 107:20.            [68] Isa. 63:9 (LXX)

come to pass. To expose the godlessness of idolatry? It is already exposed and condemned. Or to destroy death? He is already destroyed. What, then, has not come to pass that the Christ must do? What is left unfulfilled, that the Jews should now disbelieve with impunity? For if, I say—which is just what we actually see—there is no longer king, nor prophet, nor Jerusalem, nor sacrifice, nor vision, among them, but even the whole earth is filled with the knowledge of God, and Gentiles, leaving their godlessness, are now taking refuge with the God of Abraham, through the Word, even our Lord Jesus Christ, then it must be plain, even to those who are exceedingly obstinate, that the Christ is come, and that he has illumined absolutely all with his light, and given them the true and divine teaching concerning his Father.

So one can fairly refute the Jews by these and by other arguments from the divine Scriptures.

## REPLY TO OBJECTIONS: GREEK

41. But one cannot but be utterly astonished at the Gentiles, who, while they laugh at what is no matter for jesting, are themselves insensible to their own disgrace, which they do not see that they have set up in the shape of stocks and stones. Only, as our argument is not lacking in demonstrative proof, come let us put them also to shame on reasonable grounds— mainly from what we ourselves also see. For what is there on our side that is absurd, or worthy of derision? Is it merely our saying that the Word has been made manifest in the body? But this even they will join in owning to have happened without any absurdity, if they show themselves friends of truth. If, then, they deny that there is a Word of God at all, they do so gratuitously, jesting at what they know not. But if they confess that there is a Word of God, and he ruler of the universe, and that in him the Father has produced the creation, and that by his providence the whole receives light and life and being, and that he reigns over all, so that from the works of his providence he is known, and through him the Father—consider, I pray you, whether they be not unwittingly raising the jest against themselves. The philosophers of the Greeks say that the universe is a great body; and rightly so. For we see it and its parts as objects of our senses. If, then, the Word of God is in the universe, which is a body, and has united himself with the whole and with all its parts, what is there surprising or absurd

if we say that he has united himself with man also. For if it were absurd for him to have been in a body at all, it would be absurd for him to be united with the whole either, and to be giving light and movement to all things by his providence. For the whole also is a body. But if it beseems him to unite himself with the universe, and to be made known in the whole, it must beseem him also to appear in a human body, and that by him it should be illumined and work. For mankind is part of the whole as well as the rest. And if it be unseemly for a part to have been adopted as his instrument to teach men of his Godhead, it must be most absurd that he should be made known even by the whole universe.

42. For just as, while the whole body is quickened and illumined by man, supposing one said it were absurd that man's power should also be in the toe, he would be thought foolish; because, while granting that he pervades and works in the whole, he demurs to his being in the part also; thus he who grants and believes that the Word of God is in the whole universe, and that the whole is illumined and moved by him, should not think it absurd that a single human body also should receive movement and light from him. But if it is because the human race is a thing created and has been made out of nothing, that they regard that manifestation of the Saviour in man, which we speak of, as not seemly, it is high time for them to eject him from creation also; for it too has been brought into existence by the Word out of nothing. But if, even though creation be a thing made, it is not absurd that the Word should be in it, then neither is it absurd that he should be in man. For whatever idea they form of the whole, they must necessarily apply the like idea to the part. For man also, as I said before, is a part of the whole. Thus it is not at all unseemly that the Word should be in man, while all things are deriving from him their light and movement and light, as also their authors say, "In him we live and move and have our being." [69] So, then, what is there to scoff at in what we say, if the Word has used that wherein he is as an instrument to manifest himself? For were he not in it, neither could he have used it; but if we have previously allowed that he is in the whole and in its parts, what is there incredible in his manifesting himself in that wherein he is? For by his own power he is united wholly with each and all, and orders all things without stint, so that no one could have called it out of place for him to speak, and

[69] Acts 17:28.

make known himself and his Father, by means of sun, if he so willed, or moon, or heaven, or earth, or waters, or fire; inasmuch as he holds in one all things at once, and is in fact not only in all, but also in the part in question, and there invisibly manifests himself. In like manner, it cannot be absurd if, ordering as he does the whole, and giving life to all things, and having willed to make himself known through men, he has used as his instrument a human body to manifest the truth and knowledge of the Father. For humanity too is an actual part of the whole. And as mind, pervading man all through, is interpreted by a part of the body—I mean the tongue—without anyone saying, I suppose, that the essence of the mind is on that account lowered, so if the Word, pervading all things, has used a human instrument, this cannot appear unseemly. For, as I have said previously, if it be unseemly to have used a body as an instrument, it is unseemly also for him to be in the whole.

43. Now, if they ask, Why, then, did he not appear by means of other and nobler parts of creation, and use some nobler instrument, as the sun, or moon, or stars, or fire, or air, instead of man merely? let them know that the Lord came not to make a display, but to heal and teach those who were suffering. For the way for one aiming at display would be, just to appear, and to dazzle the beholders; but for one seeking to heal and teach the way is, not simply to sojourn here, but to give himself to the aid of those in want, and to appear as they who need him can bear it; that he may not, by exceeding the requirements of the sufferers, trouble the very persons that need him, rendering God's appearance useless to them. Now, nothing in creation had gone astray with regard to their notions of God, save man only. Why, neither sun, nor moon, nor heaven, nor the stars, nor water, nor air had swerved from their order; but knowing their artificer and sovereign, the Word, they remain as they were made. But men alone, having rejected what was good, then devised things of nought instead of the truth, and have ascribed the honor due to God, and their knowledge of him, to demons and men in the shape of stones. With reason, then, since it were unworthy of the divine goodness to overlook so grave a matter, while yet men were not able to recognize him as ordering and guiding the whole, he takes to himself as an instrument a part of the whole, his human body, and unites himself with that, in order that since men could not recognize him in the whole, they should not fail to know him in the part; and since they could not look up to his invisible power, might be able, at any

rate, from what resembled themselves to reason to him and to contemplate him. For, men as they are, they will be able to know his Father more quickly and directly by a body of like nature and by the divine works wrought through it, judging by comparison that they are not human but the works of God which are done by him. And if it were absurd, as they say, for the Word to be known through the works of the body, it would likewise be absurd for him to be known through the works of the universe. For just as he is in creation, and yet does not partake of its nature in the least degree, but rather all things partake of his power, so, while he used the body as his instrument, he partook of no corporeal property, but, on the contrary, himself sanctified even the body. For if even Plato, who is in such repute among the Greeks, says that its author, beholding the universe tempest-tossed, and in peril of going down to the place of chaos, takes his seat at the helm of the soul and comes to the rescue and corrects all its calamities,[70] what is there incredible in what we say, that, mankind being in error, the Word lighted down upon it and appeared as man, that he might save it in its tempest by his guidance and goodness?

44. But perhaps, shamed into agreeing with this, they will choose to say that God, if he wished to reform and to save mankind, ought to have done so by a mere fiat, without his Word taking a body, in just the same way as he did formerly, when he produced them out of nothing. To this objection of theirs a reasonable answer would be: that formerly, nothing being in existence at all, what was needed to make everything was a fiat and the bare will to do so. But when man had once been made, and necessity demanded a cure, not for things that were not, but for things that had come to be, it was naturally consequent that the physician and Saviour should appear in what had come to be, in order also to cure the things that were. For this cause, then, he has become man, and used his body as a human instrument. For if this were not the right way, how was the Word, choosing to use an instrument, to appear? or whence was he to take it, save from those already in being, and in need of his Godhead by means of one like themselves? For it was not things without being that needed salvation, so that a bare command should suffice, but man, already in existence, was going to corruption and ruin. It was then natural and right that the Word should use a human instrument and reveal himself everywhither. Secondly, you

70 Politicus 273 D.

must know this also, that the corruption which had set in was not external to the body, but had become attached to it; and it was required that, instead of corruption, life should cleave to it; so that, just as death has been engendered in the body, so life may be engendered in it also. Now if death were external to the body, it would be proper for life also to have been engendered externally to it. But if death was wound closely to the body and was ruling over it as though united to it, it was required that life also should be wound closely to the body, that so the body, by putting on life in its stead, should cast off corruption. Besides, even supposing that the Word had come outside the body, and not in it, death would indeed have been defeated by him, in perfect accordance with nature, inasmuch as death has no power against the life; but the corruption attached to the body would have remained in it none the less. For this cause the Saviour reasonably put on him a body, in order that the body, becoming bound closely to the Life,[71] should no longer, as mortal, abide in death, but, as having put on immortality, should thenceforth rise again and remain immortal. For, once it had put on corruption, it could not have risen again unless it had put on life. And death likewise could not, from its very nature, appear save in the body. Therefore he put on a body that he might find death in the body and blot it out. For how could the Lord have been proved at all to be the Life, had he not quickened what was mortal? And just as, whereas stubble is naturally destructible by fire, supposing [firstly] a man keeps fire away from the stubble, though it is not burned, yet the stubble remains, for all that, merely stubble, fearing the threat of the fire—for fire has the natural property of consuming it; while if a man [secondly] encloses it with a quantity of asbestos, the substance said to be an antidote to fire, the stubble no longer dreads the fire, being secured by its enclosure in incombustible matter; in this very way one may say, with regard to the body and death, that if death had been kept from the body by a mere command on his part, it would none the less have been mortal and corruptible, according to the nature of bodies; but, that this should not be, it put on the incorporeal Word of God, and thus no longer fears either death or corruption, for it has life as a garment, and corruption is done away in it.

45. Consistently, therefore, the Word of God took a body and has made use of a human instrument, in order to quicken

[71] Or simply, "To life."

the body also, and as he is known in creation by his works so
to work in man as well, and to show himself everywhere, leaving
nothing void of his own divinity and of the knowledge of him.
For I resume, and repeat what I said before, that the Saviour
did this in order that, as he fills all things on all sides by his
presence, so also he might fill all things with the knowledge of
him, as the divine Scripture also says, "The whole earth was
filled with the knowledge of the Lord." [72] For if a man will but
look up to heaven, he sees its order, or if he cannot raise his
face to heaven, but only to man, he sees his power, beyond
comparison with that of men, shown by his works, and learns
that he alone among men is God the Word. Or if a man is gone
astray among demons, and is in fear of them, he may see this
man drive them out, and make up his mind that he is their
master. Or if a man has sunk to the waters, and thinks that they
are God—as the Egyptians, for instance, reverence the water
—he may see its nature changed by him, and learn that the
Lord is Creator of the waters. But if a man is gone down even
to Hades, and stands in awe of the heroes who have descended
thither, regarding them as gods, yet he may see the fact of
Christ's resurrection and victory over death, and infer that
among them also Christ alone is true God and Lord. For the
Lord touched all parts of creation, and freed and undeceived
all of them from every illusion; as Paul says, "Having put off
from himself the principalities and the powers, he triumphed
on the cross" [73]; that no one might by any possibility be any
longer deceived, but everywhere might find the true Word of
God. For thus man, shut in on every side, and beholding the
divinity of the Word unfolded everywhere, that is, in heaven,
in Hades, in man, upon earth, is no longer exposed to deceit
concerning God, but is to worship Christ alone, and through
him come rightly to know the Father. By these arguments, then,
on grounds of reason, the Gentiles in their turn will fairly be
put to shame by us. But if they deem the arguments insufficient
to shame them, let them be assured of what we are saying at
any rate by facts obvious to the sight of all.

46. When did men begin to desert the worshiping of idols,
save since God, the true Word of God, has come among men?
Or when have the oracles among the Greeks, and everywhere,
ceased and become empty, save when the Saviour has manifested himself upon earth? Or when did those who are called
gods and heroes in the poets begin to be convicted of being

[72] Isa. 11:9.          [73] Or, "Stripping naked the principalities" (Col. 2:15).

merely mortal men, save since the Lord effected his conquest
of death, and preserved incorruptible the body he had taken,
raising it from the dead? Or when did the deceitfulness and
madness of demons fall into contempt, save when the power of
God, the Word, the master of all these as well, condescending
because of man's weakness, appeared on earth? Or when did
the art and the schools of magic begin to be trodden down,
save when the divine manifestation of the Word took place
among men? And, in a word, at what time has the wisdom of
the Greeks become foolish, save when the true Wisdom of God
manifested itself on earth? For formerly the whole world and
every place was led astray by the worshiping of idols, and men
regarded nothing else but the idols as gods. But now, all the
world over, men are deserting the superstition of the idols,
and taking refuge with Christ; and, worshiping him as God,
are by his means coming to know that Father also whom they
knew not. And, marvelous fact, whereas the objects of worship
were various and of vast number, and each place had its own
idol, and he who was accounted a god among them had no
power to pass over to the neighboring place, so as to persuade
those of neighboring peoples to worship him, but was barely
served even among his own people; for no one else worshiped
his neighbor's god—on the contrary, each man kept to his own
idol, thinking it to be lord of all—Christ alone is worshiped
as one and the same among all peoples; and what the weakness
of the idols could not do—to persuade, namely, even those
dwelling close at hand—this Christ has done, persuading not
only those close at hand, but simply the entire world, to
worship one and the same Lord, and through him God, even
his Father.

47. And whereas formerly every place was full of the deceit
of the oracles, and the oracles at Delphi and Dodona, and in
Boeotia and Lycia and Libya and Egypt and those of the
Cabiri, and the Pythoness, were held in repute by men's
imagination, now, since Christ has begun to be preached everywhere, their madness also has ceased and there is none among
them to divine any more. And whereas formerly demons used
to deceive men's fancy, occupying springs or rivers, trees or
stones, and thus imposed upon the simple by their juggleries;
now, after the divine visitation of the Word, their deception
has ceased. For by the sign of the cross, though a man but use
it, he drives out their deceits. And while formerly men held to
be gods Zeus and Cronos and Apollo and the heroes mentioned

in the poets, and went astray in honoring them, now that the Saviour has appeared among men, those others have been exposed as mortal men, and Christ alone has been recognized among men as the true God, the Word of God. And what is one to say of the magic esteemed among them? that before the Word sojourned among us this was strong and active among Egyptians, and Chaldeans, and Indians, and inspired awe in those who saw it; but that by the presence of the truth, and the appearing of the Word, it also has been thoroughly confuted, and brought wholly to nought. But as to Gentile wisdom, and the sounding pretensions of the philosophers, I think none can need our argument, since the wonder is before the eyes of all that while the wise among the Greeks had written so much, and were unable to persuade even a few from their own neighborhood, concerning immortality and a virtuous life, Christ alone, by ordinary language and by men not clever with the tongue, has throughout all the world persuaded whole churches [74] full of men to despise death, and to mind the things of immortality; to overlook what is temporal and to turn their eyes to what is eternal; to think nothing of earthly glory and to strive only for the heavenly.

48. Now these arguments of ours do not amount merely to words, but have in actual experience a witness to their truth. For let him that will, go up and behold the proof of virtue in the virgins of Christ and in the young men that practice holy chastity, and the assurance of immortality in so great a band of his martyrs. And let him come who would test by experience what we have now said, and in the very presence of the deceit of demons and the imposture of oracles and the marvels of magic let him use the sign of that cross which is laughed at among them, and he shall see how by its means demons fly, oracles cease, all magic and witchcraft is brought to nought. Who, then, and how great is this Christ, who by his own name and presence casts into the shade and brings to nought all things on every side, and is alone strong against all, and has filled the whole world with his teaching? Let the Greeks tell us, who are pleased to laugh, and blush not. For if he is a man, how, then, has one man exceeded the power of all whom even themselves hold to be gods, and convicted them by his own power of being nothing? But if they call him a magician, how can it be that by a magician all magic is destroyed, instead of being confirmed? For if he conquered particular magicians, or

[74] The word can also be taken nontechnically—"assemblies."

prevailed over one only, it would be proper for them to hold that he excelled the rest by superior skill; but if his cross has won the victory over absolutely all magic, and over the very name of it, it must be plain that the Saviour is not a magician, seeing that even those demons who are invoked by the other magicians fly from him as their master. Who he is, then, let the Greeks tell us, whose only serious pursuit is jesting. Perhaps they might say that he too was a demon, and hence his strength. But say this as they will, they will have the laugh against them, for they can once more be put to shame by our former proofs. For how is it possible that he should be a demon who drives the demons out? For if he simply drove out particular demons, it might properly be held that by the chief of demons he prevailed against the lesser, just as the Jews said to him when they wished to insult him.[75] But if, by his name being named, all madness of the demons is uprooted and chased away, it must be evident that here too they are wrong, and that our Lord and Saviour Christ is not, as they think, some demoniacal power. Then, if the Saviour is neither a man simply nor a magician nor some demon, but has by his own Godhead brought to nought and cast into the shade both the doctrine found in the poets and the delusion of the demons, and the wisdom of the Gentiles, it must be plain, and will be owned by all, that this is the true Son of God, even the Word and Wisdom and Power of the Father from the beginning. For this is why his works also are no works of man, but are recognized to be above man, and truly God's works, both from the facts in themselves and from comparison with [the rest of] mankind.

49. For what man that ever was born formed a body for himself from a virgin alone? Or what man ever healed such diseases as the common Lord of all? Or who has restored what was wanting to man's nature, and made one blind from his birth to see? Asclepius was deified among them, because he practiced medicine and found out herbs for bodies that were sick, not forming them himself out of the earth, but discovering them by science drawn from nature. But what is this to what was done by the Saviour, in that, instead of healing a wound, he modified a man's original nature and restored the body whole. Heracles is worshiped as a god among the Greeks because he fought against men, his peers, and destroyed wild beasts by guile. What is this to what was done by the Word, in driving away from man diseases and demons and death

[75] Matt. 9:34 (12:24; Luke 11:15).

itself? Dionysus is worshiped among them because he has taught man drunkenness; but the true Saviour and Lord of all, for teaching temperance, is mocked by these people.[76] But let these matters pass. What will they say to the other miracles of his Godhead? At what man's death was the sun darkened and the earth shaken? Lo, even to this day men are dying, and they died also of old. When did any suchlike wonder happen in their case? Or, to pass over the deeds done through his body, and mention those after its rising again: What man's doctrine that ever was has prevailed everywhere, one and the same, from one end of the earth to the other, so that his worship has winged its way through every land? Or why, if Christ is, as they say, a man, and not God the Word, is not his worship prevented by the gods they have from passing into the same land where they are? Or why on the contrary does the Word himself, sojourning here, by his teaching stop their worship and put their deception to shame?

50. Many before this man have been kings and tyrants of the world; many are on record who have been wise men and magicians, among the Chaldeans and Egyptians and Indians; which of these, I say, not after death, but while still alive, was ever able so far to prevail as to fill the whole earth with his teaching and reform so great a multitude from the superstition of idols as our Saviour has brought over from idols to himself? The philosophers of the Greeks have composed many works with plausibility and verbal skill; what result, then, have they exhibited so great as has the cross of Christ? For the refinements they taught were plausible enough till they died; but even the influence they seemed to have while alive was subject to their mutual rivalries; and they were emulous, and declaimed against one another. But the Word of God, most strange fact, teaching in meaner language, has cast into the shade the choice sophists; and while he has, by drawing all to himself, brought their schools to nought, he has filled his own churches; and the marvelous thing is, that by going down as man to death, he has brought to nought the sounding utterances of the wise concerning idols. For whose death ever drove out demons? or whose death did demons ever fear, as they did that of Christ? For where the Saviour's name is named, there every demon is driven out. Or who has so rid men of the passions of the natural man that whoremongers are chaste, and murderers no longer

[76] Cf. the different treatment of the same figures in Justin Martyr, First Apology, 21.

hold the sword, and those who were formerly mastered by
cowardice play the man? And, in short, who persuaded men
of barbarous countries and heathen men in divers places to lay
aside their madness, and to mind peace, if it be not the faith
of Christ and the sign of the cross? Or who else has given men
such assurance of immortality as has the cross of Christ, and
the resurrection of his body? For although the Greeks have told
all manner of false tales, yet they were not able to feign a
resurrection of their idols—for it never crossed their mind
whether it be at all possible for the body again to exist after
death. And here one would most especially accept their testimony, inasmuch as by this opinion they have exposed the
weakness of their own idolatry, while leaving the possibility
open to Christ, so that hence also he might be made known
among all as Son of God.

51. Which of mankind, again, after his death, or else while
living, taught concerning virginity, and that this virtue was
not impossible among men? But Christ, our Saviour and king
of all, had such power in his teaching concerning it that even
children not yet arrived at the lawful age vow that virginity
which lies beyond the law. What man has ever yet been able
to pass so far as to come among Scythians and Ethiopians, or
Persians or Armenians or Goths, or those we hear of beyond
the ocean or those beyond Hyrcania, or even the Egyptians
and Chaldeans, men that mind magic and are superstitious
beyond nature and savage in their ways, and to preach at all
about virtue and self-control, and against the worshiping of
idols, as has the Lord of all, the Power of God, our Lord Jesus
Christ? Who not only preached by means of his own disciples,
but also carried persuasion to men's mind, to lay aside the
fierceness of their manners and no longer to serve their ancestral
gods, but to learn to know him, and through him to worship
the Father. For formerly, while in idolatry, Greeks and Barbarians used to war against each other, and were actually cruel
to their own kin. For it was impossible for anyone to cross sea
or land at all without arming the hand with swords, because
of their implacable fighting among themselves. For the whole
course of their life was carried on by arms, and the sword with
them took the place of a staff, and was their support in every
emergency; and still, as I said before, they were serving idols,
and offering sacrifices to demons, while for all their idolatrous
superstition they could not be reclaimed from this spirit. But
when they have come over to the school of Christ, then,

strangely enough, as men truly pricked in conscience, they have laid aside the savagery of their murders and no longer mind the things of war; but all is at peace with them, and from henceforth what makes for friendship is to their liking.

52. Who, then, is he that has done this, or who is he that has united in peace men that hated one another, save the beloved Son of the Father, the common Saviour of all, even Jesus Christ, who by his own love underwent all things for our salvation? For even from of old it was prophesied of the peace he was to usher in, where the Scripture says: "They shall beat their swords into plowshares, and their pikes into sickles, and nation shall not take the sword against nation, neither shall they learn war any more." [77] And this is at least not incredible, inasmuch as even now those Barbarians who have an innate savagery of manners, while they still sacrifice to the idols of their country, are mad against one another, and cannot endure to be a single hour without weapons; but when they hear the teaching of Christ, straightway instead of fighting they turn to husbandry, and instead of arming their hands with weapons they raise them in prayer, and in a word, in place of fighting among themselves henceforth they arm against the devil and against evil spirits, subduing these by self-restraint and virtue of soul. Now this is at once a proof of the divinity of the Saviour, since what men could not learn among idols they have learned from him, and no small exposure of the weakness and nothingness of demons and idols. For demons, knowing their own weakness, for this reason formerly set men to make war against one another, lest, if they ceased from mutual strife, they should turn to battle against demons. Why, they who become disciples of Christ, instead of warring with each other, stand arrayed against demons by their habits and their virtuous actions, and they rout them and mock at their captain the devil; so that in youth they are self-restrained, in temptations endure, in labors persevere, when insulted are patient, when robbed make light of it, and, wonderful as it is, they despise even death and become martyrs of Christ.

53. And, to mention one proof of the divinity of the Saviour which is indeed utterly surprising, what mere man or magician or tyrant or king was ever able by himself to engage with so many, and to fight the battle against all idolatry and the whole demoniacal host and all magic, and all the wisdom of the Greeks, while they were so strong and still flourishing and

[77] Isa. 2:4 (Micah 4:3).

imposing upon all, and at one onset to check them all, as was our Lord, the true Word of God, who, invisibly exposing each man's error, is by himself bearing off all men from them all, so that while they who were worshiping idols now trample upon them, those in repute for magic burn their books, and the wise prefer to all studies the interpretation of the Gospels? For whom they used to worship, them they are deserting, and whom they used to mock as one crucified, him they worship as Christ, confessing him to be God. And they that are called gods among them are routed by the sign of the cross, while the crucified Saviour is proclaimed in all the world as God and the Son of God. And the gods worshiped among the Greeks are falling into ill repute at their hands, as scandalous beings, while those who receive the teaching of Christ live a chaster life than they. If, then, these and the like are human works, let him who will point out similar works on the part of men of former time, and so convince us. But if they prove to be, and are, not men's works, but God's, why are the unbelievers so irreligious as not to recognize the master that wrought them? For their case is as though a man, from the works of creation, failed to know God their artificer. For if they knew his Godhead from his power over the universe, they would have known that the bodily works of Christ also are not human, but are the works of the Saviour of all, the Word of God. And did they thus know, "they would not," as Paul said, "have crucified the Lord of glory." [78]

54. As, then, if a man should wish to see God, who is invisible by nature and not seen at all, he may know and apprehend him from his works, so let him who fails to see Christ with his understanding at least apprehend him by the works of his body, and test whether they be human works or God's works. And if they be human, let him scoff; but if they are not human, but of God, let him recognize it, and not laugh at what is no matter for scoffing; but rather let him marvel that by so ordinary a means things divine have been manifested to us, and that by death immortality has reached to all, and that by the Word becoming man, the universal providence has been known, and its giver and artificer the very Word of God. For he was made man that we might be made God [79]; and he manifested himself by a body that we might receive the idea of the unseen Father; and he endured the insolence of men that

[78] I Cor. 2:8.
[79] Or "divine"; literally, "He was humanized that we might be deified."

we might inherit immortality. For while he himself was in no way injured, being impassible and incorruptible and very Word and God, men who were suffering, and for whose sakes he endured all this, he maintained and preserved in his own impassibility. And, in a word, the achievements of the Saviour, resulting from his becoming man, are of such kind and number that if one should wish to enumerate them he may be compared to men who gaze at the expanse of the sea and wish to count its waves. For as one cannot take in the whole of the waves with his eyes, for those which are coming on baffle the sense of him that attempts it, so for him that would take in all the achievements of Christ in the body, it is impossible to take in the whole, even by reckoning them up, as those which go beyond his thought are more than those he thinks he has taken in. Better is it, then, not to aim at speaking of the whole, where one cannot do justice even to a part, but, after mentioning one more, to leave the whole for you to marvel at. For all alike are marvelous, and wherever a man turns his glance, he may behold on that side the divinity of the Word, and be struck with exceeding great awe.

## EPILOGUE

55. This, then, after what we have so far said, it is right for you to realize, and to take as the sum of what we have already stated, and to marvel at exceedingly; namely, that since the Saviour has come among us, idolatry not only has no longer increased, but what there was is diminishing and gradually coming to an end; and not only does the wisdom of the Greeks no longer advance, but what there is is now fading away; and demons, so far from cheating any more by illusions and prophecies and magic arts, if they so much as dare to make the attempt, are put to shame by the sign of the cross. And, to sum the matter up, behold how the Saviour's doctrine is everywhere increasing, while all idolatry and everything opposed to the faith of Christ is daily dwindling, and losing power, and falling. And thus beholding, worship the Saviour, "who is above all" [80] and mighty, even God the Word, and condemn those who are being worsted and done away by him. For as, when the sun is come, darkness no longer prevails, but if any be still left anywhere it is driven away, so, now that the divine appearing of the Word of God is come, the darkness of the

[80] Rom. 9:5.

idols prevails no more, and all parts of the world in every direction are illumined by his teaching. And as, when a king is reigning in some country without appearing but keeps at home in his own house, often some disorderly persons, abusing his retirement, proclaim themselves; and each of them, by assuming the character, imposes on the simple as king, and so men are led astray by the name, hearing that there is a king, but not seeing him, if for no other reason, because they cannot enter the house; but when the real king comes forth and appears, then the disorderly impostors are exposed by his presence, while men, seeing the real king, desert those who previously led them astray: in like manner, the evil spirits formerly used to deceive men, investing themselves with God's honor; but when the Word of God appeared in a body, and made known to us his own Father, then at length the deceit of the evil spirits is done away and stopped, while men, turning their eyes to the true God, Word of the Father, are deserting the idols and now coming to know the true God. Now this is a proof that Christ is God the Word, and the Power of God. For whereas human things cease, and the Word of Christ abides, it is clear to all eyes that what ceases is temporary, but that he who abides is God, and the true Son of God, his only-begotten Word.

56. Let this, Christ-loving man, then, be our offering to you, just for a rudimentary sketch and outline, in a short compass, of the faith of Christ and of his divine appearing to usward. But you, taking occasion by this, if you light upon the text of the Scriptures, by genuinely applying your mind to them, will learn from them more completely and clearly the exact detail of what we have said. For they were spoken and written by God, through men who spoke of God. But we impart of what we have learned from inspired teachers who have been conversant with them, who have also become martyrs for the deity of Christ, to your zeal for learning, in turn. And you will also learn about his second glorious and truly divine appearing to us, when no longer in lowliness but in his own glory, no longer in humble guise but in his own magnificence, he is to come, no more to suffer, but thenceforth to render to all the fruit of his own cross, that is, the resurrection and incorruption; and no longer to be judged, but to judge all, by what each has done in the body, whether good or evil; where there is laid up for the good the Kingdom of Heaven, but for them that have done evil everlasting fire and outer darkness. For thus the Lord

himself also says, "Henceforth ye shall see the Son of Man sitting at the right hand of power, and coming on the clouds of heaven in the glory of the Father." [81] And for this very reason there is also a word of the Saviour to prepare us for that day, in these words: "Be ye ready and watch, for he cometh at an hour ye know not." [82] For, according to the blessed Paul, "We must all stand before the judgment seat of Christ, that each one may receive according as he hath done in the body, whether it be good or bad." [83]

57. But for the searching of the Scriptures and true knowledge of them an honorable life is needed, and a pure soul, and that virtue which is according to Christ; so that the intellect, guiding its path by it, may be able to attain what it desires, and to comprehend it, in so far as it is accessible to human nature to learn concerning the Word of God. For without a pure mind and a modeling of the life after the saints a man could not possibly comprehend the words of the saints. For just as, if a man wished to see the light of the sun, he would at any rate wipe and brighten his eye, purifying himself in some sort like what he desires, so that the eye, thus becoming light, may see the light of the sun; or as, if a man would see a city or country, he at any rate comes to the place to see it—thus he that would comprehend the mind of those who speak of God must needs begin by washing and cleansing his soul, by his manner of living, and approach the saints themselves by imitating their works; so that, associated with them in the conduct of a common life, he may understand also what has been revealed to them by God, and thenceforth, as closely knit to them, may escape the peril of the sinners and their fire at the Day of Judgment, and receive what is laid up for the saints in the Kingdom of Heaven, which "eye hath not seen, nor ear heard, neither have entered into the heart of man," [84] whatsoever things are prepared for them that live a virtuous life, and love the God and the Father, in Christ Jesus our Lord: through whom and with whom be to the Father himself, with the Son himself, in the Holy Spirit, honor and might and glory for ever and ever. Amen.

[81] Mark 14:62 (Matt. 26:64).
[83] II Cor. 5:10; Rom. 14:10.
[82] Matt. 24:42.
[84] I Cor. 2:9 (Isa. 54:4).

# GREGORY OF NAZIANZUS

# Introduction to Gregory of Nazianzus

THE CAPPADOCIAN FATHERS ARE THE CHIEF glory of their province of east-central Asia Minor in the history of the Roman Empire as well as in that of the Church. Under the Republic and the early Empire, Cappadocia was a vassal kingdom. In A.D. 18 it became a province, but still retained some of the character of frontier territory. Its cities were relatively few, and except for the capital, Mazaca, renamed Caesarea, of little importance. Large areas of former royal domain became part of the imperial estates. The leading Cappadocian families were country gentlemen rather than Greek citizens. Their sons went to study rhetoric, law, or philosophy in the great centers of the Empire, and then returned to administer the family property or occupy the position to which they might be called in public life. From such a family in the neighboring province of Pontus to the north came the law student Gregory, who turned to the gospel instead under the teaching of Origen and returned to be the missionary bishop of his home town of Neocaesarea. From the stories of his miracles he was known in later times as the Wonder-worker. But the historical Gregory already illustrates the qualities that were to distinguish the Cappadocians—the combination of theological and practical interests, the union of ascetic piety and literary culture, and the devotion to the Church of abilities of leadership which might otherwise have led to important positions in civil life.

From such a family, already Christian for several generations, came the elder Basil, a gentleman with properties in both Cappadocia and Pontus. Of his ten children, three became bishops—Basil of Caesarea, Gregory of Nyssa, and the youngest,

Peter, of Sebasteia—and the devout life of their oldest sister, Macrina, won her, along with their affection, the reputation of sanctity. Basil was born about 330, probably at Caesarea. At about the same time his future friend and colleague saw the light of day in the smaller city of Nazianzus, or, rather, at his family's country home in the nearby village of Arianzus. His father also bore the confusingly popular Christian name of Gregorios, "the watchful" (cf. Matt. 24:42), but had adhered for some time to the Hypsistarii, "worshipers of the Most High," an obscure sect that practiced an eclectic cult. The elder Gregory was obviously a leading citizen of Nazianzus. When his wife's influence brought him into the Church, his baptism, administered in the presence of several bishops on their way to the Council of Nicaea, was rapidly followed by his consecration to the episcopate, apparently with no previous service as presbyter or deacon.[1] Shortly after his ordination came the birth of his namesake.[2]

The world in which Gregory and Basil were growing up brought new conditions to their province as well as to the Church. On the highroad between the two centers of the Eastern Empire, Constantinople and Antioch, Cappadocia came more into the center of public affairs than at any other time in its history. Officials, imperial messengers, now and again a prefect or the emperor himself, passed through it. For Christians the age of the martyrs was still a vivid memory, but was rapidly being succeeded by that of the imperial Church, with its new set of problems. Persecution had produced martyrs; patronage was almost equally dangerous, and was met in turn by the protest of the monks. The Church was no longer wholly out of the world, and yet there was much doubt whether the Christian life could be lived in contact with the affairs of the world. Even devout families postponed the baptism of their sons, and gave them a pagan classical education. The young Gregory was still unbaptized when he began his higher studies at Caesarea and there met Basil. In the same condition the two friends went to Athens, the university town of the East, sometime about A.D. 350.

Gregory has left us a vivid description of student life at Athens, with its hazing and parties, but fewer details of his

---

[1] As narrated by his son in Oration 18, 5–16.
[2] In his autobiographical poem Gregory has his father say that the son had not lived as long as the father had been a priest (Poems ii, 11, 512, 513).

studies.[3] But it is clear that at Athens Basil and Gregory met Christian as well as pagan learning, and found their way to an intelligent acceptance of the faith which their more conspicuous fellow student the prince Julian was preparing to renounce. It is worth reflecting that, though they came to opposite solutions, Gregory and Julian as men of their age shared a common spiritual and theological problem—what intermediary can put us surely in touch with the ineffable supreme being? Julian, like other pagan Neo-Platonists (and Arian Christians), resorted to deities of a lower rank than the ultimate: Gregory, to the eternal Son of the eternal Father, the "mediator between God and men, the man Christ Jesus."[4]

After some ten years of studies abroad Gregory returned home in 358 or 359. His baptism seems to have taken place at about this time, or perhaps in his last years at Athens. For a short time, just enough to show that his education was not wasted, he engaged in the teaching of rhetoric, and then prepared to give himself to the work of the Lord, either in monastic solitude or in some active work—he was for the rest of his life to move between the two. The next few years were spent partly in helping his now aged father at Nazianzus, partly with Basil in the monastic retreat he had set up on the family estate near Neocaesarea in Pontus. At the end of 361 the elder Gregory demanded his son's assistance in the ministry and almost forcibly ordained him to the presbyterate. Gregory fled to Pontus, partly in protest, partly for final preparation, then returned to Nazianzus and there preached his first sermon at Easter of 362.

Though in a minor position in a small church, Gregory was now brought into contact with public events in Church and State. The apparent victory of Arianism under Constantius had just been ended by the pagan reaction of Julian's brief reign. The shift from a pagan to an orthodox emperor (Jovian), and then to another Arianizing ruler in the East (Valens, 365–378), kept Church affairs in a state of confusion. Gregory secured a reconciliation between his father and the monks of Nazianzus, who had renounced the communion of their bishop on account of his temporary acceptance of the Arianizing Creed of Ariminum. He similarly reconciled Basil, now a presbyter of Caesarea, with his bishop, the timid Eusebius, and in

[3] In his eulogy of Basil, Oration 43, 15–24.
[4] I Tim. 2:5, a favorite text of the age; cf. Theological Orations, iv, 14, and Augustine, *Confessions* x, 43.

370 helped to smooth the way for Basil's election as Eusebius' successor.

Basil rapidly became a leading figure among the orthodox bishops of Asia Minor, expounding the faith in his sermons and treatises, laboring in the active ministry of his diocese and his monasteries, endeavoring by a correspondence that stretched as far as Rome to settle the personal misunderstandings that divided the adherents of the Nicene faith. The death of Athanasius in 373 left him the leader of orthodoxy in the East; at Caesarea he was almost a prince-bishop, with the "new city" of his charitable institutions rivaling the old town and with the numerous assistant bishops—Gregory with poetic license says fifty [5]—of his extensive diocese.

It was not surprising that the division of the province of Cappadocia which Valens ordered in 371–372 was interpreted by Basil and his friends as an attack on the archbishop's position. The canons of Nicaea assumed that the civil province would also be an ecclesiastical unit, headed by the bishop of the metropolitan city. The new arrangement seems to have put all the cities of southern and western Cappadocia in the new province of Cappadocia Secunda, leaving only Caesarea itself and the imperial estates in Cappadocia Prima; the metropolitan bishop of the new province, Anthimus of Tyana, acquired a natural interest in supporting his own position. Basil embarked on the defense by planting his friends in old or new bishoprics, assuming their devotion to his cause, in which, as so often happens in human affairs, his own position and the principles for which he stood were inextricably combined. His brother Gregory became bishop of Nyssa, and Gregory of Nazianzus was destined for a new diocese set up in the disputed territory at the way station of Sasima—a dusty one-horse town, as he feelingly describes it.[6] Under protest he accepted consecration from Basil and his father, but in fact never took possession of the see of Sasima, where Anthimus was already in control.

After this unhappy contretemps, for which Gregory never quite forgave his old friend, his active life seemed to be ending in tragedy. His brother and sister had died a few years before, and in 374 he lost his father and soon afterward his mother. For a short time he was acting pastor of the church of Nazianzus, but shortly left his native town and province for a life of retirement at Seleucia in the province of Isauria to the south [7]

[5] Poems ii, 11, 447, 448.          [6] Poems ii, 11, 439–445.
[7] Somewhat to Basil's annoyance, Epistle 217.

From here the march of events suddenly brought him back to the center of Church and Empire. In August of 378, Valens was defeated and killed by the Goths at Adrianople, leaving as sole emperor his young nephew Gratian. Arian pressure was removed, but what would follow was uncertain. At this juncture Basil died, worn out by his labors and austerities, on January 1, 379, just missing the general victory of his cause. Three weeks later Gratian raised the Spanish general Theodosius to the purple and sent him to the East. With him the series of orthodox emperors of Byzantium was to begin. But even before Theodosius' policy was known, the time seemed ripe for revival of the depressed orthodox congregation at Constantinople. Gregory's knowledge and abilities were well known; he was free from obligations to another church; and the faithful of Constantinople and neighboring bishops called him to the capital.

Were it not for his two years at Constantinople, Gregory would be an inconspicuous figure in Church history, if known to us at all. His work there, however, not only left its mark on external events, but made him known as one of the great teachers and preachers of the Church. In Constantinople, Arianism had been predominant for nearly forty years, and was itself divided into sects. Bishop Demophilus represented the Creed of Ariminum, while others followed Macedonius (expelled from the see of Constantinople in 360), whose followers were less conspicuous for Arian views on the Son than for the denial of the deity of the Holy Spirit; and still others, Bishop Eunomius of Cyzicus, who represented extreme Arianism with its profession to know all about the Son and his subordination to the Father. This school seems to have appealed, with its claim to settle these questions by simple reason, to what might be called the "village atheist" type of mind. It is of them in particular, at this time and place, that Gregory of Nyssa makes his famous remark that all public places were full of these amateur theologians, who, if you ask the price of bread, tell you that the Father is greater and the Son subject to him, and if you want to order a bath, reply that the Son is made out of nothing.[8]

---

[8] On the Deity of the Son and Spirit (Migne, *Patrologia Graeca*, Vol. 46, col. 557), a reference which should, I think, be quoted as typical of Constantinople at this particular time rather than of the period generally. On the other hand, this kind of interest has been known to recur; some thirty years ago one of my own teachers, on arriving at Athens for study,

The orthodox themselves, so long leaderless in the capital, were divided on personal matters. But at first all went well. Gregory began his ministry in a private chapel, which in honor of the resurrection of Christ, and as the scene of renewal of his Church, came to be called the Anastasia. Here in 379 and 380 Gregory's great discourses were delivered. He was at one time mobbed by Arians, and later troubled by an ecclesiastical adventurer named Maximus, who arrived as a rival claimant for the see under the patronage of the bishop of Alexandria. But Gregory's congregation grew, and meanwhile Theodosius had declared that he would recognize as orthodox bishops and legitimate holders of church property those who held the faith of the Trinity and were in communion with Rome or Alexandria. Deprived of official support, Arianism began to collapse, and few objected when after his arrival at Constantinople in November, 380, Theodosius expelled Demophilus, and Gregory and his congregation took over the imperial Church of the Holy Wisdom.[9]

In the following spring a council met at Constantinople to settle miscellaneous affairs of the Eastern Church. As more than provincial, this Council is called ecumenical, although it did not at the time claim the universal character which later acceptance gave to it. It apparently issued a statement of faith (not preserved), supporting Nicaea and, in what now appears as its first canon, condemning various heresies, old and new, especially those that had grown up in the different phases of the Arian controversy, Eunomianism and Macedonianism among them. It rejected the claims of Maximus and recognized Gregory as bishop of Constantinople. The difficult question of the schism at Antioch, where at this point two orthodox rivals competed, came before it. Meletius, who, with most of the Antiochene Church, had returned from Semi-Arianism to orthodoxy, presided at the opening of the Council and died during it. Paulinus, the leader of the strict orthodox remnant who had never swerved from their loyalty to Nicaea, might have been recognized as his successor. But instead Flavian was elected,

was challenged by a barber with the query, "What do people in America think about the procession of the Holy Ghost?"

[9] Rather than Holy Apostles, I think, in spite of the considerations in which most later writers have followed Ullmann, *Gregorius von Nazianz*, 2d ed., p. 153 (English translation, p. 223); in Oration 43, 26, where Gregory bids farewell to the churches of Constantinople, he seems clearly to distinguish between the Great Church "which takes its greatness from the Word" and the shrine of the apostles.

and the division continued. Meanwhile Timothy of Alexandria had arrived, and began to challenge Gregory's position as uncanonical—he had at least technically been transferred from another see, which the rules of Nicaea forbade. Disgusted by these proceedings, and perhaps feeling that his work was done, Gregory withdrew from the Council and from Constantinople after a solemn farewell sermon. In his place the mild Nectarius, a highly esteemed civil servant, still unbaptized at the time of his election, was chosen for what the Council had declared should rank as the second see of Christendom.

Back at Nazianzus, Gregory once more returned to private life. For a short time he again took charge of the local church, until in 384 a satisfactory successor to his father was finally chosen. He was now in his early fifties, but already thought of himself as aged. On the family property at Arianzus he resumed the monastic life with his household, while as an elder statesman of the Church sometimes writing about its affairs. One year he took a vow of silence for the sacred season of Lent, but this did not prevent him from using his pen or greeting visitors with a smile. His own feelings and memories he recorded in his verse, much of which seems to date from this period. Newman was certainly correct in interpreting as autobiographical the opening stanzas of one of Gregory's shorter poems in defense of the monastic life—

"Someone whispered yesterday
    Of the rich and fashionable:
Gregory, in his own small way,
    Easy was, and comfortable.

"Had he not of wealth his fill,
    Whom a garden gay did bless,
And a gently trickling rill,
    And the sweets of idleness?

"I made answer: 'Is it ease,
    Fasts to keep, and tears to shed?
Vigil hours and wounded knees—
    Call you such a pleasant bed?

" 'Thus a veritable monk
    Does to death his fleshly frame;
Be there who in sloth have sunk,
    They have forfeited the name.' " [10]

[10] Poems ii, 44, 1–8; translation by J. H. Newman, *The Church of the Fathers*, London, 1840, end of Chapter IX.

At Arianzus, Gregory died in 389.[11] One's first impression of his character is perhaps that of a sympathetic weakness, in contrast to the vigor of Basil and the straightforwardness of Gregory of Nyssa. One reads his story with a certain amount of pity, and indeed he wrote his autobiography with a certain amount of self-pity. Yet his achievements were not a few, and his weakness was made strong in Christ.

## WRITINGS

The writings of Gregory of Nazianzus fall into three groups —letters, poems, and sermons (conventionally called Orations). The letters and sermons were obviously called forth by particular occasions, and the poems scarcely less so, since many of them were written to record or express his own feelings at a certain moment. The Benedictine editors arranged them in two books, didactic and personal; the latter includes a number of short pieces of some charm—though Gregory is in general a persistent rather than an inspired poet—and a long autobiographical poem which is a principle source for Gregory's career at Constantinople. The letters, 242 in number, are of considerable interest, although not so intimate as one might expect. Gregory's position as a Father of the Church rests mainly on the sermons. They include discourses given at the striking moments in Gregory's career—his first appearance as a priest, his acceptance of the episcopate, his farewell to Constantinople; funeral or memorial discourses on his own relatives, on Basil, and on Athanasius; and the most careful exposition of his theological teaching. This is to be found most completely, though not exclusively, in the Theological Orations here reprinted, which won him from later ages the distinctive title of *Theologos*, otherwise given only to Saint John.

The study of Gregory has pursued rather a curious course. He was much read in the Greek Middle Ages, and a number of Byzantine commentators added notes to one or another section of his works. Those of Elias, a tenth century archbishop of Crete, are still of value. Gregory's character and career attracted the interest of Christian humanists of the Renaissance. After several partial publications a full edition of the Orations, with some of the letters and poems, appeared at Basel in 1550.

---

[11] Jerome, *De viris illustribus*, 117, writing in the thirteenth year of Theodosius (A.D. 391), says, "Three years ago," which by Roman calculation would be 389.

Further material was added in seventeenth century editions. But because of a series of accidents the complete edition undertaken by the French Benedictines was in preparation for over a century and a half. Volume I, containing the Orations, appeared in 1778. During the French Revolution the materials collected for Volume II passed into private hands; the volume was finally published by A.-B. Caillau in 1840, only a few years before the two volumes (and some other material, including Jahn's selections from the notes of Elias) were reprinted in Migne's *Patrologia Graeca.*

Gregory's character and career have fascinated students in the English-speaking world. "There's a Basil for you," said John Henry Newman, when one of his friends presumed on his support in a manner reminiscent of the Sasima episode. But nothing seems to have been done to make Gregory's works available in English until the inclusion of half a volume of selections in the Post-Nicene Fathers. A new edition of his works was long in preparation in Cracow and was ready to appear in 1939; it seems to have been one of the casualties of the war. The editors reported, however, that they found the Benedictine text of the Orations excellent, but were less satisfied with that of the poems and letters.[12]

## THE THEOLOGICAL ORATIONS

The five sermons commonly described as the Theological Orations of Gregory Nazianzen (Orations XXVII–XXXI as usually published) were evidently preached as a series during the middle of his Constantinople period, probably in the summer or fall of 380. They are the platform of the orthodox cause at the moment when it is fighting on equal terms with the Eunomians and Macedonians of Constantinople. Though they lack the dramatic interest of some of the other Orations, they are fair examples of the homiletic style that won Gregory his great reputation as a preacher. A recent study has suggested that his language was in fact closer to good spoken Greek of the time, less of an artificial rhetoric of the schools, than one might at first suppose.[13] Though not without art, he also allows himself a certain informality, which may account for occasional slips in quotation or reference, as when John the

[12] Letter cited in Gallay, *La vie de Saint Grégoire de Nazianze,* p. x.
[13] Henry, *The Late Greek Optative and Its Use in the Writings of Greogory Nazianzen,* pp. 91–93.

Baptist is confused with the apostle (II, 20), or when the preacher allows himself so casual a Biblical allusion as "it seems to Solomon and me" (I, 5).

Since what we have before us is what was delivered at the Anastasia, we need not be surprised that Gregory's approach to theology is closely related to the current rival ideas which he was meeting. In fact, several of the discourses follow a surprising but effective pattern of first dealing with opponents and then laying down positive principles on the topic in hand. Theology was a subject of current argument at Constantinople, so that Gregory was beginning with a theme of popular interest. His affirmative teaching is the last impression left on the minds of his congregation, and this section usually leads into or includes a rhetorical conclusion of some literary beauty, and swings naturally into the final doxology.

The First Oration is an introduction to the series. Attacking the argumentativeness of the Eunomians, Gregory warns his own congregation against replying in kind, and emphasizes that the discussion of divine things belongs to the man who is leading a life of prayer and has at least a far-off glimpse of the mystic vision. The Second approaches from this point of view the doctrine of God, *theologia* in the strict sense of the word. Nature and Scripture make us aware of the fact of God's existence, but the negative way is our best approach to the intellectual definition of his being. But he is known gloriously in his works—and this Gregory expounds in a magnificent passage. The Hexaemeron, the "six days' employ,"[14] received the attention of leading preachers of the period—Basil and Gregory of Nyssa both preached series of sermons on it, and Ambrose, drawing largely on Basil, did the same at Milan. Nazianzen avoids excessive detail in using the theme for part of one sermon, yet gives enough to impress; he skillfully weaves together Biblical, classical, and current scientific references, and ends by raising his congregation to join in adoration with the higher creation, the angelic hosts.

Two Orations are then devoted to the main battleground with Arians, the doctrine of God the Son. The Third first aims to show that the orthodox doctrine of the coequal Father and Son, one in the unity of the divine Monarchia, is both more Christian and more logical than the Arian concept of a subordinate deity. After this refutation, which cannot help being

14 John Mason Neale, "Stars of the Morning," in *Hymns of the Eastern Church*, London, 1862.

somewhat dry to those who do not confront Arianism as a present problem, the Biblical experience of and Christian faith in the one Christ, God and Man, is splendidly expounded. The Fourth Oration first refutes the conclusions drawn from a series of proof texts, which evidently circulated in a specific Eunomian manual (one of those referred to in III, 1). The Nicene faith is then clearly stated, first in theological and then in Biblical terms; the conclusion breathes the language of evangelical piety, calling on the Christian to rejoice in the manifold names of his Saviour—his "Shepherd, Guardian, Friend, Prophet, Priest, and King."

In the Fifth Oration, Gregory turns from Arians and the doctrine of the Son to Macedonians and the doctrine of the Holy Spirit. He begins with some fencing with opponents in their own terms, and gradually shifts to a more positive statement. It is here that the formal doctrine of the Trinity is finally enunciated, along with some observations about the use of language and the development of doctrine which, as has been noted, still retain their value. Once more, there is an impressive massing of Biblical testimonies, though just before the end (and it was doubtless well to move to a quieter note) comes a discussion and rejection of the traditional attempt to explain the Trinity by physical analogies.

Surely no series of doctrinal sermons has ever been so successful in simultaneously meeting the current intellectual problems of the age and making a permanent contribution to the formulation of Christian thought. Through them there run as moving themes two aspects of Gregory's interests which were represented by two of the rising young men of the Church who looked to him as their master at this time. Jerome, who spent some time under Gregory's teaching at Constantinople on his way back from the Syrian desert to Rome, looked to him primarily as one mighty in the Scriptures. Gregory's Scriptural knowledge is indeed impressive, though he works rather by piling up masses of texts than by establishing general principles. He was of course confined to the Septuagint Old Testament, which sometimes misled him. But better for the preacher perhaps than Jerome's detailed learning was Gregory's sense of the Bible as the book of redemption—and an occasional lightness of touch which did no harm, as when Jerome asked him to explain that puzzle in the Gospel of Luke, the "second-first Sabbath," and Gregory cheerfully replied, "I'd better answer this in church where you won't venture to disagree." [15]

[15] Jerome, *Epistle* 52, 8; Luke 6:1.

A closer friend of Gregory's was the deacon Evagrius of Pontus, whom he remembered with a personal memento in the will which he drew up in 382. Evagrius was a philosopher and mystic, who for the rest of his life was to be a prominent figure among the Greek and Origenistic party of the monks of Egypt. His approach to religion had much in common with Gregory's, both intellectually and spiritually. Like his second successor at Constantinople, John Chrysostom, Gregory had a special devotion among the apostles to Paul, "disciple and teacher of the fishermen," as he rather daringly calls him (I, 1). Of the many aspects of the apostle, it was the mystic whose life was hid in Christ and renewed by the Spirit, and who hints at glimpses of the ineffable things in the third heaven but quite properly does not attempt to relate them (II Cor. 12:4), who most appealed to Gregory.

## LETTERS ON APOLLINARIANISM

In his years of retirement Gregory was troubled by the appearance in Cappadocia of some of the heresies he had battled at Constantinople. There were not only the remains of Arianism, but the apparently opposite extreme of Apollinarianism. The Apollinarians were a party as well as a school of thought, and at one time went so far as to set up a rival to Gregory in the see of Nazianzus itself, while he was recovering his health at the hot baths of Xanxaris.[16] Bad health may account for the air of personal annoyance in these letters, two addressed to Cledonius, the priest who was in charge of the church of Nazianzus in Gregory's absence, and one to Nectarius of Constantinople. But the intellectual vigor of the theologian is unweakened, and the letters contain a clear statement of the essential doctrine of the full humanity of Christ which was to be a guide for the orthodox party in the debates of the following century. The teaching attacked is that which would find in the humanity of Christ body and animal soul, but with the indwelling deity replacing the higher human soul (*nous*, mind); so that Christ was indeed a "man from heaven" (I Cor. 15:47) in that it was what came from heaven that gave him full human existence. In the letter to Nectarius, Gregory quotes from a pamphlet by Apollinaris himself, although the latter seems to have repudiated the strange idea that the flesh of Christ as well was heavenly in origin. It may have been a speculation

16 Gregory, Epistle 125.

entertained briefly and then dropped—or Gregory's interpretation of what the idea of heavenly humanity would necessarily mean.

The version of the Theological Orations and Letters on Apollinarianism reprinted here is that prepared by Browne and Swallow for the Nicene and Post-Nicene Fathers, Series II, Vol. VII. I have, however, filled two apparently accidental omissions, simplified the use of capitals, corrected a few apparent misprints, and in some cases added brackets around words required by the translation but not actually expressed in the original, especially when they happened to be technical terms of theology such as "person" or "nature."

# BIBLIOGRAPHY

## Editions

Basel, 1550. Paris, 2 vols., 1609–1611.

Paris (Benedictine edition), 2 vols., 1778–1840, reprinted in Migne, *Patrologia Graeca*, Vols. 35–38, Paris, 1857–1858.

A. J. Mason, *The Five Theological Orations of Gregory of Nazianzus* (Cambridge Patristic Texts), Cambridge, 1899 (with a valuable commentary).

## Translations

*English*:

C. G. Browne and J. E. Swallow, *S. Gregory Nazianzen, Archbishop of Constantinople, Select Orations* and *Select Letters* (Nicene and Post-Nicene Fathers, Series II, Vol. VII, pp. 185–498), London and New York, 1894.

*French*:

N. Fontaine, *Orations*, 2 vols., 1693.

Paul Gallay, *Grégoire de Nazianze, Les discours théologiques*, Lyons and Paris, Vitte, 1942.

*German*:

Twenty-five orations (not including the Theological Orations) are translated by Johannes Röhm, *Ausgewählte Schriften des heiligen Gregor von Nazianz* (Bibliothek der Kirchenväter, Vols. 20 and 47), Kempten, 1874–1877, and 1–20 have appeared in Philipp Haeuser, *Des heiligen Bischofs Gregor von Nazianz Reden*, Vol. 1 (Bibliothek der Kirchenväter, new series, 59), Munich, Pustet, 1928.

## BIOGRAPHIES

Carl Ullmann, *Gregorius von Nazianz* (Darmstadt, 1825, 2d ed. Gotha, 1867; tr. G. V. Cox, *Gregory of Nazianzum*, London, 1851), is still useful; the latest formal biography is Paul Gallay, *La vie de Saint Grégoire de Nazianze*, Lyons and Paris, Vitte, 1943. Less pretentious sketches of value are those of J. H. Newman, in *The Church of the Fathers*, London, 1840 (reprinted 1900), of which Chs. 5–9 deal with Basil and Gregory; in the 4th ed., 1868, these are Chs. 1–4—reprinted in J. H. Newman, *Essays and Sketches*, ed. C. F. Harrold, Vol. III, New York and London, Longmans, Green, 1948, pp. 1–91; Frederick W. Farrar, *Lives of the Fathers*, London and New York, 1889, Vol. I, pp. 491–582; and Dorothy Brooke, *Pilgrims Were They All, Stories of Religious Adventure in the Fourth Century of Our Era*, IV, "The Saint: Gregory of Nazianzus," London, Faber and Faber, 1943.

## SPECIAL STUDIES

Adolf Donders, *Der hl. Kirchenlehrer Gregor von Nazianz als Homilet*, Münster, 1909.

E. Fleury, *Hellénisme et Christianisme, Saint Grégoire de Nazianze et son temps*, Paris, Beauchesne, 1930.

Johannes Focken, *De Gregorii Nazianzeni orationum et carminum dogmaticorum argumentandi ratione*, Berlin, 1912.

Marcel Guignet, *Saint Grégoire de Nazianze et la rhétorique*, Paris, 1911.

Rose de Lima Henry, *The Late Greek Optative and Its Use in the Works of Gregory Nazianzen* (Catholic University of America Patristic Studies 68), Washington, Catholic University Press, 1943; cf. Martin J. Higgins, "Why Another Optative Dissertation?", *Byzantion*, Vol. 15, 1940–1941, pp. 443–448.

Henri Pinault, *Le Platonisme de Saint Grégoire de Nazianze, essai sur les relations du Christianisme et de l'Hellénisme dans son oeuvre théologique*, Paris, 1925.

*On Cappadocia*:

A. H. M. Jones, *The Cities of the Eastern Roman Provinces*, Oxford, Clarendon Press, 1937, VII, "Cappadocia," pp. 175–191.

*On the Second Ecumenical Council*:

Hans Lietzmann, *The Era of the Church Fathers* (A History of the Early Church, Vol. IV), tr. B. L. Woolf, London, 1950, New York, Charles Scribner's Sons, 1952, Ch. 2.

# The Theological Orations

## THE TEXT: THE FIRST THEOLOGICAL ORATION—INTRODUCTORY

1. I am to speak against persons who pride themselves on their eloquence; so, to begin with a text of Scripture, "Behold, I am against thee, O thou proud one,"[1] not only in your system of teaching, but also in your hearing, and in your tone of mind. For there are certain persons who have not only their ears and their tongues, but even, as I now perceive, their hands too, itching for our words; who delight in profane babblings, and oppositions of science falsely so called, and strifes about words, which tend to no profit[2]; for so Paul, the preacher and establisher of the "Word cut short,"[3] the disciple and teacher of the fishermen, calls all that is excessive or superfluous in discourse. But as to those to whom we refer, would that they, whose tongue is so voluble and clever in applying itself to noble and approved language, would likewise pay some attention to actions. For then perhaps in a little while they would become less sophistical, and less absurd and strange acrobats of words, if I may use a ridiculous expression about a ridiculous subject.

2. But since they neglect every path of righteousness, and look only to this one point, namely, which of the propositions submitted to them they shall bind or loose (like those persons who in the theaters perform wrestling matches in public, but not that kind of wrestling in which the victory is won according to the rules of the sport, but a kind to deceive the eyes of those who are ignorant in such matters, and to catch applause), and

---

[1] Jer. 50:31 (LXX, ch. 27:31); surely Gregory is speaking against rather than simply to the Eunomians, in spite of Mason's note to the contrary —he both attacks their approach to the discussion of theology and endeavors to discourage his congregation from replying in the same spirit.
[2] I Tim. 6:20; II Tim. 2:14, 16.     [3] Rom. 9:28 (Isa. 10:23).

every marketplace must buzz with their talking; and every dinner party be worried to death with silly talk and boredom; and every festival be made unfestive and full of dejection, and every occasion of mourning be consoled by a greater calamity —their questions—and all the women's apartments accustomed to simplicity be thrown into confusion and be robbed of its [their] flower [4] of modesty by the torrent of their words . . . since, I say, this is so, the evil is intolerable and not to be borne, and our great mystery is in danger of being made a thing of little moment. Well then, let these spies bear with us, moved as we are with fatherly compassion, and as holy Jeremiah says, torn in our hearts [5]; let them bear with us so far as not to give a savage reception to our discourse upon this subject; and let them, if indeed they can, restrain their tongues for a short while and lend us their ears. However that may be, you shall at any rate suffer no loss. For either we shall have spoken in the ears of them that will hear, and our words will bear some fruit, namely, an advantage to you (since the sower sows the Word upon every kind of mind; and the good and fertile bears fruit), or else you will depart despising this discourse of ours as you have despised others, and having drawn from it further material for gainsaying and railing at us, upon which to feast yourselves yet more.

And you must not be astonished if I speak a language which is strange to you and contrary to your custom, who profess to know everything and to teach everything in a too impetuous and generous manner . . . not to pain you by saying ignorant and rash.

3. Not to everyone, my friends, does it belong to philosophize about God; not to everyone—the subject is not so cheap and low—and, I will add, not before every audience, nor at all times, nor on all points; but on certain occasions, and before certain persons, and within certain limits.

Not to all men, because it is permitted only to those who have been examined, and are past masters in meditation, and who have been previously purified in soul and body, or at the very least are being purified. For the impure to touch the pure is, we may safely say, not safe, just as it is unsafe to fix weak eyes upon the sun's rays. And what is the permitted occasion? It is when we are free from all external defilement or disturbance, and when

---

[4] The confusion of numbers is only in English, which has no single word for *gunaikōnitis*, the women's part of a house.
[5] Jer. 4:19 (LXX).

that which rules within us is not confused with vexatious or erring images; like persons mixing up good writing with bad, or filth with the sweet odors of unguents. For it is necessary to be truly at leisure to know God; and when we can get a convenient season, to discern the straight road of the things divine. And who are the permitted persons? They to whom the subject is of real concern, and not they who make it a matter of pleasant gossip, like any other thing, after the races, or the theater, or a concert, or a dinner, or still lower employments. To such men as these, idle jests and petty contradictions about these subjects are a part of their amusement.

4. Next, on what subjects and to what extent may we philosophize? On matters within our reach, and to such an extent as the mental power and grasp of our audience may extend. No further, lest, as excessively loud sounds injure the hearing, or excess of food the body, or, if you will, as excessive burdens beyond the strength injure those who bear them, or excessive rains the earth; so these too, being pressed down and overweighted by the stiffness, if I may use the expression, of the arguments, should suffer loss even in respect of the strength they originally possessed.

5. Now, I am not saying that it is not needful to remember God at all times; . . . I must not be misunderstood, or I shall be having these nimble and quick people down upon me again. For we ought to think of God even more often than we draw our breath; and if the expression is permissible, we ought to do nothing else. Yea, I am one of those who entirely approve that Word which bids us meditate day and night, and tell at eventide and morning and noonday, and praise the Lord at every time [6]; or, to use Moses' words, whether a man lie down, or rise up, or walk by the way, or whatever else he be doing [7]— and by this recollection we are to be molded to purity. So that it is not the continual remembrance of God that I would hinder, but only the talking about God; nor even that as in itself wrong, but only when unreasonable; nor all teaching, but only want of moderation. As of even honey, repletion and satiety, though it be of honey, produce vomiting; and, as Solomon says and I think, [8] there is a time for everything, and that which is good ceases to be good if it be not done in a good way; just as a flower is quite out of season in winter, and just as a man's dress does not become a woman, nor a woman's a man; and as

6 Ps. 1:2; 55 (54):17; 34 (33):1.
7 Deũt. 6:7; 11:19.                    8 Eccl. 3:1.

geometry is out of place in mourning, or tears at a carousal; shall we in this instance alone disregard the proper time, in a matter in which most of all due season should be respected? Surely not, my friends and brethren (for I will still call you brethren, though you do not behave like brothers). Let us not think so nor yet, like hot-tempered and hard-mouthed horses, throwing off our rider Reason, and casting away Reverence, that keeps us within due limits, run far away from the turning point,[9] but let us philosophize within our proper bounds, and not be carried away into Egypt, nor be swept down into Assyria, nor sing the Lord's song in a strange land,[10] by which I mean before any kind of audience, strangers or kindred, hostile or friendly, kindly or the reverse, who watch what we do with overgreat care, and would like the spark of what is wrong in us to become a flame, and secretly kindle and fan it and raise it to heaven with their breath and make it higher than the Babylonian flame which burned up everything around it. For since their strength lies not in their own dogmas, they hunt for it in our weak points. And therefore they apply themselves to our, shall I say, "misfortunes" or "failings," like flies to wounds. But let us at least be no longer ignorant of ourselves, or pay too little attention to the due order in these matters. And if it be impossible to put an end to the existing hostility, let us at least agree upon this, that we will utter mysteries under our breath, and holy things in a holy manner, and we will not cast to ears profane that which may not be uttered, nor give evidence that we possess less gravity than those who worship demons, and serve shameful fables and deeds; for they would sooner give their blood to the uninitiated than certain words. But let us recognize that as in dress and diet and laughter and demeanor there is a certain decorum, so there is also in speech and silence; since among so many titles and powers of God, we pay the highest honor to [the] Word. Let even our disputings then be kept within bounds.

6. Why should a man who is a hostile listener to such words be allowed to hear about the generation of God, or his creation, or how God was made out of things which had no existence, or of section and analysis and division? Why do we make our accusers judges? Why do we put swords into the hands of our enemies? How, do you think, or with what temper, will the

9 Suggested by the Platonic chariot (*Phaedrus* 246, 253, 254) here engaged in a race.
10 Cf. Hos. 9:3; Ps. 137 (136):4.

arguments about such subjects be received by one who approves of adulteries, and corruption of children, and who worships the passions and cannot conceive of aught higher than the body . . . who till very lately set up gods for himself, and gods too who were noted for the vilest deeds? Will it not first be from a material standpoint, shamefully and ignorantly, and in the sense to which he has been accustomed? Will he not make your theology a defense for his own gods and passions? For if we ourselves wantonly misuse these words, it will be a long time before we shall persuade them to accept our philosophy. And if they are in their own persons inventors of evil things, how should they refrain from grasping at such things when offered to them? Such results come to us from mutual contest. Such results follow to those who fight for the Word beyond what the Word approves; they are behaving like mad people, who set their own house on fire, or tear their own children, or disavow their own parents, taking them for strangers.

7. But when we have put away from the conversation those who are strangers to it, and sent the great legion on its way to the abyss into the herd of swine,[11] the next thing is to look to ourselves, and polish our theological self to beauty like a statue. The first point to be considered is: What is this great rivalry of speech and endless talking? What is this new disease of insatiability? Why have we tied our hands and armed our tongues? We do not praise either hospitality, or brotherly love, or conjugal affection, or virginity; nor do we admire liberality to the poor, or the chanting of psalms, or nightlong vigils, or tears. We do not keep under the body by fasting, or go forth to God by prayer; nor do we subject the worse to the better— I mean the dust to the spirit—as they would do who form a just judgment of our composite nature; we do not make our life a preparation for death; nor do we make ourselves masters of our passions, mindful of our heavenly nobility; nor tame our anger when it swells and rages, nor our pride that brings to a fall, nor unreasonable grief, nor unchastened pleasure, nor meretricious laughter, nor undisciplined eyes, nor insatiable ears, nor excessive talk, nor absurd thoughts, nor aught of the occasions which the evil one gets against us from sources within ourselves; bringing upon us the death that comes through the windows, as Holy Scripture says[12]; that is, through the senses. Nay, we do the very opposite, and have given liberty to the

11 Mark 5:13; Luke 8:31–33; Matt. 8:32.
12 Jer 9:21, as commonly interpreted by the Fathers.

passions of others, as kings give releases from service in honor of a victory, only on condition that they incline to our side, and make their assault upon God more boldly, or more impiously. And we give them an evil reward for a thing which is not good, license of tongue for their impiety.

8. And yet, O talkative dialectician, I will ask you one small question, and answer me, as He says to Job who through whirlwind and cloud gives divine admonitions.[13] Are there many mansions in God's house, as you have heard, or only one? Of course you will admit that there are many, and not only one. Now, are they all to be filled, or only some, and others not; so that some will be left empty, and will have been prepared to no purpose? Of course all will be filled, for nothing can be in vain which has been done by God. And can you tell me what you will consider this mansion to be? Is it for the rest and glory which is in store there for the blessed, or something else?—No, not anything else. Since then we are agreed upon this point, let us further examine another also. Is there anything that procures these mansions, as I think there is; or is there nothing? —Certainly there is.—What is it? Is it not that there are various modes of conduct, and various purposes, one leading one way, another another way, according to the proportion of faith, and these we call ways? Must we, then, travel all, or some of these ways . . . the same individual along them all, if that be possible; or, if not, along as many as may be; or else along some of them? And even if this may not be, it would still be a great thing, at least as it appears to me, to travel excellently along even one. —You are right in your conception.—What, then, when you hear there is but one way, and that a narrow one,[14] does the word seem to you to show? That there is but one on account of its excellence. For it is but one, even though it be split into many parts. And narrow because of its difficulties, and because it is trodden by few in comparison with the multitude of the adversaries, and of those who travel along the road of wickedness.—So I think too.—Well, then, my good friend, since this is so, why do you, as though condemning our doctrine for a certain poverty, rush headlong down that one which leads through what you call arguments and speculations but I, frivolities and quackeries? Let Paul reprove you with those

13 Job 40: 7, 8 (LXX, vs. 2, 3).
14 A rather confusing combination of John 14:2 and Matt. 7:14—the idea seems to be that there is but one Christian way, comprising the variety of Christian vocations.

bitter reproaches in which, after his list of the gifts of grace, he says: Are all apostles? Are all prophets? [15] etc.

9. But, be it so. Lofty you are, even beyond the lofty, even above the clouds, if you will, a spectator of things invisible, a hearer of things unspeakable; one who has ascended after Elijah, and who after Moses has been deemed worthy of the vision of God, and after Paul has been taken up into heaven; why do you mold the rest of your fellows in one day into saints, and ordain them theologians, and as it were breathe into them instruction, and make them many councils of ignorant oracles? Why do you entangle those who are weaker in your spider's web, as if it were something great and wise? Why do you stir up wasps' nests against the faith? Why do you suddenly spring a flood of dialectics upon us, as the fables of old did the Giants? Why have you collected all that is frivolous and unmanly among men, like a rabble, into one torrent, and having made them more effeminate by flattery, fashioned a new workshop, cleverly making a harvest for yourself out of their want of understanding? Do you deny that this is so, and are the other matters of no account to you? Must your tongue rule at any cost, and can you not restrain the birth pang of your speech? You may find many other honorable subjects for discussion. To these turn this disease of yours with some advantage. Attack the silence of Pythagoras, and the Orphic beans, and the novel brag about "The Master said." Attack the ideas of Plato, and the transmigrations and courses of our souls, and the reminiscences, and the unlovely loves of the soul for lovely bodies. Attack the atheism of Epicurus, and his atoms, and his unphilosophic pleasure; or Aristotle's petty Providence, and his artificial system, and his discourses about the mortality of the soul, and the humanitarianism of his doctrine. Attack the superciliousness of the Stoa, or the greed and vulgarity of the Cynic. Attack the "Void and Full" (what nonsense), and all the details about the gods and the sacrifices and the idols and demons, whether beneficent or malignant, and all the tricks that people play with divination, evoking of gods, or of souls, and the power of the stars. And if these things seem to you unworthy of discussion as petty and already often confuted, and you will keep to your line, and seek the satisfaction of your ambition in it; then here too I will provide you with broad paths. Philosophize about the world or worlds; about matter;

15 I Cor. 12:29; the thought seems to be that only if all were apostles and prophets could people who behave like the Eunomians claim to be such.

about soul; about natures endowed with reason, good or bad; about resurrection, about judgment, about reward, or the sufferings of Christ.[16] For in these subjects to hit the mark is not useless, and to miss it is not dangerous. But with God we shall have converse, in this life only in a small degree; but a little later, it may be, more perfectly, in the same, our Lord Jesus Christ, to whom be glory forever. Amen.

16 The last items in this list are rather surprising in view of the following sentence—perhaps Gregory assumes the Christians agree on them basically and their differences are only minor and speculative.

# THE TEXT: THE SECOND THEOLOGICAL ORATION—ON GOD

1. In the former discourse we laid down clearly with respect to the theologian both what sort of character he ought to bear, and on what kind of subject he may philosophize, and when, and to what extent. We saw that he ought to be, as far as may be, pure, in order that light may be apprehended by light; and that he ought to consort with serious men, in order that his word be not fruitless through falling on an unfruitful soil; and that the suitable season is when we have a calm within from the whirl of outward things, so as not like madmen to lose our breath; and that the extent to which we may go is that to which we have ourselves advanced, or to which we are advancing. Since, then, these things are so, and we have broken up for ourselves the fallows of divinity, so as not to sow upon thorns, and have made plain the face of the ground, being molded and molding others by Holy Scripture . . . let us now enter upon theological questions, setting at the head thereof the Father, the Son, and the Holy Ghost, of whom we are to treat; that the Father may be well pleased, and the Son may help us, and the Holy Ghost may inspire us; or rather that one illumination may come upon us from the one God, one in diversity, diverse in unity, wherein is a marvel.

2. Now when I go up eagerly into the Mount[1]—or, to use a truer expression, when I both eagerly long, and at the same time am afraid (the one through my hope and the other through my weakness), to enter within the cloud, and hold converse with God, for so God commands—if any be an Aaron,[2] let him go up with me, and let him stand near, being ready, if it must be so, to remain outside the cloud. But if any be a

[1] Ex. 19:3.  [2] Ex. 19:24.

Nadab or an Abihu, or of the Order of the Elders,[3] let him go up indeed, but let him stand afar off, according to the value of his purification. But if any be of the multitude, who are unworthy of this height of contemplation, if he be altogether impure, let him not approach at all, for it would be dangerous to him; but if he be at least temporarily purified, let him remain below and listen to the voice alone, and the trumpet, the bare words of piety, and let him see the mountain smoking and lightening, a terror at once and a marvel to those who cannot get up. But if any is an evil and savage beast, and altogether incapable of taking in the subject matter of contemplation and theology, let him not hurtfully and malignantly lurk in his den among the woods, to catch hold of some dogma or saying by a sudden spring, and to tear sound doctrine to pieces by his misrepresentations, but let him stand yet afar off and withdraw from the Mount, or he shall be stoned and crushed, and shall perish miserably in his wickedness.[4] For to those who are like wild beasts true and sound discourses are stones. If he be a leopard, let him die with his spots; if a ravening and roaring lion, seeking what he may devour of our souls or of our words; or a wild boar, trampling underfoot the precious and translucent pearls of the truth; or an Arabian and alien wolf,[5] or one keener even than these in tricks of argument; or a fox, that is a treacherous and faithless soul, changing its shape according to circumstances or necessities, feeding on dead or putrid bodies, or on little vineyards when the large ones have escaped them; or any other carnivorous beast, rejected by the law as unclean for food or enjoyment, our discourse must withdraw from such and be engraved on solid tables of stone, and that on both sides because the law is partly visible, and partly hidden, the one part belonging to the mass who remain below, the other to the few who press upward into the Mount.[6]

3. What is this that has happened to me, O friends, and initiates, and fellow lovers of the truth? I was running to lay hold on God, and thus I went up into the Mount, and drew aside the curtain of the cloud, and entered away from matter and material things, and as far as I could I withdrew within myself. And then when I looked up, I scarce saw the back parts of God; although I was sheltered by the rock, the Word

[3] Ex. 24:1.
[4] Ex. 19:13, 16, mystically interpreted; cf. similar treatment of this chapter in Gregory of Nyssa, Contemplation on the Life of Moses.
[5] Hab. 1:8 (LXX).      [6] Ex. 32:15; a rather strange interpretation.

that was made flesh for us.[7] And when I looked a little closer,
I saw, not the first and unmingled nature, known to itself—to
the Trinity, I mean; not that which abides within the first veil,
and is hidden by the cherubim; but only that nature, which at
last even reaches to us. And that is, as far as I can learn, the
majesty, or, as holy David calls it, the glory which is manifested
among the creatures, which it has produced and governs.[8] For
these are the back parts of God, which he leaves behind him,
as tokens of himself, like the shadows and reflection of the sun
in the water, which show the sun to our weak eyes, because we
cannot look at the sun himself, for by his unmixed light he is
too strong for our power of perception. In this way then you
shall discourse of God; even were you a Moses and a god to
Pharaoh; even were you caught up like Paul to the third heaven,
and had heard unspeakable words;[9] even were you raised above
them both, and exalted to angelic or archangelic place and
dignity. For though a thing be all heavenly, or above heaven,
and far higher in nature and nearer to God than we, yet it is
farther distant from God, and from the complete comprehension of his nature, than it is lifted above our complex and lowly
and earthward-sinking composition.

4. Therefore we must begin again thus: It is difficult to conceive God, but to define him in words is an impossibility, as
one of the Greek teachers of divinity taught, not unskillfully, as
it appears to me;[10] with the intention that he might be thought
to have apprehended him; in that he says it is a hard thing to
do; and yet may escape being convicted of ignorance because
of the impossibility of giving expression to the apprehension.
But in my opinion it is impossible to express him, and yet more
impossible to conceive him. For that which may be conceived
may perhaps be made clear by language, if not fairly well, at
any rate imperfectly, to anyone who is not quite deprived of
his hearing, or slothful of understanding. But to comprehend
the whole of so great a subject as this is quite impossible and
impracticable, not merely to the utterly careless and ignorant,
but even to those who are highly exalted, and who love God,
and in like manner to every created nature; seeing that the
darkness of this world and the thick covering of the flesh is an

---

[7] Ex. 33:21–23; the Christian mystic glimpses God only because he has
taken refuge in the Rock of Ages, Christ (Matt. 16:18).
[8] The psalms, as Gregory correctly observes, speak of God's manifested
glory rather than of his abstract greatness; cf. Ps. 8:2; 145 (144):5, 12.
[9] Ex. 7:1; II Cor. 12:2.          [10] Plato, *Timaeus* 28E.

obstacle to the full understanding of the truth. I do not know whether it is the same with the higher natures and purer intelligences which because of their nearness to God, and because they are illumined with all his light, may possibly see, if not the whole, at any rate more perfectly and distinctly than we do; some perhaps more, some less than others, in proportion to their rank.

5. But enough has been said on this point. As to what concerns us, it is not only the peace of God which passes all understanding and knowledge, nor only the things which God has stored up in promise for the righteous, which "eye hath not seen, nor ear heard, nor mind conceived" [11] except in a very small degree, nor the accurate knowledge of the Creation. For even of this I would have you know that you have only a shadow when you hear the words, "I will consider the heavens, the work of thy fingers, the moon and the stars," [12] and the settled order therein; not as if he were considering them now, but as destined to do so hereafter. But far before them is that nature which is above them, and out of which they spring, the incomprehensible and illimitable—not, I mean, as to the fact of his being, but as to its nature. For our preaching is not empty, nor our faith vain, [13] nor is this the doctrine we proclaim; for we would not have you take our candid statement as a starting point for a quibbling denial of God, or of arrogance on account of our confession of ignorance. For it is one thing to be persuaded of the existence of a thing, and quite another to know what it is.

6. Now our very eyes and the law of nature teach us that God exists and that he is the efficient and maintaining cause of all things: our eyes, because they fall on visible objects, and see them in beautiful stability and progress, immovably moving and revolving if I may so say; natural law, because through these visible things and their order it reasons back to their author. For how could this universe have come into being or been put together unless God had called it into existence, and held it together? For everyone who sees a beautifully made lute, and considers the skill with which it has been fitted together and arranged, or who hears its melody, would think of none but the lutemaker, or the luteplayer, and would recur to him in mind, though he might not know him by sight. And thus to us also is manifested that which made and moves and

11 Phil. 4:7; I Cor. 2:9.                    12 Ps. 8:4 (LXX).
13 I Cor. 15:14, 17.

preserves all created things, even though he be not comprehended by the mind. And very wanting in sense is he who will
not willingly go thus far in following natural proofs; but not
even this which we have fancied or formed, or which reason
has sketched for us, proves the existence of a God. But if anyone has got even to some extent a comprehension of this, how
is God's being to be demonstrated? Who ever reached this
extremity of wisdom? Who was ever deemed worthy of so
great a gift? Who has opened the mouth of his mind and
drawn in the Spirit, so as by him that searches all things, yea,
the deep things of God,[14] to take in God, and no longer to
need progress, since he already possesses the extreme object of
desire, and that to which all the social life and all the intelligence of the best men press forward?

7. For what will you conceive the Deity to be, if you rely
upon all the approximations of reason? Or to what will reason
carry you, O most philosophic of men and best of theologians,
who boast of your familiarity with the unlimited? Is he a body?
How, then, is he the infinite and limitless, and formless, and
intangible, and invisible? or are these attributes of a body?
What arrogance, for such is not the nature of a body! Or will
you say that he has a body, but not these attributes? O stupidity,
that a deity should possess nothing more than we do! For how
is he an object of worship if he be circumscribed? Or how shall
he escape being made of elements, and therefore subject to be
resolved into them again, or even altogether dissolved? For
every compound is a starting point of strife, and strife of
separation, and separation of dissolution. But dissolution is
altogether foreign to God and to the first nature. Therefore
there can be no separation, that there may be no dissolution,
and no strife that there may be no separation, and no composition that there may be no strife. Thus also there must be
no body, that there may be no composition, and so the argument is established by going back from last to first.

8. And how shall we preserve the truth that God pervades
all things and fills all, as it is written, "Do not I fill heaven and
earth? saith the Lord," and "The Spirit of the Lord filleth the
world," [15] if God partly contains and partly is contained? For
either he will occupy an empty universe, and so all things will
have vanished for us, with this result, that we shall have
insulted God by making him a body, and by robbing him of
all things which he has made; or else he will be a body con-

[14] I Cor. 2:10.        [15] Jer. 23:24; Wisdom 1:7.

tained in other bodies, which is impossible; or he will be en-
folded in them, or contrasted with them, as liquids are mixed,
and one divides and is divided by another—a view which is
more absurd and anile than even the atoms of Epicurus—and
so this argument concerning the body will fall through, and
have no body and no solid basis at all. But if we are to assert
that he is immaterial (as, for example, that fifth element which
some have imagined), and that he is carried round in the
circular movement . . . let us assume that he is immaterial,
and that he is the fifth element; and, if they please, let him be
also bodiless in accordance with the independent drift and
arrangement of their argument; for I will not at present differ
with them on this point; in what respect, then, will he be one
of those things which are in movement and agitation, to say
nothing of the insult involved in making the creator subject
to the same movement as the creatures, and him that carries
all (if they will allow even this) one with those whom he carries.
Again, what is the force that moves your fifth element, and
what is it that moves all things, and what moves that, and
what is the force that moves that? [16] And so on ad infinitum.
And how can he help being altogether contained in space if
he be subject to motion? But if they assert that he is something
other than this fifth element: suppose it is an angelic nature
that they attribute to him, how will they show that angels
are corporeal, or what sort of bodies they have? And how far
in that case could God, to whom the angels minister, be
superior to the angels? And if he is above them, there is again
brought in an irrational swarm of bodies, and a depth of nonsense that has no possible basis to stand upon.

9. And thus we see that God is not a body. For no inspired
teacher has yet asserted or admitted such a notion, nor has
the sentence of our own court [17] allowed it. Nothing then
remains but to conceive of him as incorporeal. But this term
"incorporeal," though granted, does not yet set before us—or
contain within itself—his essence, any more than "unbegotten,"
or "unoriginate," or "unchanging," or "incorruptible," or any
other predicate which is used concerning God or in reference
to him. For what effect is produced upon his being or substance
by his having no beginning, and being incapable of change or
limitation? Nay, the whole question of his being is still left

[16] An Aristotelian idea of the elements, though not of the Deity.
[17] Or, "the language (*logos*) of our fold," i.e., neither the Biblical writers
nor the teachers of the Church so teach.

for the further consideration and exposition of him who truly has the mind of God and is advanced in contemplation. For just as to say, "It is a body," or, "It was begotten," is not sufficient to present clearly to the mind the various objects of which these predicates are used, but you must also express the subject of which you use them, if you would present the object of your thought clearly and adequately (for every one of these predicates, "corporeal," "begotten," "mortal," may be used of a man, or a cow, or a horse), just so he who is eagerly pursuing the nature of the self-existent will not stop at saying what he is not, but must go on beyond what he is not, and say what he is; inasmuch as it is easier to take in some single point than to go on disowning point after point in endless detail, in order both by the elimination of negatives and the assertion of positives to arrive at a comprehension of this subject.

But a man who states what God is not without going on to say what he is acts much in the same way as one would who, when asked how many twice five make, should answer, "Not two, nor three, nor four, nor five, nor twenty, nor thirty, nor in short any number below ten, nor any multiple of ten"; but would not answer, "Ten," nor settle the mind of his questioner upon the firm ground of the answer. For it is much easier, and more concise, to show what a thing is not from what it is than to demonstrate what it is by stripping it of what it is not. And this surely is evident to everyone.

10. Now since we have ascertained that God is incorporeal, let us proceed a little further with our examination. Is he nowhere or somewhere? For if he is nowhere, then some person of a very inquiring turn of mind might ask, How is it, then, that he can even exist? For if the nonexistent is nowhere, then that which is nowhere is also perhaps nonexistent. But if he is somewhere, he must be either in the universe, or above the universe. And if he is in the universe, then he must be either in some part or in the whole. If in some part, then he will be circumscribed by that part which is less than himself; but if everywhere, then by one which is further and greater—I mean the universal, which contains the particular; if the universe is to be contained by the universe, and no place is to be free from circumscription. This follows if he is contained in the universe. And besides, where was he before the universe was created, for this is a point of no little difficulty. But if he is above the universe, is there nothing to distinguish this from the universe,

and where is this above situated? And how could this tran-scendence and that which is transcended be distinguished in thought if there is not a limit to divide and define them? Is it not necessary that there shall be some mean to mark off the universe from that which is above the universe? And what could this be but place, which we have already rejected? For I have not yet brought forward the point that God would be altogether circumscript if he were even comprehensible in thought: for comprehension is one form of circumscription.

11. Now, why have I gone into all this, perhaps too minutely for most people to listen to, and in accordance with the present manner of discourse, which despises noble simplicity and has introduced a crooked and intricate style? That the tree may be known by its fruits;[18] I mean, that the darkness which is at work in such teaching may be known by the obscurity of the arguments. For my purpose in doing so was, not to get credit for myself for astonishing utterances, or excessive wisdom, through tying knots and solving difficulties (this was the great miraculous gift of Daniel),[19] but to make clear the point at which my argument has aimed from the first. And what was this? That the divine nature cannot be apprehended by human reason, and that we cannot even represent to ourselves all its greatness. And this is not out of envy, for envy is far from the divine nature, which is passionless and only good and Lord of all; especially envy of that which is the most honorable of all his creatures. For what does the Word prefer to the rational and speaking creatures? Why, even their very existence is a proof of his supreme goodness. Nor yet is this incomprehen-sibility for the sake of his own glory and honor, who is full, as if his possession of his glory and majesty depended upon the impossibility of approaching him. For it is utterly sophistical and foreign to the character, I will not say of God, but of any moderately good man, who has any right ideas about himself, to seek his own supremacy by throwing a hindrance in the way of another.

12. But whether there be other causes for it also, let them see who are nearer God, and are eyewitnesses and spectators of his unsearchable judgments; if there are any who are so eminent in virtue, and who walk in the paths of the infinite, as the saying is. As far, however, as we have attained, who measure with our little measure things hard to be understood, perhaps one reason is to prevent us from too readily throwing

18 Matt. 7:20.                              19 Dan. 5:12.

away the possession because it was so easily come by. For
people cling tightly to that which they acquire with labor;
but that which they acquire easily they quickly throw away,
because it can be easily recovered. And so it is turned into a
blessing, at least to all men who are sensible that this blessing
is not too easy. Or perhaps it is in order that we may not share
the fate of Lucifer, who fell, and in consequence of receiving
the full light make our necks stiff against the Lord Almighty,[20]
and suffer a fall, of all things most pitiable, from the height
we had attained. Or perhaps it may be to give a greater reward
hereafter for their labor and glorious life to those who have
here been purified, and have exercised long patience in respect
of that which they desired.

Therefore this darkness of the body has been placed between
us and God, like the cloud of old between the Egyptians and
the Hebrews; and this is perhaps what is meant by, "He made
darkness his secret place,"[21] namely, our dullness, through
which few can see even a little. But as to this point, let those
discuss it whose business it is; and let them ascend as far as
possible in the examination. To us who are (as Jeremiah says)
"prisoners of the earth,"[22] and covered with the denseness of
carnal nature, this at all events is known, that as it is impossible
for a man to step over his own shadow, however fast he may
move (for the shadow will always move on as fast as it is being
overtaken), or, as it is impossible for the eye to draw near to
visible objects apart from the intervening air and light, or for
a fish to glide about outside of the waters, so it is quite impracticable for those who are in the body to be conversant with
objects of pure thought apart altogether from bodily objects.
For something in our own environment is ever creeping in,
even when the mind has most fully detached itself from the
visible, and collected itself and is attempting to apply itself to
those invisible things which are akin to itself.

13. This will be made clear to you as follows: Are not spirit,
and fire, and light, love, and wisdom, and righteousness, and
mind and reason, and the like, the names of the first nature?
What, then? Can you conceive of spirit apart from motion and
diffusion; or of fire without its fuel and its upward motion,
and its proper color and form? or of light unmingled with air,
and loosed from that which is as it were its father and source?
And how do you conceive of a mind? Is it not that which is

[20] Isa. 14:12; Job 15:25.    [21] Ex. 14:20; Ps. 18 (17):12.
[22] Lam. 3:34.

inherent in some person not itself, and are not its movements thoughts, silent or uttered? And reason . . . what else can you think it than that which is either silent within ourselves or else outpoured (for I shrink from saying loosed)? And if you conceive of wisdom, what is it but the habit of mind which you know as such, and which is concerned with contemplations either divine or human? And justice and love, are they not praiseworthy dispositions, the one opposed to injustice, the other to hate, and at one time intensifying themselves, at another relaxed, now taking possession of us, now letting us alone, and in a word, making us what we are, and changing us as colors do bodies? Or are we rather to leave all these things, and to look at the Deity absolutely, as best we can, collecting a fragmentary perception of it from its images? What, then, is this subtile thing, which is of these, and yet is not these, or how can that unity which is in its nature uncomposite and incomparable, still be all of these, and each one of them perfectly? Thus our mind faints to transcend corporeal things, and to consort with the incorporeal, stripped of all clothing of corporeal ideas, as long as it has to look with its inherent weakness at things above its strength. For every rational nature longs for God and for the first cause, but is unable to grasp him, for the reasons I have mentioned. Faint therefore with the desire, and as it were restive and impatient of the disability, it tries a second course, either to look at visible things, and out of some of them to make a god . . . (a poor contrivance, for in what respect and to what extent can that which is seen be higher and more godlike than that which sees, that this should worship that?), or else through the beauty and order of visible things to attain to that which is above sight; but not to suffer the loss of God through the magnificence of visible things.

14. From this cause some have made a god of the sun, others of the moon, others of the host of stars, others of heaven itself with all its hosts, to which they have attributed the guiding of the universe, according to the quality or quantity of their movement. Others again of the elements, earth, air, water, fire, because of their useful nature, since without them human life cannot possibly exist. Others again have worshiped any chance visible objects, setting up the most beautiful of what they saw as their gods. And there are those who worship pictures and images, at first indeed of their own ancestors—at least, this is the case with the more affectionate and sensual

—and honor the departed with memorials; and afterward even those of strangers are worshiped by men of a later generation separated from them by a long interval; through ignorance of the first nature, and following the traditional honor as lawful and necessary; for usage when confirmed by time was held to be law. And I think that some who were courtiers of arbitrary power and extolled bodily strength and admired beauty made a god in time out of him whom they honored, perhaps getting hold of some fable to help on their imposture.

15. And those of them who were most subject to passion deified their passions, or honored them among their gods—anger and bloodthirstiness, lust and drunkenness, and every similar wickedness—and made out of this an ignoble and unjust excuse for their own sins. And some they left on earth, and some they hid beneath the earth (this being the only sign of wisdom about them), and some they raised to heaven. O ridiculous distribution of inheritance! Then they gave to each of these concepts the name of some god or demon, by the authority and private judgment of their error, and set up statues whose costliness is a snare, and thought to honor them with blood and the steam of sacrifices, and sometimes even by most shameful actions, frenzies, and manslaughter. For such honors were the fitting due of such gods. And before now men have insulted themselves by worshiping monsters, and four-footed beasts, and creeping things, of the very vilest and most absurd, and have made an offering to them of the glory of God;[23] so that it is not easy to decide whether we ought most to despise the worshipers or the objects of their worship. Probably the worshipers are far the most contemptible, for though they are of a rational nature, and have received grace from God, they have set up the worse as the better. And this was the trick of the evil one, who abused good to an evil purpose, as in most of his evil deeds. For he laid hold of their desire in its wandering in search of God, in order to distort to himself the power, and steal the desire, leading it by the hand, like a blind man asking a road; and he hurled down and scattered some in one direction and some in another, into one pit of death and destruction.

16. This was their course. But reason[24] receiving us in our desire for God, and in our sense of the impossibility of being without a leader and guide, and then making us apply ourselves to things visible and meeting with the things which have

[23] Rom. 1:23; Wisdom 11:15.    [24] Or perhaps, "the Word."

been since the beginning, does not stay its course even here. For it was not the part of wisdom to grant the sovereignty to things which are, as observation tells us, of equal rank. By these, then, it leads to that which is above these, and by which being is given to these. For what is it which ordered things in heaven and things in earth, and those which pass through air, and those which live in water; or rather the things which were before these, heaven and earth, air and water? Who mingled these, and who distributed them? What is it that each has in common with the other, and their mutual dependence and agreement? For I commend the man, though he was a heathen, who said, "What gave movement to these, and drives their ceaseless and unhindered motion?" [25] Is it not the artificer of them who implanted reason in them all, in accordance with which the universe is moved and controlled? Is it not he who made them and brought them into being? For we cannot attribute such a power to the accidental. For, suppose that its existence is accidental, to what will you let us ascribe its order? And if you like, we will grant you this: to what, then, will you ascribe its preservation and protection in accordance with the terms of its first creation? Do these belong to the accidental, or to something else? Surely not to the accidental. And what can this something else be but God? Thus reason that proceeds from God, that is implanted in all from the beginning and is the first law in us, and is bound up in all, leads us up to God through visible things. Let us begin again, and reason this out.

17. What God is in nature and essence, no man ever yet has discovered or can discover. Whether it will ever be discovered is a question which he who will may examine and decide. In my opinion it will be discovered when that within us which is godlike and divine, I mean our mind and reason, shall have mingled with its like, and the image shall have ascended to the archetype, of which it has now the desire. And this I think is the solution of that vexed problem as to "We shall know even as we are known." [26] But in our present life all that comes to us is but a little effluence, and as it were a small effulgence from a great light. So that if anyone has known God, or has had the testimony of Scripture to his knowledge of God, we are to understand such a one to have possessed a degree of knowledge which gave him the appearance of being more fully enlightened than another who did not enjoy the

[25] A reference to theistic views of some Greek writer; the quotation, if meant to be specific, has not been identified.    [26] I Cor. 13:12.

same degree of illumination; and this relative superiority is spoken of as if it were absolute knowledge, not because it is really such, but by comparison with the power of that other.

18. Thus Enos "hoped to call upon the name of the Lord." [27] Hope was that for which he is commended; and that, not that he should know God, but that he should call upon him. And Enoch was translated, but it is not yet clear whether it was because he already comprehended the divine nature or in order that he might comprehend it. And Noah's glory was that he was pleasing to God; he who was entrusted with the saving of the whole world from the waters, or rather of the seeds of the world, escaped the deluge in a small ark. And Abraham, great patriarch though he was, was justified by faith, and offered a strange victim, the type of the great sacrifice. Yet he saw not God as God, but gave him food as a man. [28] He was approved because he worshiped as far as he comprehended. And Jacob dreamed of a lofty ladder and stair of angels, and in a mystery anointed a pillar—perhaps to signify the rock that was anointed for our sake—and gave to a place the name of the house of God in honor of Him whom he saw; and wrestled with God in human form; whatever this wrestling of God with man may mean . . . possibly it refers to the comparison of man's virtue with God's; and he bore on his body the marks of the wrestling, setting forth the defeat of the created nature; and for a reward of his reverence he received a change of his name, being named, instead of Jacob, Israel—that great and honorable name. Yet neither he nor anyone on his behalf, unto this day, of all the twelve tribes who were his children, could boast that he comprehended the whole nature or the pure sight of God.

19. To Elijah neither the strong wind nor the fire, nor the earthquake, as you learn from the story, but a light breeze adumbrated the presence of God, and not even this his nature. And who was this Elijah? The man whom a chariot of fire took up to heaven, signifying the superhuman excellency of the righteous man. And are you not amazed at Manoah the judge of yore, and at Peter the disciple in later days: the one being unable to endure the sight even of one in whom was a representation of God, and saying, "We are undone, O wife, we have seen God"—speaking as though even a vision of God could not be grasped by human beings, let alone the nature of God [29]—and the other unable to endure the presence of

[27] Gen. 4:26; the LXX reads "hoped" instead of "began."
[28] Gen. 15:6; 22:13; 18:8.        [29] Judg. 13:22.

Christ in his boat and therefore bidding him depart, and this though Peter was more zealous than the others for the knowledge of Christ, and received a blessing for this and was entrusted with the greatest gifts?[30] What would you say of Isaiah or Ezekiel, who was an eyewitness of very great mysteries, and of the other prophets: for one of these saw the Lord of Sabaoth sitting on the throne of glory, and encircled and praised and hidden by the six-winged seraphim, and was himself purged by the live coal, and equipped for his prophetic office, and the other describes the cherubic chariot of God, and the throne upon them, and the firmament over it, and him that showed himself in the firmament, and voices, and forces, and deeds.[31] And whether this was an appearance by day, only visible to saints, or an unerring vision of the night, or an impression on the mind holding converse with the future as if it were the present, or some other ineffable form of prophecy, I cannot say; the God of the prophets knows, and they know who are thus inspired. But neither these of whom I am speaking, nor any of their fellows, ever stood before the council and essence of God, as it is written,[32] or saw, or proclaimed the nature of God.

20. If it had been permitted to Paul to utter what the third heaven contained, and his own advance, or ascension, or assumption thither, perhaps we should know something more about God's nature, if this was the mystery of the rapture. But since it was ineffable, we too will honor it by silence. Thus much we will hear Paul say about it, that we know in part, and we prophesy in part. This and the like to this are the confessions of one who is not rude in knowledge, who threatens to give proof of Christ speaking in him, the great doctor and champion of the truth. Wherefore he estimates all knowledge on earth only as through a glass darkly, as taking its stand upon little images of the truth.[33] Now, unless I appear to anyone too careful, and overanxious about the examination of this matter, perhaps it was of this and nothing else that the Word himself intimated that there were things which could not now be borne, but which should be borne and cleared up hereafter, and which John the forerunner of the Word and great voice of the truth declared even the whole world could not contain.[34]

[30] Luke 5:8; Matt. 16:17–19.
[31] Isa., ch. 6; Ezek., ch. 1.      [32] II Cor. 12:2; I Cor. 13:9, 12.
[33] I Cor. 13:9, 12; II Cor. 11:6; 12:2; 13:3.
[34] John 16:12; 21:25—with a curious confusion of the Baptist and the Evangelist.

21. The truth, then—and the whole word—is full of difficulty and obscurity; and, as it were, with a small instrument we are undertaking a great work, when with merely human wisdom we pursue the knowledge of the self-existent, and in company with, or not apart from, the senses, by which we are borne hither and thither, and led into error, we apply ourselves to the search after things which are only to be grasped by the mind, and we are unable by meeting bare realities with bare intellect to approximate somewhat more closely to the truth, and to mold the mind by its concepts.

Now the subject of God is more hard to come at, in proportion as it is more perfect than any other, and is open to more objections, and the solutions of them are more laborious. For every objection, however small, stops and hinders the course of our argument, and cuts off its further advance, just like men who suddenly check with the rein the horses in full career, and turn them right round by the unexpected shock. Thus Solomon, who was the wisest of all men, whether before him or in his own time, to whom God gave breadth of heart, and a flood of contemplation more abundant than the sand, even he, the more he entered into the depth, the more dizzy he became, and declared the furthest point of wisdom to be the discovery of how very far off she was from him.[35] Paul also tries to arrive at, I will not say the nature of God, for this he knew was utterly impossible, but only the judgments of God; and since he finds no way out, and no halting place in the ascent, and moreover, since the earnest searching of his mind after knowledge does not end in any definite conclusion, because some fresh unattained point is being continually disclosed to him (O marvel, that I have a like experience!), he closes his discourse with astonishment, and calls this the riches of God, and the depth, and confesses the unsearchableness of the judgments of God, in almost the very words of David, who at one time calls God's judgments the great deep whose foundations cannot be reached by measure or sense, and at another says that his knowledge of him and of his own constitution was marvelous, and had attained greater strength than was in his own power or grasp.[36]

22. For if, he says, I let everything else alone, and consider myself and the whole nature and constitution of man, and how

[35] Cf. I Kings 3:12; 4:29; Eccl. 7:23, 24.
[36] Rom. 11:33; Ps. 36 (35):6; 139 (138):6; the following chapter begins by paraphrasing this psalm.

we are mingled, and what is our movement, and how the mortal was compounded with the immortal, and how it is that I flow downward and yet am borne upward, and how the soul is circumscribed; and how it gives life and shares in feelings; and how the mind is at once circumscribed and unlimited, abiding in us and yet traveling over the universe in swift motion and flow; how it is both received and imparted by word, and passes through air, and enters with all things; how it shares in sense, and enshrouds itself away from sense—and, even before these questions—what was our first molding and composition in the workshop of nature, and what is our last formation and completion? What is the desire for and imparting of nourishment, and who brought us spontaneously to those first springs and sources of life? How is the body nourished by food, and the soul by reason? What is the drawing of nature, and the mutual relation between parents and children, that it should be held together by a spell of love? How is it that species are permanent, and are different in their characteristics, although there are so many that their individual marks cannot be described? How is it that the same animal is both mortal and immortal, the one by decease, the other by coming into being? For one departs, and another takes its place, just like the flow of a river, which is never still, yet ever constant. And you might discuss many more points concerning men's members and parts, and their mutual adaptation both for use and beauty, and how some are connected and others disjoined, some are more excellent and others less comely, some are united and others divided, some contain and others are contained, according to the law and reason of nature. Much too might be said about voices and ears. How is it that the voice is carried by the vocal organs, and received by the ears, and both are joined by the smiting and resounding of the medium of the air? Much too of the eyes, which have an indescribable communion with visible objects, and which are moved by the will alone, and that together, and are affected exactly as is the mind. For with equal speed the mind is joined to the objects of thought, the eye to those of sight. Much too concerning the other senses, not objects of the research of reason. And much concerning our rest in sleep, and the figments of dreams, and of memory and remembrance; of calculation, and anger, and desire; and, in a word, all by which this little world called man is swayed.

23. Shall I reckon up for you the differences of the other animals, both from us and from each other—differences of

nature, and of production, and of nourishment, and of region, and of temper, and, as it were, of social life? How is it that some are gregarious and others solitary, some herbivorous and others carnivorous, some fierce and others tame, some fond of man and domesticated, others untamable and free? And some we might call bordering on reason and power of learning, while others are altogether destitute of reason, and incapable of being taught. Some with fuller senses, others with less; some immovable, and some with the power of walking, and some very swift, and some very slow; some surpassing in size or beauty, or in one or other of these respects, others very small or very ugly, or both; some strong, others weak, some apt at self-defense, others timid and crafty and others, again, unguarded. Some are laborious and thrifty, others altogether idle and improvident. And before we come to such points as these, how is it that some are crawling things, and others upright; some attached to one spot, some amphibious; some delight in beauty and others are unadorned; some are married and some single; some temperate and others intemperate; some have numerous offspring and others not; some are long-lived and others have but short lives? It would be a weary discourse to go through all the details.

24. Look also at the fishy tribe gliding through the waters, and, as it were, flying through the liquid element, and breathing its own air, but in danger when in contact with ours, as we are in the waters; and mark their habits and dispositions, their intercourse and their births, their size and their beauty, and their affection for places, and their wanderings, and their assemblings and departings, and their properties which so nearly resemble those of the animals that dwell on land—in some cases community, in others contrast of properties, both in name and shape. And consider the tribes of birds, and their varieties of form and color, both of those which are voiceless and of songbirds. What is the reason of their melody, and from whom came it? Who gave to the grasshoppers the lutes in their breasts, and the songs and chirruping on the branches, when they are moved by the sun to make their midday music, and sing among the groves, and escort the wayfarer with their voices? Who wove the song for the swan when he spreads his wings to the breezes, and makes melody of their rustling? For I will not speak of the forced voices, and all the rest that art contrives against the truth. Whence does the peacock, that boastful bird of Media, get his love of beauty and of praise

(for he is fully conscious of his own beauty), so that when he sees anyone approaching, or when, as they say, he would make a show before his hens, raising his neck and spreading his tail in a circle around him, glittering like gold and studded with stars, he makes a spectacle of his beauty to his lovers with pompous strides?

Now Holy Scripture admires the cleverness in weaving even of women, saying, "Who gave to woman skill in weaving and cleverness in the art of embroidery?" [37] This belongs to a living creature that has reason, and exceeds in wisdom and makes way even as far as the things of heaven. 25. But I would have you marvel at the natural knowledge even of irrational creatures, and, if you can, explain its cause. How is it that birds have for nests rocks and trees and roofs, and adapt them both for safety and beauty, and suitably for the comfort of their nurslings? Whence do bees and spiders get their love of work and art, by which the former plan their honeycombs, and join them together by hexagonal and co-ordinate tubes, and construct the foundation by means of a partition and an alternation of the angles with straight lines; and this, as is the case, in such dusky hives and dark combs; and the latter weave their intricate webs by such light and almost airy threads stretched in divers ways, and this from almost invisible beginnings, to be at once a precious dwelling, and a trap for weaker creatures with a view to enjoyment of food? What Euclid ever imitated these, while pursuing philosophical inquiries with lines that have no real existence, and wearying himself with demonstrations? From what Palamedes came the tactics, and, as the saying is, the movements and configurations of cranes, and the systems of their movement in ranks and their complicated flight? Who were their Phidiae and Zeuxides, and who were the Parrhasii and Aglaophons who knew how to draw and mold excessively beautiful things? What harmonious Gnossian chorus of Daedalus, wrought for a girl to the highest pitch of beauty? What Cretan Labyrinth, hard to get through, hard to unravel, as the poets say, and continually crossing itself through the tricks of its construction? I will not speak of the ants' storehouses and storekeepers, and of their treasurings of wood in quantities corresponding to the time for which it is wanted, and all the other details which we know are told of their marches and leaders and their good order in their works. 26. If this knowledge has come within your reach and you

[37] Job 38:36 (LXX).

are familiar with these branches of science, look at the differences of plants also, up to the artistic fashion of the leaves, which is adapted both to give the utmost pleasure to the eye and to be of the greatest advantage to the fruit. Look too at the variety and lavish abundance of fruits, and most of all at the wondrous beauty of such as are most necessary. And consider the power of roots, and juices, and flowers, and odors, not only so very sweet, but also serviceable as medicines; and the graces and qualities of colors; and again the costly value, and the brilliant transparency of precious stones; since nature has set before you all things as in an abundant banquet free to all, both the necessaries and the luxuries of life, in order that, if nothing else, you may at any rate know God by his benefits, and by your own sense of want be made wiser than you were. Next, I pray you, traverse the length and breadth of earth, the common mother of all, and the gulfs of the sea bound together with one another and with the land, and the beautiful forests, and the rivers and springs abundant and perennial, not only of waters cold and fit for drinking, and on the surface of the earth; but also such as running beneath the earth, and flowing under caverns, are then forced out by a violent blast, and repelled, and then filled with heat by this violence of strife and repulsion, burst out by little and little wherever they get a chance, and hence supply our need of hot baths in many parts of the earth, and in conjunction with the cold give us a healing which is without cost and spontaneous. Tell me how and whence are these things? What is this great web unwrought by art? These things are no less worthy of admiration in respect of their mutual relations than when considered separately.

How is it that the earth stands solid and unswerving? On what is it supported? What is it that props it up, and on what does that rest? For indeed even reason has nothing to lean upon, but only the will of God. And how is it that part of it is drawn up into mountain summits, and part laid down in plains, and this in various and differing ways? And because the variations are individually small, it both supplies our needs more liberally, and is more beautiful by its variety; part being distributed into habitations, and part left uninhabited, namely, all the great height of mountains, and the various clefts of its coast line cut off from it. Is not this the clearest proof of the majestic working of God?

27. And with respect to the sea, even if I did not marvel at

its greatness, yet I should have marveled at its gentleness, in that although loose it stands within its boundaries; and if not at its gentleness, yet surely at its greatness; but since I marvel at both, I will praise the power that is in both. What collected it? What bounded it? How is it raised and lulled to rest, as though respecting its neighbor earth? How, moreover, does it receive all the rivers, and yet remain the same, through the very superabundance of its immensity, if that term be permissible? How is the boundary of it, though it be an element of such magnitude, only sand? Have your natural philosophers with their knowledge of useless details anything to tell us— those men, I mean, who are really endeavoring to measure the sea with a wineglass, and such mighty works by their own conceptions? Or shall I give the really scientific explanation of it from Scripture concisely, and yet more satisfactorily and truly than by the longest arguments? "He hath fenced the face of the water with His command." [38] This is the chain of fluid nature. And how does he bring upon it the Nautilus that inhabits the dry land [i.e., man] in a little vessel, and with a little breeze (do you not marvel at the sight of this—is not your mind astonished?), that earth and sea may be bound together by needs and commerce, and that things so widely separated by nature should be thus brought together into one for man? What are the first foundations of springs? Seek, O man, if you can trace out or find any of these things. And who was it who cleft the plains and the mountains for the rivers, and gave them an unhindered course? And how comes the marvel on the other side, that the sea never overflows, nor the rivers cease to flow? And what is the nourishing power of water, and what the difference therein; for some things are irrigated from above and others drink from their roots, if I may luxuriate a little in my language when speaking of the luxuriant gifts of God.

28. And now, leaving the earth and the things of earth, soar into the air on the wings of thought, that our argument may advance in due path; and thence I will take you up to heavenly things, and to heaven itself, and things which are above heaven; for to that which is beyond my discourse hesitates to ascend, but still it shall ascend as far as may be. Who poured forth the air, that great and abundant wealth, not measured to men by their rank or fortunes; not restrained by boundaries; not divided out according to people's ages; but, like the distribution

[38] Job 26:10.

of the manna, received in sufficiency, and valued for its
equality of distribution; the chariot of the winged creation;
the seat of the winds; the moderator of the seasons; the
quickener of living things, or rather the preserver of natural
life in the body; in which bodies have their being, and by which
we speak; in which is the light and all that it shines upon, and
the sight which flows through it? And mark, if you please, what
follows. I cannot give to the air the whole empire of all that is
thought to belong to the air. What are the storehouses of the
winds? What are the treasuries of the snow? Who, as Scripture
has said, has begotten the drops of dew? Out of whose womb
came the ice? and who binds the waters in the clouds,[39] and,
fixing part in the clouds (O marvel!), held by his word though
its nature is to flow, pours out the rest upon the face of the whole
earth, and scatters it abroad in due season, and in just pro-
portions, and neither suffers the whole substance of moisture
to go out free and uncontrolled (for sufficient was the cleansing
in the days of Noah; and he who cannot lie is not forgetful of
his own covenant); . . . nor yet restrains it entirely that we
should not again stand in need of an Elijah to bring the drought
to an end? If he shall shut up heaven, it says, who shall open it?
If he open the floodgates, who shall shut them up?[40] Who can
bring an excess or withhold a sufficiency of rain, unless he
govern the universe by his own measures and balances? What
scientific laws, pray, can you lay down concerning thunder
and lightning, O you who thunder from the earth, and cannot
shine with even little sparks of truth? To what vapors from
earth will you attribute the creation of cloud, or is it due to
some thickening of the air, or pressure or crash of clouds of
excessive rarity, so as to make you think the pressure the cause
of the lightning, and the crash that which makes the thunder?
Or what compression of wind having no outlet will account to
you for the lightning by its compression, and for the thunder
by its bursting out?

Now if you have in your thought passed through the air
and all the things of air, reach with me to heaven and the
things of heaven. And let faith lead us rather than reason, if
at least you have learned the feebleness of the latter in matters
nearer to you, and have known reason by knowing the things
that are beyond reason, so as not to be altogether on the earth
or of the earth, because you are ignorant even of your ignorance.

29. Who spread the sky around us, and set the stars in order?

39 Job 38:22, 28, 29; 26:8.          40 Job 12:14; Gen. 7:11.

Or rather, first, can you tell me, of your own knowledge of the things in heaven, what are the sky and the stars; you who know not what lies at your very feet, and cannot even take the measure of yourself, and yet must busy yourself about what is above your nature, and gape at the illimitable? For, granted that you understand orbits and periods, and waxings and wanings, and settings and risings, and some degrees and minutes, and all the other things which make you so proud of your wonderful knowledge, you have not arrived at comprehension of the realities themselves, but only at an observation of some movement, which when confirmed by longer practice, and drawing the observations of many individuals into one generalization, and thence deducing a law, has acquired the name of science (just as the lunar phenomena have become generally known to our sight), being the basis of this knowledge. But if you are very scientific on this subject, and have a just claim to admiration, tell me what is the cause of this order and this movement. How came the sun to be a beacon fire to the whole world, and to all eyes like the leader of some chorus, concealing all the rest of the stars by his brightness, more completely than some of them conceal others? The proof of this is that they shine against him, but he outshines them and does not even allow it to be perceived that they rose simultaneously with him, fair as a bridegroom, swift and great as a giant—for I will not let his praises be sung from any other source than my own Scriptures—so mighty in strength that from one end to the other of the world he embraces all things in his heat, and there is nothing hid from the feeling thereof, but it fills both every eye with light, and every embodied creature with heat[41]; warming, yet not burning, by the gentleness of its temper, and the order of its movement, present to all, and equally embracing all.

30. Have you considered the importance of the fact that a heathen writer speaks of the sun as holding the same position among material objects as God does among objects of thought?[42] For the one gives light to the eyes, as the other does to the mind; and is the most beautiful of the objects of sight, as God is of those of thought. But who gave him motion at first? And what is it which ever moves him in his circuit, though in his nature stable and immovable, truly unwearied,[43] and the giver and sustainer of life, and all the rest of the titles

---

[41] Ps. 19 (18):5, 6.          [42] Plato, *Republic* 507, 508, 517.
[43] *Iliad* xviii, 239; the other poetic references are obscure.

which the poets justly sing of him, and never resting in his course or his benefits? How comes he to be the creator of day when above the earth, and of night when below it? or whatever may be the right expression when one contemplates the sun? What are the mutual aggressions and concessions of day and night, and their regular irregularities—to use a somewhat strange expression? How comes he to be the maker and divider of the seasons, that come and depart in regular order, and as in a dance interweave with each other, or stand apart by a law of love on the one hand and of order on the other, and mingle little by little, and steal on their neighbor, just as nights and days do, so as not to give us pain by their suddenness? This will be enough about the sun.

Do you know the nature and phenomena of the moon, and the measures and courses of light, and how it is that the sun bears rule over the day, and the moon presides over the night; and while she gives confidence to wild beasts, he stirs man up to work, raising or lowering himself as may be most serviceable? [44] Know you the bond of Pleiades, or the fence of Orion, as he who counts the number of the stars and calls them all by their names? [45] Know you the differences of the glory of each,[46] and the order of their movement, that I should trust you, when by them you weave the web of human concerns, and arm the creature against the Creator?

31. What say you? Shall we pause here, after discussing nothing further than matter and visible things, or, since the Word knows the Tabernacle of Moses to be a figure of the whole creation—I mean the entire system of things visible and invisible—shall we pass the first veil, and, stepping beyond the realm of sense, shall we look into the holy place, the intellectual and celestial creation? [47] But not even this can we see in an incorporeal way, though it is incorporeal, since it is called—or is—fire and spirit. For he is said to make his angels spirits, and his ministers a flame of fire . . . though perhaps this "making" means preserving by that Word by which they came into existence.[48] The angel then is called spirit and fire: spirit, as being a creature of the intellectual sphere; fire, as being of a

---

[44] Gen. 1:16; Ps. 104 (103):20–23.    [45] Job 38:31; Ps. 147 (146):4.
[46] I Cor. 15:41.
[47] Heb. 9:1, 3, with which Gregory shares the established interpretation of the structure of the Tabernacle as a symbol of the universe.
[48] Ps. 104 (103):4; Heb. 1:7; Gregory hesitates to think of the angelic natures as undergoing further "making" or changing after their creation.

purifying nature; for I know that the same names belong to the first nature. But, relatively to us at least, we must reckon the angelic nature incorporeal, or at any rate as nearly so as possible. Do you see how we get dizzy over this subject, and cannot advance to any point, unless it be as far as this, that we know there are angels and archangels, thrones, dominions, princedoms, powers,[49] splendors, ascents, intelligent powers or intelligences, pure natures and unalloyed, immovable to evil, or scarcely movable; ever circling in chorus round the first cause (or how should we sing their praises?), illuminated thence with the purest illumination, or one in one degree and one in another, proportionally to their nature and rank . . . so conformed to beauty and molded that they become secondary lights, and can enlighten others by the overflowings and largesses of the first light? Ministrants of God's will, strong with both inborn and imparted strength, traversing all space, readily present to all at any place through their zeal for ministry and the agility of their nature . . . different individuals of them embracing different parts of the world, or appointed over different districts of the universe, as He knows who ordered and distributed it all. Combining all things in one, solely with a view to the consent of the Creator of all things; hymners of the majesty of the Godhead, eternally contemplating the eternal glory, not that God may thereby gain an increase of glory, for nothing can be added to that which is full—to him, who supplies good to all outside himself—but that there may never be a cessation of blessings to these first natures after God. If we have told these things as they deserve, it is by the grace of the Trinity, and of the one Godhead in three Persons; but if less perfectly than we have desired, yet even so our discourse has gained its purpose. For this is what we were laboring to show, that even the secondary natures surpass the power of our intellect; much more then the first and (for I fear to say merely that which is above all) the only nature.[50]

[49] Cf. Col. 1:16; Rom. 8:38, though Gregory adds further titles to the traditional list; his vision of the praise and service of the angels is used, almost phrase by phrase, in the Greek hymns which inspired J. M. Neale's "Stars of the Morning."

[50] The divine nature should not be listed with others as even the first of a series.

# THE TEXT: THE THIRD THEOLOGICAL
# ORATION—ON THE SON

1. This, then, is what might be said to cut short our opponents' readiness to argue and their hastiness, with its consequent insecurity in all matters but above all in those discussions which relate to God. But since to rebuke others is a matter of no difficulty whatever, but a very easy thing, which anyone who likes can do; whereas to substitute one's own belief for theirs is the part of a pious and intelligent man, let us, relying on the Holy Ghost, who among them is dishonored but among us is adored, bring forth to the light our own conceptions about the Godhead, whatever these may be, like some noble and timely birth. Not that I have at other times been silent, for on this subject alone I am full of youthful strength and daring, but the fact is that under present circumstances I am even more bold to declare the truth, that I may not (to use the words of Scripture) by drawing back fall into the condemnation of being displeasing to God.[1] And since every discourse is of a twofold nature, the one part establishing one's own and the other overthrowing one's opponents' position, let us first of all state our own position, and then try to controvert that of our opponents; and both as briefly as possible, so that our arguments may be taken in at a glance (like those of the elementary treatises which they have devised to deceive simple or foolish persons), and that our thoughts may not be scattered by reason of the length of the discourse, like water which is not contained in a channel, but flows to waste over the open land.

2. The three most ancient opinions concerning God are Anarchia, Polyarchia, and Monarchia. The first two are the

[1] Heb. 10:38, 39.

sport of the children of Hellas, and may they continue to be so. For anarchy is a thing without order; and the rule of many is factious, and thus anarchical, and thus disorderly. For both these tend to the same thing, namely, disorder; and this to dissolution, for disorder is the first step to dissolution.

But monarchy is that which we hold in honor. It is, however, a monarchy that is not limited to one person, for it is possible for unity if at variance with itself to come into a condition of plurality; but one that is made of an equality of nature, and a union of mind, and an identity of motion, and a convergence of its elements to unity—a thing which is impossible to the created nature—so that though numerically distinct there is no severance of essence. Therefore unity, having from all eternity arrived by motion at duality, found its rest in trinity. This is what we mean by Father and Son and Holy Ghost. The Father is the begetter and the emitter; without passion, of course, and without reference to time, and not in a corporeal manner. The Son is the begotten, and the Holy Ghost the emission; for I know not how this could be expressed in terms altogether excluding visible things. For we shall not venture to speak of "an overflow of goodness," as one of the Greek philosophers dared to say, as if it were a bowl overflowing,[2] and this in plain words in his Discourse on the First and Second Causes. Let us not ever look on this generation as involuntary, like some natural overflow, hard to be retained, and by no means befitting our conception of deity. Therefore let us confine ourselves within our limits; and speak of the unbegotten and the begotten and that which proceeds from the Father, as somewhere God the Word himself says.[3]

3. When did these come into being? They are above all "when," but—if I am to speak with something more of boldness—when the Father did. And when did the Father come into being? There never was a time when he was not. And the same thing is true of the Son and the Holy Ghost. Ask me again, and again I will answer you, When was the Son begotten? When the Father was not begotten. And when did the Holy Ghost proceed? When the Son was—not proceeding, but begotten—beyond the sphere of time, and above the grasp of reason; although we cannot set forth that which is above time, if we avoid as we desire any expression which conveys

2 The simile occurs in Plato, *Timaeus* 41D, but the reference here is probably to some unknown author.
3 John 15:26.

the idea of time. For such expressions as "when" and "before" and "after" and "from the beginning" are not timeless, however much we may force them; unless indeed we were to take the aeon, that interval which is coextensive with the eternal things, and is not divided or measured by any motion, or by the revolution of the sun, as time is measured.

How, then, are they not alike unoriginate, if they are co-eternal? Because they are from him, though not after him. For that which is unoriginate is eternal, but that which is eternal is not necessarily unoriginate, so long as it may be referred to the Father as its origin. Therefore in respect of cause they are not unoriginate; but it is evident that the cause is not necessarily prior to its effects, for the sun is not prior to its light. And yet they are in some sense unoriginate, in respect of time, even though you would scare simple minds with your quibbles, for the sources of time are not subject to time.

4. But how can this generation be passionless? In that it is incorporeal. For if corporeal generation involves passion, incorporeal generation excludes it. And I will ask of you in turn, How is he God if he is created? For that which is created is not God. I refrain from reminding you that here too is passion if we take the creation in a bodily sense, as time, desire, imagination, thought, hope, pain, risk, failure, success, all of which and more than all find a place in the creature, as is evident to everyone. Nay, I marvel that you do not venture so far as to conceive of marriages and times of pregnancy, and dangers of miscarriage, as if the Father could not have begotten at all if he had not begotten thus; or again, that you did not count up the modes of generation of birds and beasts and fishes, and bring under some one of them the divine and ineffable generation, or even eliminate the Son out of your new hypothesis. And you cannot even see this, that as his generation according to the flesh differs from all others (for where among men do you know of a virgin mother?), so does he differ also in his spiritual generation; or rather he, whose existence is not the same as ours, differs from us also in his generation.

5. Who, then, is that Father who had no beginning? One whose very existence had no beginning; for one whose existence had a beginning must also have begun to be a father. He did not then become a father after he began to be, for his being had no beginning. And he is Father in the absolute sense, for he is not also Son; just as the Son is Son in the absolute sense, because he is not also Father. These names do not belong to

us in the absolute sense, because we are both, and not one more than the other; and we are of both, and not of one only; and so we are divided, and by degrees become men, and perhaps not even men, and such as we did not desire, leaving and being left, so that only the relations remain, without the underlying facts.

But, the objector says, the very form of the expression, "He begot," and, "He was begotten," brings in the idea of a beginning of generation. But what if you do not use this expression, but say, "He had been begotten from the beginning," so as readily to evade your farfetched and time-loving objections? Will you bring Scripture against us, as if we were forging something contrary to Scripture and to the truth? Why, everyone knows that in practice we very often find tenses interchanged when time is spoken of; and especially is this the custom of Holy Scripture, not only in respect of the past tense, and of the present, but even of the future, as, for instance: "Why did the heathen rage?" when they had not yet raged; and, "They shall cross over the river on foot," [4] where the meaning is they did cross over. It would be a long task to reckon up all the expressions of this kind which students have noticed.

6. So much for this point. What is their next objection, how full of contentiousness and impudence? He, they say, either voluntarily begot the Son or else involuntarily. Next, as they think, they bind us on both sides with cords; these, however, are not strong, but very weak. For, they say, if it was involuntarily, he was under the sway of someone, and who exercised this sway? And how is he, over whom it is exercised, God? But if voluntarily, the Son is a son of will—how, then, is he of the Father?—and they thus invent a new sort of mother for him, the will, in place of the Father. There is one good point which they may allege about this argument of theirs, namely, that they desert passion and take refuge in will. For will is not passion.

Secondly, let us look at the strength of their argument. And it were best to wrestle with them at first at close quarters. You yourself, who so recklessly assert whatever takes your fancy, were you begotten voluntarily or involuntarily by your father? If involuntarily, then he was under some tyrant's sway (O terrible violence!) and who was the tyrant? You will hardly say it was nature, for nature is tolerant of chastity. If it was voluntarily, then by a few syllables your father is done away with, for you are shown to be the son of will, and not of your

4 Ps. 2:1; 66 (65):6. (The LXX here is overliteral.)

father. But I pass to the relation between God and the creature, and I put your own question to your own wisdom. Did God create all things voluntarily or under compulsion? If under compulsion, here also is the tyranny, and one who played the tyrant; if voluntarily, the creatures also are deprived of their God, and you before the rest, who invent such arguments and tricks of logic. For a partition is set up between the Creator and the creatures in the shape of will. And yet I think that the person who wills is distinct from the act of willing, he who begets from the act of begetting, the speaker from the speech—or else we are all very stupid. On the one side we have the mover, and on the other that which is, so to speak, the motion. Thus the thing willed is not the child of will, for it does not always result therefrom; nor is that which is begotten the child of generation, nor that which is heard the child of speech, but of the person who willed, or begat, or spoke. But the things of God are beyond all this, for with him perhaps the will to beget is generation, and there is no intermediate action (if we may accept this altogether, and not rather consider generation superior to will).

7. Will you, then, let me play a little upon this word "Father," for your example encourages me to be so bold? The Father is God either willingly or unwillingly; and how will you escape from your own excessive acuteness? If willingly, when did he begin to will? It could not have been before he began to be, for there was nothing prior to him. Or is one part of him will and another the object of will? If so, he is divisible. So the question arises, as the result of your argument, whether he himself is not the child of will. And if unwillingly, what compelled him to exist, and how is he God if he was compelled —and that to nothing less than to be God? How, then, was he begotten? says my opponent. How was he created, if, as you say, he was created? For this is a part of the same difficulty. Perhaps you would say, by will and word. You have not yet solved the whole difficulty; for it yet remains for you to show how will and word gained the power of action. For man was not created in this way.

8. How, then, was he begotten? This generation would have been no great thing, if you could have comprehended it who have no real knowledge even of your own generation, or at least who comprehend very little of it, and of that little you are ashamed to speak; and then do you think you know the whole? You will have to undergo much labor before you

discover the laws of composition formation, manifestation, and the bond whereby soul is united to body, mind to soul, and reason to mind; and movement, increase, assimilation of food, sense, memory, recollection, and all the rest of the parts of which you are compounded; and which of them belongs to the soul and body together, and which to each independently of the other, and which is received from each other. For those parts whose maturity comes later, yet received their laws at the time of conception. Tell me what these laws are? And do not even then venture to speculate on the generation of God; for that would be unsafe. For even if you knew all about your own, yet you do not by any means know about God's. And if you do not understand your own, how can you know about God's? For in proportion as God is harder to trace out than man, so is the heavenly generation harder to comprehend than your own. But if you assert that because you cannot comprehend it therefore he cannot have been begotten, it will be time for you to strike out many existing things which you cannot comprehend; and first of all God himself. For you cannot say what he is, even if you are very reckless, and excessively proud of your intelligence. First, cast away your notions of flow and divisions and sections, and your conceptions of immaterial as if it were material birth, and then you may perhaps worthily conceive of the divine generation. How was he begotten?—I repeat the question in indignation. The begetting of God must be honored by silence. It is a great thing for you to learn that he was begotten. But the manner of his generation we will not admit that even angels can conceive, much less you. Shall I tell you how it was? It was in a manner known to the Father who begot, and to the Son who was begotten. Anything more than this is hidden by a cloud, and escapes your dim sight.

9. Well, but the Father begot a Son who either was or was not in existence. What utter nonsense! This is a question which applies to you or me, who on the one hand were in existence, as, for instance, Levi in the loins of Abraham[5]; and on the other hand came into existence; and so in some sense we are partly of what existed, and partly of what was nonexistent; whereas the contrary is the case with the original matter, which was certainly created out of what was nonexistent, nowithstanding that some pretend that it is unbegotten. But in this case "to be begotten," even from the beginning is concurrent with "to be." On what then will you base this captious question? For what

5 Heb. 7:10.

is older than that which is from the beginning, if we may place there the previous existence or nonexistence of the Son? In either case we destroy its claim to be the beginning. Or perhaps you will say, if we were to ask you whether the Father was of existent or nonexistent substance, that he is twofold, partly pre-existing, partly existing; or that his case is the same with that of the Son; that is, that he was created out of nonexisting matter, because of your ridiculous questions and your houses of sand, which cannot stand against the merest ripple.[6]

I do not admit either solution, and I declare that your question contains an absurdity, and not a difficulty to answer. If, however, you think, in accordance with your dialectic assumptions, that one or other of these alternatives must necessarily be true in every case, let me ask you one little question: Is time in time, or is it not in time? If it is contained in time, then in what time? What is that surpassing wisdom which can conceive of a time which is timeless? Now, in regard to this expression, "I am now telling a lie," admit one of these alternatives, either that it is true or that it is a falsehood, without qualification (for we cannot admit that it is both). But this cannot be. For necessarily he either is lying, and so is telling the truth, or else he is telling the truth, and so is lying. What wonder is it, then, that, as in this case contraries are true, so in that case they should both be untrue, and so your clever puzzle prove mere foolishness? Solve me one more riddle. Were you present at your own generation, and are you now present to yourself, or is neither the case? If you were and are present, who were you, and with whom are you present? And how did your single self become thus both subject and object? But if neither of the above is the case, how did you get separated from yourself, and what is the cause of this disjoining? But, you will say, it is stupid to make a fuss about the question whether or not a single individual is present to himself, for the expression is not used of oneself but of others. Well, you may be certain that it is even more stupid to discuss the question whether that which was begotten from the beginning existed before its generation or not. For such a question arises only as to matter divisible by time.

10. But, they say, the unbegotten and the begotten are not the same; and if this is so, neither is the Son the same as the Father. It is clear, without saying so, that this line of argument manifestly excludes either the Son or the Father from the God-

6 Or, literally "breezes"; cf. Matt. 7:26, 27.

head. For if to be unbegotten is the essence of God, to be begotten is not that essence; if the opposite is the case, the unbegotten is excluded. What argument can contradict this? Choose then whichever blasphemy you prefer, my good inventor of a new theology, if indeed you are anxious at all costs to embrace a blasphemy. In the next place, in what sense do you assert that the unbegotten and the begotten are not the same? If you mean that the uncreated and the created are not the same, I agree with you; for certainly the unoriginate and the created are not of the same nature. But if you say that he that begot and that which is begotten are not the same, the statement is inaccurate. For it is in fact a necessary truth that they are the same. For the nature of the relation of father to child is this: that the offspring is of the same nature with the parent. Or we may argue thus again: What do you mean by unbegotten and begotten, for if you mean the simple fact of being unbegotten or begotten, these are not the same; but if you mean those to whom these terms apply, how are they not the same? For example, wisdom and unwisdom are not the same in themselves, but yet both are attributes of man, who is the same; and they mark not a difference of essence, but one external to the essence. Are immortality and innocence and immutability also the essence of God? If so, God has many essences and not one; or deity is a compound of these. For he cannot be all these without composition, if they be essences.

11. They do not, however, assert this, for these qualities are common also to other beings. But God's essence is that which belongs to God alone, and is proper to him. But they, who consider matter and form to be unbegotten, would not allow that to be unbegotten is the property of God alone (for we must cast away even further the darkness of the Manichaeans). But suppose that it is the property of God alone. What of Adam? Was he not alone the direct creature of God? Yes, you will say. Was he, then, the only human being? By no means. And why, but because humanity does not consist in direct creation? For that which is begotten is also human. Just so neither is he who is unbegotten alone God, though he alone is Father. But grant that he who is begotten is God; for he is of God, as you must allow, even though you cling to your "unbegotten." Then how do you describe the essence of God? Not by declaring what it is, but by rejecting what it is not. For your word signifies that he is not begotten; it does not present to you what is the real nature or condition of that which has

no generation. What, then, is the essence of God? It is for your infatuation to define this, since you are so anxious about his generation too; but to us it will be a very great thing, if ever, even in the future, we learn this, when this darkness and dullness is done away for us, as he has promised who cannot lie. This, then, may be the thought and hope of those who are purifying themselves with a view to this. Thus much we for our part will be bold to say, that if it is a great thing for the Father to be unoriginate, it is no less a thing for the Son to have been begotten of such a Father. For not only would he share the glory of the unoriginate, since he is of the unoriginate, but he has the added glory of his generation, a thing so great and august in the eyes of all those who are not altogether groveling and material in mind.

12. But, they say, if the Son is the same as the Father in respect of essence, then if the Father is unbegotten, the Son must be so likewise. Quite so—if the essence of God consists in being unbegotten; and so he would be a strange mixture, begottenly unbegotten. If, however, the difference is outside the essence, how can you be so certain in speaking of this? Are you also your father's father, so as in no respect to fall short of your father, since you are the same with him in essence? Is it not evident that our inquiry into the nature of the essence of God, if we make it, will leave personality [7] absolutely unaffected? But that "unbegotten" is not a synonym of "God" is proved thus: If it were so, it would be necessary that since "God" is a relative term, "unbegotten" should be so likewise; or that since "unbegotten" is an absolute term, so must "God" be . . . God of no one. For words which are absolutely identical are similarly applied. But the word "unbegotten" is not used relatively. For to what is it relative? And of what things is God the God? Why, of all things. How, then, can "God" and "unbegotten" be identical terms? And again, since "begotten" and "unbegotten" are contradictories, like "possession" and "deprivation," it would follow that contradictory essences would coexist, which is impossible. Or again, since possessions are prior to deprivations, and the latter are destructive of the former, not only must the essence of the Son be prior to that of the Father, but it must be destroyed by the Father, on your hypothesis.

13. What now remains of their invincible arguments? Perhaps the last they will take refuge in is this: If God has never

7 Or "individuality," *idiōtes*.

ceased to beget, the generation is imperfect; and when will he cease? But if he has ceased, then he must have begun. Thus again these carnal minds bring forward carnal arguments. Whether he is eternally begotten or not, I do not yet say, until I have looked into the statement, "Before all the hills he begetteth me," more accurately.[8] But I cannot see the necessity of their conclusion. For if, as they say, everything that is to come to an end had also a beginning, then surely that which has no end had no beginning. What, then, will they decide concerning the soul, or the angelic nature? If it had a beginning, it will also have an end; and if it has no end, it is evident that according to them it had no beginning. But the truth is that it had a beginning, and will never have an end. Their assertion, then, that that which will have an end had also a beginning is untrue. Our position, however, is that as in the case of a horse, or an ox, or a man, the same definition applies to all the individuals of the same species, and whatever shares the definition has also a right to the name; so in the very same way there is one essence of God, and one nature, and one name; although in accordance with a distinction in our thoughts we use distinct names; and that whatever is properly called by this name really is God; and what he is in nature, that he is truly called—if at least we are to hold that truth is a matter not of names but of realities. But our opponents, as if they were afraid of leaving any stone unturned to subvert the truth, acknowledge indeed that the Son is God when they are compelled to do so by arguments and evidences; but they only mean that he is God in an ambiguous sense, and that he only shares the name.

14. And when we advance this objection against them: What do you mean to say, then? That the Son is not properly God, just as a picture of an animal is not properly an animal? And if not properly God, in what sense is he God at all? they reply, Why should not these terms be ambiguous, and in both cases be used in a proper sense? And they will give us such instances as the land dog and the dogfish, where the word "dog" is ambiguous, and yet in both cases is properly used, for there is such a species among the ambiguously named, or any other case in which the same appellative is used for two things of different nature. But, my good friend, in this case, when you include two natures under the same name, you do not assert that either is better than the other, or that the one

8 Prov. 8:25.

is prior and the other posterior, or that one is in a greater degree and the other in a lesser that which is predicated of them both, for there is no connecting link which forces this necessity upon them. One is not a dog more than the other, and one less so; either the dogfish more than the land dog, or the land dog than the dogfish. Why should they be, or on what principle? But the community of name is here between things of equal value, though of different nature. But in the case of which we are speaking, you couple the name of God with adorable majesty, and make it surpass every essence and nature (an attribute of God alone), and then you ascribe this name to the Father, while you deprive the Son of it, and make him subject to the Father, and give him only a secondary honor and worship; and even if in words you bestow on him one which is equal, yet in practice you cut off his deity, and pass malignantly from a use of the same name implying an exact equality to one that connects things that are not equal. And so the pictured and the living man are in your mouth an apter illustration of the relations of deity than the dogs which I instanced. Or else you must concede to both an equal dignity of nature as well as a common name—even though you introduced these natures into your argument as different; and thus you destroy the analogy of your dogs, which you invented as an instance of inequality. For what is the force of your instance of ambiguity if those whom you distinguish are not equal in honor? For it was not to prove an equality but an inequality that you took refuge in your dogs. How could anybody be more clearly convicted of fighting both against his own arguments, and against the Deity?

15. And if, when we admit that in respect of being the cause the Father is greater than the Son, they should assume the premise that he is the cause by nature, and then deduce the conclusion that he is greater by nature also, it is difficult to say whether they mislead most themselves or those with whom they are arguing. For it does not absolutely follow that all that is predicated of a class can also be predicated of all the individuals composing it; for the different particulars may belong to different individuals. For what hinders me—if I assume the same premise, namely, that the Father is greater by nature, and then add this other, yet not by nature in every respect greater nor yet Father—from concluding, therefore, the greater is not in every respect greater, nor the Father in every respect Father? Or, if you prefer it, let us put it in this way: God is an

essence, but an essence is not in every case God; and draw the conclusion for yourself—therefore God is not in every case God. I think the fallacy here is the arguing from a conditioned to an unconditioned use of a term, to use the technical expression of the logicians. For while we assign this word "greater" to his nature viewed as a cause, they infer it of his nature viewed in itself. It is just as if when we said that such a one was a dead man they were to infer simply that he was a man.

16. How shall we pass over the following point, which is no less amazing than the rest? Father, they say, is a name either of an essence or of an action, thinking to bind us down on both sides. If we say that it is a name of an essence, they will say that we agree with them that the Son is of another essence, since there is but one essence of God, and this, according to them, is preoccupied by the Father. On the other hand, if we say that it is the name of an action, we shall be supposed to acknowledge plainly that the Son is created and not begotten. For where there is an agent there must also be an effect. And they will say they wonder how that which is made can be identical with that which made it. I should myself have been frightened with your distinction, if it had been necessary to accept one or other of the alternatives, and not rather put both aside, and state a third and truer one, namely, that Father is not a name either of an essence or of an action, most clever sirs. But it is the name of the relation in which the Father stands to the Son, and the Son to the Father. For as with us these names make known a genuine and intimate relation, so in the case before us too they denote an identity of nature between him that is begotten and him that begets. But let us concede to you that Father is a name of essence; it will still bring in the idea of Son, and will not make it of a different nature, according to common ideas and the force of these names. Let it be, if it so please you, the name of an action; you will not defeat us in this way either. The *homoousion* would be indeed the result of this action, or otherwise the conception of an action in this matter would be absurd. You see then how, even though you try to fight unfairly, we avoid your sophistries. But now, since we have ascertained how invincible you are in your arguments and sophistries, let us look at your strength in the oracles of God, if perchance you may choose to persuade us out of them.

17. For we have learned to believe in and to teach the deity of the Son from their great and lofty utterances. And what

utterances are these? These: God—the Word—He That Was in the Beginning and with the Beginning, and the Beginning. "In the beginning was the Word, and the Word was with God, and the Word was God," and "With thee is the beginning," and "He who calleth her the beginning from generations." [9] Then the Son is only-begotten: the "only-begotten Son which is in the bosom of the Father," it says, "he hath declared him." The Way, the Truth, the Life, the Light. "I am the way, the truth, and the life"; and "I am the light of the world." [10] Wisdom and Power, "Christ, the wisdom of God, and the power of God." [11] The Effulgence, the Impress, the Image, the Seal: "Who being the effulgence of his glory and the impress of his essence," and "the image of his goodness," and "him hath God the Father sealed." [12] Lord, King, He That Is, the Almighty. "The Lord rained down fire from the Lord"; and "A sceptre of righteousness is the sceptre of thy kingdom"; and "Which is and was and is to come, the Almighty" [13]— all which are clearly spoken of the Son, with all the other passages of the same force, none of which is an afterthought, or added later to the Son or the Spirit, any more than to the Father himself. For their perfection is not affected by additions. There never was a time when he was without the Word, or when he was not the Father, or when he was not true, or not wise, or not powerful, or devoid of life, or of splendor, or of goodness.

18. But, in opposition to all these, do you reckon up for me the expressions which make for your ignorant arrogance, such as "My God and your God," or "greater," or "created," or "made," or "sanctified"; add, if you like, "servant" and "obedient" and "gave" and "learned," and "was commanded," "was sent," "can do nothing of himself," either say, or judge, or give, or will. [14] And further, these—his "ignorance," "subjection," "prayer," "asking," "increase," "being made perfect." [15] And, if you like, even more humble than these: such as speak of his sleeping, hungering, being in an agony, and fear-

[9] John 1:1; Ps. 110 (109):3; Isa. 41:4 (a variant LXX reading); "beginning" is grammatically feminine in Greek.
[10] John 1:18; 14:6; 8:12.          [11] I Cor. 1:24.
[12] Heb. 1:3; Wisdom 7:26; John 6:27.
[13] Gen. 19:24; Ps. 45 (44):6; Rev. 1:8.
[14] John 20:17; 14:28; Prov. 8:22; Acts 2:36; John 10:36; Phil. 2:7, 18; John 18:11; Heb. 5:8; John 15:10; 5:36; 20:21; 5:19; 8:28; 8:15; Matt. 20:23; John 5:20.
[15] Mark 13:32; Luke 2:51; Luke 3:21; 22:41; John 11:34; Heb. 2:10.

ing;[16] or perhaps you would make even his cross and death a matter of reproach to him. His resurrection and ascension I fancy you will leave to me, for in these is found something to support our position. A good many other things too you might pick up, if you desire to put together that equivocal and intruded god of yours, who to us is true God, and equal to the Father. For every one of these points, taken separately, may very easily, if we go through them one by one, be explained to you in the most reverent sense, and the stumbling block of the letter be cleansed away—that is, if your stumbling at it be honest, and not willfully malicious. To give you the explanation in one sentence: What is lofty you are to apply to the Godhead, and to that nature in him which is superior to sufferings and incorporeal; but all that is lowly to the composite condition of him who for your sakes made himself of no reputation and was incarnate—yes, for it is no worse thing to say—was made man, and afterwards was also exalted. The result will be that you will abandon these carnal and groveling doctrines, and learn to be more sublime, and to ascend with his Godhead, and you will not remain permanently among the things of sight, but will rise up with him into the world of thought, and come to know which passages refer to his nature, and which to his assumption of human nature.[17]

19. For he whom you now treat with contempt was once above you. He who is now man was once the uncompounded. What he was he continued to be; what he was not he took to himself. In the beginning he was, uncaused; for what is the cause of God? But afterward for a cause he was born. And that cause was that you might be saved, who insult him and despise his Godhead, because of this, that he took upon him your denser nature, having converse with flesh by means of mind. While his inferior [nature], the humanity, became God, because it was united to God,[18] and became one [person] because the higher nature prevailed ... in order that I too might be made God so far as he is made man.[19] He was born —but he had been begotten: he was born of a woman—but she was a virgin. The first is human; the second, divine. In his human nature he had no father, but also in his divine

16 Matt. 8:24; 21:18; John 4:6; 11:35; Luke 22:44.
17 "What belongs to [his] nature and what to the dispensation."
18 Or, punctuating differently, "And becoming man, God on earth, because [his humanity] was united to God."
19 Cf. Athanasius, On the Incarnation, 54.

nature no mother. Both these belong to Godhead. He dwelt in the womb—but he was recognized by the prophet, himself still in the womb, leaping before the Word, for whose sake he came into being.[20] He was wrapped in swaddling clothes—but he took off the swathing bands of the grave by his rising again. He was laid in a manger—but he was glorified by angels, and proclaimed by a star, and worshiped by the Magi. Why are you offended by that which is presented to your sight, because you will not look at that which is presented to your mind? He was driven into exile into Egypt—but he drove away the Egyptian idols.[21] He had no form nor comeliness in the eyes of the Jews—but to David he is fairer than the children of men.[22] And on the mountain he was bright as the lightning, and became more luminous than the sun, initiating us into the mystery of the future.[23]

20. He was baptized as man—but he remitted sins as God —not because he needed purificatory rites himself, but that he might sanctify the element of water. He was tempted as man, but he conquered as God; yea, he bids us be of good cheer, for he has overcome the world.[24] He hungered—but he fed thousands; yea, he is the bread that gives life, and that is of heaven. He thirsted—but he cried, "If any man thirst, let him come unto me and drink." Yea, he promised that fountains should flow from them that believe.[25] He was wearied, but he is the rest of them that are weary and heavy-laden.[26] He was heavy with sleep, but he walked lightly over the sea. He rebuked the winds, he made Peter light as he began to sink.[27] He pays tribute, but it is out of a fish; yea, he is the king of those who demanded it.[28]

He is called a Samaritan and a demoniac, but he saves him that came down from Jerusalem and fell among thieves[29]; the demons acknowledge him, and he drives out demons, and sinks in the sea legions of foul spirits, and sees the prince of demons falling like lightning.[30] He is stoned, but is not taken.[31] He prays, but he hears prayer. He weeps, but he causes tears to cease. He asks where Lazarus was laid, for he was man; but

[20] Luke 1:41.
[21] Cf. Athanasius, On the Incarnation, 36, 37.
[22] Isa. 53:2; Ps. 45 (44):2.     [23] Matt. 17:2; Luke 9:29.
[24] John 16:33.     [25] John 6:51.
[26] Matt. 11:28.     [27] Matt. 14:25, 31.
[28] Matt. 17:27.
[29] John 8:48; Luke 10:30–37, interpreted symbolically.
[30] Mark 5:9 and parallels.     [31] John 8:59.

he raises Lazarus, for he was God.[32] He is sold, and very cheap, for it is only for thirty pieces of silver; but he redeems the world, and that at a great price, for the price was his own blood. As a sheep he is led to the slaughter, but he is the shepherd of Israel, and now of the whole world also.[33] As a lamb he is silent, yet he is the Word, and is proclaimed by the voice of one crying in the wilderness. He is bruised and wounded, but he heals every disease and every infirmity.[34] He is lifted up and nailed to the tree, but by the tree of life he restores us[35]; yea, he saves even the robber crucified with him; yea, he wrapped the visible world in darkness. He is given vinegar to drink mingled with gall. Who? He who turned the water into wine, who is the destroyer of the bitter taste, who is sweetness and altogether desired.[36] He lays down his life, but he has power to take it again[37]; and the veil is rent, for the mysterious doors of heaven are opened; the rocks are cleft, the dead arise.[38] He dies, but he gives life, and by his death destroys death. He is buried but he rises again; he goes down into hell, but he brings up the souls[39]; he ascends to heaven, and shall come again to judge the quick and the dead, and to put to the test such words as yours. If the one give you a starting point for your error, let the others put an end to it.

21. This, then, is our reply to those who would puzzle us—not given willingly indeed (for light talk and contradictions of words are not agreeable to the faithful, and one adversary is enough for us), but of necessity, for the sake of our assailants (for medicines exist because of diseases), that they may be led to see that they are not all-wise, nor invincible in those superfluous arguments which make void the gospel. For when we leave off believing, and protect ourselves by mere strength of argument, and destroy the claim which the Spirit has upon our faith by questionings, and then our argument is not strong enough for the importance of the subject (and this must necessarily be the case, since it is put in motion by an organ of so little power as is our mind), what is the result? The weakness of the argument appears to belong to the mystery, and thus elegance of language makes void the cross,[40] as Paul also

[32] John 11:34, 35, 43.
[33] Isa. 53:7; Ps. 80 (79):1.
[34] Matt. 9:35.
[35] Rev. 22:2; Gen. 2:9.
[36] S. of Sol. 5:16.
[37] John 10:18.
[38] Matt. 27:51, 52.
[39] Cf. I Peter 3:19; the idea is already somewhat further developed.
[40] I Cor. 1:17.

thought. For faith is that which completes our argument. But may He who proclaims unions and looses those that are bound, and who puts into our minds to solve the knots of their unnatural dogmas, if it may be, change these men and make them faithful instead of rhetoricians, Christians instead of that which they now are called. This indeed we entreat and beg for Christ's sake: "Be ye reconciled to God,"[42] and quench not the Spirit; or rather, may Christ be reconciled to you, and may the Spirit enlighten you, though so late. But if you are too fond of your quarrel, we at any rate will hold fast to the Trinity, and by the Trinity may we be saved, remaining pure and without offense until the more perfect showing forth of that which we desire, in him, Christ our Lord, to whom be the glory forever. Amen.

[42] II Cor. 5:20.

# THE TEXT: THE FOURTH THEOLOGICAL ORATION—WHICH IS THE SECOND ON THE SON

1. Since I have by the power of the Spirit sufficiently overthrown the subtleties and intricacies of the arguments, and already solved in the mass the objections and oppositions drawn from Holy Scripture, with which these sacrilegious robbers of the Bible and thieves of the sense of its contents draw over the multitude to their side, and confuse the way of truth; and that not without clearness, as I believe all candid persons will say, attributing to the Deity the higher and diviner expressions, and the lower and more human to Him who for us men was the second Adam, and was God made capable of suffering [to strive] against sin; yet we have not yet gone through the passages in detail, because of the haste of our argument. But since you demand of us a brief explanation of each of them, that you may not be carried away by the plausibilities of their arguments, we will therefore state the explanations summarily, dividing them into numbers for the sake of carrying them more easily in mind.

2. In their eyes the following is only too ready to hand: "The Lord created me at the beginning of his ways with a view to his works." [1] How shall we meet this? Shall we bring an accusation against Solomon, or reject his former words because of his fall in afterlife? Shall we say that the words are those of wisdom herself, as it were of knowledge and the creator-word, in accordance with which all things were made? For Scripture often personifies many even lifeless objects; as, for instance, "The sea said" so and so; [2] and, "The heavens declare the glory of god"; and again a command is given to the sword; and the mountains and hills are asked the reason of their

[1] Prov. 8:22.        [2] Job 28:14.

skipping.[3] We do not allege any of these, though some of our predecessors used them as powerful arguments. But let us grant that the expression is used of our Saviour himself, the true wisdom. Let us consider one small point together. What among all things that exist is unoriginate? The Godhead. For no one can tell the origin of God, that otherwise would be older than God. But what is the cause of the manhood, which for our sake God assumed? It was surely our salvation. What else could it be? Since, then, we find here clearly both the "created" and the "begetteth me," the argument is simple. Whatever we find joined with a cause we are to refer to the manhood, but all that is absolute and unoriginate we are to reckon to the account of his Godhead. Well, then, is not this "created" said in connection with a cause? He created me, it so says, as the beginning of his ways, with a view to his works. Now, the works of his hands are verity and judgment; for whose sake he was anointed with Godhead; for this anointing is of the manhood; but the "He begetteth me" is not connected with a cause; or it is for you to show the adjunct.[4] What argument, then, will disprove that wisdom is called a creature, in connection with the lower generation, but begotten in respect of the first and more incomprehensible?

3. Next is the fact of his being called servant and serving many well, and that it is a great thing for him to be called the child of God.[5] For in truth he was in servitude to flesh and to birth and to the conditions of our life with a view to our liberation, and to that of all those whom he has saved, who were in bondage under sin. What greater destiny can befall man's humility than that he should be intermingled with God, and by this intermingling should be deified, and that we should be so visited by the "dayspring from on high" that even that holy thing that should be born should be called the Son of the Highest, and that there should be bestowed upon him "a name which is above every name"? And what else can this be than God—and that every knee should bow to him that was made of no reputation for us, and that mingled the form of God with the form of a servant, and that all the house of Israel should know that God has made him both Lord and Christ?[6] For all

---

[3] Ps. 19 (18):1; Zech. 13:7; Ps. 114 (113):6.
[4] Prov. 8:25 (LXX), "Before the hills he begetteth me"; Gregory's text may have read "anointed" for "established" in v. 23, or the reference be to Ps. 45 (44):7.
[5] Isa. 53:11; 49:6.             [6] Luke 1:78, 32, 35; Phil. 2:7–11; Acts 2:36.

this was done by the action of the begotten, and by the good pleasure of Him that begot him.

4. Well, what is the second of their great irresistible passages? "He must reign," till such and such a time . . . and "be received by heaven until the time of restitution," and "have the seat at the right hand until the overthrow of his enemies." [7] But after this? Must he cease to be king, or be removed from heaven? Why, who shall make him cease, or for what cause? What a bold and very anarchical interpreter you are; and yet you have heard that of his Kingdom there shall be no end. Your mistake arises from not understanding that "until" is not always exclusive of that which comes after, but asserts up to that time, without denying what comes after it. To take a single instance, how else would you understand, "Lo, I am with you always, even unto the end of the world"? [8] Does it mean that he will no longer be so afterwards? And for what reason? But this is not the only cause of your error; you also fail to distinguish between the things that are signified. He is said to reign in one sense as the Almighty King, both of the willing and the unwilling; but in another as producing in us submission, and placing us under his kingship as willingly acknowledging his sovereignty. "Of his Kingdom," considered in the former sense, "there shall be no end." But in the second sense, what end will there be? His taking us as his servants, on our entrance into a state of salvation. For what need is there to work submission in us when we have already submitted? After which he arises to judge the earth, and to separate the saved from the lost. [9] After that he is to stand as God in the midst of gods, that is, of the saved, distinguishing and deciding of what honor and of what mansion each is worthy.

5. Take, in the next place, the subjection by which you subject the Son to the Father. What, you say, is he not now subject, or must he, if he is God, be subject to God? You are fashioning your argument as if it concerned some robber, or some hostile deity. But look at it in this manner: that as for my sake he was called a curse who destroyed my curse, and sin who takes away the sin of the world, and became a new Adam to take the place of the old, just so he makes my disobedience his own as head of the whole body. As long, then, as I am disobedient and rebellious, both by denial of God and by my passions, so long Christ also is called disobedient on my

[7] I Cor. 15:25; Acts 3:21; Ps. 110 (109):1.
[8] Matt. 28:20.                    [9] Ps. 82 (81): 8, 1.

account. But when all things shall be subdued unto him on the one hand by acknowledgment of him and on the other by a reformation, then he himself also will have fulfilled his submission, bringing me whom he has saved to God.[10] For this, according to my view, is the subjection of Christ, namely, the fulfilling of the Father's will. But as the Son subjects all to the Father, so does the Father to the Son, the one by his work, the other by his good pleasure, as we have already said. And thus he who subjects presents to God that which he has subjected, making our condition his own. Of the same kind, it appears to me, is the expression, "My God, my God, why hast thou forsaken me?" It was not he who was forsaken either by the Father or by his own Godhead, as some have thought, as if it were afraid of the Passion, and therefore withdrew itself from him in his sufferings (for who compelled him either to be born on earth at all or to be lifted up on the cross?). But, as I said, he was in his own person representing us. For we were the forsaken and despised before, but now, by the sufferings of Him who could not suffer, we were taken up and saved. Similarly, he makes his own our folly and our transgressions; and says what follows in the psalm, for it is very evident that the Twenty-first Psalm refers to Christ.[11]

6. The same consideration applies to another passage, "He learned obedience by the things which he suffered," and to his "strong crying and tears," and his "entreaties," and his "being heard," and his "reverence," [12] all of which he wonderfully wrought out, like a drama whose plot was devised on our behalf. For in his character of the Word he was neither obedient nor disobedient. For such expressions belong to servants, and inferiors, and the one applies to the better sort of them, while the other belongs to those who deserve punishment. But, in the character of the form of a servant, he condescends to his fellow servants, nay, to his servants, and takes upon him a strange form, bearing all me and mine in himself, that in himself he may exhaust the bad, as fire does wax, or as the sun does the mists of earth; and that I may partake of his nature by the blending. Thus he honors obedience by his action, and proves it experimentally by his Passion. For to possess the disposition is not enough, just as it would not be enough for us,

[10] I Cor. 15:28, interpreted of what Augustine calls "the whole Christ,' head and members; cf. Gal. 3:13; II Cor. 5:21; I Cor. 15:45.
[11] Ps. 22 (21 in LXX):1, with a reference to Gnostic ideas of Christ's Godhead leaving him on the cross.          [12] Heb. 5:7, 8.

unless we also proved it by our acts; for action is the proof of disposition.

And perhaps it would not be wrong to assume this also, that by the art of his love for man he gauges our obedience, and measures all by comparison with his own sufferings, so that he may know our condition by his own, and how much is demanded of us, and how much we yield, taking into account, along with our environment, our weakness also. For if the light shining through the veil upon the darkness, that is, upon this life, was persecuted by the other darkness [13] (I mean, the evil one and the tempter), how much more will the darkness be persecuted, as being weaker than it? And what marvel is it, that though he entirely escaped, we have been, at any rate in part, overtaken? For it is a more wonderful thing that he should have been chased than that we should have been captured—at least to the minds of all who reason aright on the subject. I will add yet another passage to those I have mentioned, because I think that it clearly tends to the same sense. I mean, "In that he hath suffered being tempted, he is able to succor them that are tempted." [14] But God will be all in all [15] in the time of restitution; not in the sense that the Father alone will be, and the Son be wholly resolved into him, like a torch into a great pyre, from which it was reft away for a little space, and then put back (for I would not have even the Sabellians injured by such an expression); but the entire Godhead . . . when we shall be no longer divided (as we now are by movements and passions), and containing nothing at all of God, or very little, but shall be entirely like [16] God, ready to receive [into our hearts] the whole God and him alone. This is the perfection to which we press on. Paul himself indeed bears witness to this. For what he here says in general of God he elsewhere specifically applies to Christ. What does he say [about this]? "Where there is neither Greek nor Jew, circumcision nor uncircumcision, barbarian, Scythian, bond or free; but Christ is all and in all." [17]

7. As your third point you count the word "greater" [18]; and as your fourth, "[to] my God and your God." [19] And, indeed, if he had been called greater, and the word "equal" had not occurred, this might perhaps have been a point in their favor.

[13] Cf. John 1:5.  [14] Heb. 2:18.  [15] I Cor. 15:28.
[16] The remainder of this chapter is missing in the Post-Nicene Fathers, p. 312.
[17] Heb. 6:1; Col. 3:11.  [18] John 14:28.  [19] John 20:17.

But if we find both words clearly used, what will these gentlemen have to say? How will it strengthen their argument? How will they reconcile the irreconcilable? For that the same thing should be at once both greater than and equal to the same thing is an impossibility; and the evident solution is that the "greater" refers to the origination, while the "equal" belongs to the nature; and this we acknowledge with much good will. But perhaps someone else will back up our attack on your argument, and assert that that which is from such a cause is not inferior to that which has no cause; for it would share the glory of the unoriginate, because it is from the unoriginate. And there is, besides, the generation, which is to all men a matter so marvelous and of such majesty. For to say that he is greater than the [Son] considered as man is true indeed, but is no great thing. For what marvel is it if God is greater than man? Surely that is enough to say in answer to their talk about "greater."

8. As to the other passages, "my God" would be used in respect, not of the Word, but of the visible Word. For how could there be a God of him who is properly God? In the same way he is Father, not of the visible, but of the Word; for our Lord was of two [natures]; so that one expression is used properly, the other improperly in each of the two cases; but exactly the opposite way to their use in respect of us. For with respect to us God is properly our God, but not properly our Father. And this is the cause of the error of the heretics, namely, the joining of these two names, which are interchanged because of the union [of the natures]. And an indication of this is found in the fact that wherever the natures are distinguished in our thoughts from one another, the names are also distinguished; as you hear in Paul's words, "The God of our Lord Jesus Christ, the Father of Glory." [20] The God of Christ, but the Father of Glory. For although these two terms express but one person, yet this is not by a unity of nature, but by a union of the two. What could be clearer?

9. Fifthly, let it be alleged that it is said of him that he receives life, judgment, inheritance of the Gentiles, or power over all flesh, or glory, or disciples,[21] or whatever else is mentioned. This also belongs to the manhood; and yet if you were to ascribe it to the Godhead it would be no absurdity. For you would not so ascribe it as if it were newly acquired,

[20] Eph. 1:17, "Glory" being taken as a title of the Son; cf. James 2:1.
[21] John 5:26, 22, 27; Ps. 2:8; John 17:1, 2, 5, 6.

but as belonging to him from the beginning by reason of nature, and not as an act of favor.

10. Sixthly, let it be asserted that it is written, "The Son can do nothing of himself, but what he sees the Father do."[22] The solution of this is as follows: "Can" and "cannot" are not words with only one meaning, but have many meanings. On the one hand, they are used sometimes in respect of deficiency of strength, sometimes in respect of time, and sometimes relatively to a certain object; as, for instance, a child who cannot be an athlete, or, a puppy cannot see, or fight with so and so. Perhaps someday the child will be an athlete, the puppy will see, will fight with that other, though it may still be unable to fight with any other. Or again, they may be used of that which is generally true. For instance, "a city that is set on a hill cannot be hid"; while yet it might possibly be hidden by another higher hill being in a line with it. Or in another sense they are used of a thing that is not reasonable, as, Can the children of the bridechamber fast while the bridegroom is with them?[23] whether he be considered as visible in bodily form (for the time of his sojourning among us was not one of mourning, but of gladness), or, as the Word. For why should they keep a bodily fast who are cleansed by the Word? Or, again, they are used of that which is contrary to the will; as in, "He could do no mighty works there because of their unbelief,"[24] i.e., of those who should receive them. For since in order to healing there is need of both faith in the patient and power in the healer, when one of the two failed the other was impossible. But probably this sense also is to be referred to the head of the unreasonable. For healing is not reasonable in the case of those who would afterwards be injured by unbelief. The sentence "The world cannot hate you"[25] comes under the same head, as does also "How can ye, being evil, speak good things?"[26] For in what sense is either impossible, except that it is contrary to the will? There is a somewhat similar meaning in the expressions which imply that a thing impossible by nature is possible to God if he so wills; as that a man cannot be born a second time, or that a needle will not let a camel through it.[27] For what could prevent either of these happening if God so willed?

[22] John 5:19          [23] Matt. 5:14; Mark 2:19.          [24] Mark 6:5.
[25] John 7:7; the MSS. of Gregory insert another negative ("not hate you"), probably by mistake, without changing the meaning.
[26] Matt. 12:34.                    [27] John 3:4; Matt. 19:24, 26.

11. And besides all this, there is the absolutely impossible and inadmissible, as that which we are now examining. For as we assert that it is impossible for God to be evil, or not to exist—for this would be indicative of weakness in God rather than of strength—or for the nonexistent to exist, or for two and two to make both four and ten, so it is impossible and inconceivable that the Son should do anything that the Father does not. For all things that the Father has are the Son's; and on the other hand, all that belongs to the Son is the Father's. Nothing, then, is peculiar, because all things are in common. For their being itself is common and equal, even though the Son receive it from the Father. It is in respect of this that it is said, "I live by the Father"[28]; not as though his life and being were kept together by the Father, but because he has his being from Him beyond all time, and beyond all cause. But how does he see the Father doing, and do likewise? Is it like those who copy pictures and letters, because they cannot attain the truth unless by looking at the original and being led by the hand by it? But how shall wisdom stand in need of a teacher, or be incapable of acting unless taught? And in what sense does the Father "do" in the present or in the past? Did he make another world before this one, or is he going to make a world to come? And did the Son look at that and make this? Or will he look at the other, and make one like it? According to this argument there must be four worlds, two made by the Father, and two by the Son. What an absurdity! He cleanses lepers, and delivers men from evil spirits and diseases, and quickens the dead, and walks upon the sea, and does all his other works; but in what case or when did the Father do these acts before him? Is it not clear that the Father impressed the ideas of these same actions, and the Word brings them to pass, yet not in slavish or unskillful fashion, but with full knowledge and in a masterly way, or, to speak more properly, like the Father? For in this sense I understand the words that whatsoever is done by the Father, these things does the Son likewise; not, that is, because of the likeness of the things done, but in respect of the authority. This might well also be the meaning of the passage which says that the Father works hitherto and the Son also[29]; and not only so, but it refers also to the government and preservation of the things which he has made; as is shown by the passage which says that he makes his angels spirits, and that the earth is founded upon its steadfastness (though once

[28] John 16:5; 17:10; 6:57.    [29] John 5:17, 19.

for all these things were fixed and made), and that the thunder is made firm and the wind created.³⁰ Of all these things the Word was given once, but the action is continuous even now.

12. Let them quote in the seventh place that the Son came down from heaven, not to do his own will, but the will of Him that sent him.³¹ Well, if this had not been said by himself who came down, we should say that the phrase was modeled as issuing from the human nature, not from Him who is conceived of in his character as the Saviour, for his human will cannot be opposed to God, seeing it is altogether taken into God; but conceived of simply as in our nature, inasmuch as the human will does not completely follow the divine, but for the most part struggles against and resists it. For we understand in the same way the words, "Father, if it be possible, let this cup pass from me; nevertheless let not what I will but thy will prevail."³² For it is not likely that he did not know whether it was possible or not, or that he would oppose will to will. But since, as this is the language of him who assumed our nature (for he it was who came down), and not of the nature which he assumed, we must meet the objection in this way, that the passage does not mean that the Son has a special will of his own, besides that of the Father, but that he has not; so that the meaning would be, "Not to do mine own will, for there is none of mine apart from, but that which is common to, me and thee; for as we have one Godhead, so we have one will." For many such expressions are used in relation to this community,³³ and are expressed not positively but negatively; as, e.g., "God giveth not the Spirit by measure,"³⁴ for as a matter of fact he does not give the Spirit to the Son, nor does he measure it, for God is not measured by God; or again, "Not my transgression nor my sin." The words are used not because he has these things, but because he has them not. And again, "Not for our righteousness which we have done," for we have not done any.³⁵ And this meaning is evident also in the clauses which follow. For what, says he, is the will of my Father? That everyone that believes on the Son should be saved, and obtain the final resurrection. Now is this the will of the Father, but not of the Son? Or does he preach the gospel, and receive men's faith against his will? Who could

³⁰ Ps. 104 (103):4, 5; Amos 4:13.   ³¹ John 6:38.
³² Matt. 26:39; Luke 22:42.   ³³ Or simply, "in common usage."
³⁴ John 3:34, with (as in the Authorized Version) "to him" assumed to be implied.   ³⁵ Ps. 59 (58):3; Titus 3:5.

believe that? Moreover, that passage, too, which says that the Word which is heard is not the Son's but the Father's has the same force. For I cannot see how that which is common to two can be said to belong to one alone, however much I consider it, and I do not think anyone else can. If, then, you hold this opinion concerning the will, you will be right and reverent in your opinion, as I think, and as every right-minded person thinks.

13. The eighth passage is, "That they may know thee the only true God, and Jesus Christ, whom thou hast sent"; and, "There is none good save one, that is, God."[36] The solution of this appears to me very easy. For if you attribute this only to the Father, where will you place the very truth? For if you conceive in this manner of the meaning of "To the only wise God," or "Who only hath immortality, dwelling in the light which no man can approach unto," or of "To the king of the ages, immortal, invisible, and only wise God,"[37] then the Son has vanished under sentence of death, or of darkness, or at any rate condemned to be neither wise nor king, nor invisible, nor God at all, which sums up all these points. And how will you prevent his goodness, which especially belongs to God alone, from perishing with the rest? I, however, think that the passage "That they may know thee the only true God" was said to overthrow those gods which are falsely so called, for he would not have added, "And Jesus Christ, whom thou hast sent," if the only true God were contrasted with him, and the sentence did not proceed upon the basis of a common Godhead. The "none is good" meets the tempting lawyer, who was testifying to his goodness viewed as man. For perfect goodness, he says, is God's alone, even if a man is called perfectly good: as, for instance, "A good man out of the good treasure of his heart bringeth forth good things."[38] And, "I will give the kingdom to one who is good above thee"—words of God, speaking to Saul about David.[39] Or again, "Do good, O Lord, unto the good"[40] . . . and all other like expressions concerning those of us who are praised, upon whom it is a kind of effluence from the supreme good, and has come to them in a secondary degree. It will be best of all if we can persuade you of this. But if not, what will you say to the suggestion on the other side, that on your hypothesis the Son has been called the only God?

36 John 17:3; Mark 10:18.          37 Rom. 16:27; I Tim. 6:16; 1:17.
38 Matt. 12:35.                    39 I Sam. 15:28.
40 Ps. 125 (124):4.

In what passage? Why, in this: "This is your God; no other shall be accounted of in comparison with him," and a little further on: "After this did he show himself upon earth, and conversed with men."[41] This addition proves clearly that the words are used not of the Father, but of the Son; for it was he who in bodily form companied with us, and was in this lower world. Now, if we should determine to take these words as said in contrast with the Father, and not with the imaginary gods, we lose the Father by the very terms which we were pressing against the Son. And what could be more disastrous than such a victory?

14. Ninthly, they allege, "Seeing he ever liveth to make intercession for us."[42] O how beautiful and mystical and kind! For to intercede does not imply to seek for vengeance, as is most men's way (for in that there would be something of humiliation), but it is to plead for us by reason of his mediatorship, just as the Spirit also is said to make intercession for us. For "there is one God, and one mediator between God and man, the man Christ Jesus."[43] For he still pleads even now as man for my salvation; for he continues to wear the body which he assumed, until he make me God by the power of his incarnation; although he is no longer known after the flesh—I mean, the passions of the flesh—the same, except sin, as ours. Thus, too, we have an advocate, Jesus Christ,[44] not indeed prostrating himself for us before the Father, and falling down before him in slavish fashion—away with a suspicion so truly slavish and unworthy of the Spirit! For neither is it seemly for the Father to require this nor for the Son to submit to it; nor is it just to think it of God. But by what he suffered as man, he as the Word and the counselor persuades [him][45] to be patient. I think this is the meaning of his advocacy.

15. Their tenth objection is the ignorance, and the statement that "of the last day and hour knoweth no man, not even the Son himself, but the Father."[46] And yet how can wisdom be ignorant of anything—that is, wisdom who made the worlds, who perfects them, who remodels them, who is the limit of all things that were made, who knows the things of God as the spirit of a man knows the things that are in him? For what can be more perfect than this knowledge? How, then, can you say

41 Baruch 3:35–37.   42 Heb. 7:25.   43 Rom. 8:26; I Tim. 2:5.
44 II Cor. 5:16; Heb. 4:15; I John 2:1; Christ's intercession is paralleled to that of delegates to the emperor, but equally contrasted; he is no mere suppliant.   45 Or [us].   46 Mark 13:32.

that all things before that hour he knows accurately, and all things that are to happen about the time of the end, but of the hour itself he is ignorant? For such a thing would be like a riddle; as if one were to say that he knew accurately all that was in front of the wall, but did not know the wall itself; or that, knowing the end of the day, he did not know the beginning of the night—where knowledge of the one necessarily brings in the other. Thus everyone must see that he knows as God, and knows not as man—if one may separate the visible from that which is discerned by thought alone. For the absolute and unconditioned use of the name "the Son" in this passage, without the addition of whose Son, gives us this thought, that we are to understand the ignorance in the most reverent sense, by attributing it to the manhood, and not to the Godhead.

16. If, then, this argument is sufficient, let us stop here, and not inquire further. But if not, our second argument is as follows: Just as we do in all other instances, so let us refer his knowledge of the greatest events, in honor of the Father, to the cause. And I think that anyone, even if he did not read it in the way that one of our own students did,[47] would soon perceive that not even the Son knows the day or hour otherwise than as the Father does. For what do we conclude from this? That since the Father knows, therefore also does the Son, as it is evident that this cannot be known or comprehended by any but the first nature. There remains for us to interpret the passage about his receiving commandment, and having kept His commandments and done always those things that please Him[48]; and further concerning his being made perfect, and his exaltation, and his learning obedience by the things which he suffered; and also his high priesthood, and his oblation, and his betrayal, and his prayer to Him that was able to save him from death, and his agony and bloody sweat and prayer,[49] and suchlike things; if it were not evident to everyone that such words are concerned, not with that nature which is unchangeable and above all capacity of suffering, but with the passible humanity. This, then, is the argument concerning these objections, so far as to be a sort of foundation and memorandum for the use of those who are better able to conduct the inquiry to a more complete working out. It may,

47 The interpretation of Basil, Epistle 236—the Son does not know these things as Son, but by the divine nature which he shares with the Father.
48 Cf. John 12:49; 15:10; 8:29.
49 Cf. Heb. 2:10, 17; 5:7, 8; 8:3; Gal. 2:20; Acts 2:33; Luke 22:44.

however, be worth-while, and will be consistent with what has been already said, instead of passing over without remark the actual titles of the Son (there are many of them, and they are concerned with many of his attributes), to set before you the meaning of each of them, and to point out the mystical meaning of the name.

17. We will begin thus: The Deity cannot be expressed in words. And this is proved to us, not only by argument, but by the wisest and most ancient of the Hebrews, so far as they have given us reason for conjecture. For they appropriated certain characters to the honor of the Deity, and would not even allow the name of anything inferior to God to be written with the same letters as that of God, because to their minds it was improper that the Deity should even to that extent admit any of his creatures to a share with himself.[50] How, then, could they have admitted that the invisible and separate nature can be explained by divisible words? For neither has anyone yet breathed the whole air, nor has any mind entirely comprehended, or speech exhaustively contained, the being of God. But we sketch him by his attributes, and so obtain a certain faint and feeble and partial idea concerning him, and our best theologian is he who has, not indeed discovered the whole, for our present chain does not allow of our seeing the whole, but conceived of him to a greater extent than another, and gathered in himself more of the likeness or adumbration of the truth, or whatever we may call it.

18. As far, then, as we can reach, "He who is" and "God" are the special names of his essence; and of these especially "He who is," not only because when he spake to Moses in the mount, and Moses asked what his name was, this was what he called himself, bidding him say to the people, "I am hath sent me," [51] but also because we find that this name is the more strictly appropriate. For the name *theos* [God], even if, as those who are skillful in these matters say, it were derived from *theein* [to run] or from *aithein* [to blaze], from continual motion, and because he consumes evil conditions of things (from which fact he is also called a consuming fire),[52] would still be one of the relative names, and not an absolute one; as again is the case with "Lord," which also is called a name of God. "I am the Lord thy God," he says, "that is my name"; and, "The

50 A confused impression, apparently, of the Jewish reluctance to pronounce the proper name of God.
51 Ex. 3:14.                     52 Deut. 4:24; Heb. 12:29.

Lord is his name." [53] But we are inquiring into a nature whose being is absolute and not [into being] bound up with something else. But being is in its proper sense peculiar to God, and belongs to him entirely, and is not limited or cut short by any before or after, for indeed in him there is no past or future.

19. Of the other titles, some are evidently names of his authority, others of his government of the world, and of this viewed under a twofold aspect: the one before, the other in, the incarnation. [54] For instance, the Almighty, the King of Glory, or of the Ages, or of the Powers, or of the Beloved, [55] or of Kings. Or again, the Lord of Sabaoth, that is, of hosts, or of powers, or of lords [56]; these are clearly titles belonging to his authority. But the God either of salvation or of vengeance, or of peace, or of righteousness [57]; or of Abraham, Isaac, and Jacob, and of all the spiritual Israel that sees God [58]—these belong to his government. For since we are governed by these three things, the fear of punishment, the hope of salvation and of glory besides, and the practice of the virtues by which these are attained, the name of the God of vengeance governs fear, and that of the God of salvation our hope, and that of the God of virtues our practice; that whoever attains to any of these may, as carrying God in himself, [59] press on yet more unto perfection, and to that affinity which arises out of virtues. Now these are names common to the Godhead, but the proper name of the unoriginate is "Father," and that of the unoriginately begotten is "Son," and that of the unbegottenly proceeding or going forth is "the Holy Ghost." Let us proceed, then, to the names of the Son, which were our starting point in this part of our argument.

20. In my opinion he is called Son because he is identical with the Father in essence; and not only for this reason, but also because he is of him. And he is called only-begotten, not because he is the only Son and of the Father alone, and only a Son, but also because the manner of his Sonship is peculiar

---

53 Ex. 20:2 and Isa. 42:8; Ex. 15:3.
54 Literally, "above the body" and "in body."
55 Ps. 24 (23):7; I Tim. 1:17; "the powers of the beloved" in LXX of Ps. 68 (67):12—several MSS. of Gregory omit "or."
56 I Tim. 6:15.
57 Ps. 68 (67):20; 94 (93):1; Rom. 15:33; Mal. 2:17; Ps. 4:1.
58 Ex. 3:6; Ps. 68 (67):8, 35; interpreted with reference to the meaning of Israel, Gen. 32:28, 30.
59 From the presence of God follows our sanctification; as Ignatius in the salutations of his Epistles calls himself *Theophoros*.

to himself and not shared by bodies. And [he is called] the
Word, because he is related to the Father as word to mind;
not only on account of his passionless generation, but also
because of the union, and of his declaratory function. Perhaps
too this relation might be compared to that between the definition and the thing defined since this also is called *logos*. For,
it says, he that has mental perception of the Son (for this is
the meaning of "hath seen") has also perceived the Father;
and the Son is a concise demonstration and easy setting forth
of the Father's nature. For everything that is begotten is a
silent word of him that begot it. And if anyone should say that
this name was given him because he exists in all things that are,
he would not be wrong. For what is there that consists but by
the word? [He is] also [called] Wisdom, as the knowledge of
things divine and human. For how is it possible that he who
made all things should be ignorant of the reasons of what he
has made? And Power, as the sustainer of all created things,
and the furnisher to them of power to keep themselves together.[60] And Truth,[51] as being in nature one and not many
(for truth is one and falsehood is manifold), and as the pure
seal of the Father and his most unerring impress. And the
Image,[62] as of one substance with him, and because he is of
the Father, and not the Father of him. For this is of the nature
of an image, to be the reproduction of its archetype, and of
that whose name it bears; only that there is more here. For
in ordinary language an image is a motionless representation
of that which has motion; but in this case it is the living
reproduction of the living one, and is more exactly like than
was Seth to Adam,[63] or any son to his father. For such is the
nature of simple existences that it is not correct to say of them
that they are like in one particular and unlike in another;
but they are a complete resemblance, and should rather be
called identical than like. Moreover [he is called] Light, as
being the brightness of souls cleansed by word and life. For if
ignorance and sin be darkness, knowledge and a godly life
will be light. And [he is called] Life because he is Light, and
is the constituting and creating power of every reasonable
soul.[64] For "in him we live, and move, and have our being,"
according to the double power of that breathing into us; for we
were all inspired by him with breath, and as many of us as

[60] John 14:9; Col. 1:17; I Cor. 1:24.          [61] John 14:6
[62] Heb. 1:3; II Cor. 4:4; Col. 1:15.           [63] Gen. 5:3.
[64] John 1:9; 11:25; 14:6.

were capable of it, and in so far as we open the mouth of our mind, with the Holy Ghost.[65] He is righteousness, because he distributes according to that which we deserve, and is a righteous arbiter both for those who are under the law and for those who are under grace, for soul and body, so that the former should rule, and the latter obey, and the higher have supremacy over the lower; that the worse may not rise in rebellion against the better. He is sanctification, as being purity, that the pure may be contained by purity. And redemption, because he sets us free who were held captive under sin, giving himself a ransom for us, the sacrifice to make expiation for the world. And resurrection, because he raises up from hence, and brings to life again, us who were slain by sin.[66]

21. These names, however, are still common to Him who is above us, and to Him who came for our sake. But others are peculiarly our own, and belong to that nature which he assumed. So he is called man, not only that through his body he may be apprehended by embodied creatures, whereas otherwise this would be impossible because of his incomprehensible nature; but also that by himself he may sanctify humanity, and be as it were a leaven to the whole lump; and by uniting to himself that which was condemned may release it from all condemnation, becoming for all men all things that we are, except sin—body, soul, mind, and all through which death reaches—and thus he became man, who is the combination of all these; God in visible form, because he retained that which is perceived by mind alone. He is son of man, both on account of Adam, and of the Virgin from whom he came: from the one as a forefather, from the other as his mother, both in accordance with the law of generation, and apart from it. He is Christ because of his Godhead. For this is the anointing of his manhood, and does not, as is the case with all other anointed ones, sanctify by its action, but by the presence in his fullness of the anointing one[67]; the effect of which is that that which anoints is called man, and makes that which is anointed God. He is the way, because he leads us through himself; the door, as letting us in; the shepherd, as making us dwell in a place of green pastures, and bringing us up by waters of rest, and leading

---

[65] Acts 17:28; "breath" and "spirit" are clearly cognate in Greek, *pnoē* and *pneuma*.
[66] I Cor. 1:30; Mark 10:45; John 11:25.
[67] Prophets, kings, and priests were anointed by divine power; the anointing of Christ was the personal union of God and man.

us there,[68] and protecting us from wild beasts, converting the erring, bringing back that which was lost, binding up that which was broken, guarding the strong, and bringing them together in the fold beyond,[69] with words of pastoral knowledge. The sheep, as the victim; the lamb, as being perfect[70]; the high priest, as the offerer; Melchizedek, as without mother in that nature which is above us, and without father in ours; and without genealogy above (for who, it says, shall declare his generation?)[71] and, moreover, as king of Salem, which means peace, and king of righteousness, and as receiving tithes from patriarchs, when they prevail over powers of evil.[72] They are the titles of the Son. Walk through them, those that are lofty in a godlike manner; those that belong to the body in a manner suitable to them; or rather, altogether in a godlike manner, that thou mayest become a god, ascending from below, for his sake who came down from on high for ours. In all and above all keep to this, and you shall never err, either in the loftier or the lowlier names; Jesus Christ is the same yesterday and today in the incarnation, and in the Spirit forever and ever.[73] Amen.

[68] John 14:6; 10:9, 11; Ps. 23 (22):2, 3.
[69] Ezek. 34:16 ("guard" instead of "destroy" as in LXX).
[70] Isa. 53:7; the lamb as the spotless victim (John 1:36; Heb. 9:14).
[71] Isa. 53:8.
[72] Heb. 7:1–10; 8:1; Abraham's victory over the kings is also taken as a type.
[73] Heb. 13:8.

# THE TEXT: THE FIFTH THEOLOGICAL
## ORATION—ON THE SPIRIT

1. Such, then, is the account of the Son, and in this manner he has escaped those who would stone him, passing through the midst of them.[1] For the Word is not stoned, but casts stones when he pleases; and uses a sling against wild beasts—that is, words—approaching the Mount in an unholy way.[2] But, they go on, what have you to say about the Holy Ghost? From whence are you bringing in upon us this strange God, of whom Scripture is silent? And even they who keep within bounds as to the Son speak thus. And just as we find in the case of roads and rivers, that they split off from one another and join again, so it happens also in this case, through the superabundance of impiety, that people who differ in all other respects have here some points of agreement, so that you never can tell for certain either where they are of one mind or where they are in conflict.

2. Now the subject of the Holy Spirit presents a special difficulty, not only because when these men have become weary in their disputations concerning the Son they struggle with greater heat against the Spirit (for it seems to be absolutely necessary for them to have some object on which to give expression to their impiety, or life would appear to them no longer worth living), but further because we ourselves also, being worn out by the multitude of their questions, are in something of the same condition with men who have lost their appetite; who, having taken a dislike to some particular kind of food, shrink from all food; so we in like manner have an aversion from all discussions. Yet may the Spirit grant it to us, and then the discourse will proceed, and God will be glorified. Well, then, we will leave to others who have worked upon this

[1] John 8:59; Luke 4:30.    [2] Ex. 19:13; cf. Oration ii, 2.

subject for us as well as for themselves, as we have worked upon it for them, the task of examining carefully and distinguishing in how many senses the word "Spirit" or the word "holy" is used and understood in Holy Scripture, with the evidence suitable to such an inquiry; and of showing how, besides these, the combination of the two words—I mean, "Holy Spirit"—is used in a peculiar sense; but we will apply ourselves to the remainder of the subject.

3. They, then, who are angry with us on the ground that we are bringing in a strange or interpolated God, viz., the Holy Ghost, and who fight so very hard for the letter, should know that they are afraid where no fear is; and I would have them clearly understand that their love for the letter is but a cloak for their impiety, as shall be shown later on, when we refute their objections to the utmost of our power. But we have so much confidence in the deity of the Spirit whom we adore, that we will begin our teaching concerning his Godhead by fitting to him the names which belong to the Trinity, even though some persons may think us too bold. The Father was "the true Light, which lighteth every man coming into the world." The Son was "the true Light, which lighteth every man coming into the world." The other Comforter was "the true Light, which lighteth every man coming into the world." [3] Was and was and was, but was one thing. Light thrice repeated; but one light and one God. This was what David represented to himself long before when he said, "In thy light shall we see light." [4] And now we have both seen and proclaim concisely and simply the doctrine of God the Trinity, comprehending out of light [the Father], light [the Son], in light [the Spirit]. He that rejects it, let him reject it; and he that does iniquity, let him do iniquity; we proclaim that which we have understood. We will get us up into a high mountain, and will shout, if we be not heard, below; we will exalt the Spirit; we will not be afraid; or if we are afraid, it shall be of keeping silence, not of proclaiming.

4. If ever there was a time when the Father was not, then there was a time when the Son was not. If ever there was a time when the Son was not, then there was a time when the Spirit was not. If the one was from the beginning, then the three were so too. If you throw down the one, I am bold to assert that you do not set up the other two. For what profit is there in an imperfect Godhead? Or rather, what Godhead can

[3] John 1:9; 14:16.          [4] Ps. 36 (35):9.

there be if it is not perfect? And how can that be perfect which lacks something of perfection? And surely there is something lacking if it has not the Holy, and how would it have this if it were without the Spirit? For either holiness is something different from him, and if so let someone tell me what it is conceived to be; or if it is the same, how is it not from the beginning, as if it were better for God to be at one time imperfect and apart from the Spirit? If he is not from the beginning, he is in the same rank with myself, even though a little before me; for we are both parted from Godhead by time. If he is in the same rank with myself, how can he make me God, or join me with Godhead?

5. Or rather, let me reason with you about him from a somewhat earlier point, for we have already discussed the Trinity. The Sadducees altogether denied the existence of the Holy Spirit, just as they did that of angels and the resurrection,[5] rejecting, I know not upon what ground, the important testimonies concerning him in the Old Testament. And of the Greeks, those who are more inclined to speak of God, and who approach nearest to us, have formed some conception of him, as it seems to me, though they have differed as to his name, and have addressed him as the mind of the world, or the external mind,[6] and the like. But of the wise men among ourselves, some have conceived of him as an activity, some as a creature, some as God; and some have been uncertain which to call him, out of reverence for Scripture, they say, as though it did not make the matter clear either way. And therefore they neither worship him nor treat him with dishonor, but take up a neutral position, or rather a very miserable one, with respect to him. And of those who consider him to be God, some are orthodox in mind only, while others venture to be so with the lips also. And I have heard of some who are even more clever, and measure deity; and these agree with us that there are three conceptions; but they have separated these from one another so completely as to make one of them infinite both in essence and power, and the second in power but not in essence, and the third circumscribed in both; thus imitating in another way those who call them the creator, the co-operator, and the minister, and consider that the same order and

---

[5] Acts 23:8, assuming the "spirit" there referred to to be the Holy Spirit.
[6] Platonic ideas of the world-soul; the second phrase is Aristotle's (*De generatione animalium* ii, 3, 736b), with reference to the entrance of the divine rational soul "from outside" into the embryo.

dignity which belongs to these names is also a sequence in the facts.

6. But we cannot enter into any discussion with those who do not even believe in his existence, nor with the Greek babblers (for we would not be enriched in our argument with the oil of sinners).[7] With the others, however, we will argue thus: The Holy Ghost must certainly be conceived of either as in the category of the self-existent or as in that of the things which are contemplated in another; of which classes those who are skilled in such matters call the one substance and the other accident. Now if he were an accident, he would be an activity of God, for what else, or of whom else, could he be, for surely this is what most avoids composition?[8] And if he is an activity, he will be effected, but will not effect and will cease to exist as soon as he has been effected, for this is the nature of an activity. How is it, then, that he acts and says such and such things, and defines, and is grieved, and is angered,[9] and has all the qualities which belong clearly to one that moves, and not to movement? But if he is a substance and not an attribute of substance, he will be conceived of either as a creature of God or as God. For anything between these two, whether having nothing in common with either or a compound of both, not even they who invented the goat-stag could imagine. Now, if he is a creature, how do we believe in him, how are we made perfect in him? For it is not the same thing to believe in a thing and to believe about it. The one belongs to deity, the other to —any thing. But if he is God, then he is neither a creature, nor a thing made, nor a fellow servant, nor any of these lowly appellations.

7. There—the word is with you. Let the slings be let go; let the syllogism be woven. Either he is altogether unbegotten or else he is begotten. If he is unbegotten, there are two un-originates. If he is begotten, you must make a further sub-division. He is so either by the Father or by the Son. And if by the Father, there are two Sons, and they are brothers. And you may make them twins if you like, or the one older and the other younger, since you are so very fond of the bodily conceptions. But if by the Son, then such a one will say, we get a glimpse of a grandson God, than which nothing could be more absurd.

---

7 Ps. 141 (140):5; Gregory will not add apparent force to his discourse by attacking these non-Christian ideas, as mere men of straw.

8 I.e., describes the Spirit most simply and clearly.

9 Acts 13:2; Eph. 4:30; Isa. 63:10.

[Let them think] such things, who are wise to do evil, but will not write what is good.[10] For my part, however, if I saw the necessity of the distinction, I should have acknowledged the facts without fear of the names. For it does not follow that because the Son is the Son in some higher relation (inasmuch as we could not in any other way than this point out that he is of God and consubstantial), it would also be necessary to think that all the names of this lower world and of our kindred should be transferred to the Godhead. Or maybe you would consider our God to be a male, according to the same arguments, because he is called God and Father, and that deity is feminine, from the gender of the word, and Spirit neuter, because it has nothing to do with generation; but if you would be silly enough to say, with the old myths and fables, that God begot the Son by a marriage with his own will, we should be introduced to the hermaphrodite god of Marcion and Valentinus who imagined these newfangled Aeons.[11]

8. But since we do not admit your first division, which declares that there is no mean between begotten and unbegotten, at once, along with your magnificent division, away go your brothers and your grandsons, as when the first link of an intricate chain is broken they are broken with it, and disappear from your system of divinity. For, tell me, what position will you assign to that which proceeds, which has started up between the two terms of your division, and is introduced by a better theologian than you, our Saviour himself? Or perhaps you have taken that word out of your Gospels for the sake of your third Testament, "the Holy Ghost, which proceedeth from the Father"[12]; who, inasmuch as he proceeds from that source, is no creature; and inasmuch as he is between the unbegotten and the begotten is God. And thus escaping the toils of your syllogisms, he has manifested himself as God, stronger than your divisions. What, then, is procession? Do you tell me what is the unbegottenness of the Father, and I will explain to you the physiology of the generation of the Son and the procession of the Spirit, and we shall both of us be frenzy-stricken for prying into the mystery of God. And who are we to do these

10 Jer. 4:22; sentence missing in Post-Nicene Fathers; "write" for "do," perhaps because Gregory is thinking of the numerous writings of his opponents (cf. Oration iii, 1).

11 Cf. Valentinus' generations of Aeons as described by Irenaeus; Marcion's system was different, and the name may be a slip for Marcus, to whom it would better apply (cf. Irenaeus, *Adversus haereses*, I. 11).

12 John 15:26.

things, we who cannot even see what lies at our feet, or number the sand of the sea, or the drops of rain, or the days of eternity, much less enter into the depths of God,[13] and supply an account of that nature which is so unspeakable and transcending all words?

9. What, then, say they, is there lacking to the Spirit which prevents his being a Son, for if there were not something lacking he would be a Son? We assert that there is nothing lacking— for God has no deficiency. But the difference of manifestation, if I may so express myself, or rather of their mutual relations one to another, has caused the difference of their names. For indeed it is not some deficiency in the Son which prevents his being Father (for Sonship is not a deficiency), and yet he is not Father. According to this line of argument there must be some deficiency in the Father, in respect of his not being Son. For the Father is not Son, and yet this is not due to either deficiency or subjection of essence; but the very fact of being unbegotten or begotten, or proceeding, has given the name of Father to the first, of the Son to the second, and to the third, him of whom we are speaking, of the Holy Ghost, that the distinction of the three persons may be preserved in the one nature and dignity of the Godhead. For neither is the Son Father, for the Father is one, but he is what the Father is; nor is the Spirit Son because he is of God, for the only-begotten is one, but he is what the Son is. The three are one in Godhead, and the one three in properties; so that neither is the unity a Sabellian one, nor does the Trinity countenance the present evil distinction.

10. What, then? Is the Spirit God? Most certainly. Well, then, is he consubstantial? Yes, if he is God. Grant me, says my opponent, that there spring from the same source one who is a Son and one who is not a Son, and these of one substance with the source, and I admit a God and a God. Nay, if you will grant me that there is another God and another nature of God, I will give you the same Trinity with the same name and facts. But since God is one and the supreme nature is one, how can I present to you the likeness? Or will you seek it again in lower regions and in your own surroundings? It is very shameful, and not only shameful but very foolish, to take from things below a guess at things above, and from a fluctuating nature at the things that are unchanging, and, as Isaiah says to seek the living among the dead.[14] But yet I will try, for your sake, to give you some assistance for your argument, even from

13 Ecclesiasticus 1:2; I Cor. 2:10.    14 Isa. 8:19; cf. Luke 24:5.

that source. I think I will pass over other points, though I might bring forward many from animal history, some generally known, others known only to a few, of what nature has contrived with wonderful art in connection with the generation of animals. For not only are likes said to beget likes, and things diverse to beget things diverse, but also likes to be begotten by things diverse, and things diverse by likes. And if we may believe the story, there is yet another mode of generation, when an animal is self-consumed and self-begotten. There are also creatures which depart in some sort from their true natures, and undergo change and transformation from one creature into another, by a magnificence of nature. And indeed sometimes in the same species part may be generated and part not, and yet all of one substance; which is more like our present subject. I will just mention one fact of our own nature which everyone knows, and then I will pass on to another part of the subject.

11. What was Adam? A creature of God. What, then, was Eve? A fragment of the creature. And what was Seth? The begotten of both. Does it, then, seem to you that creature and fragment and begotten are the same thing? Of course it does not. But were not these persons consubstantial? Of course they were. Well, then, here it is an acknowledged fact that different persons may have the same substance. I say this, not that I would attribute creation or fraction or any property of body to the Godhead (let none of your contenders for a word be down upon me again), but that I may contemplate in these, as on a stage, things which are objects of thought alone. For it is not possible to trace out any image exactly to the whole extent of the truth. But, they say, what is the meaning of all this? For is not the one an offspring, and the other a something else of the one? Did not both Eve and Seth come from the one Adam? And were they both begotten by him? No; but the one was a fragment of him, and the other was begotten by him. And yet the two were one and the same thing; both were human beings; no one will deny that. Will you, then, give up your contention against the Spirit, that he must either be altogether begotten, or else cannot be consubstantial, or be God; and admit from human examples the possibility of our position? I think it will be well for you, unless you are determined to be very quarrelsome, and to fight against what is proved to demonstration.

12. But, he says, who in ancient or modern times ever

worshiped the Spirit? Who ever prayed to him? Where is it written that we ought to worship him, or to pray to him, and whence have you derived this tenet of yours? We will give the more perfect reason hereafter, when we discuss the question of the unwritten[15]; for the present it will suffice to say that it is the Spirit in whom we worship, and in whom we pray. For Scripture says, "God is a Spirit, and they that worship him must worship him in spirit and in truth." And again, "We know not what we should pray for as we ought; but the Spirit itself maketh intercession for us with groanings which cannot be uttered"; and, "I will pray with the spirit, and I will pray with the understanding also"[16]—that is, in the mind and in the Spirit. Therefore to adore or to pray to the Spirit seems to me to be simply himself offering prayer or adoration to himself. And what godly or learned man would disapprove of this, because in fact the adoration of one is the adoration of the three, because of the equality of honor and deity between the three? So I will not be frightened by the argument that all things are said to have been made by the Son; as if the Holy Spirit also were one of these things. For it says all things that were made,[17] and not simply all things. For the Father was not, nor were any of the things that were not made. Prove that he was made, and then give him to the Son, and number him among the creatures; but until you can prove this you will gain nothing for your impiety from this comprehensive phrase. For if he was made, it was certainly through Christ; I myself would not deny that. But if he was not made, how can he be either one of the "all" or through Christ? Cease, then, to dishonor the Father in your opposition to the only-begotten (for it is no real honor, by presenting to him a creature to rob him of what is more valuable, a Son), and to dishonor the Son in your opposition to the Spirit. For he is not the maker of a fellow servant, but he is glorified with one of coequal honor. Rank no part of the Trinity with yourself, lest you fall away from the Trinity; cut not off from either the one and equally august nature; because if you overthrow any of the three you will have overthrown the whole. Better to take a meager view of the unity than to venture on a complete impiety.

13. Our argument has now come to its principal point; and I am grieved that a problem that was long dead, and that had

---

[15] This promise is fulfilled in the discussion of the "unwritten," i.e., extra-Biblical, experience of the Spirit, Chs. 26–28.
[16] John 4:24; Rom. 8:26; I Cor. 14:15.          [17] John 1:3.

given way to faith, is now stirred up afresh; yet it is necessary to stand against these praters, and not to let judgment go by default, when we have the Word on our side, and are pleading the cause of the Spirit. If, say they, there is God and God and God, how is it that there are not three Gods, or how is it that what is glorified is not a plurality of principles? Who is it who say this? Those who have reached a more complete ungodliness, or even those who have taken the secondary part; I mean, who are moderate in a sense in respect of the Son. For my argument is partly against both in common, partly against these latter in particular. What I have to say in answer to these is as follows: What right have you who worship the Son, even though you have revolted from the Spirit, to call us Tritheists? Are not you Ditheists? For if you deny also the worship of the only-begotten, you have clearly ranged yourself among our adversaries. And why should we deal kindly with you as not quite dead? But if you do worship him, and are so far in the way of salvation, we will ask you what reasons you have to give for your Ditheism, if you are charged with it? If there is in you a word of wisdom, answer, and open to us also a way to an answer. For the very same reason with which you will repel a charge of Ditheism will prove sufficient for us against one of Tritheism. And thus we shall win the day by making use of you, our accusers, as our advocates, than which nothing can be more generous.

14. What is our quarrel and dispute with both? To us there is one God, for the Godhead is one, and all that proceeds from him is referred to one, though we believe in three Persons. For one is not more and another less God; nor is one before and another after; nor are they divided in will or parted in power; nor can you find here any of the qualities of divisible things; but the Godhead is, to speak concisely, undivided in separate Persons; and there is one mingling of lights, as it were of three suns joined to each other. When, then, we look at the Godhead, or the first cause, or the monarchia, that which we conceive is one; but when we look at the Persons in whom the Godhead dwells, and at those who timelessly and with equal glory have their being from the first cause, there are three whom we worship.

15. What of that, they will say perhaps? Do not the Greeks also believe in one Godhead, as their more advanced philosophers declare? And with us humanity is one, namely, the entire race; but yet they have many gods, not one, just as there are many men. But in this case the common nature has a

unity which is only conceivable in thought; and the individuals are parted from one another very far indeed, both by time and by dispositions, and by power. For we are not only compound beings, but also contrasted beings, both with one another and with ourselves; nor do we remain entirely the same for a single day, to say nothing of a whole lifetime, but both in body and in soul are in a perpetual state of flow and change. And perhaps the same may be said of the angels and the whole of that superior nature which is second to the Trinity alone; although they are simple in some measure and more fixed in good, owing to their nearness to the highest good.

16. Nor do those whom the Greeks worship as gods, and (to use their own expression) daemons, need us in any respect for their accusers, but are convicted upon the testimony of their own theologians, some as subject to passion, some as given to faction, and full of innumerable evils and changes, and in a state of opposition, not only to one another, but even to their first causes, whom they call Oceani and Tethyes and Phanetes,[18] and by several other names; and last of all a certain god[19] who hated his children through his lust of rule, and swallowed up all the rest through his greediness that he might become the father of all men and gods whom he miserably devoured, and then vomited forth again. And if these are but myths and fables, as they say in order to escape the shamefulness of the story, what will they say in reference to the dictum that all things are divided into three parts,[20] and that each god presides over a different part of the universe, having a distinct province as well as a distinct rank? But our faith is not like this, nor is this the portion of Jacob,[21] says my theologian. But each of these Persons possesses unity, not less with that which is united to it than with itself, by reason of the identity of essence and power. And this is the account of the unity, so far as we have apprehended it. If, then, this account is the true one, let us thank God for the glimpse he has granted us; if it is not, let us seek for a better.

17. As for the arguments with which you would overthrow the union which we support, I know not whether we should say you are jesting or in earnest. For what is this argument? Things of one essence, you say, are counted together, and by this "counted together" you mean that they are collected into

18 The "gods before the gods," Oceanus and Tethys in Homeric (*Iliad* 14: 201), Phanetes in Orphic, mythology.
19 Cronus (Saturn).          20 *Iliad* 15:189.          21 Jer. 10:16.

one number. But things which are not of one essence are not thus counted . . . so that you cannot avoid speaking of three gods, according to this account, while we do not run any risk at all of it, inasmuch as we assert that they are not consubstantial. And so by a single word you have freed yourselves from trouble, and you have gained a pernicious victory, for in fact you have done something like what men do when they hang themselves for fear of death. For to save yourselves trouble in your championship of the monarchia you have denied the Godhead, and abandoned the question to your opponents. But for my part, even if labor should be necessary, I will not abandon the object of my adoration. And yet on this point I cannot see where the difficulty is.

18. You say things of one essence are counted together, but those which are not consubstantial are reckoned one by one. Where did you get this from? From what teachers of dogma or mythology? Do you not know that every number expresses the quantity of what is included under it, and not the nature of the things? But I am so old-fashioned—or perhaps I should say so unlearned—as to use the word "three" of that number of things, even if they are of a different nature, and to use one and one and one in a different way of so many units, even if they are united in essence, looking not so much at the things themselves as at the quantity of the things in respect of which the enumeration is made. But since you hold so very close to the letter (although you are contending against the letter), pray take your demonstrations from this source. There are in the book of Proverbs three things which go well: a lion, a goat, and a cock; and to these is added a fourth: a king making a speech before the people,[22] to pass over the other sets of four which are there counted up, although things of various natures. And I find in Moses two cherubim counted singly.[23] But now, in your technology, could either the former things be called three, when they differ so greatly in their nature, or the latter be treated as units, when they are so closely connected and of one nature? For if I were to speak of God and Mammon as two masters,[24] reckoned under one head, when they are so very different from each other, I should probably be still more laughed at for such a connumeration.

19. But to my mind, he says,[25] those things are said to be

22 Prov. 30:29.          23 Ex. 25:19; 37:8.          24 Matt. 6:24.
25 I.e., Gregory's Macedonian opponent, elsewhere addressed in the second person.

connumerated and of the same essence of which the names also correspond, as three men, or three gods, but not three this and that. What does this concession amount to? It is suitable to one laying down the law as to names, not to one who is asserting the truth. For I also will assert that Peter and James and John are not three or consubstantial, so long as I cannot say three Peters, or three Jameses, or three Johns; for what you have reserved for common names we demand also for proper names, in accordance with your arrangement; or else you will be unfair in not conceding to others what you assume for yourself. What about John, then, when in his Catholic Epistle he says that there are three that bear witness, the Spirit and the water and the blood?[26] Do you think he is talking nonsense? First, because he has ventured to reckon under one numeral things which are not consubstantial, though you say this ought to be done only in the case of things which are consubstantial. For who would assert that these are consubstantial? Secondly, because he has not been consistent in the way he has happened upon his terms; for after using three in the masculine gender he adds three words which are neuter, contrary to the definitions and laws which you and your grammarians have laid down. For what is the difference between putting a masculine three first, and then adding one and one and one in the neuter, or after a masculine one and one and one to use the three not in the masculine but in the neuter, which you yourself disclaim in the case of deity? What have you to say about the crab, which may mean either an animal or an instrument or a constellation? And what about the dog, now terrestrial, now aquatic, now celestial? Do you not see that three crabs or dogs are spoken of? Why, of course it is so. Well, then, are they therefore of one substance? None but a fool would say that. So you see how completely your argument from connumeration has broken down, and is refuted by all these instances. For if things that are of one substance are not always counted under one numeral, and things not of one substance are thus counted, and the pronunciation of the name once for all is used in both cases, what advantage do you gain towards your doctrine?

20. I will look also at this further point, which is not without its bearing on the subject. One and one added together make two; and two resolved again becomes one and one, as is perfectly evident. If, however, elements which are added together must, as your theory requires, be consubstantial, and

[26] I John 5:8.

those which are separate be heterogeneous, then it will follow that the same things must be both consubstantial and heterogeneous. No: I laugh at your counting before and your counting after, of which you are so proud, as if the facts themselves depended upon the order of their names. If this were so, according to the same law, since the same things are in consequence of the equality of their nature counted in Holy Scripture, sometimes in an earlier, sometimes in a later, place,[27] what prevents them from being at once more honorable and less honorable than themselves? I say the same of the names "God" and "Lord," and of the prepositions "of whom," and "by whom," and "in whom,"[28] by which you describe the Deity according to the rules of art for us, attributing the first to the Father, the second to the Son, and the third to the Holy Ghost. For what would you have done if each of these expressions were constantly allotted to each Person, when, the fact being that they are used of all the Persons, as is evident to those who have studied the question, you even so make them the ground of such inequality both of nature and dignity? This is sufficient for all who are not altogether wanting in sense. But since it is a matter of difficulty for you, after you have once made an assault upon the Spirit, to check your rush, and not rather like a furious boar to push your quarrel to the bitter end and to thrust yourself upon the knife until you have received the whole wound in your own breast, let us go on to see what further argument remains to you.

21. Over and over again you turn upon us the silence of Scripture. But that it is not a strange doctrine, nor an afterthought, but acknowledged and plainly set forth both by the ancients and many of our own day, is already demonstrated by many persons who have treated of this subject, and who have handled the Holy Scriptures, not with indifference or as a mere pastime, but have gone beneath the letter and looked into the inner meaning, and have been deemed worthy to see the hidden beauty, and have been irradiated by the light of knowledge. We, however, in our turn will briefly prove it as far as may be, in order not to seem to be overcurious or improperly ambitious, building on another's foundation. But since the fact that Scripture does not very clearly or very often write him God in express words, as it does first the Father and afterwards the Son, becomes to you an occasion of blasphemy and of this excessive wordiness and impiety, we will release you from this

[27] E.g., II Cor. 13:14.            [28] Cf. Rom. 11:36.

inconvenience by a short discussion of things and names, and especially of their use in Holy Scripture.

22. Some things have no existence, but are spoken of; others which do exist are not spoken of; some neither exist nor are spoken of; and some both exist and are spoken of. Do you ask me for proof of this? I am ready to give it. According to Scripture, God sleeps and is awake, is angry, walks, has the cherubim for his throne.[29] And yet when did he become liable to passion, and have you ever heard that God has a body? This, then, is, though not really fact, a figure of speech. For we have given names according to our own comprehension from our own attributes to those of God. His remaining silent apart from us, and as it were not caring for us, for reasons known to himself, is what we call his sleeping; for our own sleep is such a state of inactivity. And again, his sudden turning to do us good is the waking up; for waking is the dissolution of sleep, as visitation is of turning away. And when he punishes, we say he is angry; for so it is with us—punishment is the result of anger. And his working, now here now there, we call walking; for walking is change from one place to another. His resting among the holy hosts, and as it were loving to dwell among them, is his sitting and being enthroned; this, too, from ourselves, for God rests nowhere as he does upon the saints. His swiftness of moving is called flying, and his watchful care is called his face, and his giving and bestowing is his hand; and, in a word, every other of the powers or activities of God has depicted for us some other corporeal one.

23. Again, where do you get your "unbegotten" and "unoriginate," those two citadels of your position, or we our "immortal"? Show me these in so many words, or we shall either set them aside or erase them as not contained in Scripture; and you are slain by your own principle, the names you rely on being overthrown, and therewith the wall of refuge in which you trusted. Is it not evident that they are due to passages which imply them, though the words do not actually occur? What are these passages?—"I am the first, and I am the last," and "Before me there was no God, neither shall there be after me."[30] For all that depends on that "am" makes for my side, for it has neither beginning nor ending. When you accept this, that nothing is before him, and that he has not an older cause, you have implicitly given him the titles

29 Ps. 44 (43):23; Jer. 31:28; Gen. 3:8; Ps. 80 (79):1; 18 (17):10.
30 Isa. 44:6; 43:10.

"unbegotten" and "unoriginate." And to say that he has no end of being is to call him "immortal" and "indestructible." The first pairs, then, that I referred to are accounted for thus. But what are the things which neither exist in fact nor are said? That God is evil; that a sphere is square; that the past is present; that man is not a compound being. Have you ever known a man of such stupidity as to venture either to think or to assert any such thing? It remains to show what are the things which exist, both in fact and in language. God, man, angel, judgment, vanity (viz., such arguments as yours), and the subversion of faith and emptying of the mystery.

24. Since, then, there is so much difference in terms and things, why are you such a slave to the letter, and a partisan of the Jewish wisdom, and a follower of syllables at the expense of facts? But if, when you said twice five or twice seven, I concluded from your words that you meant ten or fourteen; or if, when you spoke of a rational and mortal animal, that you meant man, should you think me to be talking nonsense? Surely not, because I should be merely repeating your own meaning; for words do not belong more to the speaker of them than to him who called them forth. As, then, in this case, I should have been looking, not so much at the terms used as at the thoughts they were meant to convey; so neither, if I found something else either not at all or not clearly expressed in the words of Scripture to be included in the meaning, should I avoid giving it utterance, out of fear of your sophistical trick about terms. In this way, then, we shall hold our own against the semiorthodox—among whom I may not count you. For since you deny the titles of the Son, which are so many and so clear, it is quite evident that even if you learned a great many more and clearer ones, you would not be moved to reverence. But now I will take up the argument again a little way further back, and show you, though you are so clever, the reason for this entire system of secrecy.

25. There have been in the whole period of the duration of the world two conspicuous changes of men's lives, which are also called two Testaments, or, on account of the wide fame of the matter, two earthquakes; the one from idols to the law, the other from the law to the gospel. And we are taught in the gospel of a third earthquake, namely, from this earth to that which cannot be shaken or moved.[31] Now the two Testaments are alike in this respect, that the change was not made

31 Heb. 12:26.

on a sudden, nor at the first movement of the endeavor. Why not (for this is a point on which we must have information)? That no violence might be done to us, but that we might be moved by persuasion. For nothing that is involuntary is durable; like streams or trees which are kept back by force. But that which is voluntary is more durable and safe. The former is due to one who uses force, the latter is ours; the one is due to the gentleness of God, the other to a tyrannical authority. Wherefore God did not think it behooved him to benefit the unwilling, but to do good to the willing. And therefore, like a tutor or physician, he partly removes and partly condones ancestral habits, conceding some little of what tended to pleasure, just as medical men do with their patients, that their medicine may be taken, being artfully blended with what is nice. For it is no very easy matter to change from those habits which custom and use have made honorable. For instance, the first cut off the idol, but left the sacrifices; the second, while it destroyed the sacrifices did not forbid circumcision. Then, when once men had submitted to the curtailment, they also yielded that which had been conceded to them —in the first instance, the sacrifices; in the second, circumcision—and became instead of Gentiles, Jews, and instead of Jews, Christians, being beguiled into the gospel by gradual changes. Paul is a proof of this; for having at one time administered circumcision, and submitted to legal purification, he advanced till he could say, "And I, brethren, if I yet preach circumcision, why do I yet suffer persecution?"[32] His former conduct belonged to the [temporary] dispensation, his latter to maturity.

26. To this I may compare the case of theology except that it proceeds the reverse way. For in the case by which I have illustrated it the change is made by successive subtractions; whereas here perfection is reached by additions. For the matter stands thus: The Old Testament proclaimed the Father openly, and the Son more obscurely. The New manifested the Son, and suggested the deity of the Spirit. Now the Spirit himself dwells among us, and supplies us with a clearer demonstration of himself. For it was not safe, when the Godhead of the Father was not yet acknowledged, plainly to proclaim the Son; nor when that of the Son was not yet received, to burden us further (if I may use so bold an expression) with the Holy Ghost; lest perhaps people might, like men loaded with food beyond their strength, and presenting eyes as yet too weak to bear it to the

[32] Acts 16:3; 21:26; Gal. 5:11.

sun's light, risk the loss even of that which was within the reach
of their powers; but that by gradual additions, and, as David
says, goings up, and advances and progress from glory to
glory,[33] the light of the Trinity might shine upon the more
illuminated. For this reason it was, I think, that he gradually
came to dwell in the disciples, measuring himself out to them
according to their capacity to receive him, at the beginning
of the gospel, after the Passion, after the ascension, making
perfect their powers, being breathed upon them, and appearing
in fiery tongues. And indeed it is by little and little that he is
declared by Jesus, as you will learn for yourself if you will read
more carefully. "I will ask the Father," he says, "and he will
send you another Comforter, even the Spirit of truth." This he
said that he might not seem to be a rival God, or to make his
discourses to them by another authority. Again, "He shall send
him," but it is "in my name." He leaves out the "I will ask,"
but he keeps the "shall send," then again, "I will send"—his
own dignity. Then "shall come"—the authority of the Spirit.[34]

27. You see lights breaking upon us, gradually; and the order
of theology, which it is better for us to keep, neither proclaiming
things too suddenly nor yet keeping them hidden to the end.
For the former course would be unscientific, the latter atheisti-
cal; and the former would be calculated to startle outsiders,
the latter to alienate our own people. I will add another point
to what I have said—one which may readily have come into
the mind of some others, but which I think a fruit of my own
thought. Our Saviour had some things which, he said, could
not be borne at that time by his disciples (though they were
filled with many teachings), perhaps for the reasons I have
mentioned; and therefore they were hidden. And again he
said that all things should be taught us by the Spirit when he
should come to dwell amongst us.[35] Of these things one, I take
it, was the deity of the Spirit himself, made clear later on, when
such knowledge should be seasonable and capable of being
received after our Saviour's restoration, when it would no
longer be received with incredulity because of its marvelous
character. For what greater thing than this did either he
promise, or the Spirit teach—if indeed anything is to be considered great and worthy of the majesty of God, which was
either promised or taught.'

28. This, then, is my position with regard to these things,

33 Ps. 84 (83):7; cf. II Cor. 3:18.
34 John 14:16, 26; 15:26; 16:7.     35 John 14:12, 26.

and I hope it may be always my position, and that of who-soever is dear to me: to worship God the Father, God the Son, and God the Holy Ghost, three persons, one Godhead, un-divided in honor and glory and substance and kingdom,[36] as one of our own inspired philosophers not long departed showed. Let him not see the rising of the morning star,[37] as Scripture says, nor the glory of its brightness, who is otherwise minded, or who follows the temper of the times, at one time being of one mind and of another at another time, and thinking un-soundly in the highest matters. For if He is not to be worshiped, how can he deify me by baptism? but if he is to be worshiped, surely he is an object of adoration, and, if an object of adora-tion, he must be God; the one is linked to the other, a truly golden and saving chain. And indeed from the Spirit comes our new birth, and from the new birth our new creation, and from the new creation our deeper knowledge of the dignity of Him from whom it is derived.

29. This, then, is what may be said by one who admits the silence of Scripture. But now the swarm of testimonies shall burst upon you from which the deity of the Holy Ghost shall be shown to all who are not excessively stupid, or else altogether enemies to the Spirit, to be most clearly recognized in Scripture. Look at these facts: Christ is born; the Spirit is his forerunner. He is baptized; the Spirit bears witness. He is tempted; the Spirit leads him up. He works miracles; the Spirit accompanies them.[38] He ascends; the Spirit takes his place.[39] What great things are there in the idea of God which are not in his power? What titles which belong to God are not applied to him, except only unbegotten and begotten? For it was needful that the dis-tinctive properties of the Father and the Son should remain peculiar to them, lest there should be confusion in the Godhead which brings all things, even disorder itself, into due arrange-ment and good order. Indeed I tremble when I think of the abundance of the titles, and how many names they outrage who fall foul of the Spirit. He is called "the Spirit of God," "the Spirit of Christ," "the mind of Christ," "the Spirit of the Lord," and himself the Lord, "the Spirit of adoption," "of truth," "of liberty"[40]; the Spirit of wisdom, of understanding,

---

[36] Basil, in his treatise On the Holy Spirit.    [37] Job 3:9.
[38] Luke 1:35; Matt. 1:20; John 1:32, 33; Matt. 4:1; Luke 4:1, 14; Matt. 12:28.    [39] Acts 1:8, 9.
[40] Cf. I Cor. 2:11, 16; Rom. 8:9; II Cor. 3:17; Rom. 8:15; John 14:17; 15:26; 16:13.

of counsel, of might, of knowledge, of godliness, of the fear of God.[41] For he is the maker of all these, filling all with his essence, containing all things, filling the world in his essence,[42] yet incapable of being comprehended in his power by the world; good, upright, princely, by nature not by adoption[43]; sanctifying, not sanctified; measuring, not measured; shared, not sharing; filling, not filled; containing, not contained[44]; inherited, glorified, reckoned with the Father and the Son; held out as a threat; the finger of God; fire like God[45]; to manifest, as I take it, his consubstantiality; the creator-spirit, who by baptism and by resurrection creates anew[46]; the Spirit that knows all things, that teaches, that blows where and to what extent he lists[47]; that guides, talks, sends forth, separates, is angry or tempted[48]; that reveals, illumines, quickens, or rather is the very light and life[49]; that makes temples, that deifies; that perfects so as even to anticipate baptism, yet after baptism to be sought as a separate gift[50]; that does all things that God does: divided into fiery tongues; dividing gifts; making apostles, prophets, evangelists, pastors, and teachers[51]; understanding manifold, clear, piercing, undefiled, unhindered, which is the same thing as most wise and varied in his actions; and making all things clear and plain; and of independent power, unchangeable, almighty, all-seeing, penetrating all spirits that are intelligent, pure, most subtle [the angel hosts I think][52]; and also all prophetic spirits and apostolic in the same manner and not in the same places, for they lived in different places; thus showing that he is uncircumscript.

30. They who say and teach these things, and moreover call him another Paraclete in the sense of another God, who know that blasphemy against him alone cannot be forgiven, and who branded with such fearful infamy Ananias and Sapphira for having lied to the Holy Ghost, what do you think of these men[53]? Do they proclaim the Spirit God, or something else?

[41] Isa. 11:2.                    [42] Wisdom 1:7.
[43] Ps. 143 (142): 10; 51 (50):10, 12.
[44] Cf. Rom. 15:26; I Cor. 12:11; Phil. 2:1; II Cor. 13:14; Wisdom 1:7.
[45] Cf. Matt. 12:31; Luke 11:20 (Matt. 12:28); Acts 2:3 (Heb. 12:29).
[46] John 3:5; Rom. 8:11.        [47] I Cor. 2:10; John 14:26; 3:8; I John 2:27.
[48] John 16:13; Ps. 143 (142):10; Acts 13:2, 3; 20:23; Isa. 63:10; Acts 5:9.
[49] I Cor. 2:10; John 6:63; Rom. 8:10.
[50] I Cor. 3:16; 6:19; Acts 10:47; 8:16.
[51] I Cor. 12:11 and Eph. 4:11; Acts 2:3.        [52] Wisdom 7:22–27.
[53] John 14:16—not that the Spirit is really another God, but that he is given the same title as the Son; Matt. 12:31, 32; Acts 5:3, 4.

Now really, you must be extraordinarily dull and far from the Spirit if you have any doubt about this and need someone to teach you. So important, then, and so vivid are his names. Why is it necessary to lay before you the testimony contained in the very words? And whatever in this case also is said in more lowly fashion, as that he is given, sent, divided[54]; that he is the gift, the bounty, the inspiration, the promise, the intercession for us,[55] and, not to go into any further detail, any other expressions of the sort, is to be referred to the first cause, that it may be shown from whom he is, and that men may not in heathen fashion admit three principles. For it is equally impious to confuse the Persons with the Sabellians, or to divide the natures with the Arians.

31. I have very carefully considered this matter in my own mind, and have looked at it in every point of view, in order to find some illustration of this most important subject, but I have been unable to discover anything on earth with which to compare the nature of the Godhead. For even if I did happen upon some tiny likeness, it escaped me for the most part, and left me down below with my example. I picture to myself an eye, a fountain,[56] a river, as others have done before, to see if the first might be analogous to the Father, the second to the Son, and the third to the Holy Ghost. For in these there is no distinction in time, nor are they torn away from their connection with each other, though they seem to be parted by three personalities. But I was afraid in the first place that I should present a flow in the Godhead, incapable of standing still; and secondly that by this figure a numerical unity would be introduced. For the eye and the spring and the river are numerically one, though in different forms.

32. Again I thought of the sun and a ray and light. But here again there was a fear lest people should get an idea of composition in the uncompounded nature, such as there is in the sun and the things that are in the sun; and in the second place lest we should give essence to the Father but deny personality to the others, and make them only powers of God, existing in him and not personal. For neither the ray nor the light is another sun, but they are only effulgences from the sun, and

---

54 Cf. Luke 11:13; Gal. 4:6; Heb. 2:4; Acts 2:3.
55 II Tim. 1:6; John 4:10; 20:22; Luke 24:49; Acts 1:4; Rom. 8:26.
56 More clearly, "a source, a spring"; this seems to be a unique use of the Greek *ophthalmos*, "eye," for the source of a watercourse; the Hebrew *'ayin* is literally the same, but Gregory can scarcely have known this.

qualities of his essence. And lest we should thus, as far as the illustration goes, attribute both being and not-being to God, which is even more monstrous. I have also heard that someone has suggested an illustration of the following kind: A ray of the sun flashing upon a wall and trembling with the movement of the moisture which the beam has taken up in mid-air, and then, being checked by the hard body, has set up a strange quivering. For it quivers with many rapid movements, and is not one rather than it is many, nor yet many rather than one; because by the swiftness of its union and separating it escapes before the eye can see it.

33. But it is not possible for me to make use of even this, because it is very evident what gives the ray its motion, but there is nothing prior to God which could set him in motion, for he is himself the cause of all things, and he has no prior cause; and secondly because in this case also there is a suggestion of such things as composition, diffusion, and an unsettled and unstable nature . . . none of which we can suppose in the Godhead. In a word, there is nothing which presents a standing point to my mind in these illustrations from which to consider the object which I am trying to represent to myself, unless one may indulgently accept one point of the image while rejecting the rest. Finally, then, it seems best to me to let the images and the shadows go, as being deceitful and very far short of the truth; and clinging myself to the more reverent conception, and resting upon few words, using the guidance of the Holy Ghost, keeping to the end as my genuine comrade and companion the enlightenment which I have received from him, and passing through this world to persuade all others also to the best of my power to worship Father, Son, and Holy Ghost, the one Godhead and power. To him belongs all glory and honor and might forever and ever. Amen.

# Letters on the Apollinarian Controversy

## THE TEXT: TO CLEDONIUS AGAINST APOLLINARIS (EPISTLE 101)

To our most reverend and God-beloved brother and fellow priest[1] Cledonius, Gregory, greeting in the Lord.

I desire to learn what is this fashion of innovation in things concerning the Church, which allows anyone who likes, or the passer-by, as the Bible says, to tear asunder the flock[2] that has been well led, and to plunder it by larcenous attacks, or rather by piratical and fallacious teachings. For if our present assailants had any ground for condemning us in regard of the faith, it would not have been right for them, even in that case, to have ventured on such a course without giving us notice. They ought rather to have first persuaded us, or to have been willing to be persuaded by us (if at least any account is to be taken of us as fearing God, laboring for the faith, and helping the Church), and then, if at all, to innovate; but then perhaps there would be an excuse for their outrageous conduct. But since our faith has been proclaimed, both in writing and without writing, here and in distant parts, in times of danger and of safety, how comes it that some make such attempts, and that others keep silence?

The most grievous part of it is not (though this too is shocking) that the men instill their own heresy into simpler souls by means of those who are worse; but that they also tell lies about us and say that we share their opinions and sentiments; thus baiting their hooks, and by this cloak villainously fulfilling

---

[1] Or rather "sympresbyter," as in I Peter 5:1; this letter is to be dated in 382 or 383, after Gregory had finally given up the care of the Church of Nazianzus, and before the consecration of Bishop Eulalius, probably after 384, since it seems to refer to Damasus as deceased (see Gallay, *Vie de St. Grégoire*, pp. 217, 218, 229–232).    [2] Ps. 81 (80):12.

their will, and making our simplicity, which looked upon them as brothers and not as foes, into a support of their wickedness. And not only so, but they also assert, as I am told, that they have been received by the Western Synod, by which they were formerly condemned, as is well known to everyone.[3] If, however, those who hold the views of Apollinaris have either now or formerly been received, let them prove it and we will be content. For it is evident that they can only have been so received as assenting to the orthodox faith, for this were an impossibility on any other terms. And they can surely prove it, either by the minutes of the synod, or by letters of communion, for this is the regular custom of synods. But if it is mere words, and an invention of their own, devised for the sake of appearances and to give them weight with the multitude through the credit of the persons, teach them to hold their tongues, and confute them; for we believe that such a task is well suited to your manner of life and orthodoxy. Do not let the men deceive themselves and others with the assertion that the "Man of the Lord," [4] as they call him, who is rather our Lord and God, is without human mind. For we do not sever the man from the Godhead, but we lay down as a dogma the unity and identity [of person], who of old was not man but God, and the only Son before all ages, unmingled with body or anything corporeal; but who in these last days has assumed manhood also for our salvation; passible in his flesh, impassible in his Godhead; circumscript in the body, uncircumscript in the Spirit; at once earthly and heavenly, tangible and intangible, comprehensible and incomprehensible; that by one and the same [Person], who was perfect man and also God, the entire humanity fallen through sin might be created anew.

If anyone does not believe that holy Mary is the mother of God,[5] he is severed from the Godhead. If anyone should assert

---

[3] Apollinaris and his follower Timotheus had been condemned at the Roman Synod of 377 under Damasus; but further negotiations for recognition, connected with the confusing question of parties at Antioch, may have led to the claim here referred to—the condemnation is repeated by Damasus at the Synod of 382 (Theodoret, Church History, v, 10).

[4] *Kuriakos anthrōpos*, used for the humanity of Christ by Athanasius (Statement of Faith, 1), but because of its ambiguity dropped in later orthodox usage—as by Augustine, who formally withdrew his earlier use of *homo dominicus* in *Retractationes* i, 19, 8; this passage ("Do not let . . . added to the ranks of the gods, let him be anathema") was among the extracts from the Fathers read with approval at the Council of Ephesus (Schwartz, *Acta conciliorum*, Vol. i, ii, pp. 43, 44).

[5] *Theotokos*, cf. Introduction, p. 31; the term was already known to Origen

that he passed through the Virgin as through a channel, and was not at once divinely and humanly formed in her (divinely, because without the intervention of a man; humanly, because in accordance with the laws of gestation), he is in like manner godless. If any assert that the manhood was formed and afterward was clothed with the Godhead, he too is to be condemned. For this were not a generation of God, but a shirking of generation. If any introduce the notion of two sons, one of God the Father, the other of the mother, and discredits the unity and identity, may he lose his part in the adoption promised to those who believe aright. For God and man are two natures, as also soul and body are; but there are not two sons or two gods. For neither in this life are there two manhoods; though Paul speaks in some such language of the inner and outer man.[6] And (if I am to speak concisely) the Saviour is made of [elements] which are distinct from one another (for the invisible is not the same with the visible, nor the timeless with that which is subject to time), yet he is not two [persons]. God forbid! For both [natures] are one by the combination, the deity being made man, and the manhood deified or however one should express it. And I say different [elements],[7] because it is the reverse of what is the case in the Trinity; for there we acknowledge different [Persons] so as not to confound the Persons; but not different [elements], for the three are one and the same in Godhead.

If any should say that it wrought in him by grace as in a prophet, but was not and is not united with him in essence—let him be empty of the higher energy, or rather full of the opposite. If any worship not the Crucified, let him be anathema and be numbered among the deicides. If any assert that he was made perfect by works, or that after his baptism, or after his resurrection from the dead, he was counted worthy of an adoptive sonship, like those whom the Greeks interpolate as added

(cited by Socrates, *Church History*, vii, 32), and was used by Alexander of Alexandria (confession of faith in letter to Alexander of Byzantium, Theodoret, Church History, i, 3) and Athanasius (Discourses Against the Arians, iii, 14, 29, 33), but now acquires technical dogmatic significance; the idea that Christ was not really born, but merely passed through the Virgin's body, has had a surprising appeal at various periods, from the Valentinians in the second century to some of the lesser Reformers in the sixteenth.

6 Rom. 7:22; II Cor. 4:16; Eph. 3:16.
7 The distinction is between neuter and masculine—in Christ there is manhood and Godhead (*allo kai allo*) in one Person, while in the one Godhead there are different Persons (*allos kai allos*).

to the ranks of the gods, let him be anathema. For that which has a beginning or a progress or is made perfect is not God, although the expressions may be used of his gradual manifestation. If any assert that he has now put off his holy flesh, and that his Godhead is stripped of the body, and deny that he is now with his body and will come again with it, let him not see the glory of his coming. For where is his body now, if not with him who assumed it? For it is not laid by in the sun, according to the babble of the Manichaeans, that it should be honored by a dishonor; nor was it poured forth into the air and dissolved, as is the nature of a voice or the flow of an odor, or the course of a lightning flash that never stands. Where in that case were his being handled after the resurrection, or his being seen hereafter by them that pierced him, for Godhead is in its nature invisible? Nay; he will come with his body— so I have learned—such as he was seen by his disciples in the Mount, or as he showed himself for a moment, when his Godhead overpowered the carnality. And as we say this to disarm suspicion, so we write the other to correct the novel teaching. If anyone assert that his flesh came down from heaven, and is not from hence, nor of us though above us, let him be anathema. For the words, "The second man is the Lord from heaven; and, as is the heavenly, such are they that are heavenly"; and, "No man hath ascended up into heaven save he which came down from heaven, even the Son of Man which is in heaven" [8]; and the like, are to be understood as said on account of the union with the heavenly; just as that "All things were made by Christ," and that "Christ dwelleth in your hearts" is said,[9] not of the visible nature which belongs to God, but of what is perceived by the mind, the names being mingled like the natures, and flowing into one another, according to the law of their intimate union.

If anyone has put his trust in him as a man without a human mind, he is really bereft of mind, and quite unworthy of salvation. For that which he has not assumed he has not healed; but that which is united to his Godhead is also saved. If only half Adam fell, then that which Christ assumes and saves may be half also; but if the whole of his nature fell, it must be united to the whole nature of Him that was begotten, and so

[8] I Cor. 15:47, 48; John 3:13.
[9] John 1:3; Eph. 3:17; the doctrine later known as the *communicatio idiomatum*, or exchange of properties between the two natures of Christ, at least in nomenclature.

be saved as a whole. Let them not, then, begrudge us our complete salvation, or clothe the Saviour only with bones and nerves and the portraiture of humanity. For if his manhood is without soul, even the Arians admit this, that they may attribute his Passion to the Godhead, as that which gives motion to the body is also that which suffers. But if he has a soul, and yet is without a mind, how is he man, for man is not a mindless animal? And this would necessarily involve that while his form and tabernacle was human, his soul should be that of a horse or an ox, or some other of the brute creation. This, then, would be what he saves; and I have been deceived by the truth, and led to boast of an honor which had been bestowed upon another. But if his manhood is intellectual and not without mind, let them cease to be thus really mindless.

But, says such a one, the Godhead took the place of the human intellect. How does this touch me? For Godhead joined to flesh alone is not man, nor to soul alone, nor to both apart from intellect, which is the most essential part of man. Keep, then, the whole man, and mingle Godhead therewith, that you may benefit me in my completeness. But, he asserts, he could not contain two perfect [natures]. Not if you only look at him in a bodily fashion. For a bushel measure will not hold two bushels, nor will the space of one body hold two or more bodies. But if you will look at what is mental and incorporeal, remember that I in my one personality can contain soul and reason and mind and the Holy Spirit; and before me this world, by which I mean the system of things visible and invisible, contained Father, Son, and Holy Ghost. For such is the nature of intellectual existences, that they can mingle with one another and with bodies, incorporeally and invisibly. For many sounds are comprehended by one ear; and the eyes of many are occupied by the same visible objects, and the smell by odors; nor are the senses narrowed by each other, or crowded out, nor the objects of sense diminished by the multitude of the perceptions. But where is there mind of man or angel so perfect in comparison of the Godhead that the presence of the greater must crowd out the other? The light is nothing compared with a river, that we must first do away with the lesser, and take the light from a house, or the moisture from the earth, to enable it to contain the greater and more perfect. For how shall one thing contain two completenesses, either the house, the sunbeam and the sun, or the earth, the moisture and the river? Here is matter for inquiry; for indeed the question is worthy of much consideration. Do they not know, then, that what is perfect by comparison with one thing may be imperfect by comparison with another, as a hill compared with a mountain, or a grain of mustard seed with a bean or any other of the larger seeds, although it may be called larger than any of the same kind? Or, if you like, an angel compared with God, or a man with an angel. So our mind is perfect and commanding, but only in respect of soul and body; not absolutely perfect; and a servant and a subject of God, not a sharer of his princedom and honor. So Moses was a god to Pharaoh, but a servant of God, as it is written [10]; and the stars which illumine the night are hidden by the sun, so much that you could not even know of their existence by daylight; and a little torch brought near a great blaze is neither destroyed, nor seen, nor extinguished; but is all one blaze, the bigger one prevailing over the other.

But, it may be said, our mind is subject to condemnation. What, then, of our flesh? Is that not subject to condemnation? You must therefore either set aside the latter on account of sin, or admit the former on account of salvation. If he assumed the worse that he might sanctify it by his incarnation, may he not assume the better that it may be sanctified by his becoming man? If the clay was leavened and has become a new lump,[11] O ye wise men, shall not the image be leavened and mingled with God, being deified by his Godhead? And I will add this also: If the mind was utterly rejected, as prone to sin and subject to damnation, and for this reason he assumed a body but left out the mind, then there is an excuse for them who sin with the mind; for the witness of God—according to you—has shown the impossibility of healing it. Let me state the greater results. You, my good sir, dishonor my mind (you a Sarcolater, if I am an Anthropolater)[12] that you may tie God down to the flesh, since he cannot be otherwise tied; and therefore you take away the wall of partition. But what is my theory, who am but an ignorant man, and no philosopher? Mind is mingled with mind, as nearer and more closely related, and through it with flesh, being a mediator between God and carnality.

10 Ex. 7:1; Num. 12:7 (Heb. 3:5); the infinite can be joined with the finite in a way that would be impossible for another finite being, such as the Arian Christ.
11 I Cor. 5:7, mixed with Matt. 13:33, or Luke 13:21.
12 If the Apollinarian calls Gregory a "man worshiper" for seeing God in a perfect man, he is a "flesh worshiper," seeing God in a body without human mind.

Further let us see what is their account of the assumption of manhood, or the assumption of flesh, as they call it. If it was in order that God, otherwise incomprehensible, might be comprehended, and might converse with men through his flesh as through a veil, their mask and the drama which they represent is a pretty one, not to say that it was open to him to converse with us in other ways, as of old, in the burning bush and in the appearance of a man.[13] But if it was that he might destroy the condemnation by sanctifying like by like, then as he needed flesh for the sake of the flesh which had incurred condemnation, and soul for the sake of our soul, so, too, he needed mind for the sake of mind, which not only fell in Adam, but was the first to be affected, as the doctors say of illnesses. For that which received the command was that which failed to keep the command, and that which failed to keep it was that also which dared to transgress; and that which transgressed was that which stood most in need of salvation; and that which needed salvation was that which also he took upon him. Therefore, mind was taken upon him. This has now been demonstrated, whether they like it or no, by, to use their own expression, geometrical and necessary proofs. But you are acting as if, when a man's eye had been injured and his foot had been injured in consequence, you were to attend to the foot and leave the eye uncared for; or as if, when a painter had drawn something badly, you were to alter the picture, but to pass over the artist as if he had succeeded. But if they, overwhelmed by these arguments, take refuge in the proposition that it is possible for God to save man even apart from mind, why, I suppose that it would be possible for him to do so also apart from flesh by a mere act of will, just as he works all other things, and has wrought them without body. Take away, then, the flesh as well as the mind, that your monstrous folly may be complete. But they are deceived by the letter, and, therefore, they run to the flesh, because they do not know the custom of Scripture. We will teach them this also. For what need is there even to mention to those who know it the fact that everywhere in Scripture he is called "man," and "the Son of Man"?

If, however, they rely on the passage, "The Word was made flesh and dwelt among us," and because of this erase the noblest part of man (as cobblers do the thicker part of skins) that they may join together God and flesh, it is time for them

[13] Ex. 3:2; and, e.g., Gen., ch. 18.

to say that God is God only of flesh, and not of souls, because it is written, "As thou hast given him power over all flesh," and, "Unto thee shall all flesh come," and, "Let all flesh bless his holy Name," meaning every man.[14] Or, again, they must suppose that our fathers went down into Egypt without bodies and invisible, and that only the soul of Joseph was imprisoned by Pharaoh, because it is written, "They went down into Egypt with threescore and fifteen souls," and, "The iron entered into his soul,"[15] a thing which could not be bound. They who argue thus do not know that such expressions are used by synecdoche, declaring the whole by the part, as when Scripture says that the young ravens call upon God, to indicate the whole feathered race; or Pleiades, Hesperus, and Arcturus are mentioned, instead of all the stars and his providence over them.[16]

Moreover, in no other way was it possible for the love of God toward us to be manifested than by making mention of our flesh, and that for our sake he descended even to our lower part. For that flesh is less precious than soul, everyone who has a spark of sense will acknowledge. And so the passage, "The Word was made flesh," seems to me to be equivalent to that in which it is said that he was made sin, or a curse for us; not that the Lord was transformed into either of these—how could he be? But because by taking them upon him he took away our sins and bore our iniquities.[17] This, then, is sufficient to say at the present time for the sake of clearness and of being understood by the many. And I write it, not with any desire to compose a treatise, but only to check the progress of deceit; and if it is thought well, I will give a fuller account of these matters at greater length.

But there is a matter which is graver than these, a special point which is necessary that I should not pass over. I would they were even cut off that trouble you,[18] and would reintroduce a second Judaism, and a second circumcision, and a second system of sacrifices. For if this be done, what hinders

---

[14] John 1:14; 17:2; Ps. 65 (64):2; 145 (144):21.
[15] Acts 7:14 (Gen. 46:26); Ps. 105 (104): 18.
[16] Ps. 147 (146):9; Job 9:9.
[17] John 1:14; II Cor. 5:21; Gal. 3:13; Isa. 53:4, 5 (LXX).
[18] Gal. 5:12; Apollinaris apparently taught that the millennium would include a restoration of the Temple at Jerusalem (Basil, Epistles 263 and 265)—which perhaps had a special appeal in Asia Minor, where Papias and others had taught a literal interpretation of the promise of the Kingdom to come (cf. Epistle 102, p. 227).

Christ also being born again to set them aside, and again being betrayed by Judas, and crucified and buried, and rising again, that all may be fulfilled in the same order, like the Greek system of cycles, in which the same revolutions of the stars bring round the same events? For what the method of selection is, in accordance with which some of the events are to occur and others to be omitted, let these wise men who glory in the multitude of their books show us.

But since, puffed up by their theory of the Trinity, they falsely accuse us of being unsound in the faith and entice the multitude, it is necessary that people should know that Apollinaris, while granting the name of Godhead to the Holy Ghost, did not preserve the power of the Godhead. For to make the Trinity consist of great, greater, and greatest, as of light, ray, and sun, the Spirit and the Son and the Father (as is clearly stated in his writings), is a ladder of Godhead not leading to heaven, but down from heaven.[19] But we recognize God the Father and the Son and the Holy Ghost, and these not as bare titles, dividing inequalities of ranks or of power, but as there is one and the same title, so there is one nature and one substance in the Godhead.

But if anyone who thinks we have spoken rightly on this subject reproaches us with holding communion with heretics, let him prove that we are open to this charge, and we will either convince him or retire. But it is not safe to make any innovation before judgment is given, especially in a matter of such importance, and connected with so great issues. We have protested and continue to protest this before God and men. And not even now, be well assured, should we have written this if we had not seen that the Church was being torn asunder and divided, among their other tricks, by their present synagogue of vanity.[20] But if anyone when we say and protest this, either from some advantage he will thus gain, or through fear of men, or monstrous littleness of mind, or through some neglect of pastors and governors, or through love of novelty and proneness to innovations, rejects us as unworthy of credit, and attaches himself to such men, and divides the noble body of the Church, he shall bear his judgment, whoever he may be, and shall give account to God in the Day of Judgment. But if their long books, and their new psalters, contrary to that of David, and the grace of their meters, are taken for a third

19 Cf. repudiation of this analogy in Fifth Theological Oration, 32, p. 213.
20 Ps. 26 (25):4 (LXX).

Testament, we too will compose psalms, and will write much in meter. For we also think we have the spirit of God, if indeed this is a gift of the Spirit, and not a human novelty. This I will that thou declare publicly, that we may not be held responsible, as overlooking such an evil, and as though this wicked doctrine received food and strength from our indifference.

# THE TEXT: THE SECOND LETTER TO
## CLEDONIUS AGAINST APOLLINARIS
### (EPISTLE 102)

Forasmuch as many persons have come to Your Reverence seeking confirmation of their faith, and therefore you have affectionately asked me to put forth a brief definition and rule of my opinion, I therefore write to Your Reverence, what indeed you knew before, that I never have and never can honor anything above the Nicene faith, that of the holy Fathers who met there to destroy the Arian heresy; but am, and by God's help ever will be, of that faith; completing in detail that which was incompletely said by them concerning the Holy Ghost; for that question had not then been mooted, namely, that we are to believe that the Father, Son, and Holy Ghost are of one Godhead, thus confessing the Spirit also to be God.[1] Receive then to communion those who think and teach thus, as I also do; but those who are otherwise-minded refuse, and hold them as strangers to God and the Catholic Church. And since a question has also been mooted concerning the divine assumption of humanity, or incarnation, state this also clearly to all concerning me, that I join in One the Son, who was begotten of the Father, and afterward of the Virgin Mary, and that I do not call him two sons, but worship him as one and the same in undivided Godhead and honor. But if anyone does not assent to this statement, either now or hereafter, he shall give account to God at the Day of Judgment.

Now, what we object and oppose to their mindless opinion about his mind is this, to put it shortly; for they are almost alone in the condition which they lay down, as it is through want of mind that they mutilate his mind. But, that they may

[1] Gregory's Confession is thus something like the Creed now commonly called Nicene; see Introduction, pp. 25, 26.

not accuse us of having once accepted but of now repudiating the faith of their beloved Vitalius which he handed in in writing at the request of the blessed bishop Damasus of Rome,[2] I will give a short explanation on this point also. For these men, when they are theologizing among their genuine disciples, and those who are initiated into their secrets, like the Manichaeans among those whom they call the "Elect," expose the full extent of their disease, and scarcely allow flesh at all to the Saviour. But when they are refuted and pressed with the common answers about the incarnation which the Scripture presents, they confess indeed the orthodox words, but they do violence to the sense; for they acknowledge the manhood to be neither without soul nor without reason nor without mind, nor imperfect, but they bring in the Godhead to supply the soul and reason and mind, as though it had mingled itself only with his flesh, and not with the other properties belonging to us men; although his sinlessness was far above us, and was the cleansing of our passions.

Thus, then, they interpret wrongly the words, "But we have the mind of Christ,"[3] and very absurdly, when they say that his Godhead is the mind of Christ, and not understanding the passage as we do, namely, that they who have purified their mind by the imitation of the mind which the Saviour took of us, and, as far as may be, have attained conformity with it, are said to have the mind of Christ; just as they might be testified to have the flesh of Christ who have trained their flesh, and in this respect have become of the same body and partakers of Christ; and so he says, "As we have borne the image of the earthy we shall also bear the image of the heavenly."[4] And so they declare that the perfect man is not he who was in all points tempted like as we are yet without sin[5]; but the mixture of God and flesh. For what, say they, can be more perfect than this?

They play the same trick with the word that describes the incarnation, viz., He was made man—explaining it to mean, not, He was in the human nature with which he surrounded himself, according to the Scripture, "He knew what was in man"; but teaching that it means, He consorted and conversed with men, and taking refuge in the expression which says that

[2] The Apollinarian claimant to the see of Antioch, who for a time about 375 was recognized as orthodox by Damasus (cf. Jerome, *Epistles*, 16), and accepted as such by Gregory, as noted below.
[3] I Cor. 2:16.      [4] I Cor. 15:49.      [5] Heb. 4:15.

he was seen on earth and conversed with men.[6] And what can anyone contend further? They who take away the humanity and the interior image cleanse by their newly invented mask only our outside,[7] and that which is seen; so far in conflict with themselves that at one time, for the sake of the flesh, they explain all the rest in a gross and carnal manner (for it is from hence that they have derived their second Judaism and their silly thousand years' delight in paradise, and almost the idea that we shall resume again the same conditions after these same thousand years)[8]; and at another time they bring in his flesh as a phantom rather than a reality, as not having been subjected to any of our experiences, not even such as are free from sin; and use for this purpose the apostolic expression, understood and spoken in a sense which is not apostolic, that our Saviour "was made in the likeness of men and found in fashion as a man," [9] as though by these words was expressed, not the human form, but some delusive phantom and appearance.

Since, then, these expressions, rightly understood, make for orthodoxy, but wrongly interpreted are heretical, what is there to be surprised at if we received the words of Vitalius in the more orthodox sense, our desire that they should be so meant persuading us, though others are angry at the intention of his writings? This is, I think, the reason why Damasus himself, having been subsequently better informed, and at the same time learning that they hold by their former explanations, excommunicated them and overturned their written confession of faith with an anathema; as well as because he was vexed at the deceit which he had suffered from them through simplicity.

Since, then, they have been openly convicted of this, let them not be angry, but let them be ashamed of themselves; and let them not slander us, but abase themselves and wipe off from their portals that great and marvelous proclamation and boast of their orthodoxy, meeting all who go in at once with the question and distinction that we must worship, not a God-bearing man, but a flesh-bearing God. What could be more unreasonable than this, though these new heralds of truth think a great deal of the title? For though it has a certain sophistical grace through the quickness of its antithesis, and a sort of juggling quackery grateful to the uninstructed, yet it is the most absurd of absurdities and the most foolish of follies. For

---

[6] John 2:25; Baruch 3:37.     [7] Cf. Matt. 23:25, 26.
[8] Cf. p. 222, n. 18.     [9] Phil. 2:7, 8.

if one were to change the word man or flesh into God (the first would please us, the second them), and then were to use this wonderful antithesis, so divinely recognized, what conclusion should we arrive at? That we must worship, not a God-bearing flesh, but a man-bearing God.[10] O monstrous absurdity! They proclaim to us today a wisdom hidden ever since the time of Christ—a thing worthy of our tears. For if the faith began thirty years ago, when nearly four hundred years had passed since Christ was manifested, vain all that time will have been our gospel, and vain our faith; in vain will the martyrs have borne their witness, and in vain have so many and so great prelates presided over the people; and grace is a matter of meters and not of the faith.

And who will not marvel at their learning, in that on their own authority they divide the things of Christ, and assign to his manhood such sayings as, he was born, he was tempted, he was hungry, he was thirsty, he was wearied, he was asleep[11]; but reckon to his divinity such as these: he was glorified by angels, he overcame the tempter, he fed the people in the wilderness, and he fed them in such a manner, and he walked upon the sea[12]; and say on the one hand that the "Where have ye laid Lazarus?" belongs to us, but the loud voice "Lazarus, come forth," and the raising him that had been four days dead,[13] is above our nature; and that while "He was in an agony,[14] he was crucified, he was buried," belong to the veil, on the other hand, "He was confident,[15] he rose again, he ascended," belong to the inner treasure; and then they accuse us of introducing two natures, separate or conflicting, and of dividing the supernatural and wondrous union. They ought either not to do that of which they accuse us or not to accuse us of that which they do; so at least if they are resolved to be consistent and not to propound at once their own and their opponents' principles.[16] Such is their want of reason; it conflicts both with itself and with the truth to such an extent that

---

[10] The orthodox retort to Apollinarianism, as the previous antithesis is the Apollinarian retort to orthodoxy; the absurdity is what follows, not what precedes.

[11] Matt. 4:2; Luke 4:2; John 19:28; 4:6; Mark 4:38.

[12] Luke 2:14 or Mark 1:13; Mark 6:35–51 and parallels.

[13] John 11:34, 43.          [14] Luke 22:44.

[15] Cf. Mark 6:50; John 16:33.

[16] I.e., the division of the actions of Christ between his two natures, natural for the orthodox (cf. Third Theological Oration, 17–20), should not be permissible on Apollinarian principles.

they are neither conscious nor ashamed of it when they fall out with themselves. Now, if anyone thinks that we write all this willingly and not upon compulsion, and that we are dissuading from unity, and not doing our utmost to promote it, let him know that he is very much mistaken, and has not made at all a good guess at our desires, for nothing is or ever has been more valuable in our eyes than peace, as the facts themselves prove; though their actions and brawlings against us altogether exclude unanimity.

## THE TEXT: TO NECTARIUS, BISHOP OF CONSTANTINOPLE (EPISTLE 202)

The care of God, which throughout the time before us guarded the Churches, seems to have utterly forsaken this present life. And my soul is immersed to such a degree by calamities that the private sufferings of my own life hardly seem to be worth reckoning among evils (though they are so numerous and great, that if they befell anyone else I should think them unbearable); but I can only look at the common sufferings of the churches; for if at the present crisis some pains be not taken to find a remedy for them, things will gradually get into an altogether desperate condition. Those who follow the heresy of Arius or Eudoxius (I cannot say who stirred them up to this folly) are making a display of their disease, as if they had attained some degree of confidence by collecting congregations as if by permission. And they of the Macedonian party have reached such a pitch of folly that they are arrogating to themselves the name of bishops, and are wandering about our districts babbling of Eleusius as to their ordinations.[1] Our bosom evil, Eunomius, is no longer content with merely existing; but unless he can draw away everyone with him to his ruinous heresy, he thinks himself an injured man. All this, however, is endurable. The most grievous item of all in the woes of the Church is the boldness of the Apollinarians, whom Your Holiness has overlooked, I know not how, when providing themselves with authority to hold meetings on an equality with myself.

[1] Leaders of the variations of Arianism found at or near Constantinople; Eudoxius of Constantinople (360–370) and Eunomius of Cyzicus (360–393) represented extreme Arianism; Macedonius of Constantinople (352–362) gave his name to the more moderate Semi-Arians or *pneumatomachi*, whose clergy evidently claimed to derive their orders from their last conspicuous leader, Eleusius of Cyzicus (358–383).

However, you being, as you are, thoroughly instructed by the grace of God in the divine mysteries on all points, are well informed, not only as to the advocacy of the true faith, but also as to all those arguments which have been devised by the heretics against the sound faith; and yet perhaps it will not be unseasonable that Your Excellency should hear from my littleness that a pamphlet by Apollinaris has come into my hands, the contents of which surpass all heretical pravity. For he asserts that the flesh which the only-begotten Son assumed in the incarnation for the remodeling of our nature was no new acquisition, but that that carnal nature was in the Son from the beginning. And he puts forward as a witness to this monstrous assertion a garbled quotation from the Gospels, namely, "No man hath ascended up into heaven save he which came down from heaven, even the Son of Man which is in heaven." [2] As though even before he came down he was the Son of Man, and when he came down he brought with him that flesh, which it appears he had in heaven, as though it had existed before the ages, and been joined with his essence. For he alleges another saying of an apostle, which he cuts off from the whole body of its context, that the second man is the Lord from heaven.[3] Then he assumes that that man who came down from above is without a mind, but that the Godhead of the only-begotten fulfills the function of mind, and is the third part of this human composite, inasmuch as soul and body are in it on its human side, but not mind, the place of which is taken by God the Word. This is not yet the most serious part of it; that which is most terrible of all is that he declares that the only-begotten God, the judge of all, the prince of life, the destroyer of death, is mortal, and underwent the Passion in his proper Godhead; and that in the three days' death of his body, his Godhead also was put to death with his body, and thus was raised again from the dead by the Father.[4] It would be tedious to go through all the other propositions which he adds to these monstrous absurdities. Now, if they who hold such views have authority to meet, your wisdom approved in Christ must see that, inasmuch as we do not approve their views, any permission of assembly granted to them is nothing less than a declaration that their view is thought more true than ours.

[2] John 3:13.
[3] I Cor. 15:47.
[4] As with later Monophysites, the doctrine of the single nature of Christ involved the passibility of the Godhead.

For if they are permitted to teach their view as godly men, and with all confidence to preach their doctrine, it is manifest that the doctrine of the Church has been condemned, as though the truth were on their side. For nature does not admit of two contrary doctrines on the same subject being both true. How then, could your noble and lofty mind submit to suspend your usual courage in regard to the correction of so great an evil? But even though there is no precedent for such a course, let your inimitable perfection in virtue stand up at a crisis like the present, and teach our most pious emperor that no gain will come from his zeal for the Church on other points if he allows such an evil to gain strength from freedom of speech for the subversion of sound faith.[5]

5 As a result of this letter, or similar representations, a law of 388 (Codex Theodosianus 16.5.14) applied specially to Apollinarians the laws previously enacted against heretics generally.

# GREGORY OF NYSSA

# Introduction to Gregory of Nyssa

THE IMPORTANCE OF GREGORY OF NYSSA FOR the development of Christian thought is very great and has often been overlooked. This man who was hailed by the Second Council of Nicaea as "Father of Fathers" and "Star of Nyssa," of whom his friend Gregory of Nazianzus could write (Ep. 74) that he was "the column supporting the whole Church," whom Maximus the Confessor calls "Doctor of the Universe," and whom Scotus Eriugena cites no less frequently than Augustine, deserves more study than he has received. It is, indeed, only within very recent years that a sound critical edition of his works has been begun.[1] Yet he is coming into his own; and two important studies of his thought have lately appeared.[2]

He belonged to that group of theologians of the later fourth century who are termed the "Cappadocians," and who were responsible for the final triumph of the Nicene orthodoxy over Arianism and Apollinarianism. His elder brother, Basil, bishop of Caesarea, was a more gifted man of affairs and an abler Biblical scholar. His lifelong friend Gregory Nazianzen, bishop of Sasima and later of Constantinople, was more cultured and a more eloquent rhetorician. Yet Gregory of Nyssa was distinguished by a keen philosophic mind, and his writings reveal a depth and a breadth of thought which outdistances that of the other two. He accomplished for Eastern orthodoxy what Origen (a more brilliant and productive writer, to be sure) had attempted and yet not fully succeeded in doing—to relate the faith to the Greek classical heritage. Where in Origen the

[1] By Werner Jaeger. See Bibliography.
[2] By H. V. de Balthasar and Jean Daniélou. See Bibliography.

Greek spirit sometimes triumphs over the Christian, in Gregory of Nyssa philosophy becomes the handmaiden of faith.

It is, however, particularly in his mystical writings that Gregory showed originality and had his most enduring influence. He laid the foundations of Eastern mysticism with its emphasis upon the *via negativa*, in his Life of Moses and in his commentaries on Ecclesiastes and the Song of Songs. Nor was his work along this line unknown in the West. As late as the twelfth century both Bernard of Clairvaux and William of St. Thierry were indebted to him.

## LIFE

Gregory came of well-to-do Christian parents, and was born probably in Caesarea of Cappadocia, around A.D. 334. He was one of a family of ten children, which was remarkable for giving to the Church three bishops (Basil, Gregory, and Peter), and for having as its spiritual mentor their elder sister Macrina, whose intellectual gifts, earnest piety, and ascetic life so influenced the brothers.

Unlike Basil, Gregory did not have the advantages of a formal university education. He studied at home and in local schools. Shy and retiring by nature and prone to sickness, he settled down to a life of literary leisure. In his early years he was not particularly inclined toward religion; and his first profession of it, which led to his being baptized and appointed a lector in the Church, was due to a dream. His mother had urged him to take part in a family festival in honor of the Forty Martyrs of Sebaste, for whose relics she had provided a chapel. He came only reluctantly and slept through the ceremony, which lasted all night. He dreamed he was trying to enter a garden and was prevented by the Forty Martyrs, who beat him with rods. On awaking, stung by remorse for his indifference to the glorious martyrs, he made recompense by entreating their mercy and taking up the Christian life.

But his resolution was short-lived. Soon he "cast away the sacred and delightful books" he once had read in church, and became a professor of rhetoric. His friend Gregory Nazianzen wrote to reproach him for this ambitious "descent to the lower life" (Ep. 11). Probably under his influence Gregory of Nyssa turned his back on this secular occupation and, following his brother Basil and his sister Macrina, retired to a monastery in Pontus. There he devoted himself to study and prayer, having

Basil (whom he often terms "the Master") for his tutor. Among the authors he read at this time Origen was the most influential on his mind. Indeed, Gregory of Nyssa is distinguished from the other Cappadocians by his greater dependence on this writer.

It is probable that Gregory was married during the period when he was professor of rhetoric. In one of his early works, On Virginity, he regrets the "gulf that divides" him "from glorious virginity," and we have a letter of Gregory Nazianzen (Ep. 97), written much later (about A.D. 381), consoling him on the death of a certain Theosebeia to whom he refers as "truly consort [suzugos] of a priest." While these references have been otherwise interpreted by some scholars, they point in the direction that Gregory contracted a marriage which forbade him fully to follow the monastic life.

It was in A.D. 372 that Gregory's public labors for the faith began. His brother Basil, in order to surround himself with bishops favorable to the Nicene cause, engineered the consecration of the two Gregorys to the episcopate. This cost Basil the friendship of Nazianzen, and brought Nyssa into the arena of Church politics, for which he was peculiarly unfitted. The see of Nyssa was as obscure as the trials before him were uncongenial. Yet he won a notable reputation. Basil truthfully prophesied that Gregory did not derive dignity from the see, but would confer dignity on it (Ep. 98). Indeed, we should never have heard of Nyssa, had its bishop not become so distinguished.

Gregory's episcopate was set in troublous times. Within four years he had been banished by Valens on trumped-up Arian charges about the illegitimacy of his ordination and his misappropriation of Church funds. Forced from his see, he wandered from place to place, depressed and sick in body and spirit. With Gratian's accession, however, he was back again; and he has left us a vivid account (Ep. 6) of his reception by his diocese. In the pouring rain the people flocked to greet him, so that he had difficulty in getting out of his carriage. Choirs of virgins preceded him into the church, which was ablaze with the splendor of their torches.

The following year was one of personal sorrow. Basil died in January, and Macrina in September. Gregory's last hours with that brave spirit Macrina are poignantly described in his Life of St. Macrina and in his dialogue On the Soul and the Resurrection.

He continued to be involved in diocesan troubles, and possibly at this time he undertook his travels to Transjordan and the Holy Land, despite his ill-health. A council of Antioch had commissioned him to visit and reform the Church in "Arabia" (apparently Transjordan), and the emperor provided him with facilities for the journey. During his visit to the Holy Land he was so abashed by the evils he witnessed that he was quickly cured of the growing passion for pilgrimages. Indeed, his experiences provoked a letter (Ep. 2) so strong in tone on the subject that its authenticity was at one time disputed.

But Gregory's labors for the Nicene orthodoxy had their reward. He was present as a leading theologian at the Council of Constantinople (A.D. 381), where he read to Nazianzen and Jerome the first draft of his great work Against Eunomius (*De vir. ill.* 128). In the decree of Theodosius by which the question of heresy was to be settled in terms of communion with recognized orthodox sees, that of Nyssa is one of the few mentioned (Cod. Theod. 16.1.3). Further recognition came to Gregory four years later when he preached the funeral orations of the princess Pulcheria and of the empress Flacilla, in Constantinople. There, too, he developed his friendship with the remarkable deaconess Olympias, under whose inspiration he undertook his commentary on the Song of Songs. He died around A.D. 395, his feast being celebrated in the East on January 10 and in the West on March 9.

In some ways Gregory's character is not so inspiring as his mind. He was a naïve and simple soul, more fitted for the study than for the episcopal throne. He forged letters in a vain attempt to heal a rift between Basil and their uncle (another Gregory: Basil, Ep. 58); and with good intentions, but with complete ignorance of practical affairs, he embarrassed Basil by summoning a council at Ancyra (Basil, Ep. 100). Basil rightly speaks of his "simplicity" and his "inexperience in ecclesiastical affairs," in view of which he urged against his appointment as a delegate to wait on Pope Damasus (Basil, Ep. 215). The account which Gregory himself gives of the discourteous reception accorded him by his metropolitan, Helladius, indicates a person who was not able to handle difficult situations (Ep. 1). But the most startling of Gregory's attitudes is that toward marriage. How, we may ask, could a married man write the *De virginitate*? While it may be justifiable to laud virginity as a state preferable to marriage, how is it possible for a man who was happily married (to judge by Nazianzen's letter) to have nothing good to say about marriage, and to fail to appreciate the deeper spiritual aspects of that union? All Gregory does is to harp on the dangers, uncertainties, and distractions which marriage entails.

## WRITINGS

Gregory has left us a considerable number of writings. The exegetical ones are important, in the first place, for the development of mystical theology. To those already mentioned we should add the homilies On the Lord's Prayer, On the Beatitudes, and On the Titles of the Psalms. The strong Platonic element in his mystical and ascetical theology finds peculiarly marked expression in his tract On Virginity, where Plato's imagery of the ascent of the soul by a ladder to the Form of the Beautiful is applied to the ascent of the Christian soul to God, above the distractions of evil and passion (Ch. 11). In these mystical works Gregory outlines some three stages of this ascent. The first is that of "apathy" or "liberty"—freedom, that is, from the slavery of passion. The second is "gnosis" or mystical knowledge, the night of the senses, whereby one passes from the visible to the invisible world. Finally, there is *theoria*, the highest stage of contemplation, but one that involves a negative element. The created soul can never really see God or reach the Divine Essence, for this is without limit. And so *theoria* implies the Divine Darkness. It is the destiny of the soul ever to strive for the vision of God, but never fully to attain it. There is a limitless progress in this ascent to the Divine, where the soul is ever aflame with desire but never fully satisfied.

Then there are Gregory's exegetical works on creation. He wrote a defense of Basil's Hexaemeron, and continued that work in two homilies on Gen. 1:26,[3] and in his important treatise On the Making of Man. In this latter he deals extensively with man's original state and with the doctrine of the resurrection. It is notable for the development of the idea that sexuality is a main root of man's troubles. While not evil in itself, it was provided by God for the propagation of the race when he foresaw that man would fall away from his original angelic nature (16.14; 17.3). When Gregory throughout his work speaks of *aphtharsia* (incorruptibility) he has the overcoming of sexuality primarily in mind. In considering the ascent of the soul to God,

[3] Frequently appended to Basil's Hexaemeron. While their authenticity has been disputed, it has recently been defended by E. von Ivanka in *Byz. Zeitschrift*, 1936, pp. 46–57.

he thinks of the first step as freedom from the passions which sexuality engenders.

Of Gregory's dogmatic works the most important is his great treatise Against Eunomius. Here he gives a detailed answer to the extreme Arian position which emphasized the unlikeness of the Son to the Father, and which was accordingly known as the "Anomoean" view, from *anomoios*, "unlike." The work is less one of originality than of penetration. In it Gregory sets forth the full implications of Eunomius' teaching, and defends his lately deceased brother Basil from charges that Eunomius had brought against him. Then there is his vehement reply to Apollinaris, *Antirrheticus adversus Apollinarem*, dealing with the union of the two natures in Christ. While affirming the fullness of the human nature of Christ against Apollinaris, Gregory is forced into language that comes perilously near Monophysitism at times. The complete blending of the two natures, so that the human is deified, has a double significance in Gregory. On the one hand it is the ground of that general deification of human nature which was the Eastern way of regarding salvation. On the other hand, it answered the objection of Apollinaris that, were the human nature in Christ complete, the Trinity would become a Quaternary. It may be noted, however, that in other passages Gregory displays an equally Nestorian tendency. He can speak of "the man" whom the Word assumed (cf. Catechetical Oration 16 fin.; 32). While he means by this the concrete instance of human nature, the phrase can be read in a Nestorian sense. However, it was for a later century to ponder this problem more fully and to reach the orthodox answer.

Of Gregory's Address on Religious Instruction we shall say more later. He has also left a number of shorter theological treatises which expound the doctrine of the Trinity. They are: On the Holy Spirit, Against the Macedonians, On the Holy Trinity, On the Faith, and That We Should Not Think of Saying There Are Three Gods (translated here). There is also his oration, delivered at the Synod of Constantinople in A.D. 383, On the Deity of the Son and the Holy Spirit. Notable, too, is his tract addressed to the Greeks, On Universal Ideas, in which he treats of the various expressions used for the Trinity.

Finally, there are extant a number of funeral orations (one being on his brother Basil), panegyrics (three being on the Forty Martyrs), and letters. We have previously mentioned his

Life of St. Macrina and his theological dialogue On the Soul and the Resurrection.[4]

# ON NOT THREE GODS

The first treatise of Gregory presented in this volume is one addressed to a certain ecclesiastic, Ablabius, on the issue of the Trinity. Ablabius had raised the question why we should not speak of three Gods when we recognize the deity of Father, Son, and Holy Spirit. In his reply Gregory gives a clear and brief exposition of the Cappadocian theology on this question. It is the point at which these Fathers made their most significant contribution to the orthodox cause. The classic Christian definition of the Godhead as three Persons and one Substance is the fruit of Cappadocian thinking.

The date of this tract is traditionally given as A.D. 375. It may, however, be a little later as Gregory was then only forty-one years old and we should hardly expect a man, just approaching middle age and newly consecrated a bishop, to write in quite the fatherly tone that Gregory adopts to his correspondent in the opening sentence. The precise date, however, cannot be determined and is not a matter of consequence. It is clear in the tract that the Arian issue is still a lively danger, so it was probably written before the Council of Constantinople in A.D. 381.

The problem the Cappadocians faced was this: to preserve the central idea of Athanasius that man's salvation depends upon the full deity of the Son, and yet to avoid the pitfall of Sabellianism. Athanasius, while escaping this danger, had never devised a satisfactory way of speaking of the distinctions of Person in the Godhead. It was this that the Cappadocians accomplished.

It was the horror of Sabellianism, which tended to identify the Son with the Father, and so endangered the principle of the distance of the Unbegotten from the created world, that led them to emphasize the distinctions in the Godhead. Both principles of God *in* relations and of God *above* relations had to be maintained. As inheritors of Origen's system, they were

---

4 Many of Gregory's treatises will be found translated in the fifth volume of the Nicene and Post-Nicene Fathers, Series II (see Bibliography). References we have given to Gregory of Nyssa's letters follow the enumeration in Migne, *P.G.* 46. The numbers in this English translation do not correspond.

familiar with the sharp distinction between begotten and unbegotten; and yet they avoided Origen's subordinationism
(which was one root of Arius' view), by seeing that "begotten"
and "created" were not necessarily synonymous. Origen had
tended to confuse them, regarding the Son as a "second god,"
created by the Father and so subordinate to him. Arianism had
developed this idea to its logical conclusion, and thereby made
apparent its full and dire consequences for the doctrine of
redemption. In response, the champions of the Nicene orthodoxy had to make a clear distinction between "created" and
"begotten."

But how, then, could the right relations within the Godhead
be expressed? The Cappadocian answer was to make a further
sharp distinction, this time between the words *hypostasis* (person)
and *ousia* (substance). They thought primarily in terms of
plurality, but they managed to reach a definition that equally
avoided Arianism and Sabellianism.

Originally these terms *ousia* and *hypostasis* were used synony-
mously to refer to "being" or "nature," and this confusion was
furthered by the fact that the Latin equivalent for the Greek
*hypostasis* was *substantia*. It was the work of the Cappadocians
to unravel this confusion and to stamp once and for all the
orthodox expression.

For them "substance" (*ousia*) refers to the nature of the
Godhead. It is that essential being which Father, Son, and
Spirit have in common. But it is not, properly speaking, a
"universal," in the same sense in which all men share in a
universal humanity, of which each is a particular instance. It
is true that some Cappadocian expressions are open to this
danger, one, in short, of tritheism.[5] But in three ways these
Fathers attempt to avoid it. For one thing they regard the
divine nature as ineffable, and hence even the term "Godhead" does not refer to the divine nature in itself, but only to
an attribute of it (his power of overseeing).[6] Then again, the
distinctions to be observed between particular men are not
applicable to the Godhead. For these depend upon individual
circumscription. Different men undertake different matters
according to their diverse environments and talents. But such
distinctions are not permissible in the Deity. Finally, the unity
of the Godhead is preserved by the identity of the attributes

---

5 See especially Basil, Ep. 214.4.
6 Taking *theos* (god) from *thea* (beholding). See Gregory's tract here
translated.

and operations of all the Persons. The goodness of the Father is the same as that of the Son and of the Spirit. As Gregory observes, "no activity is distinguished in the Persons as if it were brought to completion individually by each of them or separately apart from their joint supervision." It is this aspect of the divine unity that Gregory of Nyssa developed with some originality. It came to be known as the *perichōrēsis* (coinherence) or *circuminsessio*. On other points he is more clearly dependent upon Basil and Gregory Nazianzen.

Yet there are distinctions in the Godhead; but they are not such that this basic unity is endangered. They are expressed by the term *hypostasis* (person). This means *modes of being*, ways in which the Deity, identical in the three Persons, exists. It does not mean elements of being; nor does it refer to a circumscription of the one *ousia* so that it is divided between three separate entities. The only way in which there are three *hypostases* in the Godhead is in terms of causality. The Father is uncaused: the Son and the Spirit are caused. But this defines different modes of being in the Godhead: it does not divide the nature of the Godhead itself.

In consequence, *ousia* is not to be regarded merely as a universal, and *hypostasis* as a particular instance of it. That would surely lead to tritheism. The Cappadocian idea is far more subtle. The nature of the Godhead more nearly corresponds in their thought to Aristotle's idea of a particular, concrete existence (*prōtē ousia*), not to the *deutera ousia* which members of a species have in common. The *ousia* in the Godhead is *identical* in each Person: the common humanity in men is only *generic*.

It is for this reason that the chief charge brought against the Cappadocian theology by Adolf Harnack[7] and other writers[8] is far from fair. They claim that what triumphed at the Council of Constantinople in A.D. 381, with the victory of the Cappadocian position, was really a form of the Homoean view—"the community of substance in the sense of likeness (or equality) of substance, not in that of unity of substance."[9]

[7] *History of Dogma*, English tr., Williams and Norgate, London, 1898, Vol. 4, pp. 97 ff.

[8] The view was first put forward by Zahn. Its most notable expression is in F. Loofs, *Leitfaden zum Studium der Dogmengeschichte*, 4th ed., M. Niemeyer, Halle, 1906. He is followed by F. W. Green, in his essay "The Later Development of the Doctrine of the Trinity" in *Essays in the Trinity and Incarnation*, ed. by A. E. J. Rawlinson, Longmans, Green & Company, Inc., 1933, pp. 241–300.  [9] Harnack, *op. cit.*, Vol. 4, p. 97.

*Homoousios* (of the same substance) was really taken in the sense of *homoiousios* (of like substance). But this surely is to fail to appreciate the ways in which the Cappadocians affirmed the unity of the Godhead.[10]

It is certainly true that the danger of tritheism exists whenever one emphasizes (as did the Cappadocians) the distinctions of the Persons. It was to answer this charge that Gregory of Nyssa wrote his tract That We Should Not Think of Saying There Are Three Gods. If we attend carefully to what he says, we shall, I think, appreciate that Harnack's view is misleading.

Throughout the course of Christian history two chief types of analogy have been used in reference to the Trinity. The West (following Augustine) has distinguished the Persons in terms of internal relations within *a* person (e.g., memory, will, and intelligence). The Cappadocians most frequently begin from a consideration of *three* persons (Peter, James, and John). Now just as the latter needs qualification in order to avoid the dangers of tritheism, so the former needs equal qualification to avoid the errors of Unitarianism and Sabellianism. It is noteworthy, moreover, that many theologians used *both* types of analogy, because of the inherent dangers in each. This is true of Tertullian[11] and it is true of Gregory of Nyssa. While his tract on Not Three Gods develops the theme from a consideration of three people, the opening chapters of his Address on Religious Instruction develop it in reference to a man's capacity for thought and speech. In the first instance the distinctions within the Godhead are seen to be both *less* than and *different* from those between Peter, James, and John. In the latter, the differences again are *greater*. Thus the Godhead means *more* than *a* Person and *less* than *three* Persons, when we use the analogy of human personality to describe God.

## AN ADDRESS ON RELIGIOUS INSTRUCTION

The other treatise of Gregory translated in this volume is his Address on Religious Instruction (often called Catechetical Oration). Harnack referred to it as "the only writing of the fourth century which can be compared to the work *De principiis*"[12]; and there is, indeed, justice in this comparison. Gregory's

[10] An able reply to this thesis has been given by J. F. Bethune-Baker in *The Meaning of Homoousios in the "Constantinopolitan" Creed*, Texts and Studies 8, Cambridge University Press, 1901.
[11] Cf. *Adv. Praxeam* 3 and 5.          [12] *Op. cit.*, Vol. 4, p. 334.

Address is a compendium of Christian doctrine, which seeks to establish its truth on the basis of Greek philosophic thought. It is not, to be sure, as bold and original a creation as Origen's, nor is its scope as wide, since Gregory had in mind the practical needs of the catechist. Moreover, Gregory's own dependence upon Origen, Athanasius, and Methodius is often very clear. Yet, for all that, his Address is a notable achievement. Particularly in the doctrines of the atonement and the Eucharist does it show originality; and there is no better instance to be found of the spirit of Greek theology. It is more faithful to the orthodox tradition than was Origen, and while Gregory (as F. Ueberweg has remarked [13]) "sought to establish by rational considerations the whole complex of orthodox doctrines," we observe that in him the primary starting point is the faith of the Church rather than philosophic speculation.

That is not to say, however, that at some points he did not deviate from the orthodox position. Indeed, his tract was later regarded as having been interpolated by Origenists because of its universalist teaching on the Last Things.[14] It is true, too, that the general tendency of Eastern Christian thought, imbued as it was with the Hellenic spirit, did not fully appreciate some Biblical elements which the West developed, as, for instance, the significance of history. The final end of man is seen from the mystical point of view of the vision of God, rather than conceived in terms of the Kingdom. Gregory's teachings on creation, sexuality, and mortality may also be open to some question as reflecting too largely the basic ontological dualism of Greek culture, rather than the religious dualism of Scripture. There can be no doubt, however, that this Address gives, in its relatively small compass, a remarkable survey of Christian doctrine and reflects the genius of Eastern theology at its best. The teaching of the Church is adapted to the Hellenic environment and made intelligible to the Greek.

Gregory's Address appears to have been widely circulated in the Eastern Church, and to have influenced later writers. There are references to it in Theodoret and Leontius of Byzantium, while John of Damascus in his work On the Orthodox Faith is dependent upon Gregory's treatment of the Trinity and

[13] History of Philosophy, English trans., Charles Scribner's Sons, 1903, Vol. 1, p. 326.
[14] See Chs. 26 and 35. The charge was first made by Germanus, the eighth century patriarch of Constantinople (see Photius, Bibl. Cod., 233), and is quite unfounded.

the Eucharist. The Eucharistic chapter is also cited in the twelfth century by the Byzantine theologian Euthymius Zigabenus and by Nerses, catholicos of Armenia.[15]

The address is one of Gregory's later works and was written around A.D. 383. While it cannot be dated precisely, it would appear to have been composed after his great treatise Against Eunomius, and perhaps after the address given in Constantinople in A.D. 383., On the Deity of the Son and the Holy Spirit. It is probably to these works that he refers in Ch. 38.

Gregory's style is that of the rhetorician. The sentences are frequently long, and at times digressions and parentheses interrupt the flow of the argument. Synonyms and similes abound. A number of the latter are taken from medicine, and many of them are elaborated unduly. Translation is often rendered difficult for these reasons. In the one offered here the attempt has been made to present the exact sense in fluent English, by abbreviating the original sentence structure and by occasionally omitting the synonyms.

Aimed to assist the catechetical teacher, the Address covers the central elements of the Christian faith, and falls into four main sections:

Chs. 1– 4: The Doctrine of God and the Trinity.
Chs. 5– 7: The Creation of Man, the Nature of Evil, and the Fall.
Chs. 8–32: The Restoration of Man, the Incarnation and Atonement.
Chs. 33–40: Baptism, Eucharist, Faith, and Repentance.

In the first part of the work Gregory shows how the Christian doctrine of God represents the mean between Judaism and paganism,[16] and he indicates how Jew and Greek are to be approached with different arguments to convince them of the truth.

He then passes to consider the nature of evil. This he explains, like Origen, in terms of nonbeing. Evil arises from the privation of the good. A double significance attaches to this approach. On the one hand it avoids an ontological dualism between God and evil; on the other, it gives great emphasis to the freedom of the will. Both these were important to maintain against Gnostic and Manichaean tenets.

15 See J. H. Srawley's edition of the Greek text, pp. xlvii-xlviii, for these and other references.
16 For this idea, see Gregory Nazianzen, Orat. 23.8.

The large body of the work deals with the incarnation and the atonement. It answers the stock objections brought against these doctrines, and develops in an original manner the way in which the divine attributes of goodness, power, wisdom, and justice were united in the economy of redemption (Chs. 20–26). The most interesting feature of Gregory's treatment here is his elaboration of the ransom theory of the atonement. He works out the myth to the following effect: Satan had enslaved man through pleasure. God, being just, could not rescue him by an arbitrary and sovereign act of will. He had to provide a ransom which the devil would accept. Accordingly the Son became incarnate. The Godhead was veiled in flesh so that Satan would not be overawed by the direct vision of God. Yet the miracles of Christ showed him to be a man of such significance that the devil desired to take him captive in exchange for mankind which he had enslaved. For he thought thereby to get the better of the bargain. Little did he realize that it was God himself he was trying vainly to make a captive! God had veiled himself in human nature so that the devil, "like a greedy fish, might swallow the Godhead like a fishhook along with the flesh which was the bait" (24). In such a transaction the unity of God's attributes is apparent. His goodness is evident in his desire to save man; his power, in saving him; his justice, in not resorting to arbitrary force; and finally his wisdom, in contriving a suitable method.

Did God, then, use deceit? Not really, answers Gregory (26), for the devil himself finally profits from the encounter. Contact with the divine leads to even the devil's purification. Ultimately all creation must be restored to its original state.[17]

There is an obvious ingenuity in Gregory's myth, despite its repellent nature on the surface. Nor is it wholly original. The idea of the blood of Christ as a ransom paid to the devil is found in Origen (in *Rom.* 2:13), as is also the conception that the transaction involved some deceit (in *Matt.* 13:9).[18] But Gregory has worked the myth out more fully. It is significant in that it tries to express the objective and cosmic nature of the atonement, and to relate this to the divine attributes. Its defect lies in its somewhat grotesque imagery, and in its failure to introduce the theme of propitiation for sin.

[17] Here Gregory's dependence on Origen's universalism is very clear. He teaches the final restoration of all things in Chs. 26 and 35.
[18] So also Gregory Nazianzen, Orat. 39.13, but he rejects the myth of a ransom paid either to the devil or to the Father, Orat. 45.22.

In his general teaching on the incarnation Gregory shows significant dependence on Athanasius and on Methodius. He uses many of Athanasius' arguments in answering the question, Why did God become man? Then, too, the basic idea of man's deification he takes from Athanasius, though he does not develop the latter's thought that the incarnation restored to man the true knowledge of God. To Methodius, Gregory is indebted for his interpretation of the "coats of skin" (Gen. 3:21; Address, Ch. 8) as mortality,[19] for his idea that death was ordained by God for the purpose of dissolving the evil in our nature,[20] and for several illustrations and metaphors—e.g., that of the potter, which he uses in an identical way (Ch. 8).[21]

The most notable element in the last section of the Address is the treatment of the Eucharist (Ch. 37). Here Gregory displays his originality, and, as we have already indicated, this part of his work had no small influence on the Eastern development of Eucharistic doctrine.

His main idea is this: Since the salvation of man involves both soul and body, a way must be provided for our bodies to have an intimate union with the Saviour. This is what the Eucharist fulfills. The consecrated elements, by being the body of Christ, transform our nature, so that it comes to share the immortal quality of his body.

How can this happen? Gregory does not, on the surface at any rate, advance a view that anticipates the Latin doctrine of transubstantiation. Rather does he work out his theory in terms of the Aristotelian concept of nutrition. When we assimilate food, what occurs is that the basic elements (*stoicheia*) of bread and wine, for instance, are rearranged to take on a new form in so far as they now become human flesh and blood. The change they undergo is one of rearrangement, in which a new form (*eidos*) emerges. The constituent elements remain the same, but this regrouping of them gives them new potency and sets them in new relations.

This principle Gregory now applies to the human nature of Christ. Since this was supported in the usual manner by food,

---

[19] Methodius, *De res.* 1.39, ed. G. N. Bonwetsch, *Die griechischen christlichen Schriftsteller*, Vol. 27, J. C. Hinrichs, Leipzig, 1917, pp. 282 ff. Here Methodius attacks Origen's view that the "coats of skin" referred to the bodies men received as fetters after the Fall (cf. *Con. Cels.* 4.40).

[20] Ch. 8, Methodius, *op. cit.*, 1.39 ff.

[21] Methodius, *op. cit.*, 1.44, pp. 292, 293. See also the illustration of the human seed, Gregory, Address, Ch. 33, Methodius, *op. cit.*, 2.20, pp. 272, 273.

e.g., bread and wine, these things were in a way potentially his body, for by assimilation that is what they became. By being, moreover, the body of the Word, they acquired the divine property of immortality.

Now in the Eucharist something similar happens. Bread, which is potentially the body of Christ, becomes such by the word of God, i.e., the consecration. It is the same process by which it became his body in the days of his flesh, but with this difference: where then the process was a lengthy one of assimilation, it is now immediate by the consecration. But what is involved is identical in both cases—the rearrangement of the elements of which bread is composed into a new form, the body of Christ. And by means of our receiving this body, our bodies become deified and share in its immortal nature, just as his body, by being united with him in the incarnation, was deified.

The change, then, that consecration effects is not one of "substance" (transubstantiation), but of "form." From one point of view, this looks like the reverse of transubstantiation. It is not by the change of an underlying "substance" that bread becomes the body of Christ, but by a rearrangement of its constituent elements, so that these acquire new potency and new relations. Like transubstantiation, Gregory's view is a realistic one of a sort. But it starts from the presupposition that the reality of a thing has to do with the "form" in which its material elements are arranged, and not with its underlying substance.

Yet there is a point at which these two views are closer to each other than appears on the surface. The medieval view of "substance," basic to the doctrine of transubstantiation, is not unrelated to the idea of "form." For what characterizes the "substance" of a thing and gives it its essential being is the "form" in which it participates. The difficulty that arises in contrasting these two doctrines goes back to confusions in Aristotle himself. He views material things as composed not only of matter and form. They imply also a third conception —an underlying substance (something between matter and form) which Aristotle calls *hypokeimenon*. Now the Latin idea of substance involves both this and form. Thus, to oversimplify a very complex problem, we could compare Gregory's view with transubstantiation in this way. Since the *stoicheia* are not changed but only rearranged, Gregory does not go so far as the Latin doctrine. But the latter view approaches his, since it is the change of "form" in an object that is the really important factor in giving it its essential nature.

## SUMMARY

The significance of Gregory of Nyssa can be summed up in this: He continued the Origenist tradition of interpreting Christianity in terms of Greek culture, but he saw the necessity of subordinating philosophy to the faith. Less daring and original than Origen, he was more successful in using philosophy to support Christian truth, because, speculative though he was, he was less inclined to make Christianity *into* a philosophy. His contribution lay in three areas: First, in the realm of the mystical theology. He developed the doctrine of the Divine Darkness, which was to reach its fullest expression in Pseudo-Dionysius. Secondly, in elaborating the Trinitarian definition of three Persons and one Substance, stressing particularly the unity of the Persons. And thirdly, in offering a somewhat original presentation of the doctrines of the atonement and the Eucharist.

It would be difficult to find a Church Father who so admirably expresses the full round of Eastern Orthodox teaching: its clear Trinitarianism, its mysticism, its asceticism, its realistic sacramentalism, its idea of man's deification, and its blending of Platonic and Aristotelian forms of thought. In Gregory, too, is to be seen the weakness sometimes apparent in Eastern theology: its failure to grasp the meaning of history, and its difficulty in freeing itself fully from Hellenic elements in its approach to creation, sexuality, and death.

# BIBLIOGRAPHY

## TEXTS AND TRANSLATIONS

The need for a modern critical edition of the works of Gregory of Nyssa has long been felt. Happily the task has now been begun under the direction of Werner Jaeger. So far, however, only the Greek text of the work Against Eunomius and of the letters and ascetic works has appeared. *Gregorii Nysseni opera,* Vol. I, *Contra Eunomium libri,* was edited by Werner Jaeger, 2 vols., Weidmann, Berlin, 1921. The text is based on a study of eighteen MSS., dating from the eleventh to the sixteenth centuries. Vol. 8, Fasc. 2, *Gregorii Nysseni epistulae,* was edited by G. Pascali, Weidmann, Berlin, 1925, and Vol. 8, Pt. 1, *Gregorii Nysseni opera ascetica,* by W. Jaeger, J. V. Cavarnos, and V. W. Callahan, Brill, Leiden, 1952. A foretaste of the critical work by Jean Daniélou on the Life of Moses has been given by him in an article in *Recherches de science religieuse,* Vol. 30, July, 1940, pp. 328–347.

For the rest we are almost entirely dependent upon much older and less trustworthy editions, though there is one notable exception to this. The earliest edition was published in Paris from Claude Morel's press, in 1615, under the editorship of Fronto Ducaeus. Three years later an appendix was added from materials supplied by Jacob Gretser. A second edition issued from the same press in 1638, but was inferior in accuracy as well as in format to the original one. Between this period and the nineteenth century a number of new works of Gregory were published in the patristic collections of L. A. Zacagni (some letters, Rome, 1698), A. Gallandi (Venice, 1765–1781), and Cardinal Mai (Rome, 1825 ff., and 1847). Almost all this material was incorporated in the edition of J. P. Migne, *Patrologiae cursus completus:* Series Graeca, Vols. 44–46, Paris, 1863.

Attempts to produce emended texts of Gregory's works were made by J. C. Krabinger (including the *Oratio catechetica*, Leipzig, 1837), by G. H. Forbes (Burntisland, 1855–1861), and F. Oehler (Halle, 1865). While all these scholars contemplated complete critical editions, in each case they published only a few treatises. For an emended text of the Oration on Basil see below.

The notable exception, to which we referred above, is the text of the Catechetical Oration of Gregory of Nyssa, produced by J. H. Srawley for the Cambridge Patristic Studies, Cambridge University Press, 1903. This was based on a study of some sixteen MSS., and has been used for the translation offered here. It contains an excellent introduction and most useful notes.

The text of the tract On Not Three Gods has been translated from the edition of F. Oehler, Bibliothek der Kirchenväter, *Eine Auswahl aus deren Werken*, Part 1, Vol. 1, pp. 186–217, Wilhelm Engelmann, Leipzig, 1858. The text is that of Morel, 1638, with a few suggested emendations, but no new collation of MSS. was made for the edition. It is provided with a rendering into German.

A considerable number of Gregory's works have been translated into English by William Moore and Henry A. Wilson in the Select Library of Nicene and Post-Nicene Fathers of the Christian Church, Series II, Vol. 5, New York, 1893. This useful volume has a good introduction and the translations are accurate. Both Gregory's works offered here are included.

There is a French edition of the Address, with introduction, critical notes, and translation by Louis Meridier, in Hemmer and Lejay's "Textes et Documents": *Grégoire de Nysse, Discours catéchétique*, Alfonse Picard et Fils, Paris, 1908. The Greek text given is that by Srawley.

There is a free, but very helpful, rendering of the Address into German by Karl Weiss, in the Bibliothek der Kirchenväter, Vol. 56, Josef Kösel and Friedrich Pustet, Munich, 1927, pp. 1–85. Oehler's text (based on that of 1638) was used.

J. H. Srawley produced an English translation for the Early Church Classics: *The Catechetical Oration of St. Gregory of Nyssa*, S.P.C.K., London, 1917. This has a good introduction, and Dr. Srawley's rendering has been of considerable aid to the present editor. It is extremely accurate, even frequently retaining the lengthy and rhetorical sentence structure of the original.

Mention may also be made of the French translation of *The*

*Creation of Man* for Sources chrétiennes. This has been done by Jean Laplace, with notes by Jean Daniélou, *Grégoire de Nysse, La Création de l'homme*, Éditions du Cerf, Paris, 1943. The text used is that in Migne, with some of Forbes's emendations. The introduction is very informative. Jean Daniélou has also provided a translation, with introduction and notes, of the *Contemplation sur la vie de Moïse* in the same series, Éditions du Cerf, Paris, 1943. Finally, there are English renderings of the Life of St. Macrina by W. K. Lowther Clarke, Early Church Classics, S.P.C.K., London, 1916, and of the *Encomium of Saint Gregory, Bishop of Nyssa, on His Brother Saint Basil, Archbishop of Cappadocian Caesarea*, by J. A. Stein, Catholic University, Washington, 1928, with revised text (i.e., Migne corrected by reference to six MSS.) and commentary.

### WORKS ON GREGORY OF NYSSA

Important early works are by Julius Rupp, *Gregors des Bischofs von Nyssa Leben und Meinungen*, Dyk, Leipzig, 1834, and S. P. Heyns, *Disputatio historico-theologica de Gregorio Nysseno*, Weidmann, Leyden, 1835.

There is a careful and informative article on "Gregorius Nyssenus" in the *Dictionary of Christian Biography* by Edmund Venables, Vol. 2, John Murray, London, 1880. It is particularly good on Gregory's life. The article by F. Loofs, "Gregor von Nyssa," in the *Realencyclopädie für protestantische Theologie und Kirche*, Vol. 7, J. C. Hinrichs, Leipzig, 1899, is a patient survey of his life and writings, but does not discuss his thought.

Two important modern works on Gregory's thought are by H. V. de Balthasar, *Présence et pénsée, Essai sur la philosophie religieuse de Grégoire de Nysse*, Gabriel Beauchesne, Paris, 1942, and Jean Daniélou, *Platonisme et théologie mystique*: *Essai sur la doctrine spirituelle de Saint Grégoire de Nysse*, Aubier, Paris, 1944. The first is an illuminating study of Gregory's underlying ideas, though it is a little artificial in its systematization. It has a very full bibliography. The other work is a basic study of his mystical theology. A clear summary of this latter (based on Daniélou) is given by J. Trinick in his lecture *Gregory of Nyssa and the Rise of Christian Mysticism*, Burning Glass Papers 26, Ridgeway House, Shorne, Kent, no date.

The best introduction to the Cappadocian theology in English is the article by J. H. Srawley in the *Encyclopaedia of Religion and Ethics*, edited by James Hastings, Charles Scribner's

Sons, 1919, Vol. 3, pp. 212–217. Reference should also be made to the relevant sections in G. L. Prestige, *God in Patristic Thought*, Heinemann, London, 1936; in Reinhold Seeberg, *Text-Book of the History of Doctrines*, tr. by Charles E. Hay, United Lutheran Publication House, Philadelphia, 1905; and in Adolf Harnack, *History of Dogma*, Vol. 4, tr. by E. B. Speirs and James Millar, Williams and Norgate, London, 1898. J. F. Bethune-Baker's monograph, *The Meaning of Homoousios in the "Constantinopolitan" Creed*, Texts and Studies, Vol. 8, No. 1, Cambridge University Press, 1901, is very important. There is an article "The Later Development of the Doctrine of the Trinity," by F. W. Green, in *Essays in the Trinity and Incarnation*, edited by A. E. J. Rawlinson, Longmans, Green & Company, Inc., New York, 1933, pp. 239–300. The theology of Gregory is studied in K. Holl, *Amphilochius von Ikonium in seinem Verhältnis zu den grossen Kappadoziern*, J. C. B. Mohr, Tübingen, 1904, especially pp. 196–235. Some interesting observations on the Cappadocians and Iranian religion will be found in Endre Ivanka's *Hellenisches und Christliches im Frühbyzantinischen Geistesleben*, Herder, Vienna, 1948, pp. 28–67. Other monographs on the Trinitarian question are F. Diekamp, *Die Gotteslehre des hl. Gregors von Nyssa*, Aschendorff, Munich, 1896; J. Bayer, *Gregors von Nyssa Gottesbegriff*, Diss, Giessen, 1935; M. G. de Castro, *Die Trinitätslehre des heiligen Gregors von Nyssa*, Freiburg Theological Studies, 50, Herder, Freiburg, 1938; and S. Gonzalez, *La fórmula* mia phusis treis hypostaseis *en San Gregorio de Nisa*, Gregorian University, Rome, 1939.

Gregory's style has been studied by L. Méridier, *L'Influence de la seconde sophistique sur l'oeuvre de Grégoire de Nysse*, Rennes, 1906. For his philosophy see H. F. Cherniss, *The Platonism of Gregory of Nyssa*, University of California Press, Berkeley, 1930.

For the doctrine of man in Gregory see Roger Leys, *L'Image de Dieu chez Saint Grégoire de Nysse*, Nauwelaerts, Louvain, 1952; J. T. Muckle, "The Doctrine of Gregory of Nyssa on Man as the Image of God," in *Mediaeval Studies*, 7, 1945, pp. 55–84; J. B. Schoemann, "Gregors von Nyssa theologische Anthropologie als Bildtheologie," in *Scholastik*, 1943, pp. 31–53, 175–200; W. Vollert, *Die Lehre Gregors von Nyssa vom Guten und Bösen*, Leipzig, 1897; F. Hilt, *Des hl. Gregors von Nyssa Lehre von Menschen*, Cologne, 1890, and the French edition of The Creation of Man already noted.

The Eucharistic teaching has been treated by J. Maier, *Die Eucharistielehre der drei grossen Kappadocier*, Herder, Freiburg,

1915; and note the interpretation given by J. H. Srawley in his edition of the Greek text (pp. xxxvi–xlii).

On the atonement see J. B. Aufhauser, *Die Heilslehre des hl. Gregors von Nyssa*, Munich, 1910, and the relevant sections of R. S. Franks, *History of the Doctrine of the Work of Christ*, Vol. 1, New York, 1918, and G. Aulén, *Christus Victor*, tr. by A. G. Hebert, The Macmillan Company, 1931.

A factual summary of various aspects of the life of the fourth century is given by T. A. Goggin in her dissertation *The Times of Gregory of Nyssa as Reflected in the Letters and the Contra Eunomium*, Catholic University, Washington, 1947.

# An Answer to Ablabius:
# That We Should Not Think
# of Saying
# There Are Three Gods[1]

## THE TEXT

By rights it is you, who are in the prime of all your inner powers, who ought to continue the war against the enemies of truth and not to shrink from the task. Thus we fathers may be gladdened by the noble efforts of our children. For this is what the law of nature presupposes. But since you have turned your ranks and direct toward us the assaults of those darts which are hurled by the opponents of truth, and bid us old men to quench with the shield of faith their "hot, burning coals"[2] and their missiles sharpened by knowledge (as they falsely call it), we accept the challenge. We make ourselves a pattern of ready obedience so that you, yourself, Ablabius, Christ's noble soldier, may give us an equal response to a similar challenge, should we ever summon you to such a contest.

It is no small matter which you have broached with us; nor is it such as to involve little damage if it is not properly examined. For the force of the question, on the surface, compels us to accept one of two totally incongruous views. Either we must say there are three gods, which is blasphemy; or else we must deny divinity to the Son and the Holy Spirit, which is irreligious and absurd.

The argument you state runs like this: Peter, James, and John are called three men, despite the fact they share in a single humanity. And there is nothing absurd in using the word for their nature in the plural, if those who are thus united in nature be many. If, then, general usage grants this, and no one forbids us to speak of two as two, or of more than two as three,

1 Ablabius: a younger bishop to whom two of Gregory's letters are addressed, Epistles 6 and 21.          2 Ps. 120:4.

how is it that we in some way compromise our confession, by saying on the one hand that the Father, the Son, and the Holy Spirit have a single Godhead, and by denying on the other that we can speak of three gods? For in speaking of the mysteries [of the faith], we acknowledge three Persons and recognize there is no difference in nature between them.

As I have already said, it is very difficult to deal with the question. If, indeed, we could find something to support the mind in its uncertainty, so that it no longer doubted and wavered in the face of this extraordinary dilemma, it would be well. But if our rather feeble powers of reason prove unequal to the problem, we must guard the tradition we have received from the Fathers, as ever sure and immovable, and seek from the Lord a means of defending our faith. If this should be discovered by anyone endowed with grace, we shall give thanks to Him who granted the grace. If not, we shall none the less hold on to our unchangeable faith in those points which have been established.

Why is it, then, that we are accustomed to use the plural when we make a count of those who are shown to have the same nature? We say there are "so many men," and we do not call them all "one." And yet, when we refer to the divine nature, why does our dogma exclude a multitude of gods, and while enumerating the Persons, not admit their plural significance? Were one speaking superficially to simple folk, one might seem to give an answer by this, viz., that our doctrine refused to enumerate a number of gods in order to avoid similarity with Greek polytheism. Were we to speak of the Deity not in the singular, but in the plural, as they are accustomed to do, there might be thought to be some kinship between their doctrine and ours. Such an answer, given to rather naïve people, might seem satisfactory. To others, however, who demand that one or other of the alternatives must stand— either that we should not acknowledge the divinity of the three Persons, or that we should, without hesitation, count as three those who share the same divinity—such an answer as we have just given would not suffice to resolve the problem. We must, therefore, make our reply at greater length, tracking down the truth as best we can, for the question is no ordinary one.

Our first point is this: To use in the plural the word for the nature of those who do not[3] differ in nature, and to speak of "many men," is a customary misuse of language. It is like

[3] Adding *mē*.

saying that there are many human natures. That this is so is
clear from the following instance. When we address someone,
we do not call him by the name of his nature. Since he would
have that name in common with others, confusion would
result; and everyone within hearing would think that he was
being addressed. For the summons was not by an individual
name, but by the name of a common nature. Rather do we
distinguish him from the multitude by using his proper name,
that name, I mean, which signifies a particular subject. There
are many who have shared in the same nature—disciples,
apostles, martyrs, for instance—but the "man" in them all is
one. Hence, as we have said, the term "man" does not refer
to the particularity of each, but to their common nature. For
Luke is a man, as is Stephen. But that does not mean that if
anyone is a man he is therefore Luke or Stephen. Rather does
the distinction of persons arise from the individual differences
we observe in each. When we see them together, we can count
them. Yet the nature is one, united in itself, a unit completely
indivisible, which is neither increased by addition nor diminished
by subtraction, being and remaining essentially one, inseparable
even when appearing in plurality, continuous and entire, and
not divided by the individuals who share in it.

Just as we speak of a people, a mob, an army, and an
assembly always in the singular, and yet each of them entails
plurality, so even the term "man" should properly and most
accurately be used in the singular, even if those we observe to
share in the same nature constitute a plurality. Thus it would
be much better to correct our misguided habit and no longer
use the word for a nature in the plural than by bondage to it
to transfer the same error to our teaching about God. Yet it is
impracticable to correct the habit, for how could you persuade
anyone not to call those he observes having the same nature
"many men"? Habit, indeed, is always hard to change. Hence,
in not resisting the prevailing habit in the case of a lower
nature, we should not go very far wrong. No damage arises
from such a misguided use of words. In the case, however, of
our teaching about God the indiscriminate [4] use of words entails
no similar freedom from danger. For trifles here are far from
trifling. Therefore we must confess one God, as Scripture bears
witness, "Hear, O Israel, the Lord thy God is one Lord," [5]
even though the term "Godhead" embraces the holy Trinity.
This I say in accordance with the principle which we have

4 Reading *adiaphoros* for *diaphoros*.     5 Deut. 6:4.

given in reference to human nature and by which we have learned that we must not use the word for this nature in the plural. We must now make a more careful examination of the word "Godhead," in order that from the meaning attaching to the word we may get some help in clarifying the matter in hand.

Most people think that the word "Godhead" refers to God's nature in a special way. Just as the heaven, the sun, or any other of the world's elements is denoted by a proper name which signifies its subject, so they say that, in reference to the transcendent and divine nature, the word "Godhead" is fitly applied, like some proper name, to what it represents. We, however, following the suggestions of Holy Scripture, have learned that His nature cannot be named and is ineffable. We say that every name, whether invented by human custom or handed down by the Scriptures, is indicative of our conceptions of the divine nature, but does not signify what that nature is in itself. It is not very difficult to prove that this is the case. For, even without going into their origins, you will find that all terms that refer to the created world are accidentally applied to their subjects. We are content, in whatever way, to signify things by their names so as to avoid confusion in our knowledge of the things we refer to. But whatever terms there are to lead us to the knowledge of God, each of them contains a particular idea of its own; and you will not find any word among the terms especially applied to God which is without some meaning. From this it is clear that the divine nature in itself is not signified by any of these terms. Rather is some attribute declared by what is said. For we say, perhaps, that the divine is incorruptible or powerful or whatever else we are in the habit of saying. But in each of these terms we find a particular idea which by thought and expression we rightly attribute to the divine nature, but which does not express what that nature essentially is. For the subject, whatever it may be, is incorruptible, but our idea of incorruptibility is this: that that which is is not resolved into decay. In saying, then, that He is incorruptible, we tell what his nature does not suffer. But what that is which does not suffer corruption we have not defined. Or again, even if we say he is the creator of life, while we indicate by the expression what it is he creates, we do not reveal by the word what creates it. By the same principle, we find in all other cases that the significance attaching to divine names lies either in their forbidding wrong conceptions of the divine nature or in their teaching right ones. But they do not contain an explanation of the nature in itself.

We perceive, then, the varied operations of the transcendent power, and fit our way of speaking of him to each of the operations known to us. Now one of these is the power of viewing and seeing, or, one might say, of beholding.[6] By it God surveys all things and oversees them all. He discerns our thoughts, and by his power of beholding penetrates even what is invisible. From this we suppose that "Godhead" (*theotēs*) is derived from "beholding" (*thea*), and that by general custom and the teaching of the Scriptures, he who is our beholder (*theatēs*) is called God (*theos*). Now if anyone admits that to behold and see are the same thing, and that the God who oversees all things both is and is called the overseer of the universe, let him consider whether this operation belongs to one of the Persons we believe to constitute the holy Trinity, or whether the power extends to the three Persons. For if our interpretation of "Godhead" is the right one, and the things which are seen are said to be beheld (*theata*), and that which beholds them is called God (*theos*), no one of the Persons of the Trinity could properly be excluded from this form of address on the ground of the meaning of the word. For Scripture attributes sight equally to Father, Son, and Holy Spirit. David says, "See, O God our defender."[7] From this we learn that the power of sight is proper to the idea of God so far as he is conceived. For David said, "See, O Lord." But Jesus, too, sees the thoughts of those who condemn him because he forgives men's sins on his own authority. For it says, "Jesus, seeing their thoughts."[8] And in reference to the Holy Spirit, Peter says to Ananias, "Why has Satan filled your heart to lie to the Holy Spirit?"[9] Thus he shows that the Holy Spirit, by whom the secret was disclosed to Peter, was a faithful witness and privy to what Ananias dared to do in secret. For Ananias became a thief of his own property, imagining he was escaping everyone's notice and hiding his sin. But at the same moment the Holy Spirit was in Peter and discerned his degraded and avaricious intention and Himself gave Peter the power to penetrate the secret; which He clearly could not have done had He been unable to discern what is hidden.

But someone will say that our manner of argument does not yet touch the question raised. For even granted that the term "Godhead" has reference to the common nature, that is no

---

[6] *Theatikē.*        [7] Ps. 84:9.        [8] Matt. 9:4.        [9] Acts 5:3.

proof we should not speak of "gods." On the contrary, it rather forces us to do so. For we find that people are not accustomed to use the singular when referring to many—not only when these share a common nature, but even when they are in the same business. Thus we speak of "many orators," or "surveyors," or "farmers," or "shoemakers," and so on. If, indeed, "Godhead" were a way of talking about God's nature, it would be more proper, following the line of reasoning given, to include the three Persons in the singular, and to speak about one God, since the nature is indivisible and inseparable. But since we have proved by the foregoing that the word "Godhead" signifies an operation and not a nature, our argument seems to be driven to the contrary conclusion. Hence we must rather speak of three gods who are beheld in the same operation, just as they do who speak of "three philosophers" or "three orators," or any other name derived from a profession, when there are many who share it.

I have taken pains to go into this matter fully by adducing our adversaries' objections, so that our teaching may be the more firmly fixed, being strengthened by the forcefulness of their contradictions. Let us now resume our argument.

We have fairly well proved by our argument that the word "Godhead" does not refer to a nature, but to an operation. Perhaps, then, someone might with good cause adduce the following reason why men who share the same profession with one another can be counted and referred to in the plural, while the Deity is spoken of in the singular as one God and one Godhead, despite the fact that the three Persons are not excluded from the significance attaching to "Godhead." He might argue that in the case of men, even if many share the same operation, each one separately and by himself undertakes the matter at hand. By his individual action each contributes nothing to the others engaged in the same task. For if there are many orators, their pursuit, being identical, bears the same name despite their plurality. Yet each one who follows this pursuit goes about it on his own. This one pleads in his special way, that one in his. In the case of men, therefore, since we can differentiate the action of each while they are engaged in the same task, they are rightly referred to in the plural. Each is distinguished from the others by his special environment and his particular way of handling the task.

With regard to the divine nature, on the other hand, it is otherwise. We do not learn that the Father does something on his own, in which the Son does not co-operate. Or again, that the Son acts on his own without the Spirit. Rather does every operation which extends from God to creation and is designated according to our differing conceptions of it have its origin in the Father, proceed through the Son, and reach its completion by the Holy Spirit. It is for this reason that the word for the operation is not divided among the persons involved. For the action of each in any matter is not separate and individualized. But whatever occurs, whether in reference to God's providence for us or to the government and constitution of the universe, occurs through the three Persons, and is not three separate things.

We can grasp this by reference to a single instance. From Him, I say, who is the source of gifts, all things that share in this grace have obtained life. When, then, we inquire whence this good gift came to us, we find through the guidance of the Scriptures that it was through the Father, the Son, and the Holy Spirit. But though we take it for granted that there are three Persons and names, we do not imagine that three different lives are granted us—one from each of them. Rather is it the same life which is produced by the Father, prepared by the Son, and depends on the will of the Holy Spirit.

Thus the holy Trinity brings to effect every operation in a similar way. It is not by separate action according to the number of the Persons; but there is one motion and disposition of the good will which proceeds from the Father, through the Son, to the Spirit. For we do not call those who produce a single life three life-givers; nor do we say they are three good beings who are seen to share the same goodness; nor do we speak of them in the plural in reference to all their other attributes. In the same way we cannot enumerate as three gods those who jointly, inseparably, and mutually exercise their divine power and activity of overseeing us and the whole creation.

When we learn from Scripture that it is the God of the universe who judges all the earth,[10] we say he is the judge of all things through the Son. And again, when we hear that the Father judges no one,[11] we do not think that Scripture is at variance with itself. For he who judges all the earth does this through the Son to whom he has given all judgment. And everything done by the Only-begotten has reference to the Father, so that he both is the judge of all and yet judges no

[10] Cf. Rom. 3:6.      [11] John 5:22.

one. For, as was said, he has committed all judgment to the Son; and all the judgment of the Son is not something alien to the Father's will. Hence no one can properly say either that there are two judges or that one of them is excluded from the authority and power of judgment.

In the same way, with reference to the word "Godhead," Christ is the power of God and the wisdom of God. And the Father exercises his power of overseeing or beholding (*theatikēn*), which we call "Godhead" (*theotēta*), through the Only-begotten, who by the Holy Spirit makes all power perfect, and who judges, as Isaiah says,[12] by the spirit of judgment and the spirit of fire. Thus he acts in accordance with the gospel saying made to the Jews. For he says, "If I by the Spirit of God cast out demons."[13] By the unity of the action, he embraces every form of doing good in this instance. For the word for the operation cannot be divided among many when they mutually bring to effect a single action.

As we have already said, the principle of the overseeing and beholding (*theatikēs*) power is a unity in Father, Son, and Holy Spirit. It issues from the Father, as from a spring. It is actualized by the Son; and its grace is perfected by the power of the Holy Spirit. No activity is distinguished among the Persons, as if it were brought to completion individually by each of them or separately apart from their joint supervision. Rather is all providence, care and direction of everything, whether in the sensible creation or of heavenly nature, one and not three. The preservation of what exists, the rectifying of what is amiss, the instruction of what is set right, is directed by the holy Trinity. But it is not divided into three parts according to the number of the Persons acknowledged by the faith, so that each operation, viewed by itself, should be the work of the Father alone, or of the Only-begotten by himself, or of the Holy Spirit separately. But while, as the apostle says,[14] the one and the same Spirit distributes his benefits to each one severally, this beneficent movement of the Spirit is not without beginning. Rather do we find that the power we conceive as preceding it, namely, the only-begotten God, effects everything. Apart from him nothing comes into being; and again, this source of goodness issues from the Father's will.

Every good thing and everything we name as good depends on the power and purpose which is without beginning. And it is brought to completion by the power of the Holy Spirit and

[12] Isa. 4:4.  [13] Matt. 12:28.  [14] Cf. I Cor. 12:11.

through the only-begotten God, immediately and independent of time. No delay exists or is to be conceived in the movement of the divine will from the Father through the Son and to the Holy Spirit. Now the Godhead is one of these good names and concepts; and hence the word cannot be rightly used in the plural, since the unity of operation forbids the plural number.

The Saviour of all men, especially of believers, is spoken of by the apostle [15] as one. Yet no one argues from this expression that the Son does not save believers, or that those who share in salvation receive it apart from the Spirit. But God who is over all is the Saviour of all, while the Son brings salvation to effect by the grace of the Spirit. Yet on this account Scripture does not call them three Saviours, although salvation is recognized to come from the holy Trinity. In the same way they are not three gods according to the meaning we have given to the term "Godhead," although this expression attaches to the holy Trinity.

It does not seem to me entirely necessary for the proof of my present argument to refute opponents who claim that "Godhead" should not be conceived in terms of operation. For we believe that the divine nature is unlimited and incomprehensible, and hence we do not conceive of its being comprehended. But we declare that the nature is in every way to be thought of as infinite. What is altogether infinite is not limited in one respect and not in another, but infinity entirely transcends limitation. Therefore that which is without limit is certainly not limited by the word we use for it. In order, then, that our conception of the divine nature should remain unlimited, we say that the divine transcends every name for it. And one of these names is "Godhead." The same thing, then, cannot on the one hand be identical with the name, and yet on the other be conceived as transcending every name.

If, however, our opponents want to claim that "Godhead" refers to nature and not to operation, we shall revert to our former argument. [We shall say] that the habit of giving a plural significance to the word for a nature is mistaken. When a nature is observed in a larger or in a smaller number, neither increase nor diminution properly attaches to it. Only those things are enumerated by addition which are seen to be individually circumscribed. This circumscription is noted by bodily appearance, by size, by place, and by distinction of form and color. What is observed to transcend these things is beyond

15 Cf. I Tim. 4:10. The reference is to the Father.

circumscription by means of these categories. What is not circumscribed cannot be numbered; and what is not numbered cannot be observed in quantities.

We say of gold, when it is made into small coins, that it is one and that it is spoken of as such. While we speak of many coins or many staters,[16] we find no multiplication of the nature of gold by reason of the numbers of staters. That is why we speak of "much gold" in view of a large quantity of plate or coins. But we do not say "many golds" on account of the quantity of the material, unless one speaks this way of "many gold [pieces]," [17] such as darics or staters. In which case it is not the material but the coins which admit of the plural signification. For properly speaking we should not say "many gold [pieces]," but "many golden ones."

As, then, there may be many golden staters, but gold is one, so we may be confronted with many who individually share in human nature, such as Peter, James, and John, yet the "man" [the human nature] in them is one. Even if the Scripture extends the word to a plural significance by saying, "Men swear by the greater," [18] or, "sons of men," and so on, we must realize that it here uses the prevailing mode of speech. It does not lay down rules how words ought to be used in one way or another. It does not record these phrases by way of giving technical instruction in the use of words. But it uses the word according to prevailing custom, having only this in view, that the word may be helpful to those who receive it. It does not use language with precision in matters where no harm arises in the understanding of the phrases. Indeed, it would be a lengthy task to list the inaccurate expressions from Scripture to prove my point. But where there is danger of a point of truth being perverted, we no longer find this careless and indifferent use of words in Scripture.

It is for this reason that Scripture allows "men" to be used in the plural because, by such an expression, no one would be misled to suppose there is a multitude of "humanities," or to think that, by the plural use of the word for that nature, many human natures are signified. But the word "God" it carefully uses in the singular, guarding against introducing different natures in the divine essence by the plural significance of "gods." Wherefore it says, "The Lord God is one Lord." [19] By the word "Godhead" it proclaims, too, the only-begotten

[16] A small gold coin.                    [17] In the Greek, "many golds."
[18] Heb. 6:16.                    [19] Deut. 6:4.

God, and does not divide the unity into a duality so as to call the Father and the Son two gods, although each is called God by holy writers. The Father is God and the Son is God; and yet by the same affirmation God is one, because no distinction of nature or of operation is to be observed in the Godhead.

For if, as those who are misled suppose, there are differences of nature in the holy Trinity, it would follow that their number would be extended to a plurality of gods and divided by the divinity of essence in their subjects. But since the divine, single, and unchanging nature eschews all diversity of essence, in order to guard its unity, it admits of itself no plural significance. But as it is said to be one nature, so all the other attributes are numbered in the singular—God, good, holy, saviour, righteous, judge, and any other conceivable attribute of God, whether one says these refer to his nature or to his operation—a point we shall not dispute.

Should anyone cavil at our argument that, by refusing to acknowledge distinctions in the nature, it makes for an admixture and confusion of the Persons, we will give the following answer to such a charge. Although we acknowledge the nature is undifferentiated, we do not deny a distinction with respect to causality. That is the only way by which we distinguish one Person from the other, by believing, that is, that one is the cause and the other depends on the cause. Again, we recognize another distinction with regard to that which depends on the cause. There is that which depends on the first cause and that which is derived from what immediately depends on the first cause. Thus the attribute of being only-begotten without doubt remains with the Son, and we do not question that the Spirit is derived from the Father. For the mediation of the Son, while it guards his prerogative of being only-begotten, does not exclude the relation which the Spirit has by nature to the Father.

When we speak of a cause and that which depends on it, we do not, by these words, refer to nature. For no one would hold that cause and nature are identical. Rather do we indicate a difference in manner of existence. For in saying the one is caused and the other uncaused, we do not divide the nature by the principle of causality, but only explain that the Son does not exist without generation, nor the Father by generation. It is necessary for us first to believe that something exists, and then to examine in what way the object of our belief exists. The question of what exists is one thing: the manner of its existence is another. To say that something exists without generation explains the mode of its existence. But what it is is not made evident by the expression. If you asked a gardener about some tree, whether it was planted or grew wild, and he replied either that it had or had not been planted, would his answer tell you what sort of tree it was? By no means. In telling you how it grew, he would leave the question of its nature obscure and unexplained. In the same way here, when we learn that he is unbegotten, we are taught the mode of his existence and how we must think of it. But we do not learn from the expression what he is.

When, then, we acknowledge such a distinction in the holy Trinity that we believe that one is the cause and the other depends on it, we can no longer be charged with dissolving the distinction of the Persons in the common nature. The principle of causality distinguishes, then, the Persons of the holy Trinity. It affirms that the one is uncaused, while the other depends on the cause. But the divine nature is in every way understood to be without distinction or difference. For this reason we rightly say there is one Godhead and one God, and express all the other attributes that befit the divine in the singular.

# An Address on Religious Instruction[1]

## THE TEXT

### INTRODUCTION

Religious instruction is an essential duty of the leaders "of the mystery of our religion." [2] By it the Church is enlarged through the addition of those who are saved, while "the sure word which accords with the [traditional] teaching" [3] comes within the hearing of unbelievers. The same method of teaching, however, is not suitable for everyone who approaches this word. Rather must we adapt religious instruction to the diversities of religion. While we keep in view the same objective in our teaching, we cannot use the same arguments in each case. A man of the Jewish faith has certain presuppositions; a man reared in Hellenism, others. The Anomoean, the Manichaean, the followers of Marcion, Valentinus, and Basilides, and the rest on the list of those astray in heresy,[4] have their preconceptions, and make it necessary for us to attack their underlying ideas in each case. For we must adapt our method of therapy to the form of the disease. You will not heal the polytheism of the Greek in the same way as the Jew's disbelief about the only-begotten God. Nor, in the case of those astray in heresy, will you refute their erroneous doctrinal inventions all in the same way. For the arguments which might correct a Sabellian are of no help to an Anomoean; nor is our contro-

---

[1] *Logos katēchētikos*: generally rendered "Catechetical Oration." In some manuscripts the title reads "The Great Catechism."

[2] I Tim. 3:16.  [3] Titus 1:9.

[4] The Anomoeans were extreme Arians who emphasized that the Son was unlike (*anomoios*) the Father. The Manichaeans were dualists who distinguished the ultimate principles of light and darkness and attributed the sensible creation to the latter. Marcion, Valentinus, and Basilides were the leaders of second century Gnosticism. Sabellian, in this same paragraph, refers to the doctrine which confused the Son with the Father.

268

versy with the Manichaean of benefit to the Jew. But, as I have said, we must have in view men's preconceptions and address ourselves to the error in which each is involved. We must put forward certain principles and reasonable propositions in each discussion, so that the truth may finally emerge from what is admitted on both sides.

Therefore, when the discussion is with a Hellenist, it would be well to begin the argument in this way: Does he presuppose God's existence, or does he agree with the view of atheists? If he says God does not exist, then from the skillful and wise arrangement of the world he can be led to acknowledge the existence of some power which is manifested by it and which transcends the universe. But if he has no doubt of God's existence and is carried away by ideas of a plurality of gods, we should use with him some such argument as follows: Does he think the divine is perfect or imperfect? If, as he probably will, he testifies to the perfection of the divine nature, we must require him to acknowledge that this perfection extends to every aspect of the Deity, so that the divine may not be regarded as a mixture of opposites, of defect and perfection. Now, whether it be with respect to power, or the idea of goodness, or wisdom or incorruption or eternity or any other relevant attribute of God, he will agree, as a reasonable inference, that we must think of the divine nature as perfect in every case.

Once this is granted, it would not be difficult to bring round his 'thinking, with its diffuse ideas of a multitude of gods, to the acknowledgment of a single deity. For if he grants that perfection is to be entirely attributed to the subject of our discussion, and yet claims there are many perfect beings with the same characteristics, this follows. In the case of things marked by no differences but considered to have identical attributes, it is absolutely essential for him to show the particularity of each. Or else, if the mind cannot conceive particularity in cases where there are no distinguishing marks, he must give up the idea of any distinction. Indeed, because the idea of God is one and the same and no particularity can reasonably be discovered in any respect, the erroneous notion of a plurality of gods must of necessity give way to the acknowledgment of a single deity. For he cannot find a difference with respect to greater or less, since the idea of perfection does not admit of "less." Nor with respect to worse or better, since he would not have the conception of God where the term "worse" was not, excluded. Nor in respect to ancient and modern, since what does not always exist is alien to the idea of God.

If, then, goodness, righteousness, wisdom, and power are equally ascribed [to the Deity], and incorruption, eternity, and every thought compatible with religion are similarly acknowledged, all difference is in every way excluded. Excluded, too, from his doctrine is a plurality of gods, for the identity throughout brings him round to the conviction of the unity.

## THE DOCTRINE OF GOD AND HIS WORD

1. Our religious teaching, however, is able to discern some distinction of Persons [5] in the unity. Therefore, in order to guard our controversy with the Greeks from lapsing into Judaism, we must rectify any error in this regard by making a further fine distinction. Now, those who do not accept our teaching do not suppose the divine to be without reason [6]; and this acknowledgment of theirs will make our doctrine sufficiently intelligible to them. For he who grants that God is not without reason will agree that one who is not without reason certainly has it. The same term to be sure, we use of human reason. Therefore, if he says that he conceives God's reason by analogy with our nature, he will thus be driven to a higher conception. For it is necessary to hold that reason, like all the other attributes, corresponds to the nature [involved].

In humanity we observe a certain power and life and wisdom. But, by using the same words, no one would attribute to God the same life, power, and wisdom [as ours]. Rather are such expressions reduced in meaning to correspond to the measure of our nature. For since our nature is corruptible and weak, for this reason our life is fleeting, our power unsubstantial, and our reason unstable. In reference, however, to the transcendent nature, everything said of it is raised to a higher degree by virtue of the greatness of the object we contemplate.

If, then, we attribute the spoken word [7] to God, it will not be thought to derive its subsistence from the impulse of the

5 *Hypostasis*, in the sense of a distinct center of being.
6 *Alogos*, not having his Logos or Word. The difficulties of translation here are insuperable. Gregory plays on the double meaning of *logos* as reason and a spoken word. God's Word, in Gregory, being a distinct center of being, is personal. Hence the corresponding pronoun should properly be "he." In the translation, however, "it" has been frequently, but not always, used to bring out the analogy he makes between God's Word and "a spoken word." 7 *Logos*.

speaker, and like our speech to pass into nonexistence. But just as our nature, by being perishable, has a speech which is perishable, so the incorruptible and eternal nature has a speech which is eternal and substantial. If, accordingly, it is granted that God's spoken word subsists eternally, it is necessary to admit that the subsistence of the Word is endued with life. For it is irreverent to suppose that the Word subsists in a lifeless state in the way of stones. But if it subsists as something capable of thought and immaterial, it certainly possesses life; whereas, if it is deprived of life, it certainly has no subsistence. But we have proved that it is impious to say that God's Word does not subsist. Accordingly, we have also established that we must think of this Word as possessed of life.

Now, since the nature of the Word is with good cause held to be simple and evidences neither a double nor a composite character, one cannot consider that it possesses life by participating in it. For such a conception, which holds that one thing participates in another, would not exclude the idea of a composite character. Rather are we compelled to admit, having acknowledged its simplicity, that the Word possesses its own life, and does not participate in life.

If, then, the Word has life because it *is* life, it certainly has the faculty of will; for no living thing is without it. It is religious, too, to conclude that this faculty of will has the power to act. For if one were to deny that it had this power, one would surely imply that it was powerless. But impotence is very remote from our conception of the divine. For the divine nature displays no incongruity, and we are compelled to admit that the Word has power to carry out its purpose. Otherwise, a mixture or concurrence of opposites would be observed in a simple nature. The same purpose would display both power and lack of it, if it were capable of one thing and incapable of another.

We must, too, admit that the will of the Word, though capable of everything, has no inclination toward evil. For inclination toward evil is foreign to the divine nature. But whatever is good, it wills; and having willed it, it is altogether able to do it. Being able, it is not inoperative; but it brings to effect every good purpose.

Now, the world, and all the wise and skillful arrangement it displays, is something good. All this, then, is the work of the Word, which, living and subsisting because it is God's Word, has the faculty of will because it lives. It is capable of doing whatever it purposes, and it chooses what is absolutely good and wise and everything else indicative of excellence. The world, then, is admitted to be something good, and we have already proved it is the work of the Word, which both chooses the good and can do it. This Word, however, is different from Him whose it is. For in a way it is a relative term, since "the Word" certainly implies the Father of the Word. For there cannot be a word without its being someone's word. If, then, by its relative significance, those who hear the term mentally distinguish between the Word itself and Him from whom it comes, our religion is no longer in danger, by virtue of our controversy with Greek notions, of agreeing with those who espouse the tenets of Judaism. Rather do we equally avoid the absurdity of both viewpoints. We acknowledge God's living Word as active and creative—a doctrine the Jew does not accept; and we admit no distinction in nature between the Word and Him from whom it comes.

In our own case we say that a spoken word comes from the mind, and is neither entirely identical with it nor altogether different. For by being derived from something else, it is different and not identical with it. Yet, since it reflects the mind, it can no longer be thought to be different from it, but is one with it in nature, though distinct as a subject. So the Word of God, by having its own subsistence, is distinct from Him from whom it derives its subsistence. On the other hand, by manifesting in itself the attributes to be seen in God, it is identical in nature with Him who is recognized by the same characteristics. In whatever way one indicates the conception of the Father, whether by goodness, or power, or wisdom, or eternal being, or freedom from evil, death, and corruption, or complete perfection, by the same attributes he will recognize the Word derived from him.

## THE HOLY SPIRIT

2. Our knowledge of the Word comes from applying, in a raised degree, [8] our own attributes to the transcendent nature. In just the same way we shall be brought to the conception of the Spirit, by observing in our own nature certain hints and likenesses of this ineffable power. In our own case, indeed,

---

[8] *Anagōgikōs.* A technical phrase to indicate the mystical process of ascent by which one rises to a consideration of the noetic world from the facts of the phenomenal word. Origen uses the term frequently in connection with the mystical interpretation of Scripture.

"spirit" (i.e., breath) [9] is a drawing in of the air; and we are so constructed that something foreign to the constitution of the body is inhaled and exhaled. In the moment we give expression to a word, our breath becomes an intelligible utterance which indicates what we have in mind. In the case of the divine nature, too, we think it reverent to hold that God has a Spirit, just as we admitted that he has a Word. For it is not right that God's Word should be more defective than our own, which would be the case if, since our word is associated with breath (spirit), we were to believe he lacked a Spirit. Yet we must not imagine that, in the way of our own breath, something alien and extraneous to God flows into him and becomes the divine Spirit in him.

When we heard of the Word of God, we did not suppose that the Word was something without subsistence, that it was dependent on acquired knowledge, or uttered by a voice, or ceased to exist when once uttered. We did not think that it was subject to such conditions as we observe in the case of our own word; but [we contended] that it had its own real subsistence, and, having the faculty of will, was active and all-powerful.

In the same way, when we learn that God has a Spirit, which accompanies his Word and manifests his activity, we do not think of it as an emission of breath. For we should degrade the majesty of God's power were we to conceive of his Spirit in the same way as ours. On the contrary, we think of it as a power really existing by itself and in its own special subsistence. It is not able to be separated from God in whom it exists, or from God's Word which it accompanies. It is not dissipated into non-existence; but like God's Word it has its own subsistence, is capable of willing, and is self-moved and active. It ever chooses the good; and to fulfill its every purpose it has the power that answers to its will.

## THE MEAN BETWEEN JUDAISM AND HELLENISM

3. In effect, a studied examination of the depths of this mystery does, in a veiled way, give a man a fair, inward apprehension of our teaching on the knowledge of God. He cannot, of course, express the ineffable depth of the mystery in words, how the same thing is subject to number and yet escapes it; how it is observed to have distinctions and is yet grasped as a unity; how it admits distinction of Persons, and yet is not

[9] *Pneuma*, which has the double sense of breath and spirit.

divided in underlying essence. For the Person of the Spirit is one thing, that of the Word another; and different yet is the Person of Him whose Word and Spirit they are. But when once these distinctions are grasped, the unity of the nature still does not admit of division. Thus the power of the divine monarchy is not split up and divided into a variety of divinities; neither does our teaching conform to Jewish doctrine. Rather does the truth lie between these two conceptions. It invalidates both ways of thinking, while accepting what is useful from each. The teaching of the Jew is invalidated by the acceptance of the Word and by belief in the Spirit; while the polytheistic error of the Greeks is done away, since the unity of the nature cancels the notion of plurality. Yet again, the unity of the nature must be retained from the Jewish conception, while the distinction of Persons, and that only, from the Greek. The irreligious opinion on each side finds a corresponding remedy. For the triune number is, as it were, a remedy for those in error about the unity; while the affirmation of the unity is a remedy for those who scatter their beliefs among a multitude [of gods].

## REPLY TO THE JEW

4. If, however, this is contested by the Jew, we shall not find it equally as hard to answer him [as the Greek]. For we shall show him the truth out of the very teachings in which he has been reared. For that God has a Word and a Spirit—powers which have an independent being and which created and embrace all that exists—can be very clearly shown from the divinely inspired Scriptures. It is sufficient for us to mention a single proof text, and to leave those who are more ambitious to discover others.

Scripture says, "By the Word of the Lord were the heavens established, and all their power by the Spirit [breath] of his mouth." [10] By what Word? By what Spirit? For "the Word" [in this passage] is not an utterance, and "the Spirit" is not a breath. The divine, indeed, would be degraded to the level of our human nature, were it held that the Creator of the universe used such a word and such a breath. What power do words or breath have that would suffice to make the heavens and the powers in them? For, did God's Word resemble our utterance, and his Spirit our breath, their power would be altogether similar; and God's Word would have only as much force as

10 Ps. 33:6.

ours. But our utterances, and the breath which accompanies them, are inoperative and without subsistence. Absolutely ineffective, then, and without subsistence do they prove God's Word and Spirit to be, who degrade the divine to resemble our word. But if, as David says, the heavens were established by the Word of the Lord and their powers were fashioned by the Spirit of God, then that mystery of the truth is substantiated which leads us to speak of a Word with essential being and a Spirit with subsistence.

## THE CREATION OF MAN

5. Neither Greek nor Jew, perhaps, will contest the existence of God's Word and Spirit—the one depending on his innate ideas, the other on the Scriptures. Both, however, will equally reject the plan by which God's Word became man, as something incredible and unbefitting to say of God. We shall, then, take a different point of departure in order to convince our opponents about this.

Either they believe that with reason and wisdom all things were created by Him who fashioned the universe, or else they find even this hard to believe. Now, if they will not grant that reason and wisdom govern the constitution of things, they will set up unreason and unskillfulness as the ruling principle of the universe. But if this is absurd and irreligious, it is clearly admitted that they will acknowledge that reason and wisdom govern existing things.

From what we have already said we have proved that the Word of God is no mere utterance or a state of possessing some knowledge or wisdom. It is a power existing in its own right, able to will all good and having the power to do everything it wills. Since, too, the world is good, this power which prefers[11] and creates the good is the cause of it. Now if the existence of the whole universe depends on the power of the Word, as our argument has indicated, we must necessarily suppose that there is no other cause by which the different parts of the universe were created than the Word himself. Through him they all came into being.

If anyone wants to call him Word or Wisdom or Power or God or any other sublime or dignified title, we shall not contest the point. For whatever word or name is invented to indicate this subject, it expresses the same thing, viz., the eternal Power

11 *Proektikēn*, meaning uncertain.

of God, which creates what exists, contrives what is non-existent, sustains what is created, and foresees the future. This, then, is the implication of our argument: that he who is God the Word and Wisdom and Power created human nature. He was not, indeed, driven by any necessity to form man; but out of his abundant love he fashioned and created such a creature. For it was not right that light should remain unseen, or glory unwitnessed, or goodness unenjoyed, or that any other aspect we observe of the divine nature should lie idle with no one to share or enjoy it.

If, then, man came into being for these reasons, viz., to participate in the divine goodness, he had to be fashioned in such a way as to fit him to share in this goodness. For just as the eye shares in light through having by nature an inherent brightness in it, and by this innate power attracts what is akin to itself,[12] so something akin to the divine had to be mingled with human nature. In this way its desire [for divine goodness] would correspond to something native to it. Even the natures of irrational creatures, whose lot is to live in water or air, are fashioned to correspond with their mode of life. In each case the particular way their bodies are formed makes the air or the water appropriate and congenial to them. In the same way man, who was created to enjoy God's goodness, had to have some element in his nature akin to what he was to share. Hence he was endowed with life, reason, wisdom, and all the good things of God, so that by each of them his desires might be directed to what was natural to him. And since immortality is one of the good attributes of the divine nature, it was essential that the constitution of our nature should not be deprived of this. It had to have an immortal element, so that it might, by this inherent faculty, recognize the transcendent and have the desire for God's immortality.

The account of creation sums all this up in a single expression when it says that man was created "in the image of God." [13] For the likeness implied by the term "image" comprehends all the divine attributes; and whatever Moses relates by way of a narrative, presenting doctrines in the form of a story, has the same teaching in mind. For the Garden he mentions and the particular fruits, the eating of which does not satisfy the belly but grants to those who taste of them knowledge and eternal

[12] The idea is that the eye attracts light by having a corresponding inner light of its own. See Plato, *Timaeus* 45 B–D.
[13] Gen. 1:27.

life—all this corresponds to what we have been saying about man, how our nature in its origin was good and set in the midst of goodness.

## THE NATURE OF EVIL AND THE FALL OF MAN

But someone perhaps, with an eye to our present situation, will contest what we have said. He will imagine he can refute the truth of our argument by the fact that we do not now see man in this original state, but in an almost entirely opposite condition. For where is the soul's likeness to God? Where is the body's freedom from suffering? Where is eternal life? Man's life is fleeting, subject to passion, mortal, liable in soul and body to every type of suffering. Saying this sort of thing and running down our nature, he will suppose he can refute our contention about man. To this our reply will be brief, in order not to interrupt the sequence of our argument.

The fact that human life is at present in an unnatural condition is insufficient proof that man was never created in a state of goodness. For since man is a work of God, who out of his goodness brought this creature into being, one cannot rightly suppose that he was made by his Creator in a state of evil. For his constitution had its origin in goodness. The cause of our present condition and of our being deprived of our former preferable state is to be found elsewhere. Here again the point of departure for our argument is not something with which our opponents will disagree. He who made man to share in His own goodness and so equipped his nature with the means of acquiring everything excellent that his desires might, in each case, correspond to that to which they were directed, would not have deprived him of the most excellent and precious of blessings—I mean the gift of liberty and free will. For were human life governed by necessity, the "image" would be falsified in that respect and so differ from the archetype. For how can a nature subject to necessity and in servitude be called an image of the sovereign nature? What, therefore, is in every respect made similar to the divine, must certainly possess free will and liberty by nature, so that participation in the good may be the reward of virtue.

But, you will ask, how came it that he who was honored with all excellence exchanged these blessings for something worse? The answer to this, too, is clear. The existence of evil did not have its origin in the divine will. For no blame, indeed, would attach to evil, could it claim God as its creator and father. But evil in some way arises from within. It has its origin in the will, when the soul withdraws from the good. For as sight is an activity of nature and blindness is a privation of natural activity, so virtue is in this way opposed to vice. For the origin of evil is not otherwise to be conceived than as the absence of virtue. Just as darkness follows the removal of light and disappears in its presence, so, as long as goodness is present in a nature, evil is something nonexistent. But when there is a withdrawal from the good, its opposite arises. Since, then, it is the mark of free will to choose independently what it wants, God is not the cause of your present woes. For he made your nature independent and free. The cause is rather your thoughtlessness in choosing the worse instead of the better.

6. But perhaps you will ask the cause of this error in judgment, for our argument leads up to this. Again we can reasonably expect to find some principle by which to elucidate this issue. We have received from the Fathers some such traditional explanation as this: It is not a fanciful story[14]; but our very nature makes it convincing. Our experience and observation of existing things is twofold, being divided between the intelligible and the sensible. Besides these, nothing in the nature of existing things can be apprehended, if it falls outside this classification. The gulf that separates them is very great, so that the sensible does not bear the marks of the intelligible, nor the intelligible of the sensible. Rather are they characterized by contraries. For the intelligible nature is incorporeal, impalpable, and formless; while the sensible nature, as the very word indicates, is apprehended by the senses. In the sensible world itself, despite the strong opposition between the elements, a certain harmony of these contraries has been contrived by the wisdom which governs the universe. The whole of creation is in inward harmony, since the bond of concord is nowhere broken by the natural opposition [between the elements]. In the same way the divine wisdom also provides a blending and admixture of the sensible with the intelligible nature, so that all things equally participate in the good, and no existing thing is deprived of a share in the higher nature. Now the sphere corresponding to the intelligible nature is a subtle and mobile essence, which by virtue of its special nature and its transcending the world has a great affinity with the intelligible. Yet, for the reason given, a superior wisdom pro-

14 I.e., a "myth" in the Platonic sense.

vides a mingling of the intelligible with the sensible creation. In that way, as the apostle says, "no part of creation is to be rejected," [15] and no part fails to share in the divine fellowship.

On this account the divine nature produces in man a blending of the intelligible and the sensible, just as the account of Creation teaches. For God, it says, [16] made man by taking dust from the ground, and with his own breath planted life in the creature he had formed. In that way the earthly was raised to union with the divine, and a single grace equally extends through all creation, inasmuch as the lower nature is blended with that which transcends the world.

When the intelligible creation was already in existence, and the authority which governs all things had assigned a certain activity in connection with the framing of the universe to each of the angelic powers, one of them was appointed to maintain and take charge of the region of earth. He was equipped for this very purpose by the power which governs the universe. Then there was created that object formed of earth, which was an image of the power above; and this creature was man. In him was the divine excellence of the intelligible nature, an excellence blended with a certain ineffable power. In consequence that angelic power, which had been given the government of earth, took it amiss as something insufferable that, out of the nature subject to him, there should be produced a being to resemble the transcendent dignity.

It is irrelevant to our present purpose to explain in detail how one who was created for no evil end by Him who framed the universe in goodness fell into the passion of envy. Yet we may offer a brief explanation to those who care to hear it. We must not think of virtue as opposed to vice in the way of two existing phenomena. To illustrate: nonbeing is opposed to being; but we cannot say that the former is opposed to the latter as something existing in its own right. Rather do we say that there is a logical opposition between what does not exist and what exists. In the same way vice is opposed to the principle of virtue. It does not exist in its own right, but we think of it as the absence of the good. Again, we say that blindness is logically opposed to sight. But blindness does not by nature have real existence. On the contrary it is the privation of a former capacity. Similarly we say that vice should be viewed as the privation of the good, just as a shadow follows upon the withdrawal of the sun's rays.

[15] I Tim. 4:4.          [16] Gen. 2:7.

Uncreated nature is incapable of the movement implied in mutability, change, and variation. But everything that depends upon creation for its existence has an innate tendency to change. For the very existence of creation had its origin in change, non-being becoming being by divine power. Now that [angelic] power we have already mentioned was created, and by the movement of its own free will chose whatever it cared to. But it closed its eyes to the good and the generous; and just as one only sees darkness when one closes the eyelids in sunlight, so that power by its unwillingness to acknowledge the good contrived its opposite. That is how envy arose.

Now it is recognized that the first cause of a thing is responsible for what duly follows in its train. For instance, being in trim and at work, and leading a happy life, are consequent upon health; whereas weakness, inactivity, and feeling unwell follow upon sickness. All other things in the same way are consequent upon their particular causes. Just as freedom from passion, then, is the beginning and foundation of a life of virtue, so inclination to evil, arising through envy, paves the way for all the evils which are seen to follow it.

Now that angelic power who begot envy in himself by turning from the good developed an inclination toward evil. When this had once happened, he was like a rock breaking off from a mountain ridge and hurled headlong by its own weight. Divorced from his natural affinity with the good, he became prone to evil; and as if by a weight he was spontaneously impelled and carried to the final limit of iniquity. The capacity for thought, which he received from his Creator to help him to share in the good, he used to further his evil devices. Cunningly he cheats and deceives man by persuading him to become his own murderer and assassin.

Empowered by God's blessing, man held a lofty position. He was appointed to rule over the earth and all the creatures on it. His form was beautiful, for he was created as the image of the archetypal beauty. By nature he was free from passion, for he was a copy of Him who is without passion. He was full of candor, reveling in the direct vision of God. But all this was tinder for the adversary's passionate envy. He could not fulfill his purpose by force or violence, for the power of God's blessing was superior to such force. For this reason he contrived to tear man from the power which strengthened him, and so to render him an easy prey to his intrigue. Now in the case of a lamp, when the flame has caught the wick too much and one is unable to blow it out, one mixes water with the oil, and by this means dims the flame. In just such a way the adversary deceitfully mingled evil with man's free will and thus in some measure quenched and obscured God's blessing. When this failed, the opposite necessarily entered in. Now the opposite of life is death; of power, weakness; of blessing, cursing; of candor, shame; and of every good thing, its contrary. That is why humanity is in its present plight; for that beginning provided the occasion for such a conclusion.

## God and Evil

7. Now we ought not to ask how God came to create man when he foresaw the disaster that would result from this thoughtlessness, since it would, perhaps, have been better for him not to have been made than to be in such a plight. Those who are deceived and carried away by Manichaean teachings urge such objections to support their own error and to prove that the Creator of man's nature was evil. If God is ignorant of nothing and man is in such a plight, the principle of His goodness cannot be upheld, if He brought man to life when he was fated to live in troubles. For, they contend, if a good nature always directs its activity toward the good, we cannot refer the creation of this wretched and transient life to one who is good. Rather must we suppose that such a life has a different origin, in a nature which is inclined to evil. By their surface plausibility all these and similar arguments seem to have a certain force to those who are imbued, as it were, with the indelible dye of the deceit of heresy. Those, however, who are more perceptive of the truth, clearly recognize that they are unsound and that they afford a ready proof of their deceptive character. I think it right, too, to support our condemnation of them by bringing forward the apostle. In addressing the Corinthians [17] he makes a distinction between fleshly and spiritual states of the soul. By what he says I think he intimates that it is not right to make judgments about good and evil on the basis of sensation. Rather must we divert the mind from bodily phenomena, and distinguish what is essentially good from its opposite. For, he says, "the spiritual man is judge of all things."

The reason, I think, that they adduce these fabulous doctrines is this: They define the good by reference to the enjoyment of bodily pleasure. Hence, because the nature of the body is

17 Cf. I Cor. 2:14, 15.

necessarily subject to suffering and sickness (being composite and liable to dissolution), and because a painful sensation is in some way the result of such suffering, they imagine that the creation of man is the work of an evil god. But had they directed their minds to what is transcendent and, by diverting them from states of pleasure, considered the nature of things dispassionately, they would have thought that nothing was evil save wickedness. For all wickedness is marked by the privation of the good. It does not exist in its own right, nor is it observed to have subsistence. For nothing evil lies outside the will as if it existed by itself; but it gets its name from the absence of the good. Nonbeing has no subsistence; and the Creator of what exists is not the Creator of what has no subsistence. The God, therefore, of what exists is not responsible for evil, since he is not the author of what has no existence. Sight he made and not blindness: virtue he brought forth and not its privation. In the contest of free will he has appointed his blessings as the reward for those who live virtuously. Hence he has not subjected human nature to some forcible compulsion to do his will, dragging it unwillingly, like some lifeless object, toward the good. If a man in broad daylight of his own free will closes his eyes, the sun is not responsible for his failure to see.

## The Restoration of Man

8. Nevertheless a man who is mindful of the dissolution of the body is in any case resentful, and takes it hard that our life is dissolved by death. This, he claims, is the final evil, that death should extinguish our life. Let him, then, reflect upon God's exceeding goodness even in this melancholy prospect. For it may be that this will induce him all the more to marvel at God's gracious care for man. Those who share in life find that life is desirable because they can enjoy what they like. Hence, if a man passes his life in pain, he reckons it far preferable not to exist than to exist in a state of suffering. Let us then inquire whether He who gives us life has any other intention than that we should live under the best possible conditions.

It was by a movement of free will that we became associated with evil. To indulge some pleasure we mingled evil with our nature, like some deadly drug sweetened with honey. By this means we fell from that blessed state we think of as freedom from passion, and were changed into evil. That is the reason that man, like a clay pot, is again resolved into earth; in order that he may be refashioned into his original state through the resurrection, when once he has been separated from the filth now attaching to him.

Such a doctrine, it is, that Moses[18] expounds to us by way of a story and in a veiled manner. But what the veiled allegories teach is quite clear. For since, he says, the first men became implicated in things forbidden and were stripped naked of blessedness, the Lord clothed his first creatures in suits of skins. I do not think he uses the word "skins" in its literal sense. For to what sort of animals, when slain and flayed, did this covering contrived for them belong? But since every skin taken from an animal is a dead thing, I am sure the skins mean the attribute of death. This is the characteristic mark of irrational nature; and in His care for man, He who heals our wickedness subsequently provided him with the capacity to die, but not to die permanently. For a suit is an external covering for us. The body is given the opportunity to use it for a while, but it is not an essential part of its nature.

Mortality, then, derived from the nature of irrational creatures, provisionally clothed the nature created for immortality. It enveloped his outward, but not his inward, nature. It affected the sentient part of man, but not the divine image. The sentient part, to be sure, is dissolved; but it is not destroyed. For destruction means passing into nonbeing, while dissolution means separation once more into those elements of the world from which something was constituted. When this happens, it does not perish, even if we cannot grasp this with our senses.

Now the cause of this dissolution is clear from the illustration we have given. Appropriate to sensation is what is thick and earthly. But by nature the intellect is superior to and transcends the movements of the senses. Hence, since our judgment of the good went astray by the prompting of the senses, and this departure from the good produced a contrary state of things, that part of us which was rendered useless by partaking of its opposite is dissolved. We can put our illustration about the clay pot in this way: Suppose it has been treacherously filled with molten lead, which has hardened and cannot be poured out. Suppose, too, the owner recovers the pot, and being skilled in ceramics, he pounds to pieces the clay surrounding the lead. He then remolds the pot, now rid of the intruding matter, into its former shape and for his own use. In the same

[18] Cf. Gen. 3:21.

way the Creator of our vessel, I mean our sentient and bodily nature, when it became mingled with evil, dissolved the material which contained the evil. And then, once it has been freed from its opposite, he will remold it by the resurrection, and will reconstitute the vessel into its original beauty.

Now there is a certain bond and fellowship in the sinful passions between soul and body, and a certain analogy between bodily and spiritual death. Just as we call the body's separation from sentient life "death," so we give the same name to the soul's separation from genuine life. As we have said, soul and body are observed to share together in evil. For by means of both of them wickedness is translated into action. Yet from being clothed with dead skins the soul is not affected by death which implies dissolution. For how could the soul be dissolved when it is not composite? But since it, too, has to be freed by some remedy from the stains contracted through sin, on this account the medicine of virtue in this present life has to be applied to it to heal these wounds. But if it remains unhealed, provision has been made for its cure in the life to come.

Now there are differences in bodily ailments, some of them readily responding to treatment, others with more difficulty. In the latter case knives, cauteries, and bitter medicines are used to remove the sickness which has attacked the body. Something similar, in reference to the healing of the soul's sickness, is indicated by the future judgment. To thoughtless persons this is a threat and a harsh means of correction, so that by fear of a painful retribution we may be brought to our senses and flee evil. The more thoughtful, however, believe it to be a healing remedy provided by God, who thus restores his own creation to its original grace. Those who, by excisions or cauteries, remove moles and warts which have unnaturally grown on the body do not benefit and heal the patient painlessly, although they do not use the knife to hurt him. In the same way, whatever material excrescences have hardened on the surface of our souls, which have become fleshly through their association with the passions, are, at the time of judgment, cut off and removed by that ineffable wisdom and power of Him who (as the gospel says) heals the sick. For "those who are well," it says,[19] "do not need a doctor, but those who are sick."

Now the excision of a wart causes a sharp pain in the surface of the body, since an unnatural growth on a nature affects the

[19] Matt. 9:12.

subject by a kind of sympathy. There arises an unexpected union between what is our own and what is foreign to us, so that we feel a stinging pain when the unnatural excrescence is removed. In the same way, due to the fact that the soul has developed a great affinity for evil, it pines and wastes away, being convicted of sin, as prophecy somewhere says.[20] Because of its deep kinship with evil, there necessarily follow unspeakable pangs, which are as incapable of description as the nature of the blessings we hope for. Neither the one nor the other can be put into words nor have we an inkling of either.

Anyone, therefore, who bears in mind the wise purpose of Him who governs the universe could not be so unreasonable and shortsighted as to attribute the cause of evil to the Creator of man. He could not say either that He was ignorant of the future or that by knowing it and by creating man He was involved in the impulse toward evil. For He knew what was going to happen and yet did not prevent what led it to happen. He who is able to grasp all things within his knowledge, and sees the future equally with the past, was not ignorant that man would deviate from the good. But just as He saw man's perversion, so he perceived his restoration once more to the good. Which, then, was better? Not to have brought our nature into being at all, since he knew in advance that the one to be created would stray from the good? Or, having brought him into being, to restore him by repentance, sick as he was, to his original grace?

It is the height of shortsightedness to call God the author of evil because of the body's sufferings, which are a necessary accompaniment of our fluctuating nature; or to imagine that he is not the creator of man at all, in order to avoid attributing to him the cause of our sufferings. Such people distinguish good and evil on the basis of sensation, and do not realize that that alone is good by nature which is unaffected by sensation, and that alone is evil which is alien to what is genuinely good. To judge good and evil on the basis of pain and suffering is appropriate in the case of irrational natures, since by not sharing in intelligence and understanding they are unable to grasp what is genuinely good. But that man is a work of God, created good and for the noblest ends, is evident not only from what we have already said, but for thousands of other reasons, most of which we must disregard since their number is infinite.

When we call God the creator of man, we are not unmindful

[20] Ps. 39:11.

of the careful distinctions we made in [that part of] our introduction addressed to the Greeks. We showed there that God's
Word is a substantial and personal being, and is both God and
Word. In himself he embraces all creative power, or rather he
is absolute power. His impulses are directed toward everything
good, and by having power commensurate with his will, he
brings to effect whatever he desires. The life of existing things
is his will and his work. By him man was brought to life, and
endowed with every noble attribute to resemble God.

Now that alone is unchangeable by nature which does not
originate through creation. But whatever is derived from the
uncreated nature has its subsistence out of nonbeing. Once it
has come into being through change, it constantly proceeds
to change. If it acts according to its nature, this continual
change is for the better. But if it is diverted from the straight
path, there succeeds a movement in the opposite direction.
Such was man's condition. His mutable nature lapsed in the
opposite direction. His departure from the good at once introduced as a consequence every form of evil. By his turning from
life, death came in instead. Privation of light engendered darkness. Absence of virtue brought in wickedness; and in the place
of every form of goodness there was now to be reckoned the list
of opposing evils. Into just such a condition man fell by his
thoughtlessness. For it was not possible for him to be discreet,
once he had turned from discretion, or to form any wise
decision once he had departed from wisdom. By whom did he
have to be restored once more to his original grace? To whom
did it belong to raise him up when he had fallen, to restore
him when he was lost, to lead him back when he had gone
astray? To whom, but to the very Lord of his nature? For
only the one who had originally given him life was both able
and fitted to restore it when it was lost. This is what the
revelation [21] of the truth teaches us, when we learn that God
originally made man, and saved him when he had fallen.

## THE INCARNATION

9. One who has followed the course of our argument up to
this point will probably agree with it, since we do not appear
to have said anything unbefitting a right conception of God.
He will not, however, take a similar view of what follows,

[21] *Mystērion*, mystery, in the sense of a hidden truth of God now revealed
in the gospel.

although it substantiates the revelation of the truth in a special way. I refer to the human birth, the advance from infancy to manhood, the eating and drinking, the weariness, the sleep, the grief, the tears, the false accusations, the trial, the cross, the death, and the putting in the tomb. For these facts included as they are in the revelation, in some way blunt the faith of little minds, so that they do not accept the sequel of our argument because of what precedes. Owing to the unworthiness connected with the death, they do not admit that the resurrection from the dead was worthy of God.

For myself, however, I think we must for a moment divert our thoughts from the coarseness of the flesh, and consider what real goodness and its contrary are, and by what distinctive marks each is known. For I imagine that no one who has seriously thought about it will gainsay that one thing alone in the universe is by nature shameful, viz., the malady of evil, while no shame at all attaches to what is alien to evil. What is unmixed with shame is certainly understood to be comprised in the good, and what is genuinely good is unmixed with its opposite.

Now everything we see included in the good is fitting to God. In consequence, either our opponents must show that the birth, the upbringing, the growth, the natural advance to maturity, the experience of death and the return from it are evil. Or else, if they concede that these things fall outside the category of evil, they must of necessity acknowledge there is nothing shameful in what is alien to evil. Since we have shown that what is good is altogether free from all shame and evil, must we not pity the stupidity of those who claim that the good is unbefitting to God?

10. But, they object, is not human nature paltry and circumscribed, while Deity is infinite? How, then, could the infinite be contained in an atom? But who claims that the infinity of the Godhead was contained within the limits of the flesh as in a jar? For in our own case the intellectual nature is not enclosed in the limits of the flesh. The body's bulk, to be sure, is circumscribed by its particular parts, but the soul is free to embrace the whole creation by the movement of thought. It ascends to the heavens, sets foot in the depths, traverses the dimensions of the world, and in its constant activity makes its way to the underworld. Often it is involved in contemplating the marvels of the heavens, and it is not loaded down by being attached to the body.

If, then, the soul of man, although united to the body by natural necessity, is free to roam everywhere, why do we have to say that the Godhead is confined in a fleshly nature? Why should we not rather rely on examples we can understand, in order to form some sort of proper conception of God's plan of salvation? To illustrate: We see the flame of a lamp laying hold of the material which feeds it. Now reason distinguishes between the flame on the material, and the material which kindles the flame, though we cannot actually divorce the one from the other and point out the flame as something separate from the material. The two together form a single whole. So it is with the incarnation. (My illustration must not be pressed beyond the point where it is appropriate. What is incongruous must be omitted, and the perishable character of fire must not be taken as part of the example.) Just, then, as we see the flame hugging the material and yet not encased in it, what prevents us from conceiving of a similar union and connection of the divine nature with the human? Can we not preserve a right idea of God even when we hold to this connection, by believing that the divine is free from all circumscription despite the fact he is in man?

11. If you inquire how the Deity is united with human nature, it is appropriate for you first to ask in what way the soul is united to the body. If the manner in which your soul is joined to your body is a mystery, you must certainly not imagine this former question is within your grasp. In the one case, while we believe the soul to be something different from the body because on leaving the flesh it renders it dead and inactive, we are ignorant of the manner of the union. Similarly in the other case we realize that the divine nature by its greater majesty differs from that which is mortal and perishable; but we are unable to detect how the divine is mingled with the human. Yet we have no doubt, from the recorded miracles, that God underwent birth in human nature. But *how* this happened we decline to investigate as a matter beyond the scope of reason. While we believe that the corporeal and intelligent creation owes its being to the incorporeal and uncreated nature, our faith in this regard does not involve an examination of the source and manner of this. The fact of creation we accept; but we renounce a curious investigation of the way the universe was framed as a matter altogether ineffable and inexplicable.

## THE INCARNATION AND THE MIRACLES

12. One who is looking for proofs that God manifested himself to us in the flesh must look to his activities. For of God's very existence he can get no other proof than the testimony of his actions themselves. When we survey the universe and note the orderly government of the world and the blessings we receive in life from God, we recognize the existence of some transcendent power which both created and maintains existing things. It is the same with regard to God's manifesting himself in our flesh. The wonders evident in his actions we regard as sufficient proof of the presence of the Godhead, and in the deeds recorded we mark all those attributes by which the divine nature is characterized.

It is a mark of God to give man life; to preserve by his providence all existing things; to afford food and drink to those who have been granted life in the flesh; to care for those in want; by health to restore to itself the nature perverted by sickness; to exercise an equal sway over all creation, over land, sea, and air, and over the heavenly regions; to possess power sufficient for everything, and above all to be the vanquisher of death and corruption. If, then, the record about him were defective in any of these or suchlike things, unbelievers would have good reason to take exception to our religion. But if everything by which we know God is evident in the record about him, what stands in the way of believing?

13. But, it is objected, birth and death belong to the nature of flesh. Yes, indeed. But what preceded His birth and followed his death lies outside the nature we share. When we look at the two limits of our human life, we observe the nature of our beginning and our end. Man begins his existence in weakness and similarly ends his life through weakness. But in God's case, the birth did not have its origin in weakness, neither did the death end in weakness. For sensual pleasure did not precede the birth and corruption did not follow the death.

Do you fail to believe the miracle? I welcome your incredulity. For by your very recognition that what we have said surpasses belief, you acknowledge that the miracles transcend nature. This very fact, then, that the gospel proclamation transcends natural categories, should be proof to you that He who was manifested was God. For had the narratives of the Christ been confined within the limits of nature, where would the divine be? But if the account transcends nature, then the proof that the one we preach is God is evident in the very things you disbelieve.

Man is born through copulation, and after death lies in corruption. Were these elements comprised in the gospel preaching, you would certainly not imagine Him to be God of whom it was said he only had the properties of our nature. But since you learn that, while he was born, he transcended our nature both in manner of birth and in not being subject to the change of corruption, it would be well for you to exercise your incredulity in a different direction. It would be consistent for you to refuse to think of him as a mere man, as one instance among others of human nature.

Now by refusing to believe such a one was a mere man, a person is forced to acknowledge him to be God. For the one who recorded his birth, recorded also his birth from a virgin. If, then, the account of his birth is credible, there is surely nothing incredible, in the same account, about its manner. For the one who told of his birth told also of his birth from a virgin. And the one who mentioned his death also bore witness to his resurrection along with the death. If, then, on the basis of what you are told, you grant that he both died and was born, you must similarly admit his birth and death were free from weakness. These things, however, transcend nature. In consequence, he, whom we have shown to be born supernaturally, cannot possibly be confined within nature.

14. Why, then, they ask, did the divine stoop to such humiliation? Our faith falters when we think that God, the infinite, incomprehensible, ineffable reality, transcending all glory and majesty, should be defiled by associating with human nature, and his sublime powers no less debased by their contact with what is abject.

15. We are not at a loss to find a fitting answer even to this objection. Do you ask the reason why God was born among men? If you exclude from life the benefits which come from God, you will have no way of recognizing the divine. It is from the blessings we experience that we recognize our benefactor, since by observing what happens to us, we deduce the nature of Him who is responsible for it. If, then, the love of man is a proper mark of the divine nature, here is the explanation you are looking for, here is the reason for God's presence among men. Our nature was sick and needed a doctor. Man had fallen and needed someone to raise him up. He who had lost life

needed someone to restore it. He who had ceased to participate in the good needed someone to bring him back to it. He who was shut up in darkness needed the presence of light. The prisoner was looking for someone to ransom him, the captive for someone to take his part. He who was under the yoke of slavery was looking for someone to set him free. Were these trifling and unworthy reasons to impel God to come down and visit human nature, seeing humanity was in such a pitiful and wretched state?

## Why Did Not God Redeem Man by a Sovereign Act?

But, it is objected, man could have been benefited and yet God could have remained at the same time free from weakness and suffering. By his will he framed the universe: by a mere act of will he brought into existence that which was not. Why, then, if he loved man, did he not wrest him from the opposing power and restore him to his original state by some sovereign and divine act of authority? Why did he take a tedious, circuitous route, submit to a bodily nature, enter life through birth, pass through the various stages of development, and finally taste death, and so gain his end by the resurrection of his own body? Could he not have remained in his transcendent and divine glory, and saved man by a command, renouncing such circuitous routes?

To such objections we must oppose the truth, so that those who are seriously searching for the rational basis of our religion may find no obstacle in the way of their faith.

We must inquire first—and we have already done this in part—what it is that stands in opposition to virtue. As darkness is the contrary of light and death of life, so it is clear that vice and nothing else is the contrary of virtue. We observe many things in the created order, but none of them—not stone, wood, water, man, or anything else—is the contrary of light and life except their precise opposites, i.e., darkness and death. So it is with respect to virtue. One cannot say that any created thing is to be thought of as its opposite, except the idea of vice.

Did, then, our teaching represent the divine as born in a state of evil, our opponents would have occasion to criticize our faith, on the ground that we hold views inconsistent and incongruous with the divine nature. For it certainly would not be right to say that he who is wisdom itself and goodness and incorruption and every other sublime idea and title had been changed into the opposite. God is genuine virtue, and vice alone is by nature opposed to virtue. If, then, God entered not a state of evil but human nature, and if shame and indecency alone attach to the weakness of vice and God neither entered such a state nor can by his nature enter it, why are our opponents ashamed to acknowledge God's contact with human nature? There is nothing in man's constitution which is opposed to the principle of virtue. Neither his capacity for reason or thought or understanding nor any similar attribute peculiar to his nature stands opposed to the principle of virtue.

16. But, it is urged, our body is subject to change and hence to weakness. He who is born in such a state is born in weakness; but the divine is above weakness. It is therefore an idea foreign to God to contend that he who is by nature above weakness came to share in weakness.

In answering this objection we shall use an argument already employed, viz., that "weakness"[22] can be used in a strictly proper sense and also in an extended sense. What affects the will and perverts it toward evil and away from virtue is weakness, properly speaking. On the other hand, the successive changes we observe in nature as it proceeds on its way are more properly referred to as modes of activity than of weakness. I mean birth, growth, continuance of life[23] through taking in and expelling food, the union, and then later the dissolution, of the body's constituent parts, and its return to its kindred elements. With what, then, does our religion contend the divine came into contact? Was it weakness in its strict sense, that is, evil, or was it the changing movement of nature? Were our teaching to affirm that the divine entered a state which is morally forbidden, it would be our duty to avoid such a preposterous doctrine, implying, as it does, an unsound view of the divine nature. But if we affirm that he had contact with our nature, which derived its original being and subsistence from him, in what way does the gospel proclamation fail to have a fitting conception of God? In our faith we introduce no element of weakness in our ideas of God. For we do not say

22 *Pathos*. No English word can adequately render *pathos*, which has several nuances. Gregory regards its primary sense as moral. It is the condition of weakness by which the soul is drawn to wickedness. In an extended sense it refers to the natural changes and vicissitudes of existence, to which moral issues are irrelevant.

23 Literally, "the continuance of the subject." The idea is that one's identity remains unchanged despite the changes implied in bodily nourishment.

that a doctor incurs weakness when he heals someone in a state of weakness. Even though he comes into contact with sickness, the doctor remains free from such weakness.

If birth in itself is not weakness, one cannot call life weakness. It is the sensual pleasure which precedes human birth that is weakness, and it is the impulse to evil in living beings that is the sickness of our nature. But our religion claims He was pure from both of these. If, then, his birth was free from sensual pleasure and his life from wickedness, what weakness remains for God to have shared in, according to our devout religion? If you call the separation of the body from the soul weakness, you would be much more justified in so naming their union. For if the separation of united elements is weakness, then the union of separated elements will equally be weakness. For the union of things that are separate and the separation of things conjoined or united implies motion and change.

The name, therefore, we give to the final change ought also to apply to that which precedes it. And if the first change, which we call birth, does not involve weakness, neither can the second change, which we call death and which dissolves the union of body and soul, be logically called weakness.

We hold that God was involved in both these changes of our nature, by which the soul is united to the body and separated from it. He was united with both elements in man's make-up—I mean the sensible and intelligible elements. And by means of this ineffable and inexpressible union he brought it about that, once these elements of soul and body were united, the union would remain permanent. For when, in his case too, soul and body had been separated by that successive movement of change our nature undergoes, he joined the parts together again with a kind of glue—I mean by divine power. And so he united what was separated in an unbreakable union. This is what the resurrection means—the restoration of elements into an indissoluble union after their separation, so that they can grow together. In this way man's primal grace was restored and we retrieved once more eternal life. By our dissolution the wickedness mingled with our nature was poured off like a liquid which, when the vessel holding it is broken to pieces, is dispersed and lost, since there is nothing more to contain it.

Now just as the principle of death had its origin in a single person and passed to the whole of human nature, similarly the principle of the resurrection originated in one Man and extends to all humanity. He who united again the soul he had assumed, with his own body, did so by means of his own power which was fused with each element at their first formation. In the same way he conjoined the intelligible and sensible nature on a larger scale, the principle of the resurrection extending to its logical limits.[24] For when in the case of the man in whom he was incarnate[25] the soul returned once more to the body after the dissolution, a similar union of the separated elements potentially passed to the whole of human nature, as if a new beginning had been made. This is the mystery of God's plan with regard to death, and of the resurrection from the dead. He does not prevent the soul's separation from the body by death in accordance with the inevitable course of nature. But he brings them together again by the resurrection. Thus he becomes the meeting point of both, of death and of life. In himself he restores the nature which death has disrupted, and becomes himself the principle whereby the separated parts are reunited.

17. But, someone urges, the objection raised to our viewpoint has not yet been answered. Rather has the argument put forward by unbelievers been strengthened by what we have said. For if he was as powerful as we have indicated, so that he could destroy death and gain entrance to life, why did he not do what he wanted to by a mere act of will? Why did he effect our salvation in a devious way, by being born and nurtured and by experiencing death in the process of saving man? He could have saved us without submitting to these things.

In addressing reasonable persons it should suffice to answer such an objection in this way: Sick people do not prescribe to doctors their manner of treatment. They do not argue with their benefactors about the form of their cure, asking why the doctor felt the ailing part and devised this or that remedy to relieve the sickness, when something different was needed. Rather do they keep in view the aim of his kind services and accept them gratefully.

But, as the prophet[26] says, God's abounding goodness aids us in a hidden way, and in the present life it is not clearly evident. For every objection of unbelievers would be removed, could we actually see what we only hope for. But our hopes await the ages to come, so that there may then be revealed

---

[24] I.e., to all humanity.
[25] Literally, "The man he assumed," the concrete instance of human nature.          [26] Ps. 31:19, in the LXX rendering.

what at present our faith alone apprehends. In consequence we must search out, as far as we can, some reasonable solution of the question posed, and one in harmony with our preceding line of thought.

18. And yet it is perhaps superfluous for us who already believe that God entered human life to criticize the manner of his appearing, on the ground that it lacked something in wisdom and superior judgment. For those who do not strongly oppose the truth have no small proof that God dwelt with us. Even in advance of the life to come, it is evident in this present life; I mean we have the testimony of the facts themselves.

Who does not know that the deceit of demons filled every corner of the world and held sway over man's life by the madness of idolatry? Who does not realize that every people on earth was accustomed to worship demons under the form of idols, by sacrificing living victims and making foul offerings on their altars? But, as the apostle says,[27] from the moment that God's saving grace appeared among men and dwelt in human nature, all this vanished into nothing, like smoke. The madness of their oracles and prophecies has ceased. Their annual processions and foul and bloody hecatombs have been done away. Among many peoples altars, temple porches, and precincts and shrines have entirely disappeared, along with the ceremonies practiced by the devotees of demons for their own deceit and that of their friends. The result is that in many places where such things were once current they are not even remembered. Throughout the world, churches and altars have been erected instead in the name of Christ; and the holy and bloodless priesthood and the sublime philosophy which consists in deeds rather than words now flourish. The life of the body is held in contempt; death is despised. Those who were forced by tyrants to renounce their faith gave clear testimony to this. Bodily torture and the sentence of death they reckoned as nothing. Clearly they would not have endured such things had they not had a clear and indubitable proof of the incarnation.

For Jews the following fact is a sufficient indication of the presence of Him whom they renounce. Up to the time that God appeared in Jesus Christ they could see in Jerusalem the splendor of royal palaces, the famous Temple, and the customary sacrifices through the year. And all that the law enjoined in mysteries for those who grasp their inner meaning up to that moment went on unhindered in accordance with the ritual

[27] Titus 2:11.

originally imposed on them by their religion. But when they saw the One they expected (for they had already learned of him through the Prophets and the Law), they held what from now on was a mere superstition in higher esteem than faith in him who had come. For they misconstrued their religion. They kept the letter of the law and were in bondage to custom rather than to right reason. As a consequence they refused to accept the grace made manifest; and all that is left of their holy religion is barren narratives. Not a trace of their Temple remains. The splendor of their city is left in ruins. There survives to the Jews none of their ancient customs the law enjoined; and access to their holy city, Jerusalem, is denied them by imperial decree.[28]

19. However, neither Hellenists nor the leaders of Judaism are willing to regard these things as proof of God's presence. Hence it will be well, in the face of the objections urged, to give a more particular reason why the divine nature became joined to ours, and saved man by its own presence and did not execute its purpose by a mere command. What starting point, then, shall we adopt in order to bring our argument satisfactorily to the proposed conclusion? What other starting point is there than to give a brief review of spiritual conceptions of God?

## The Union of God's Goodness, Wisdom, Justice, and Power in the Incarnation

20. It is universally agreed that we should believe the Divine to be not only powerful, but also just and good and wise and everything else that suggests excellence. It follows, therefore, in the plan of God we are considering, that there should not be a tendency for one of his attributes to be present in what happened, while another was absent. For not a single one of these sublime attributes by itself and separated from the others constitutes virtue. What is good is not truly such unless it is associated with justice, wisdom, and power. For what is unjust and stupid and impotent is not good. Power, too, if it is separated from justice and wisdom, cannot be classed as virtue. Rather is it a brutal and tyrannical form of power. The same holds good of the other attributes. If wisdom exceeds the bounds of justice, or if righteousness is not associated with power and goodness, one would more properly call them wickedness. For how can we reckon as good what is deficient in excellence?

[28] The decree of Hadrian in A.D. 134 forbade Jews access to Jerusalem.

If, then, in our idea of God all the attributes must be combined, let us inquire whether his plan for man is deficient in any of these appropriate conceptions. We seek above all, in the case of God, signs of his goodness. Now what could be clearer evidence of this than the fact that he reclaimed him who had deserted to the enemy's side, and did not allow the fickleness of man's will to influence his own immutable nature with its constant purpose of goodness? For, as David says,[29] he would not have come to save us, had his intention not been rooted in goodness. But the goodness of his intention would have availed nothing had not wisdom made his love of man effective. In the case of the sick there are probably many who wish the patient were not sick; but only those can bring their good intentions for the sick to effect who have the technical capacity actually to cure them. Wisdom, then, certainly needs to be allied with goodness. How is this alliance of wisdom with goodness evident in what happened [in the incarnation]? A good purpose, to be sure, cannot be detected in the abstract. How, then, can it be evident except in the actual facts that occurred? These facts proceed in a logical chain and sequence, and exhibit the wisdom and skill of God's plan.

As we have already indicated, it is the union of justice with wisdom that really constitutes virtue. Separated and taken by itself, justice is not goodness. Accordingly it will be well for us to take the two together (I mean wisdom and justice) in our consideration of God's plan for man.

21. What, then, is justice? We recall, doubtless, the points we made in the early course of our argument, that man was created in the image of the divine nature, and along with other blessings he retains this divine likeness by having free will. Yet his nature is necessarily mutable. For it was not possible that one who derived his existence from change should be altogether free from it. The passage from nonbeing to being is a kind of change, nonexistence being transformed into existence by God's power. In another way, too, we observe that man is necessarily subject to change. For he is the image of the divine nature; and an image would be entirely identical with what it resembled, were it not in some way different from it. The difference between the one made "in the image" and the archetype lies in this: that the latter by nature is not subject to change, while the former is. Through change it derived its subsistence,

---

[29] Cf. Ps. 119:68. There are several passages of the LXX which Gregory may have in mind.

as we have shown; and being subject to change, its being is not entirely permanent.

Now change is a perpetual movement toward a different state. And it takes two forms. In the one case it is always directed toward the good; and here its progress is continual, since there is no conceivable limit to the distance it can go. In the other case it is directed toward the opposite, the essence of which lies in nonexistence. For the opposite of the good, as we have already indicated, implies some such notion of opposition as we intend when we oppose being to nonbeing and existence to nonexistence. By reason, then, of its impulse toward change and movement, our nature cannot remain essentially unchanged. Rather does the will drive it toward some end, desire for the good naturally setting it in motion.

Now the good is of two kinds: what is really good in the nature of things, and what is not such, but has only an outward and artificial appearance of the good. It is the mind, with which we have been endowed, that discriminates between these. In this way we run the risk either of gaining what is essentially good, or else, by being diverted from it by some misleading prospect, of lapsing into the opposite. This is what happened in the pagan fable about the dog which saw in the water the reflection of what it had in its mouth. It let go the real food, and, opening its mouth to swallow the reflection, remained hungry.

Being cheated of the desire for the genuine good, the mind was thus diverted to nonbeing. By the deceit of the advocate and contriver of wickedness, it was convinced that good was its opposite. Nor would this deception have succeeded, had not the fishhook of evil been furnished with an outward appearance of good, as with a bait. Of his own free will man fell into this misfortune, and through pleasure became subject to the enemy of life.

Let us now, in this connection, study all the appropriate attributes of God—goodness, wisdom, justice, power, incorruption, and everything else that indicates excellence. As good he has pity on him who has fallen; as wise he is not ignorant of the way to restore him. For it belongs to wisdom to make just decisions, since one would not associate genuine justice with stupidity.

22. Wherein, then, did [God's] justice consist in this matter? In His not exercising an arbitrary authority over him who held us in bondage. Also, in His not wresting us from him who held

us, by His superior power, and so leaving him who had enslaved man through pleasure, with a just cause of complaint.
Those who give up their liberty for money become the slaves
of their purchasers. By their selling themselves, neither they nor
anyone else can reclaim their freedom, even when those who
reduce themselves to this wretched state are nobly born. And
should anyone, out of concern for one so sold, exercise force
against the purchaser, he would seem unjust in dictatorially
freeing one legally acquired. On the other hand, no law stands
in the way of his buying back the man's freedom, if he wants to.
In the same way, when once we had voluntarily sold ourselves,
he who undertook out of goodness to restore our freedom had
to contrive a just and not a dictatorial method to do so. And
some such method is this: to give the master the chance to take
whatever he wants to as the price of the slave.

23. What, then, was it likely that our overlord would choose
to take? It is possible to make a reasonable guess about his
wishes, if we proceed from facts already clear. We argued at
the beginning that he envied man his happiness and closed his
eyes to the good. He begot in himself the darkness of wickedness, and sickened with the love of power. This was the origin
of his decline toward evil, and the foundation and, as it were,
the mother of all other wickedness. What, then, would he
exchange for the one in his power, if not something clearly
superior and better? Thus, by getting the better of the bargain
he might the more satisfy his pride.

Among those whom history records from the beginning, he
was aware of none who was connected with such circumstances
as he saw in His appearance. There was conception without
sexual union, birth without impurity, a virgin suckling a child,
and heavenly voices witnessing to his eminence. The healing
of natural diseases was performed by him without technical
skill, but by a mere word and act of will. There was the
restoration of the dead to life, the rescue of the condemned,[30]
the fear inspired in demons, and authority over the elements.
He walked across the sea so that the water was not parted to
lay bare the bottom for those who passed over (as happened in
Moses' miracle); but the surface of the water became like land
to his tread, and supported his footsteps by offering a firm
resistance. He ignored food as long as he wished. There were
abundant feasts in the desert, which fed many thousands.
Heaven did not rain down manna; nor did the earth naturally

[30] Possibly a reference to those possessed by demons.

bring forth wheat to fill their need. But from the secret store-houses of God's power this abundance proceeded. Bread was produced ready-made in the hands of those who served it, and, indeed, increased as it satisfied those who ate of it. Then there were the relishes of fish—not that the sea supplied their need, but He who sowed the sea with its different kinds of fish.

But how can we recount in detail each of the gospel miracles? When the enemy saw such power, he recognized in Christ a bargain which offered him more than he held. For this reason he chose him as the ransom for those he had shut up in death's prison. Since, however, he could not look upon the direct vision of God, he had to see him clothed in some part of that flesh which he already held captive through sin. Consequently the Deity was veiled in flesh, so that the enemy, by seeing something familiar and natural to him, might not be terrified at the approach of transcendent power. So when he saw this power softly reflected more and more through the miracles, he reckoned that what he saw was to be desired rather than feared.

You observe here how goodness is combined with justice, and wisdom is not separated from them. Through the covering of the flesh the divine power is made accessible, so that the enemy will not take fright at God's appearing and so thwart his plan for us. All God's attributes are at once displayed in this—his goodness, his wisdom, and his justice. That he decided to save us is proof of his goodness. That he struck a bargain to redeem the captive indicates his justice. And it is evidence of his transcendent wisdom that he contrived to make accessible to the enemy what was [otherwise] inaccessible.

24. It is likely, however, that one who has followed our train of thought will inquire where the power of the Godhead and the incorruptible nature of divine power can be seen in the account we have given. That this too may be clear, let us penetrate the successive events of the gospel story, in which the union of power with love for man is displayed.

In the first place, that the omnipotent nature was capable of descending to man's lowly position is a clearer evidence of power than great and supernatural miracles. For it somehow accords with God's nature, and is consistent with it, to do great and sublime things by divine power. It does not startle us to hear it said that the whole creation, including the invisible world, exists by God's power, and is the realization of his will. But descent to man's lowly position is a supreme example of power—of a power which is not bounded by circumstances contrary to its nature.

It belongs to the nature of fire to shoot upwards; and no one would think it wonderful for a flame to act naturally. But if he saw a flame with a downward motion like that of heavy bodies, he would take it for a marvel, wondering how it could remain a flame and yet contravene its nature by its downward motion. So it is with the incarnation. God's transcendent power is not so much displayed in the vastness of the heavens, or the luster of the stars, or the orderly arrangement of the universe or his perpetual oversight of it, as in his condescension to our weak nature. We marvel at the way the sublime entered a state of lowliness and, while actually seen in it, did not leave the heights. We marvel at the way the Godhead was entwined in human nature and, while becoming man, did not cease to be God.

As we have already observed, the opposing power could not, by its nature, come into immediate contact with God's presence and endure the unveiled sight of him. Hence it was that God, in order to make himself easily accessible to him who sought the ransom for us, veiled himself in our nature. In that way, as it is with greedy fish, he might swallow the Godhead like a fishhook along with the flesh, which was the bait. Thus, when life came to dwell with death and light shone upon darkness, their contraries might vanish away. For it is not in the nature of darkness to endure the presence of light, nor can death exist where life is active.

## SUMMARY

Let us then, by way of summary, review our argument about the gospel revelation, and so make an effective reply to those who criticize God's plan because he personally intervened to save man. Throughout we must have fitting notions of God. We must not attribute to him one transcendent attribute, and then exclude another which equally befits him. But our faith must certainly include every sublime and devout thought of God, and these must be properly related to each other.

We have shown that God's goodness, wisdom, justice, power, and incorruptible nature are all to be seen in his plan for us. His goodness is evident in his choosing to save one who was lost. His wisdom and justice are to be seen in the way he saved us. His power is clear in this: that he came in the likeness of man and in the lowly form of our nature, inspiring the hope that, like man, he could be overcome by death; and yet, having come, he acted entirely in accordance with his nature. Now it belongs to light to dispel darkness, and to life to destroy death. Seeing, then, we have been led astray from the right path, with the result we were diverted from the life we once had and were involved in death, what is there improbable in what we learn from the gospel revelation? Purity lays hold of those stained with sin, life lays hold of the dead, and guidance is given to those astray, so that the stain may be cleansed, the error corrected, and the dead may return to life.

25. There is no good reason for those who do not take too narrow a view of things to find anything strange in the fact that God assumed our nature. For when he considers the universe, can anyone be so simple-minded as not to believe that the Divine is present in everything, pervading, embracing, and penetrating it? For all things depend on Him who is, and nothing can exist which does not have its being in Him who is. If, then, all things exist in him and he exists in all things, why are they shocked at a scheme of revelation which teaches that God became man, when we believe that even now he is not external to man? For, granted that God is not present in us in the same way as he was in the incarnation, it is at any rate admitted he is equally present in us in both instances. In the one case he is united to us in so far as he sustains existing things. In the other case he united himself with our nature, in order that by its union with the Divine it might become divine, being rescued from death and freed from the tyranny of the adversary. For with *his* return from death, our mortal race begins *its* return to immortal life.

## Did God Use Deceit?

26. But perhaps someone who has examined the justice and wisdom apparent in this plan is driven to conclude that such a scheme as God contrived for us involved deceit. For in a way it was a fraud and deception for God, when he placed himself in the power of the enemy who was our master, not to show his naked deity, but to conceal it in our nature, and so escape recognition. It is the mark of deceivers to divert the hopes of those they plot against to one thing, and then to do something different from what is expected. But he who penetrates the truth of the matter will agree that we have here a crowning example of justice and wisdom.

Now it is the character of justice to render to each his due. It belongs to wisdom, on the other hand, neither to pervert justice nor to divorce its just decisions from the noble end of the love of man. Both must be skillfully combined. By justice due recompense is given; by goodness the end of the love of man is not excluded. Let us then inquire whether the two are to be seen in what happened. Justice is evident in the rendering of due recompense, by which the deceiver was in turn deceived. The purpose of the action, on the other hand, testifies to the goodness of him who brought it about. For it is the mark of justice to render to everyone the results of what he originally planted, just as the earth yields fruits according to the types of seed sown. It is the mark of wisdom, however, by the way in which it returns like for like, not to exclude a higher aim. The conspirator and the one who cures the victim both mix a drug with the man's food. In the one case it is poison; in the other it is an antidote for poison. But the mode of healing in no way vitiates the kindly intention. In both instances a drug is mixed with the food; but when we catch sight of the aim, we applaud the one and are incensed at the other. So it is with the incarnation. By the principle of justice the deceiver reaps the harvest of the seeds he sowed with his own free will. For he who first deceived man by the bait of pleasure is himself deceived by the camouflage of human nature. But the purpose of the action changes it into something good. For the one practiced deceit to ruin our nature; but the other, being at once just and good and wise, made use of a deceitful device to save the one who had been ruined. And by so doing he benefited, not only the one who had perished, but also the very one who had brought us to ruin. For when death came into contact with life, darkness with light, corruption with incorruption, the worse of these things disappeared into a state of nonexistence, to the profit of him who was freed from these evils.

When a baser metal is mixed with gold, refiners restore the more precious metal to its natural brightness by consuming the alien and worthless substance with fire. The separation, indeed, does not occur without difficulty, for it takes time for the fire to consume the base element and effect its disappearance. Yet the melting away of the substance embedded in it, which detracts from its beauty, is a kind of healing of the gold. In the same way, when death, corruption, darkness, and the other offshoots of vice have attached themselves to the author of evil, contact with the divine power acts like fire and effects the disappearance of what is contrary to nature. In this way the nature is purified and benefited, even though the process of separation is a painful one. Hence not even the adversary himself can question that what occurred was just and salutary—if, that is, he comes to recognize its benefit. In this present life patients whose cure involves surgery and cautery grow incensed at their physicians when they smart under the pain of the incision. But if by these means they are restored to health and the pain of the cautery passes off, they will be grateful to those who effected their cure. It is the same with the evil which is now mingled with our nature and has become a part of it. When, over long periods of time, it has been removed and those now lying in sin have been restored to their original state, all creation will join in united thanksgiving, both those whose purification has involved punishment and those who never needed purification at all.

## Why God Assumed Human Nature

This is the sort of teaching we derive from the mighty revelation of God's becoming man. By his intimate union with humanity, he shared all the marks of our nature. He was born, reared, grew up, and went so far as even to taste death. Thus he brought about all we have mentioned. He freed man from evil, and healed the very author of evil himself. For the healing of an infirmity involves doing away with the disease, even if the process is painful.

27. Certainly it was in keeping with his intimate union with our nature that he should be united with us in all our characteristics. Those who wash off dirt from garments do not leave some of the stains and remove others. But, from top to bottom, they cleanse the whole garment of the stains, to give it a consistent character and a uniform brightness from the washing. It is the same with our human life, which from beginning to end and throughout was stained with sin. The cleansing power had to penetrate it entirely. One part could not be healed by cleansing while another was overlooked and left uncured. That is why, in view of the fact that our life is bounded by two extremities (I mean its beginning and end), the power which amends our nature had to reach to both points. It had to touch the beginning and to extend to the end, covering all that lies between.

Now for every man there is only one way of entering life.

Whence, then, did he have to take up his abode in it who was coming to us? "From heaven," is perhaps the reply of one who despises the method of human birth as something shameful and disgraceful. But in heaven there was no human nature, nor was the disease of evil prevalent in that transcendent life. He who united himself with man did so with the aim of helping him. How, then, will anyone seek in that sphere where there was no evil and man did not live his life the particular human nature [31] which God assumed—or rather, not the human nature, but some imitation of it? For how could our nature be restored if it was some heavenly being, and not this sick creature of earth, which was united with the Divine? For a sick man cannot be healed unless the ailing part of him in particular receives the cure. If, then, the diseased member was on earth, and the divine power, to preserve its own dignity, did not come into contact with it, its concern with creatures with which we have nothing in common would not have benefited man.

Indeed, if it is permissible to conceive of anything, except evil, as unworthy of God, such a situation is as unworthy of him as any other. For to one who is so narrow-minded as to define God's majesty from its inability to share the properties of our nature, his union with a heavenly body rather than an earthly would not detract less from his dignity. For every created thing is equally inferior to the Most High who, by reason of his transcendent nature, is unapproachable. The whole universe is uniformly beneath his dignity. For what is totally inaccessible is not accessible to one thing and inaccessible to another. Rather does it transcend all existing things in equal degree. Earth is not more below his dignity, and heaven less. Nor do the creatures inhabiting each of these elements differ in this respect, that some have a direct contact with his inaccessible nature, while others are distant from it. Otherwise we could not conceive of the power that governs the universe as equally pervading all things. In some it would be unduly present, in others it would be lacking. Consequently, from these differences of more and less, the divine nature would appear to be composite and inconsistent with itself, were we to conceive of it in principle as remote from us while it was near some other creature and easily accessible by this proximity.

The true way, however, of regarding the transcendent dignity does not have in view comparisons in terms of "lower"

---

[31] *Anthrōpos*: the particular instance of human nature.

and "higher." Everything is equally beneath the power that rules the universe. In consequence, if our opponents imagine that the earthly nature is unworthy of union with the Divine, they will never discover any other nature worthy of it. If, then, everything equally falls short of this dignity, the one thing which really befits God's nature still remains, namely, to come to the aid of those in need. By acknowledging, therefore, that the healing power had recourse to the very place where the disease was, what conception unworthy of God does our faith entertain?

28. But our opponents ridicule human nature, and keep stressing the manner of our birth. They imagine, by so doing, that they hold our faith up to derision, as if it were unbecoming to God to share in, and to have contact with, human life by entering it in such a way. But we have already treated this point by our previous contention that evil, and what is akin to it, are alone essentially shameful. But the whole course of our nature has been arranged by God's will and law, and hence it is far removed from the censure of evil. Otherwise the condemnation of our nature would reflect upon the Creator, if any aspect of it could be charged with being disgraceful or improper.

The only thing alien to the Divine is evil. Nature is not evil; and our religion teaches that God was incarnate in man, not that he entered a state of evil. There is only one way for a man to enter life, viz., to be begotten and brought into existence. Now our opponents acknowledge that it was right for the divine power to visit the nature which was weakened by evil, but they are offended at the means of the visitation. What other method, then, of entering life do they prescribe for God? They fail to realize that the whole anatomy of the body is uniformly to be valued, and that no factor which contributes to the maintenance of life can be charged with being dishonorable or evil. The whole organic structure of the body is devised for a single end, and that is to preserve the human race in existence. The other organs support man's present life, and are distributed among different activities by which man exercises his faculties of perception and action. But the generative organs have the future in view, and it is by them that the succession of the race is maintained. If, then, we have in mind their usefulness, to which one of the organs we generally consider honorable can they be inferior? Indeed, to which of them should we not with good reason reckon them to be superior?

For it is not by means of the eye or the ear or the tongue or
any of our senses that our race is constantly carried on. As we
have said, such senses serve our present enjoyment. But by the
generative organs the immortality of the human race is preserved, and death's perpetual moves against us are, in a way,
rendered futile and ineffectual. By her successive generations
nature is always filling up the deficiency. What unfitting notion,
then, does our religion contain, if God was united with human
life by the very means by which our nature wars on death?

### Why Was the Incarnation Delayed?

29. But taking a different line, they try to calumniate our
teaching in another way. Granting, they say, that what
occurred was good and worthy of God, why did he delay this
act of his goodness? Why did he not cut short the further
progress of evil at its very first appearance? We have a brief
reply for this: viz., that it was wise and foreseeing to delay
the benefit, for this served to the advantage of our nature.
In the case of diseases of the body, when some corrupting
humor spreads under the skin, the skillful physician does not
bind the body up with drugs before the underlying trouble is
brought completely to the surface. Rather does he wait until
the hidden humor is altogether out, and so applies his remedy
to the disease when it is uncovered. And so, when once the
disease of wickedness had infiltrated human nature, the universal Physician waited until no form of evil remained concealed in our nature.  In consequence, he did not apply his
cure to man immediately on Cain's jealousy and murder of
his brother. For the wickedness of those destroyed in Noah's
time had not yet broken out. Nor had there come to light the
terrible disease of Sodom's transgression, or the battle of the
Egyptians with God, or the arrogance of the Assyrians, or the
murder of God's saints by the Jews, or Herod's iniquitous
slaughter of the children, or all the other things which history
records or which were wrought by successive generations and
left unrecorded. For the root of wickedness produced in men's
wills a great variety of shoots. When, then, evil had reached
its highest pitch and no form of wickedness had not been
daringly attempted by man, he healed the disease. Not, indeed,
at its onset but when it had fully devloped, so that the healing
might encompass the total ailment.

30. If anyone, furthermore, imagines he can refute our

argument because human life still continues to go astray through sin, even after the application of the remedy, he may be led to the truth by means of a familiar example. In the case of a snake, should it receive a deadly blow on the head, its coil is not at once killed with its head. While the latter is dead, the tail still remains pulsing with its own life, and is not deprived of vital movement. Similarly it is possible for evil to have been struck a mortal blow, and yet for life still to be harassed by its vestiges.

## WHY DO NOT ALL BELIEVE?

When, however, they give up reproaching our religious teaching on this point, they introduce another charge, viz., that our faith does not extent to all mankind. Why is it, they say, that the grace of the gospel has not reached all men? While some have attached themselves to its teaching, the remainder constitute no small number. Either God is unwilling to distribute his benefits ungrudgingly to everyone or else he is quite incapable of doing so. Both alternatives are open to censure. For it does not befit God's nature to be defective either in willing what is good or in executing it. Why is it, then, they ask, that the grace of the gospel has not reached all men, seeing that faith is something good?

Now had we, in the course of our argument, contended that the divine will allots faith to men in such a way that some are called, while others fail to share in the calling, there would be occasion to prefer such a charge against our religion. But all are equally called without respect to rank, age, or nationality. It was, indeed, for this reason that from the very first when the gospel was preached the ministers of the Word were at once divinely inspired to speak every language,[32] so that no one might fail to share in the blessings of their teaching. In the light of this, how can anyone rightly charge God with responsibility for the fact that the Word has not prevailed with all men? Out of his high regard for man, the Sovereign of the universe left something under our own control and of which each of us is the sole master. I mean the will, a faculty which is free from bondage and independent, and is grounded in the freedom of the mind. Such a charge, then, might with greater justice be transferred to those who have not attached themselves to the faith rather than be brought against him who

[32] Cf. Acts 2:8-11.

solicited their assent to it. When Peter first preached the gospel
before a large gathering of Jews, three thousand at once
embraced the faith. But the disbelievers, who were more
numerous than those who believed, did not blame the apostle
for their lack of conviction. For, seeing the grace of the gospel
had been offered to all, it was not reasonable that those who
held aloof of their own free choice should put the blame for
their hard luck on another, rather than on themselves.

31. Our opponents, however, are not at a loss for a captious
reply to such arguments. For they contend that, had God
wanted to, he could have compelled those who were stubborn
to accept the gospel preaching. What freedom of choice would
they then have had? Wherein would virtue lie? Wherein the
praise for those who triumphed? It is a mark only of inanimate
or irrational creatures to be induced by another's will to do
his bidding. But were a reasonable and intelligent nature to
abandon its freedom of choice, it would at the same time lose
the boon of intelligence. For what use would such a one's mind
be, if his power of free choice were at the disposal of another?
If the will is inactive, virtue of necessity vanishes, being pre-
cluded by the inertness of the will. With the absence of virtue,
life loses its honor, the praise of the victorious is done away,
sin is no longer a peril, and different ways of life are in-
distinguishable. For who any longer could reasonably censure
the dissolute, or praise the self-controlled? For everyone would
be ready with this answer: that nothing we intend is in our
power, but the wills of men are induced by a higher power to
do its bidding. The fact, then, that the faith has not taken root
in all men is not to be charged against God's goodness, but
against the disposition of those to whom the gospel is preached.

## WHY DID GOD DIE?

32. What further objection do our opponents bring forward?
In its extreme form this: that the transcendent nature ought
never to have experienced death. Rather could He, with his
excessive power, have easily accomplished his purpose without
this. But even if, for some ineffable reason, this actually had to
happen, he at least did not have to be humiliated by a shameful
manner of death. For, they urge, what death could be more
shameful than that on a cross?

What do we reply to this? That the birth makes the death
necessary. He who had once decided to share our humanity

had to experience all that belongs to our nature. Now human life is encompassed within two limits, and if he had passed through one and not touched the other, he would only have half fulfilled his purpose, having failed to reach the other limit proper to our nature.

But someone, perhaps, with an accurate grasp of our religion might more reasonably claim that the death did not occur because of the birth, but that, on the contrary, the birth was accepted by Him for the sake of the death. For he who eternally exists did not submit to being born in a body because *he* was in need of life. Rather was it to recall *us* from death to life. Our whole nature had to be brought back from death. In consequence he stooped down to our dead body and stretched out a hand, as it were, to one who was prostrate. He approached so near death as to come into contact with it, and by means of his own body to grant our nature the principle of the resurrection, by raising our total humanity along with him by his power.

Not from another source, but from the lump[33] of our humanity, came the manhood[34] which received the Divine. By the resurrection it was exalted along with the Godhead. In the case of our own bodies the activity of one of our senses is felt throughout the whole system which is united to it. In just the same way, seeing that our nature constitutes, as it were, a single living organism, the resurrection of one part of it extends to the whole. By the unity and continuity of our nature it is communicated from the part to the whole. If, then, He who stands upright stoops to raise up one who has fallen, what is there in our religious teaching which is outside the realm of probability?

Regarding the cross, whether it contains some other, deeper meaning, those familiar with mystical interpretations may know. But what has come down to us from tradition is as follows: Everything spoken and done in the gospel has a higher, divine meaning. There is no exception to this principle whereby a complete mingling of the divine and the human is indicated. The word and the act proceed in a human way, but their secret meaning reveals the divine. It follows, therefore, that in this instance we should not regard the one aspect and overlook the other. In the death we should see the human element; but from its manner we should seek to penetrate its divine significance.

33 Cf. Rom. 9:21.
34 *Ho theodochos anthrōpos.* By *anthrōpos* Gregory means the concrete instance of human nature, which the Word assumed.

It is the mark of Deity to pervade everything and to extend to every part of the nature of existing things. Nothing, indeed, could continue in existence did it not have its being in that which exists. Now that which is essential and primary being is the divine nature; and the continuance of existing things compels us to believe that it pervades all that is. We learn this from the cross. In shape it is divided into four parts in such a way that the four arms converge in the middle. Now He who was extended upon it at the time God's plan was fulfilled in his death is the one who binds all things to himself and makes them one. Through himself he brings the diverse natures of existing things into one accord and harmony. For we conceive of things as either above or below, or else we think of them as extended sideways. If, then, you consider the constitution of things in heaven or beneath the earth or at either limit of the universe, everywhere the Godhead anticipates your thought. It alone is observed in every part of existence and maintains the universe in a state of being. Whether we should call this nature Godhead or Word or Power or Wisdom, or any other sublime term that better expresses transcendence, makes no difference to our argument. We shall not quibble about a name or title or mode of expression.

The eyes of all creation are set on Him and he is its center, and it finds its harmony in him. Through him the things above are united with those below, and the things at one extremity with those at the other. In consequence it was right that we should not be brought to a knowledge of the Godhead by hearing alone; but that sight too should be our teacher in these sublime matters. This was also the starting point of the great Paul when he initiated the people of Ephesus [into the Christian mysteries]. By his teaching he implanted in them the power to know what is "the depth and height and breadth and length." [35] In fact he designates each projection of the cross by its proper term, calling the top one "height," the bottom one "depth," and the side arms "breadth" and "length." It seems to me, moreover, that he brings out this idea still more clearly when he writes to the Philippians and says to them, "At the name of Jesus every knee shall bow, of things in heaven and on earth and under the earth." [36] There he uses a single term to refer to the crossbar, designating by "on earth" everything in between the things in heaven and the things under the earth.

Such, then, is the mystical meaning of the cross as we have

[35] Eph. 3:18.  [36] Phil. 2:10.

been taught it. The succeeding events, moreover, in the gospel account are consistently of such a kind that even unbelievers would admit they involve no unfitting conception of God. He did not remain dead; and the wounds the spear inflicted on his body did not prevent his living. After the resurrection he appeared at will to the disciples. Whenever he wished, he was present with them, though unobserved. He came into their midst without needing doors to give him entrance. He strengthened the disciples by breathing on them the Spirit. He promised to be with them and that nothing would separate him from them. Visibly he ascended to heaven, but to their minds he was everywhere present. These facts, and whatever the gospel story contains of a similar nature, need no supporting arguments to prove their divine quality and their connection with sublime and transcendent power. I do not think it necessary to dwell upon them in detail. The mere mention of them at once indicates their supernatural character. But since a part of our revealed teaching concerns God's plan regarding washing (whether we call this baptism or enlightenment or regeneration—we will not quibble about the word), we may as well briefly discuss this too. 33. For our opponents are incredulous when they hear us speak about it in the following way.

## BAPTISM

For the mortal creature to pass to life, another birth had to be devised, since the first birth led only to a mortal existence. This second birth could neither begin nor end in corruption, but had to bring the one who was born to immortal life. Its purpose was this: just as one born by mortal generation is of necessity mortal, so the creature begotten by an incorruptible birth might be superior to the corruption of death. Now when our opponents hear this sort of thing and learn that the way this mystery of new birth is brought about is by prayer to God and invocation of heavenly grace, and water and faith, they are incredulous. For they look only at outward appearances, and claim that the exterior act does not correspond to the divine promise. For how, they ask, can prayer and the invocation of divine power over the water become a source of life to those initiated?

Unless they prove very stubborn, a simple rejoinder will suffice to bring them round to our position. Seeing that the

manner of human generation is plain to everybody, let us ask
them in turn how it is that the initial seed of a living creature
becomes a man. No conjecture on this point can surely, by any
kind of reasoning, devise a plausible explanation. For, when
we compare them, what has a man by definition in common
with the outward appearance of the seed? Man is a creature
of reason and intelligence, with a capacity for thought and
knowledge. But the seed is seen to have a certain moist quality;
and apart from this observation it makes by the senses, the
mind cannot penetrate the matter farther.

The reply, then, that people are likely to make when asked
how a man can conceivably be derived from that seed, is the
very one *we* make when asked about the new birth by water.
In the former case they have a ready reply, viz., that the seed
becomes a man by divine power, and without it the seed
remains inert and ineffective. The underlying substance does
not produce the man; but the power of God changes the visible
material into the nature of a man. In the light of this it would
be the height of stupidity for those who acknowledge God's
power to be so great in the one instance, to imagine he is too
feeble to work his purpose in the other. What, they ask, has
water in common with life? But what, we retort to them, has
a moist substance in common with the image of God? In the
latter case we do not think it incredible if a moist substance is
changed into the most precious living creature by the will of
God. Equally we contend there is nothing marvelous if the
presence of divine power transforms what is born in a corruptible nature into a state of incorruption.

34. But they require proof that the Divine is present when
he is invoked to sanctify the procedure. He who makes this
request should review our previous researches. For the proof
which we gave that the power revealed to us by means of flesh
is genuinely divine confirms our line of argument here. For
when we proved that he who was revealed in the flesh was God,
since he disclosed his nature by the miracles he did, we also
established that he is present at every procedure where he is
invoked. Just as everything has a certain characteristic by
which its nature is indicated, so the divine nature is characterized by truth. Well, then, he has promised always to be
present with those who call upon him, to be among believers,
to abide with them all and to be intimate with each of them.
In the light of this we can need no further proof that the divine
is present in the rite of baptism. His very miracles have

convinced us of his deity. We realize that what characterizes the Godhead is its freedom from falsehood; and we do not doubt the presence of what he has promised, because his promise is true.

The fact, moreover, that the prayer of invocation anticipates the divine intention is abundant proof that what is done is brought to effect by God. For in the other type of procreation the impulses of the parents, even when God is not invoked by them in prayer, form the newborn child (as we have already said) by God's power. And without this power their effort is useless and unavailing. How much more, then, in the case of the spiritual kind of procreation, will not the object be accomplished, if we rightly solicit the help that comes by prayer? For God has promised to be present in the rite. He has (so we believe) endowed the act with his power; and our own will is directed toward the end in view.

Those who pray to God that the sun may shine on them in no way alter the fact that it will happen anyway. Yet no one will say that the zeal of those who pray is useless, if they ask God for what will occur in any case. It is the same with those who are altogether persuaded by the truthfulness of his promise that his grace is present in those who are born again through this sacramental act. [By their prayers] they either effect an increase of the grace or at any rate they do not stand in its way. For we are convinced that grace accompanies the rite in any case, since he who made the promise is God, and his deity is attested by the miracles. As a result there is no doubt whatever that the Divine is present [in baptism].

35. Now the descent into the water and the triple immersion contain another mystery. The manner of our salvation owes its efficacy less to instruction by teaching than to what He who entered into fellowship with man actually did. In him life became a reality, so that by means of the flesh which he assumed and thereby deified salvation might come to all that was akin to it. Hence it was necessary to devise some way by which, in the baptismal procedure, there might be an affinity and likeness between disciple and master. We must therefore note what characterized the Author of our life, in order that (as the apostle says [37]) those who follow may pattern themselves after the Pioneer of our salvation.

Those who learn military rhythms by observing others acquire their skill in arms from men versed in such disciplines;

[37] Heb. 2:10.

and if they fail to do what is shown to them, they remain lacking in such skill. In the same way those who have an equal zeal for the good must thoroughly imitate and follow the Pioneer of our salvation, and must put into practice what he has shown them. For the same goal cannot be reached unless similar paths are followed. People who get lost in labyrinths, if they fall in with an experienced person, extricate themselves from the various misleading passages by following from behind. And they could not, indeed, get out if they did not follow in their guide's footsteps. In the same way I bid you think of this life as a labyrinth which human nature cannot thread, unless a man takes the same course as He did who entered it and yet extricated himself from its confines.

I use the word "labyrinth" figuratively for the prison house of death, which has no way of escape and in which the wretched race of mankind was confined. What, then, did we see in the case of the Pioneer of our salvation? Death for three days, and then a return to life. For this reason something similar had to be devised in our case too. What, then, is this device by means of which we imitate his experience?

Everything dead finds its appropriate and natural place in the earth, where it is laid and hidden away. Now there is a close affinity between earth and water. They are the only elements which have weight and gravitate downwards, penetrating one another and being absorbed in each other. Seeing, then, that the Pioneer of our life died and was buried under the earth in common with our nature, the imitation we make of his death is represented in the allied element. Now after the Man from above [38] had assumed a state of death and had been buried under the earth, on the third day he returned to life once more. In the same way everyone who by his bodily nature is united to him and looks to the same successful issue —I mean the goal of life—has water instead of earth poured on him, and by being immersed three separate times reproduces the grace of the resurrection which occurred on the third day.

In our previous discussion we have already given some indication that divine providence had a purpose in bringing death upon human nature. It was this: to refashion man once more by means of the resurrection into a sound creature, free from passion, pure and with no admixture of evil, after this had been eliminated by the dissolution of body and soul. Now

[38] Cf. John 3:31; I Cor. 15:47.

in the case of the Pioneer of our salvation this design of death was fully accomplished and its essential aim completely realized. For by means of death elements previously united were separated, and then once more brought together. Thereby our nature was purified by the dissolution of elements naturally united—I refer to the soul and the body; and the reunion of the separated elements was free from any alien admixture. In the case, however, of those who follow the Pioneer, their nature does not admit of an exact imitation at every point. It receives now only as much as it is able to. The rest is stored up for the future.

Wherein, then, does the imitation consist? In bringing this about: that the evil mingled with our nature is destroyed by the representation of death in the water. It is not, indeed, completely destroyed; but there is a kind of break in the continuity of evil. Two things contribute to this destruction of evil, the repentance of the sinner and the imitation of death. By them man is released in some degree from his connection with evil. By his repentance he comes to hate sin and to avoid it, while death brings about the destruction of evil.

Now were it possible for one undergoing this imitation to die completely, what would be involved is not imitation but identity. Evil would then have totally disappeared from our nature, and we should have "died unto sin once and for all," [39] as the apostle says. But, as we have indicated, we imitate the transcendent power only to the extent that the poverty of our nature permits. Water is poured on us three times and we emerge again from the water, thus representing the saving burial and the resurrection which occurred three days later. And what we have in mind is this: that just as it is within our power to be immersed in water and to emerge again, so it was within the power of Him who is Sovereign of all, to go down into death, as we into the water, and to return again to his natural and blessed state.

If, then, we take a reasonable attitude and judge results by the inherent capacity in each case, we shall find no essential difference in these actions. Each accomplishes what he can in terms of his nature. Man can safely come into contact with water when he so desires. It is infinitely more easy for the divine power to come into contact with death, and, while being overcome by it, to suffer no injury. Thus the reason we have to enact in advance and by water the grace of the resurrection is

[39] Rom. 6:10.

to assure us that it is just as easy to be baptized in water as it is to rise again from the dead.

In the ordinary events of life there are some things that are of more primary importance than others, and without which a given result could not be attained. Yet when one contrasts the beginning of such matters with the final end, the former appears insignificant by comparison. For instance, what parity is there between a human being and the seed from which he is constituted? And yet, if the one is absent, the other does not come into being. It is the same with what happens at the great resurrection. Though essentially superior [to baptism], it has its source and origin here; and, indeed, it could not occur, did not baptism precede it. It is not possible, I contend, for a man to attain to the resurrection apart from the regeneration by washing.

I am not thinking here of the remolding and refashioning of our composite nature. For in any case, driven by inherent necessity, our nature must reach that end in accordance with the Creator's plan for it, and independent of its receiving the grace of baptism or of its failing to share in that initiation. Rather am I thinking of the restoration of our nature to a blessed and divine state, free from all sorrow and shame.

For not all who are granted a renewed existence by the resurrection will enter upon the same new life. Rather will there be a great difference between those who are purified and those who lack purification. Those who in their lifetime here have already been purified by baptism will be restored to a state akin to this. Now purity is closely related to freedom from passion, and it is not to be doubted that blessedness consists in this freedom from passion. But those, on the other hand, who have become inured to passion, and to whom nothing has been applied to cleanse the stain—neither the sacramental water nor the invocation of divine power, nor the amendment of repentance—must necessarily find their appropriate place. Now just as the appropriate place for debased gold is the furnace, so the evil mingled with these natures must be melted away in order that, after long ages, they may be restored to God in their purity. Since, then, both fire and water have a capacity to cleanse, those who have washed off the stain of sin in the sacramental water do not need the other means of purification. But those who have not been inititated into this purification must of necessity be purified by fire.

36. Both common sense and the teaching of Scripture indicate that a man cannot enter the divine fellowship unless he

has entirely washed away all stains of sin. Though a small thing in itself, this is the origin and foundation of great blessings. I call it a small thing because of the easiness with which it is accomplished. For what is there difficult about this, to believe that God is everywhere, and that, present as he is in all things, he is also present to those who invoke his life-giving power, and that being present, he acts in character? Now the salvation of those in need is characteristic of God's activity; and this is effected through the purification by water. He who is purified will share in purity, and that which is truly pure is the Godhead itself. You observe how small a thing it is to begin with and how easily accomplished—just faith and water: faith which is a matter of our own choice, and water which is natural to man's life. But what a blessing springs from these things—no less than kinship with God himself!

## THE EUCHARIST

37. Owing to man's twofold nature, composed as it is of soul and body, those who come to salvation must be united with the Author of their life by means of both. In consequence, the soul, which has union with him by faith derives from this the means of salvation; for being united with life implies having a share in it. But it is in a different way that the body comes into intimate union with its Saviour. Those who have been tricked into taking poison offset its harmful effect by another drug. The remedy, moreover, just like the poison, has to enter the system, so that its remedial effect may thereby spread through the whole body. Similarly, having tasted[40] the poison that dissolved our nature, we were necessarily in need of something to reunite it. Such a remedy had to enter into us, so that it might, by its counteraction, undo the harm the body had already encountered from the poison.

And what is this remedy? Nothing else than the body which proved itself superior to death and became the source of our life. For, as the apostle observes,[41] a little yeast makes a whole lump of dough like itself. In the same way, when the body which God made immortal enters ours, it entirely transforms it into itself. When a poison is combined with something wholesome, the whole admixture is rendered as useless as the poison. Conversely, the immortal body, by entering the one who receives it, transforms his entire being into its own nature.

[40] The reference is to Gen. 3:6.          [41] I Cor. 5:6.

Now nothing can enter the body unless it is assimilated in the system by eating and drinking. Hence the body must receive the life-giving power in the natural way. Now only that body in which God dwelt, acquired such life-giving grace; and we have already shown that our body cannot become immortal unless it shares in immortality by its association with what is immortal. We must, therefore, inquire how that one body can be perpetually distributed to so many thousands of the faithful throughout the world, and yet be received in its entirety in the portion each gets, and still remain whole in itself. In consequence, we must turn aside for a moment to discuss the physiology of the body, so that our faith, in its concern for what is reasonable, may entertain no doubts on this question.

Now who does not realize that our bodily nature does not owe its life to its own subsistence? It maintains itself and continues in existence by a power that enters it from outside. It perpetually appropriates what it needs and disposes of what is superfluous. When a skin is full of a liquid and this leaks out of the bottom, it fails to retain its shape unless something else is poured in to fill up the vacuum. In consequence, anyone seeing the outward shape of the skin recognizes that this is not a property of the skin itself, but that it is the inflowing liquid that gives it its shape. In the same way the constitution of our body possesses nothing we recognize as its own by which to maintain itself. Rather does its existence depend on a power from outside. This power is food, as we call it. It is not the same for all bodies that need nourishment; but each has been granted its appropriate food by Him who is responsible for its nature. Some animals feed on roots that they dig up; others feed on grass; others, again, on flesh. Man, however, is principally nourished by bread. Moreover, to preserve the body's moisture there is drink; not, indeed, of water only, but often of water sweetened with wine to further the body's heat. When we look at these things, then, we are looking at the potential materials of our body. In me they become blood and flesh, since in each case the food is changed by the power of assimilation into the form of the body.

Now that we have discussed these matters, we must turn our thoughts back to the issue before us. We inquired how the one body of Christ could give life to all mankind—to all, that is, who have faith—and while being distributed to them all, suffer no reduction in size. Perhaps we are close to a reasonable explanation.

All bodies derive their subsistence from nourishment, that is, from food and drink. Now bread is food, and water sweetened with wine is drink. Moreover, God's Word, as we explained at the beginning, is both God and Word and was united with human nature. When he entered this body of ours, he did not innovate on human nature, but maintained his body in the usual and appropriate way, providing for its subsistence by food and drink, the food being bread. In our case, then, as we have frequently observed, when we see bread we see, in a way, the human body, for that is what bread, by passing into it, becomes. It was the same in his case. The body in which God dwelt, by receiving bread as nourishment, was in a sense identical with it. For, as we have said, the food was changed into the nature of the body. What is recognized as a universal characteristic applied to his flesh too, i.e., that his body was maintained by bread. But by the indwelling of God the Word, that body was raised to divine dignity.

We have good reason, then, to believe that now too the bread which is consecrated by God's Word [42] is changed into the body of God the Word. For that body as well was once virtually bread, [43] though it was sanctified by the indwelling of the Word in the flesh. Therefore the means whereby the bread was changed in that body, and was converted into divine power, are identical with those which produce a similar result now. For, in the former case, the grace of the Word sanctified the body which derived its subsistence from bread, and which, in a way, was itself bread. In the latter case, similarly, the bread (as the apostle says) is consecrated by the Word of God and prayer. It is not, however, by being eaten that it gradually becomes the body of the Word. Rather is it immediately changed by the Word into the body, as the Word himself declares: "This is my body." [44]

But all flesh is nourished by the element of moisture as well; for the earthly part in us could not continue to live unless it were combined with this. Just as we sustain the solid mass of the body by firm and solid food, so we supplement its moisture from what is akin to this. By entering us it is changed into blood by assimilation; and this is especially the case if it derives from wine the capacity of being changed into heat. Now the flesh in which God dwelt used this element too to

[42] Cf. I Tim. 4:5.
[43] In the sense that bread could be converted into it.
[44] Mark 14:22.

maintain its existence. The reason, moreover, that God, when he revealed himself, united himself with our mortal nature was to deify humanity by this close relation with Deity. In consequence, by means of his flesh, which is constituted by bread and wine, he implants himself in all believers, following out the plan of grace. He unites himself with their bodies so that mankind too, by its union with what is immortal, may share in incorruptibility. And this he confers on us by the power of the blessing,[45] through which he changes[46] the nature of the visible elements into that immortal body.

## FAITH AND REPENTANCE

38. In our treatment so far we have, I think, omitted no question that bears on our religion except that of faith; and we shall give a brief exposition of this too in our present work. For those who want a fuller discussion of the matter, we have already expounded it in previous works,[47] where we have treated the subject in detail and as rigorously as we could. In those treatises we engaged in controversy with our opponents and independently investigated the issues in question. In our discussion here we have thought it well to limit ourselves to what the gospel has to say about faith, viz., that he who is born by spiritual rebirth recognizes by whom he is born, and what kind of creature he becomes.[48] For this is the only kind of birth where we can choose what we are to become.

39. In other cases those who are born owe their existence to the impulse of their parents; but spiritual birth is in the control of the one born. Since, then, everyone has a choice in this matter and there is a danger of acting unwisely, it is well, I think, for one initiating his own birth to think out in advance whom it is well to have as a father and from what it is best that his nature should consist. For, as I have said, in such a birth one is free to choose one's own parents.

Now existence is divided into what is created and what is uncreated. The uncreated nature is essentially unchanging and

---

45 I.c., the consecration prayer.
46 *Metastoicheiōsas*, by which Gregory means that the elements, of which the bread and wine are composed, are rearranged in a new form. This "transformation" parallels the change that food undergoes when its elements are rearranged by assimilation to constitute a human body.
47 The reference is to his great work Against Eunomius, and to the oration On the Deity of the Son and the Holy Spirit.
48 Cf. John 1:13; 3:6, 7.

immutable, while what is created is subject to change. Of what, then, will one who considers his own interest carefully choose to be the child: of a nature observed to be mutable or of one which is unchanging and stable and consistently good?

We are taught in the gospel that there are three Persons and Names [49] through whom believers come to be born. He who is born of the Trinity is born equally of Father, Son, and Holy Spirit. For this is how the gospel speaks about the Spirit: "That which is born of the Spirit is spirit." [50] Paul, moreover, gives birth "in Christ," [51] and the Father is the "Father of all." [52] And here I ask the reader to judge soberly, lest he make himself the offspring of an unstable nature, when he could have that which is unchangeable as the source of his life. For what happens in the sacrament of Baptism [53] depends upon the disposition of the heart of him who approaches it. If he confesses that the holy Trinity is uncreated he enters on the life which is unchanging. But if, on a false supposition, he sees a created nature in the Trinity and then is baptized into *that*, he is born once more to a life which is subject to change. For offspring and parents necessarily share the same nature. Which, then, is more advantageous: to enter upon the life which is unchanging or to be tossed about once more in a life of instability and fluctuation?

Everyone with any intelligence at all recognizes that what is stable is far preferable to what is unstable, that the perfect is to be preferred to the defective, what is in need of nothing to what is in need, what can advance no farther but is permanently and perfectly good to what progresses gradually. In consequence an intelligent person is surely faced with this choice. Either he must believe that the nature of the holy Trinity is uncreated, and so, by spiritual birth, make it the source of his own life, or else, if he imagines the Son or the Holy Spirit is excluded from the nature of the primal, real, and good God (by which I mean the Father), [54] he should not include them in the confession of faith he makes at the time of his new birth. Otherwise he may inadvertently make himself the child of a nature which is defective and needs someone to better it; and so, by withdrawing his faith from the transcendent nature, put himself back, as it were, in the same

---

[49] Cf. Matt. 28:19.   [50] John 3:6.   [51] I Cor. 4:15.
[52] Cf. Eph. 4:6.   [53] *Oikonomia.*
[54] The reference is to the extreme Arian position represented by Eunomius, whom Gregory attacks in his elaborate work, Against Eunomius.

position in which he already is. For a person who brings himself under the yoke of anything created unwittingly puts his hope of salvation in that and not in God.

All created things, by virtue of the fact that they equally proceed from nonbeing into being, are essentially akin. In the structure of the body all the members are closely allied, even though some happen to have a lower, others a higher, position. In the same way there is an essential uniformity in the world of created things, because they are all created; and this basic kinship is in no way broken by differences of excellence and deficiency among us. Even if in other respects things we conceive of as equally arising out of nonbeing have their differences, we can discover no dissimilarity in their nature on this point.

If, then, man is a created being and he thinks of the Spirit and the only-begotten God as similarly created, he would be foolish to hope for a change for the better, when he is only reverting to his own nature. His situation resembles what Nicodemus surmised.[55] When he learned from the Lord of the need to be born again, he was dragged back in his thoughts to his mother's womb, because he had not yet grasped the meaning of the revelation. And so, if a man does not ally himself with the uncreated nature, but with the creation which is akin to him and shares his bondage, his is not the birth from above. But the gospel[56] says that the birth of those who are saved is from above.

40. Yet it appears to me that the instruction we have so far given is insufficient in what it teaches. We have, I think, to consider what follows baptism. It is a point which many of those who approach its grace neglect, deluding themselves and being born in appearance only and not in reality. For the change our life undergoes through rebirth would not be a change were we to continue in our present state. I do not, indeed, see how a man who continues the same can be reckoned to have become different, when there is no noticeable alteration in him. For it is patent to everyone that we receive the saving birth for the purpose of renewing and changing our nature. Yet baptism produces no essential change in human nature. Neither reason nor understanding, nor capacity for knowledge, nor anything else that marks human nature, undergoes a change. For the change would certainly be for the worse, were any of these characteristics of our nature to be altered. If, then,

55 Cf. John 3:4.          56 Cf. John 3:3.

these faculties are not changed, and yet the birth from above does in some way refashion man, we must inquire what that change is which the grace of rebirth brings about.

Now it is clear that when the evil characteristics of our nature are done away, there is a change for the better. If, then, as the prophet says,[57] when we undergo this sacramental "washing" we become "clean" in our wills and wash away "the iniquities" of our souls, we become better and are changed for the better. But if the washing has only affected the body, and the soul has failed to wash off the stains of passion, and the life after initiation is identical with that before, despite the boldness of my assertion I will say without shrinking that in such a case the water is only water, and the gift of the Holy Spirit is nowhere evident in the action. [That is true] not only when anger deforms and dishonors the image of God, or covetous passion or unbridled and shameful thoughts and pride, envy, and arrogance, but also when a man keeps the profits of injustice, and the woman he has acquired by adultery continues to serve his lusts. If this sort of thing characterizes a man's life as much after baptism as before it, I cannot see that he has undergone any change, since he appears just the same person as before. Those who are wronged, defrauded, and deprived of their property, observe, for their part, no change when a man like this is baptized. They do not hear him saying what Zacchaeus said: "If I have defrauded anyone of anything, I will restore him fourfold."[58] What they said of him before baptism, they continue to say of him now. They call him by the same names —a covetous person, greedy for others' property, and feeding on men's misfortunes.

A man, then, who remains the same and yet prattles to himself about the change for the better he has undergone in baptism, should attend to what Paul says: "If anyone thinks he is something when he is nothing, he deceives himself."[59] For you are not what you have not become; whereas the gospel says of the regenerate that "He gave all those who received him the power to become God's children."[60] Now the child born of someone certainly shares his parent's nature. If, then, you have received God and become his child, let your way of life testify to the God within you; make it clear who your Father is! The marks by which we recognize God are the very ones by which a son of his must show his relation to him: "he

57 Cf. Isa. 1:16.                    58 Luke 19:8.
59 Gal. 6:3.                         60 John 1:12.

opens his hand and fills everything living with joy" [61]; "he overlooks iniquity" [62]; "he relents of his evil purpose" [63]; "the Lord is kind to all, and is not angry with us every day" [64]; "God is straightforward and there is no unrighteousness in him" [65]—and the similar sayings scattered through Scripture for our instruction. If you are like this, you have genuinely become a child of God. But if you persist in displaying the marks of evil, it is useless to prattle to yourself about the birth from above. Prophecy will tell you: "You are a son of man, not a son of the Most High. You love vanity, and seek lies. You fail to realize that the only way man is magnified is by becoming holy." [66]

To this we must add the further point that the promised blessings, held out to those who have lived a good life, defy description. For how can we describe "what the eye has not seen, or the ear heard, or what the heart of man has not entertained?" [67] Nor, too, does anything which afflicts the senses here equal in torment the future life of sinners. Even if we denote some of those torments by terms familiar to us here, the difference is not slight. When you hear the word "fire," you have been taught to think of it differently from ordinary fire, since a new factor is added. For that fire is not quenched, [68] while experience has devised many ways to quench the fire we know. And there is a great difference between fire which is quenched and that which admits of no quenching. They are, therefore, different, and not the same.

Then again, when a person hears the word "worm," the identity of expression must not divert his mind to the creature of earth. For the addition of the phrase "that does not die" [69] suggests the thought that it is a different creature from the one we know.

These, then, are the things we are given to expect in the life to come; and by God's righteous judgment they are the appropriate outcome of the way of life each chooses. Those, therefore, who are wise should set their eyes, not on this present life, but on that to come. In this short and fleeting existence they should lay the foundations of untold blessedness. By choosing a good way of life they should avoid all experience of evil, now in this life and afterwards when they win their eternal reward.

[61] Ps. 145:16.
[62] Micah 7:18 (LXX).
[63] Joel 2:13.
[64] Ps. 145:9; 7:12 (LXX).
[65] Ps. 92:15.
[66] Cf. Ps. 4:3, 4 (LXX); 82:6.
[67] I Cor. 2:9.
[68] Cf. Mark 9:43.
[69] Cf. Mark 9:48.

# DOCUMENTS

# Documents
# Illustrating the Christology
# of the Ecumenical Councils

## I. THE LETTER OF ARIUS TO EUSEBIUS OF NICOMEDIA

### INTRODUCTION

At an early stage in the Arian controversy, probably about 318, before his formal condemnation at Alexandria, Arius addressed this appeal to his friend and former fellow student Eusebius, recently transferred from the see of Berytus in Syria to that of the imperial residence, Nicomedia. It gives us a frank statement of Arius' own position as he was willing to express it to his friends. The letter is preserved in Epiphanius, Heresies, 69, 7, and Theodoret, *Church History*, I, 5, and is here translated from the text as given by H. G. Opitz, ed., *Athanasius Werke*, Vol. iii, 1, *Urkunden zur Geschichte des Arianischen Streites*, Berlin and Leipzig, De Gruyter, 1934, no. 1, pp. 1–3.

### THE TEXT

To my very dear lord, the faithful and orthodox man of God Eusebius, Arius, unjustly persecuted by Pope[1] Alexander for the sake of the all-conquering truth of which you also are a defender, sends greeting in the Lord.

Since my father Ammonius was coming to Nicomedia, it seemed to me fitting and proper to send you greetings by him, and also to bring to your attention, in the natural love and affection which you have for the brethren, for the sake of God and his Christ, that the bishop greatly injures and persecutes us and does all he can against us, trying to drive us out of the

---

[1] *Papa*, a title of respect for distinguished ecclesiastics, regularly given to the bishops of Alexandria from at least the time of Heraclas, A.D. 233–249 (Eusebius, Church History, vii, 7, 4).

city as godless men, since we do not agree with him when he says publicly, "Always Father, always Son," "Father and Son together," "The Son exists unbegottenly with God," "The eternal begotten," "Unbegotten-only-one,"[2] "Neither in thought nor by a single instant is God before the Son," "Always God, always Son," "The Son is of God himself."

And since your brother Eusebius in Caesarea[3] and Theodotus and Paulinus and Athanasius and Gregorius and all the bishops of the East[4] say that God exists without beginning before the Son, they are anathematized, except Philogonius, Hellanicus, and Macarius, [and such] heretical and uninstructed men, some of whom speak of the Son as an emission, others as a projection, others as co-unbegotten. But we cannot bear even to listen to such impieties, though the heretics should threaten us with a thousand deaths. What is it that we say, and think, and have taught, and teach? That the Son is not unbegotten, nor a part of the unbegotten in any way, nor [formed out] of any substratum, but that he was constituted[5] by [God's] will and counsel, before times and before ages, full (of grace and truth),[6] divine, unique,[7] unchangeable. And before he was begotten or created or ordained or founded, he was not. For he was not unbegotten. We are persecuted because we say, "The Son has a beginning, but God is without beginning." For this we are persecuted, and because we say, "He is [made] out of things that were not."[8] But this is what we say, since he is neither a

---

2 *Agennētogenēs*, an obscure term; either used carelessly by Alexander or an interpretation of what he meant, and cited to suggest the bishop's theological confusion.

3 I.e., close friend and associate; there is no reason to believe that the two Eusebii were blood relatives.

4 I.e., of the civil diocese of the East, including Syria, Palestine, and Cilicia, under the *comes orientis* at Antioch; the reference is probably not to any formal condemnation, but to the implications of Alexander's condemnation of Arius. He claims the bishops of distinguished sees for his side, but the three opponents mentioned were the bishops of Antioch, Tripolis in Phoenicia, and Jerusalem.

→ 5 Or "had his being"—the verb (active) is the cognate of *hypostasis*.

6 Following Holl, Opitz is probably correct in restoring the words "of grace and truth," as in John 1:14.

7 Or "God only-begotten" (*theos monogenēs*); but the proper meaning of *monogenēs* is "unique, only one of the kind"; though by confusion or association it often suggests "only-begotten" (from the all-but-identical root of *gennaō*, to beget) as well.

8 I.e., the Arian Son was created out of nothing like other creatures, however different from them.

part of God nor [formed] out of any substratum. For this we are persecuted, and you know the rest. So I pray that you may prosper in the Lord, remembering our afflictions, fellow Lucianist, truly Eusebius. [9]

[9] Playful references; the former students of Lucian of Antioch were bound together by a kind of school spirit; and "Eusebius," one of the first strictly Christian names, means "pious."

# II. THE CONFESSION OF THE ARIANS, ADDRESSED TO ALEXANDER OF ALEXANDRIA

## INTRODUCTION

⌐The clearest statement of early Arianism is in the letter addressed by Arius and his associates to the bishop of Alexandria at the time of their condemnation by the Synod of Egypt, as described in Sozomen, *Church History*, I, 15. The date of this event—sometime in 320–323—and the details of the early stages of the controversy are obscure; for a recent discussion, see W. Telfer, "Sozomen, I, 15; A Reply," *The Journal of Theological Studies*, Vol. 50, 1949, pp. 187–191. The letter can be read as a "considered and conciliatory statement" (*loc. cit.*, p. 189) before the condemnation, or as a sarcastic defiance, more likely to have followed it. It served for some time as a formal Arian Confession, and is so quoted by Hilary of Poitiers, *De Trinitate*, IV, 12. The text is preserved in Athanasius, On the Councils, 16, and Epiphanius, Heresies, 69, 7, and is here translated as edited by Opitz, *Urkunden*, no. 6, in *Athanasius Werke*, Vol. iii, 1, pp. 12, 13.

## THE TEXT

To our blessed pope and bishop Alexander the presbyters and deacons send greeting in the Lord.

⌐Our faith which we received from our forefathers and have also learned from you is this. We know there is one God, the only unbegotten, only eternal, only without beginning, only true, who only has immortality, only wise, only good, the only potentate,[1] judge of all, governor, dispenser, unalterable and unchangeable, righteous and good, God of the Law and the Prophets and the New Covenant. Before everlasting ages he

[1] Cf. Rom. 16:27; I Tim. 6:15, 16.

begot his unique[2] Son, through whom he made the ages and all things. He begot him not in appearance, but in truth, constituting[3] him by his own will, unalterable and unchangeable, a perfect creature of God, but not as one of the creatures —an offspring, but not as one of things begotten. Neither [was] the offspring of the Father a projection, as Valentinus taught, nor, as Manichaeus introduced, was the offspring a consubstantial part of the Father, nor [was he], as Sabellius said, dividing the Monad, a Son-Father,[4] nor, as Hieracas [taught], a lamp [kindled] from a lamp, or like a torch [divided] into two[5]; nor did he first exist, later being begotten or re-created into a Son—as you also, blessed pope, in the midst of the Church and in council[6] often refuted those who introduced these [ideas]. But as we said, by the will of God [he was] created before times and before ages and received life and being and glories from the Father, the Father so constituting him. Nor did the Father in giving him the inheritance of all things deprive himself of what he possesses unbegottenly in himself, for he is the fount of all things. Thus there are three *hypostases*.[7] God being the cause of all things is without beginning and most unique, while the Son, begotten timelessly by the Father and created before ages and established, was not before he was begotten—but, begotten timelessly before all things, he alone was constituted by the Father. He is neither eternal nor co-eternal nor co-unbegotten with the Father, nor does he have his being together with the Father, as some say "others with one," introducing [the idea of] two unbegotten sources.[8] But as

2 *Monogenēs*, see n. 7, p. 330.

3 Here and below, the verb cognate with *hypostasis*.

4 Arius thus implies that his opponents are guilty of a variety of heresies— the Valentinian Gnostic idea of emanations, the Manichaean concept of a material and divisible divine light, the Sabellian denial of distinction between Father and Son; the word Son-Father (*huiopator*) was, as Eusebius notes (Ecclesiastical Theology, I, 1, 2), not actually used by Sabellius, but was considered by his critics a fair expression of his sense.

5 The recorded heresies of the Egyptian Hieracas are not Christological, but denial of the redemption of matter and therefore of the resurrection of the body (Epiphanius, Heresies, 67); Arius is trying to brand as heretical by association a familiar figure for the relation of Father and Son, which Hieracas had perhaps used rather carelessly.

6 I.e., in public sermons and in the council of presbyters; the phraseology is suggested by Ps. 107 (106):32.

7 Epiphanius and Hilary add, perhaps correctly, "Father, Son, and Holy Spirit"—one sees why the term "three *hypostases*" was long suspect at Alexandria, as suggesting three different kinds of being.

8 *Archē*—source, beginning, origin, here of the ultimate self-existent being.

Monad and cause of all, God is thus before all. Therefore he is also prior to the Son, as we learned from what you preached in the midst of the Church.

So therefore, as he has being and glories from God, and life and all things were given him, accordingly God is his source. For he precedes him as his God, and as being before him. But if the [phrases] "of him" and "out of the womb" and "I came forth from the Father and am come" [9] are understood by some as [meaning] a part of the consubstantial himself and a projection, then according to them the Father is compound and divisible and alterable and a body, and according to them presumably, the bodiless God [is thought of as] suffering what belongs to a body.

We pray that you may fare well in the Lord, blessed pope. Arius, Aeithales, Achilleus, Carpones, Sarmatas, Arius, presbyters. Deacons, Euzoius, Lucius, Julius, Menas, Helladius, Gaius. Bishops, Secundus of Pentapolis, Theonas of Libya, Pistus (whom the Arians installed at Alexandria).[10]

[9] Rom. 11:36 (?); Ps. 110 (109):3; John 8:42; 16:28.
[10] The signatures are preserved only by Epiphanius. The two Arian bishops Secundus and Theonas were deposed by the Egyptian Synod and again at Nicaea. Pistus doubtless added his signature to this document later, when he was consecrated by Secundus as a claimant to the see of Alexandria, where an effort was made to install him in 338–339 (Athanasius, Defense Against the Arians, 24). He may have signed as bishop of Alexandria, for which an orthodox transmitter of the letter substituted the explanatory note now found at the end. The other signatures look as if each presbyter were supported by his deacon; Euzoius remained closely associated with Arius, and survived to be Arian bishop of Antioch from 361 to 378.

# III. THE LETTER OF EUSEBIUS OF CAESAREA DESCRIBING THE COUNCIL OF NICAEA

## INTRODUCTION

In the absence of its formal records, our earliest sources for the theological deliberations of the Council of Nicaea are brief accounts by Eustathius of Antioch, Athanasius,[1] and Eusebius of Caesarea. The latter is of special interest since it includes both the Caesarean Creed which he presented and the actual Creed of the Council for which it is our earliest authority; it is a letter to Eusebius' own church written immediately after or perhaps even during the sessions of the Council. The impression produced on the face of it is that Eusebius' Creed was found satisfactory, but the bishops altered it in order to introduce the word *homoousios*. Recent discoveries have shown, however, that the situation was in fact quite different. Eusebius had been condemned for his Arian sympathies by a synod held under Eustathius at Antioch.[2] At the beginning of the sessions he stood at the bar of the Council rather than appearing as one of its leaders. The vigor of his confession of faith is explained by the fact that he was on the defensive. However, his Creed was accepted as orthodox, and his position as a bishop in good standing cleared up. He probably takes advantage of a kind phrase from the emperor to imply, without quite stating, that the conciliar Creed was based on the Caesarean; comparison of texts shows that it was not—it may have been based on some other Eastern creed of a similar type, or perhaps on several. Eusebius' letter seems carefully constructed to inform those

[1] Theodoret, *Church History*, I, 7; Athanasius, Letter to the Bishops of Africa.
[2] Letter of the Council of Antioch preserved in Syriac, Opitz, *Urkunden*, 18 (*Athanasius Werke*, Vol. iii, 1, pp. 36–41), par. 14; cf. J. N. D. Kelly, *Early Christian Creeds*, pp. 223–225.

who knew of his previous condemnation that he had been cleared, while at the same time not forcing that embarrassing episode on the attention of others who might not be aware of it. The natural trend of Eusebius' own theology was in the direction which would later be called Semi-Arian; as the letter clearly states, he accepted the Creed of the Council only subject to his own interpretations, which are such as would scarcely have been accepted fifty years later when the Nicene Creed had become the palladium of orthodoxy. His letter also illustrates the imperialist Christianity which came so easily to Arians and Semi-Arians. Nevertheless it records clearly the Council's statement of faith, though shedding little light on the process by which it was arrived at—and sufficiently indicates that the conciliar decision was no mere acceptance of an imperial suggestion.

The obvious historical importance of this letter was early recognized. It is preserved in several texts—in Athanasius, On the Decrees of Nicaea, Socrates, *Church History*, I, 8, and Theodoret, *Church History*, I, 11. It is here translated as edited by Opitz, *Urkunden*, no. 22, in *Athanasius Werke*, Vol. iii, 1, pp. 42–47. Previous versions can be found in the translations of Athanasius, Socrates, and Theodoret; the best is that of Robertson in *Select Writings and Letters of Athanasius*, Library of Nicene and Post-Nicene Fathers, Vol. IV, London, 1892, pp. 74–76.

## THE TEXT

You have very likely, beloved, already learned from some other source of the action taken at the great synod convened at Nicaea with reference to the faith of the Church, since rumor commonly outruns the true account of what has been done. But lest you should receive an inaccurate impression from such reports, I [3] have found it necessary to send you, first the statement of faith which I presented, and then the second which [the bishops] issued, making some additions to our phrases. My document, then, which was read in the presence of our most pious emperor and declared to be sound and approved, read as follows:

[3] Eusebius, as a bishop, uses the plural of dignity throughout; except in the Caesarean Creed I have translated it by the singular, since he is obviously referring to himself—though when he speaks of his reservations in accepting the conciliar Creed he may wish to include others who agreed with him.

"As I received my tradition from the bishops before me, both in my first instruction and when I was baptized, and as I have learned from the divine Scriptures, and as I believed and taught both in the [office of] the presbyterate and in the episcopate itself—so still believing I present to you my Creed,[4] which is this:

"We believe in one God, Father, Almighty, the maker of all things visible and invisible,

"And in one Lord Jesus Christ, the Word of God, God of God, Light of Light, Life of Life, unique [5] Son, first-born of all creation, begotten of the Father before all the ages, through whom also all things came to be, who for our salvation was incarnate and dwelt among men and suffered and rose on the third day and ascended to the Father and will come again with glory to judge living and dead.

"We also believe in one Holy Spirit.

"Believing that each of these is and exists, the Father truly [as] Father, the Son truly Son, and the Holy Spirit truly Holy Spirit, as also our Lord said when sending forth his disciples for the preaching, 'Go and make disciples of all nations, baptizing them in the Name of the Father and of the Son and of the Holy Spirit'—of which I firmly assert that this is what I hold, and so I am convinced,[6] and so I have held, and will stand for this faith till death, anathematizing every godless heresy.

"That I have always been convinced of these things, heart and soul, since I was first conscious of myself, and so I am now convinced and profess—[this] I witness in truth before God Almighty and our Lord Jesus Christ, and am prepared to demonstrate and prove to you that so I believed and preached in times gone by."

When I had presented this statement of faith there was no room for opposition—indeed our most pious emperor himself, first of all, testified that its contents were very sound. He further confessed that he himself was so convinced, and urged all to agree to it and to subscribe and assent to these very teachings, with the addition of the one word "consubstantial," which he himself interpreted as follows: "The Son is not to be called 'consubstantial' according to what happens to bodies,

---

[4] *Pistis*, here in the sense of "confession of faith."

[5] *Monogenēs*.

[6] Or "think," though the Greek *phroneō* does not suggest the tentativeness that "think" implies in English.

nor is he constituted by a division or some kind of cutting up of the Father, nor can the immaterial and intellectual and bodiless nature undergo what happens to bodies, but these things must be conceived of in divine and ineffable terms." Such were the theological observations of our most learned and pious emperor. But [the bishops], on the ground [7] of adding the *homoousios*, produced the following statement:

(The Creed drawn up at the Council) [8]

"We believe in one God, Father, Almighty, maker of all things, visible and invisible,

"And in one Lord Jesus Christ, begotten of the Father uniquely,[5] that is, of the substance of the Father, God of God, Light of Light, true God of true God, begotten, not made, consubstantial with the Father, through whom all things were made, both things in heaven and those in earth, who for us men and for our salvation came down and was incarnate, [and] became man; he suffered and rose on the third day, ascended into heaven, and is coming to judge living and dead,

"And in the Holy Spirit.

"But those who say, there was once when he was not, and before he was begotten he was not and he came into being out of things that are not, or allege that the Son of God is of a different subsistence or essence, or created or alterable or changeable, the catholic and apostolic Church anathematizes."

When they formulated this statement, I did not let it pass without examination in what sense they said "of the substance of the Father" and "consubstantial with the Father." So questions were raised and answered and the meaning of the phrases was tested by reason. Thus it was declared that they used the phrase "of the substance" to indicate his being of the Father, but not as if he were a part of the Father. So I agreed to subscribe to this in the sense of the pious teaching which declares that the Son is of the Father, but not as being a part of his essence. So I agreed to this idea, not rejecting the word *homoousios*, having before me the aim of peace, and that of not falling away from the sound doctrine.

In the same way I also accepted the phrase "begotten and not made," since they alleged that "made" is a term shared with the other creatures of God which came into being through

---

[7] Or "pretext," the Greek *prophasis* being ambiguous as to whether the reason alleged is the real one or not.

[8] An explanatory heading found in Athanasius and Theodoret, and obviously not part of the original letter.

the Son, which the Son is in no way like, since he is not a work of God comparable to those things that came into being through him, but is of a nature superior to everything made, which the divine oracles teach was begotten of the Father, the manner of his generation being ineffable [9] and indescribable for every nature that came into being.

So also the phrase "the Son is consubstantial with the Father" stands up if properly examined—not in the manner of bodies or similarly to mortal animals, nor by division or cutting up of the essence—nor by any suffering or alteration or change of the essence and power of the Father; for the unbegotten nature of the Father is free from all these things. But the phrase "consubstantial with the Father" indicates that the Son of God bears no similarity with the creatures of God that came into being, but is in every way made like only to the Father who begot him, and is not of any other *hypostasis* or essence, but of the Father. It seemed proper to assent to the term itself, expounded in this manner, since I knew of some learned and distinguished bishops and writers among the ancients who made use of the term *homoousios* in the doctrinal discussion about the Father and the Son.

This will be sufficient with reference to the Creed that was set forth, to which we all assented—not without examination, but according to the senses indicated, which were inquired into in the presence of our most devout emperor himself, and supported by the arguments given above. And I did not find the anathematism set forth by them after the Creed distressing, since it forbids the use of non-Scriptural terms, from which has come almost all the disorder and confusion of the Church. For as none of the inspired Scriptures uses the phrases "Out of things that are not" and "There was once when he was not," and the others that follow, it did not seem proper to use or teach them. I agreed to this too as a sound decision, since I had not been accustomed to use these terms previously.

Nor did I think it improper to anathematize the term, "Before he was begotten he was not," since all confess that the Son of God was before [his] generation according to the flesh. Our most pious emperor similarly supported the principle that He existed before all ages according to his divine generation,

---

[9] Isa. 53:8 (LXX) reads, "Who shall declare his generation?" a favorite patristic text in this connection, though even in Greek the reference is to the contemporaries of the Suffering Servant rather than to his mysterious birth.

since before he was actually begotten he existed potentially in the Father, unbegottenly. For the Father is always Father as he is always King and Saviour, being all potentially, and always standing in the same relations and [being in himself] the same.[10]

I have thought it necessary to report to you these things, beloved, showing you the process of our examination and assent. I properly resisted up to the last moment, as long as what was written in unaccustomed language was offensive, but then I accepted without disputing what was unobjectionable, when it became clear to me, on examining fairly the meaning of the terms, that they harmonized with what I myself had professed in the Creed that I previously issued.

[10] This paragraph, one sentence in the original, is omitted by Socrates; doubtless he (or his source) found it incredible in a writer who was considered generally orthodox. As shown before, Eusebius did believe in the pre-existence of the Son, though not clearly in his eternity; but tries to argue that this anathema committed him to nothing in particular.

# IV. THE CREED OF ARIMINUM

## INTRODUCTION

During the sole reign of Constantius, 350–361, a confusing series of Arian and Semi-Arian creeds were issued, many of them prepared at what has been called "the imperial creed factory" at Sirmium in the western Balkans. The "Dated Creed" of 359 is a good statement of the Semi-Arian position, declaring the Son to be "like the Father in all respects," *kata panta*. This was propounded to the double Council for which the Western bishops were summoned to Ariminum in Italy and the Eastern to Seleucia in Isauria. But the Western bishops insisted on the Creed of Nicaea and the Easterners preferred the fairly high Christology of the Second Creed of the Council of Antioch of 341. Nevertheless delegates from Ariminum were induced to accept, at Nice in Thrace, a revision of the Dated Creed in a more definitely Arian direction, replacing "like in all respects" by simply "like." The bishops at Ariminum were forced to follow them, and on the last day of 359 delegates from Seleucia were badgered into the same action by the emperor himself at Constantinople. As formally accepted at a council at Constantinople in January, 360, this was the Creed which Ulfilas took to the Goths. It represents central or moderate Arianism, asserting the likeness of the Son to the Father, but refusing to specify the degree or quality of that likeness—the faith of the Homoeans as distinguished from the Semi-Arian Homoousians and the radical Anomoeans. It is the last of the Arian creeds, and the longest-lived, since it survived among the Germanic Arian Churches until their extinction in the seventh century. The text is to be found in Athanasius, On the Synods, 30.[1]

[1] In Migne, *Patrologia Graeca*, Vol. xxvi, cols. 745–747, reprinted in Kelly,

## THE TEXT

We believe in one God, Father almighty, from whom are all things,[2]

And in the unique[3] Son of God, who was begotten of God before all ages and before all beginning, through whom all things came into being, both visible and invisible, begotten uniquely,[3] only from the Father only, God of God, like to the Father who begot him, according to the Scriptures, whose generation no one knows[4] except only the Father who begot him. We know that this unique Son of God came from heaven, the Father sending him, as it is written, for the destruction of sin and death, and was born of [the] Holy Spirit, of Mary the Virgin according to the flesh, as it is written, and companied with the disciples, and when all the dispensation was fulfilled according to the Father's will, was crucified and died and was buried and descended into the lower regions, before whom hell [hades] itself trembled,[5] who also rose again from the dead on the third day and sojourned with the disciples, and when forty days were fulfilled was taken up into heaven, and sits on the right hand of the Father, [and] is to come on the last day, of the resurrection, in the Father's glory, to render to each according to his works,

And in the Holy Spirit, whom the unique[3] Son of God himself, Christ our Lord and God, promised to send to the race of men as a Paraclete, as it is written, "the Spirit of truth,"[6] whom he sent to them when he had ascended into heaven. But as to the word "essence" (*ousia*), which was used by the Fathers in simplicity, but, being unknown to the people caused scandal, because the Scriptures do not contain it, it seems best that it should be taken away and no mention made of it in the future, since the divine Scriptures nowhere made mention of the essence of Father and Son; nor, similarly, should the word *hypostasis* be used of Father and Son and Holy Spirit. But we say that the Son is like the Father, as the divine Scriptures say and teach; and let all heresies which have been condemned before and such recent ones as may have arisen and are contrary to this statement be anathema.

*Early Christian Creeds*, pp. 293, 294; also Socrates, *Church History*, ii, 41, and Theodoret, Church History, ii, 18; on this series of creeds generally see Kelly, *op. cit.*, Ch. ix.          [2] Rom. 11:36.
[3] *Monogenēs*.          [4] Isa. 53:8; cf. Document III, n. 9, p. 339.
[5] Job 38:17 (LXX), which the original Dated Creed quotes more literally, "the gatekeepers of Hades."          [6] John 14:16, 17.

# V. SUMMARY OF THE TOME OF CONSTANTINOPLE, 381 (IN SYNODICAL LETTER OF THE COUNCIL OF CONSTANTINOPLE, 382)

## INTRODUCTION

The purely Eastern council that met at Constantinople in 381 was not at first recognized in the West as having settled either the disciplinary or the doctrinal problems that came before it. The former were reopened in a council held at Aquileia under the leadership of Ambrose of Milan; and the Western emperor Gratian was persuaded to call a General Council to meet at Rome in the fall of 382. The Eastern bishops, once more assembled at Constantinople, excused themselves in a letter addressed to Damasus of Rome, Ambrose of Milan, and other Western bishops. Their resources were still restricted as a result of their sufferings under Valens; and in any case they had not come prepared for so long a journey. But they sent three delegates to assure the Westerners of the orthodoxy of their faith and the propriety of their disciplinary decisions. The letter is preserved in Theodoret, *Church History*, V, 9; sections 10–13, which summarize the lost doctrinal tome of 381, are here translated as edited by L. Parmentier, *Die griechischen christlichen Schriftsteller der ersten drei Jahrhunderte*, Vol. 19, Leipzig, 1911, pp. 292, 293. For the Creed commonly called Nicene, traditionally and probably correctly associated with the Council of Constantinople, see Document IX, p. 372.

## THE TEXT

... For whether we endured persecutions or afflictions, or imperial threats or the cruelties of governors, or any other trial from the heretics, we withstood all for the sake of the gospel faith[1] as authenticated by the 318[2] Fathers at Nicaea

[1] Or "creed."
[2] A number reached by adding the Arian minority of 18 that appeared at

343

in Bithynia. This [faith] should satisfy you and us, and all who do not pervert the word of truth—for it is the most ancient, it accords with the [creed of our] Baptism, and teaches us to believe in the name of the Father and of the Son and of the Holy Spirit—believing, that is to say, in one Godhead and power and substance of the Father and of the Son and of the Holy Spirit, of equal dignity and coeternal majesty, in three perfect *hypostases*,[3] that is, three perfect persons.[4] Thus no place is found for the error of Sabellius in which the *hypostases* are confused and their individualities taken away, nor does the blasphemy of the Eunomians and Arians and Pneumatomachi[5] prevail, in which the substance or nature of the Godhead is cut up and some kind of later nature, created and of a different substance, is added to the uncreated and consubstantial and coeternal Trinity.[6] We also preserve unperverted the doctrine of the incarnation of the Lord, receiving the dispensation of the flesh as neither without soul nor without mind nor incomplete,[7] but knowing that he existed as perfect[8] God, the Word, before all ages, and became perfect man in the last days for our salvation.

These [statements] are a summary in brief of the faith which is boldly proclaimed among us. You may be more fully informed about these matters if you care to consult the tome produced at Antioch by the council that assembled there,[9] and

one stage to a rough estimate of 300 bishops at Nicaea; Eustathius, writing soon afterwards, speaks of "about two hundred and seventy" (Theodoret, *Church History*, i, 7), Athanasius commonly of "the three hundred" (Defense Against the Arians, 23; History of the Arians, 66; On the Councils, 43)—in one of his last works of 318 (Letter to the Bishops of Africa, 2); but the text may have been influenced by the later tradition, which first appears in 360 in a work of Hilary of Poitiers (*Contra Constantium*, 27), who had probably heard it in the East. The number had symbolic suggestions, as Ambrose observes (*De fide*, i, Prologue); it was that of Abraham's servants (Gen. 14:14), and in Greek numerals would be written TIH, representing the cross and the name of Jesus, a combination already pointed out in the Epistle of Barnabas (9, 8).

3 The reversal of meaning is thus completed; Constantinople accepts as specific the term that Nicaea had rejected as generic.

4 Similarly, *hypostasis* and *prosōpon*, "person" in inner being and outer appearance, are declared to be interchangeable in this context.

5 "Fighters against the Spirit," the Macedonians as deniers of the deity of the Holy Ghost.

6 As was the Arian Christ or the Macedonian Spirit.

7 Thus rejecting Apollinarianism.                    8 Or "complete."

9 The Westerners are here politely referred back to themselves, since the

that issued at Constantinople last year by the Ecumenical[10] Council, in which [documents] we confessed the faith at greater length, and have produced a written anathema against the contrary heresies recently devised.[11]

[The letter proceeds to justify the decisions taken at Constantinople with reference to particular churches—the election of Nectarius as bishop of Constantinople and Flavian as bishop of Antioch, and the restoration of Cyril to the see of Jerusalem. The Roman Council of 382 did continue for a while longer the Western recognition of Paulinus, the bishop of the Eustathian minority at Antioch, which had always remained loyal to Nicaea; but it did not reopen the doctrinal questions, and so the rise of the Council of 381 to its final position as an ecumenical council accepted by the whole Church continued.]

Antiochene Council of 379 had adopted as a profession of orthodoxy statements on the Trinity and incarnation drawn up by a Roman council under Damasus ten years before (preserved fragments in J. D. Mansi, *Sacrorum conciliorum nova et amplissima .collectio*, Vol. iii, Florence, 1759, cols. 459–462, 511); this document seems to be what Canon VII of Constantinople, probably really coming from the Council of 382, calls the "Tome of the Westerners."

10 "Ecumenical" in the sense of representing a number of provinces.

11 Probably preserved as Canon I of Constantinople, which condemns the heretics referred to in this letter—Arians, Apollinarians, and Macedonians, and the followers of Marcellus of Ancyra, who carried the doctrine of consubstantiality to the point of Sabellianism, recognizing no permanent distinct being of the Son; see p. 22.

# VI. DOGMATIC LETTERS OF NESTORIUS AND CYRIL OF ALEXANDRIA— (A) THE FIRST LETTER OF NESTORIUS TO CELESTINE

## INTRODUCTION

When Nestorius came to Constantinople in 428 he was prepared to be a hammer of heretics, but soon found his own theology under attack while Cyril of Alexandria gathered the forces of rival sees against him. Cyril was already in communication with Celestine of Rome when Nestorius entered the correspondence with a rather unskillful effort to secure Roman support for his side. This letter is preserved in the Latin version of the Acts of the Council of Ephesus, and has been critically edited by Loofs[1] and Schwartz. It is here translated from Schwartz's *Acta conciliorum oecumenicorum*,[2] and I believe makes its first appearance in English. The letter begins with an inquiry about the Pelagian refugees at Constantinople—which at once led Celestine to suspect Nestorius of disingenuousness, since he professed to need information about a matter that was already well known—and then gets down to the real topic: Nestorius has his troubles with heretics too. In spite of its poor preservation in a somewhat confused translation, the letter is of value as a good brief statement of Nestorius' own ideas on the union of God and man in Christ. The only kinds of union of such different entities he could admit were conjunction and mixture; rejecting the latter, as producing some kind of demigod, he was forced back on the former.

## THE TEXT

1. We ought indeed to enjoy brotherly converse with each other, that we might, together, in harmony and concord, fight

[1] F. Loofs, ed., *Nestoriana: die Fragmente des Nestorius*, Halle, 1905, no. 24, pp. 165–168.　　[2] Vol. i, 2, Berlin and Leipzig, 1925–1926, pp. 12–14.

against the devil, the enemy of peace. Why this prelude? A certain Julian,[3] and Orontius and Fabius, saying that they are bishops from the West, have often approached our most pious and glorious emperor and bewailed their case, as orthodox men who have suffered persecution in an orthodox age. They have often addressed their laments to us and as often have been rejected, yet do not cease to repeat the same, but continue day by day filling the ears of all with their expressions of woe. We have spoken to them as is fitting, though we do not know the exact truth of their business. But since we need a fuller knowledge of their case, so that our most pious and most Christian emperor may not continue to be annoyed by them; and that we may not be uncertain about the proper measures to take in this business, being ignorant of their complaints, please give us information about them, so that people may not cause trouble [showing them] improper consideration through ignorance of the true justice in the matter, nor may expect something else after canonical sentence of Your Blessedness, given against them, I suppose, on account of religious divisions. For the rise of divisions calls for serious measures from true pastors.

2. We also have found no slight corruption of orthodoxy among some of those here, which we have treated with both sternness and gentleness [as demanded]. It is no small error, but similar to the corruption of Apollinaris and Arius, blending together the Lord's appearance as man [4] into a kind of confused combination—so much so that certain of our clergy, some from inexperience, others from heretical error long kept concealed, as often happened even in the times of the apostles, err like heretics, and openly blaspheme God the Word consubstantial with the Father, as if he took his beginning from the Christ-bearing Virgin, and grew up with his temple and was buried with [it] in the flesh; they even say that his flesh after the resurrection did not remain flesh, but was changed into the nature of Godhead. To speak briefly, they refer the Godhead of the Only-begotten to the same origin as the flesh joined [with it], and kill it with the flesh, and blasphemously say that the flesh joined with the Godhead was turned into deity by the

---

[3] Julian, bishop of Eclanum in Campania, whose treatises supporting Pelagius' denial of the absolute necessity of grace were answered by Augustine, *Contra Iulianum Pelagianum*, 422, and *Opus imperfectum contra Iulianum*, 430.

[4] *Dominicam enim in homine visionem*, which may represent *prosōpon*.

deifying Word,[5] which is nothing more nor less than to corrupt both. They even dare to treat of the Christ-bearing Virgin in a way as along with God,[6] for they do not scruple to call her *theotokos*, when the holy and beyond-all-praise Fathers at Nicaea said no more of the holy Virgin than that our Lord Jesus Christ was incarnate of the Holy Spirit and the Virgin Mary—not to mention the Scriptures, which everywhere, both by angels and apostles, speak of the Virgin as mother of Christ, not of God the Word.[7] I presume that rumor has already informed Your Blessedness what conflicts we have endured for these things, and you have also learned that we have not struggled in vain, but many of those who had gone astray have by the grace of the Lord repented, learning from us that what is born is properly consubstantial with the parent, and that it was to the creature of the Lord's humanity, joined with God, [being] of the Virgin by the Spirit, that what was seen among men [8] was committed. If anyone wishes to use this word *theotokos* with reference to the humanity which was born, joined to God the Word, and not with reference to the parent, we say that this word is not appropriate for her who gave birth, since a true mother should be of the same essence as what is born of her. But the term could be accepted in consideration of this, that the word is used of the Virgin only because of the inseparable temple of God the Word which was of her, not because she is the mother of God the Word—for none gives birth to one older than herself.

3. I suppose that rumor has already told you of these things, but we expound [9] what has been happening to us, in order to show in fact that it is in a brotherly spirit that we wish to know about the affairs of those whom we mentioned before, not out of mere importunate curiosity—since we tell you of our affairs as among brothers, sharing with each other the facts of [these] divisions, so that the beginning of this letter of mine may be indeed correct—for I said as I began this letter that we ought to enjoy brotherly converse with each other.

I and those who are with me greet all the brotherhood in Christ which is with you.

[5] *Ipso verbo deificationis.*

[6] *Virginem Christotocon ausi sunt cum deo quodam modo tractare divine*—doubtless, as Loofs suggests, representing *syntheologein*, "to include the Virgin in the topic of *theologia*." [7] Cf. Luke 1:31; John 2:1; Acts 1:14.

[8] *Illa in homine visio*; cf. n. 4 above.

[9] As represented by the translator, Nestorius shifts rather confusingly from the official plural to a more informal singular.

# (B) THE THIRD LETTER OF CYRIL TO NESTORIUS

## INTRODUCTION

In the fall of 430, Cyril, writing in the name of the Egyptian Synod, launched his final challenge to Nestorius; speaking also for Celestine and his Synod at Rome, he calls on Nestorius to retract his teaching, and instructs him in what he must believe about the unity of the Word with his own flesh, and what he must anathematize. The anathemas unhappily became the main subject of controversy; Nestorius repudiated them point by point, and others then defended the anathemas or the replies. The letter was read and acted on at Ephesus; at the Council of Chalcedon it was recognized, along with the Tome of Leo, as an orthodox statement—though, as will be noted, not wholly free of ambiguities which Monophysites resolved in one way and Chalcedonians in anothers. The key passages are here translated as edited in Schwartz, *Acta conciliorum*[1]; full text and translation are given in Bindley, *Oecumenical Documents*, pp. 105–123, 212–219.[2]

The letter begins by summoning Nestorius to remove the scandal caused to the Church by his teaching. It is not enough for him to assert his loyalty to the Creed of Nicaea, since he has misinterpreted it; and so after quoting the original Nicene Creed, Cyril continues:

## THE TEXT

. . . Following in every respect the confessions of the holy Fathers, which they drew up as the Holy Spirit spoke in them,

[1] Vol. i, 1, 1, Berlin and Leipzig, 1927, pp. 33–42.
[2] Also translation by Henry R. Percival, *The Seven Ecumenical Councils*, in Library of Nicene and Post-Nicene Fathers, Series II, Vol. xiv, New York and Oxford, 1905, pp. 201–218.

and pursuing the track of their thoughts, and taking as it were the royal road, we say that the unique[3] Word of God himself, who was begotten of the very substance of the Father, who is true God of true God, the Light of Light, through whom all things came into being, both things in heaven and things in earth, coming down for the sake of our salvation, and humbling himself even to emptying,[4] was made flesh and became man. That is, taking flesh of the holy Virgin, and making it his own from the womb, he underwent a birth like ours, and came forth a man of woman, not throwing off what he was, but even though he became [man] by the assumption of flesh and blood, yet still remaining what he was, that is, God indeed in nature and truth. We do not say that the flesh was changed into the nature of Godhead, nor that the ineffable nature of the Word of God was transformed into the nature of flesh, for he is unchangeable and unalterable, always remaining the same according to the Scriptures. But when seen as a babe and wrapped in swaddling clothes, even when still in the bosom of the Virgin who bore him, he filled all creation as God, and was enthroned with him who begot him. For the Divine cannot be numbered or measured, and does not admit of circumscription.

So confessing the Word united hypostatically to flesh, we worship one Son and Lord Jesus Christ, neither putting apart and dividing man and God, as joined with each other by a union of dignity and authority—for this would be an empty phrase and no more—nor speaking of the Word of God separately as Christ, and then separately of him who was of a woman as another Christ, but knowing only one Christ, the Word of God the Father with his own flesh. For then he was anointed[5] in human wise like us, though he himself gives the Spirit to those who are worthy to receive it, and not by measure, as says the blessed Evangelist John.[6] Neither do we say that the Word of God tabernacled in him who was begotten of the holy Virgin as in an ordinary man—lest Christ should be thought of as a God-bearing man.[7] For though the Word did tabernacle among us, and it is said that in Christ dwelt all the fullness of the Godhead bodily,[8] yet we so conceive [of this] that when he

---

[3] *Monogenēs.*          [4] *Kenōsis,* as in Phil. 2:7.
[5] I.e., as man Christ received the Spirit whom as God he bestowed; the verb "anointed" is cognate with the noun *Christos,* and so specially relevant here.          [6] John 3:34.
[7] Cf. treatment of this phrase by Gregory of Nazianzus, Epistle 102 (p. 227).
[8] John 1:14; Col. 2:9.

was made flesh, we do not define the indwelling in him in precisely the same manner as that in which one speaks of an indwelling in the saints; but being united by nature and not changed into flesh, he effected such an indwelling as the soul of man might be said to have in its own body.

[There is] therefore one Christ and Son and Lord, not as if man were conjoined with God by a union of dignity or authority. For equality of honor does not unite the natures, and Peter and John, for instance, are of equal honor with each other, as both apostles and holy disciples, but the two are not [made] into one. Nor do we think of the mode of conjunction as by association, for this is not enough for a natural union; nor as by an acquired relation, as we, being joined to the Lord, as it is written, are one spirit with him.[9] Indeed we reject the term "conjunction," as not sufficiently indicating the union . . . [nor is the Word the God or Lord of Christ, since God the Word and his flesh are united in one *hypostasis* though as man he was under God and under the law].[10]

We refuse to say of Christ, "I adore him who was born for the sake of him who bore him, I worship him who was seen for the sake of the invisible," and it is horrible to say in addition to this, "He who was assumed is styled as God with him who assumed." He who says this divides him again into two Christs, and puts a man apart separately and God similarly. For he confessedly denies the union, according to which he is not worshiped as one [person] along with another, nor does he [merely] share the style of God. But one Christ Jesus is thought of, the unique Son, honored by one worship with his own flesh. And we confess that he who was begotten from God the Father as Son and God only-begotten,[11] though being by his own nature impassible, suffered in the flesh for us, according to the Scriptures, and he was in the crucified flesh impassibly making his own the sufferings of his own flesh. So by the grace of God he tasted death for everyone, giving up his own body to it, although by nature he was life, and was himself the resurrection. . . .[12]

9 I Cor. 6:17; "natural union," *henōsis physike*, a union of natures or in nature, is in Cyril's terminology interchangeable with "union by *hypostasis*," *kath' hypostasin*; in terminology at least this is the source of the Monophysite error, in which the humanity of Christ, however complete, is considered merely adjectival to his essential divine nature.
10 Gal. 4:4.
11 Cyril evidently knew the reading *monogenēs theos* in John 1:18 instead of *monogenēs huios*, "only-begotten Son."    12 Heb. 2:9; John 11:25.

We must necessarily add this: proclaiming the death in the flesh of the unique Son of God, that is, Jesus Christ, and confessing his return to life from the dead, and his reception into heaven, we celebrate the unbloody service in the churches.[13] So we approach to the mystical gifts [14] and are sanctified, becoming partakers of the holy flesh and the honorable blood of Christ the Saviour of us all, not receiving it as ordinary flesh —God forbid—nor as that of a man sanctified and conjoined with the Word by a unity of honor, or as one who had received a divine indwelling, but as truly life-giving and the Word's own flesh. For being by nature, as God, life, when he had become one with his own flesh, he made it life-giving. . . .

We do not divide the terms used in the Gospels of the Saviour as God or man between two *hypostases*, or Persons, for the one and only Christ is not twofold, though he is thought of as out of two, and as uniting different entities into the indivisible unity—as man is thought of as of body and soul, and yet not as twofold, but one out of both. . . . For if it is necessary to believe that, being God by nature, he became flesh, that is, man ensouled with a rational soul,[15] for what reason should some be embarrassed by some of his sayings that may be such as befit humanity? [16] . . . All the terms used in the Gospels are to be referred to one Person, the one incarnate *hypostasis* of the Word.[17] There is one Lord Jesus Christ, according to the Scriptures. . . .

Since the holy Virgin gave birth after the flesh to God who was united by *hypostasis* with flesh, therefore we say that she is *theotokos*, not as though the nature of the Word had the begin-

---

[13] Liturgical phrases from the Eucharistic Prayer—closer actually to the Byzantine Liturgies than to the Alexandrian forms one might expect Cyril to quote.

[14] *Eulogiai*, gifts of compliment or blessing, here of the sacramental gifts themselves. On the significance of the Eucharist in this controversy, cf. H. Chadwick, "Eucharist and Christology in the Nestorian Controversy," *Journal of Theological Studies*, new series, vol. ii, 1951, pp. 145–164.

[15] Note Cyril's definition of what he means by "flesh."

[16] "One can understand how the Synoptic data, which formed the firmest basis of the Antiochene Christology, to some extent presented themselves to the doctors of Alexandria as difficulties to be resolved" (J. Lebon, *Le Monophysisme Sévérien*, Louvain, 1909, p. 235).

[17] Cyril could equally say "one nature (*physis*) of the incarnate Word," since he avoids speaking of a duality of either *physis* or *hypostasis* in Christ; in this form the phrase, ultimately of Apollinarian origin (Pseudo-Athanasius, On the Incarnation of the Word of God, in Migne, *Patrologia Graeca*, Vol. 28, cols. 25–30), became a Monophysite slogan.

ning of its existence from flesh . . . [nor that the Word needed human birth, but that by accepting it he blessed the beginning of our existence, and removed the curse from it]. . . . For this cause we say that he also in his [earthly] dispensation blessed marriage itself, and went when he had been invited to Cana of Galilee with the holy apostles.[18]

We have learned to hold these things from the holy apostles and Evangelists and all the God-inspired Scripture, and by the true confession of the blessed Fathers. All these it is necessary for Your Reverence to accept and support without deceit; and what Your Reverence must anathematize is subjoined to this our letter:

1. If anyone does not confess that Emmanuel is God in truth, and therefore the holy Virgin is *theotokos*—for she bore in the flesh the Word of God become flesh—let him be anathema.

2. If anyone does not confess that the Word of God the Father was united by *hypostasis* to flesh and is one Christ with his own flesh, that is, the same both God and man together, let him be anathema.

3. If anyone divides the *hypostases* in the one Christ after the union, joining them only by a conjunction in dignity, or authority or power, and not rather by a coming together in a union by nature, let him be anathema.

4. If anyone distributes between two persons or *hypostases* the terms used in the evangelical and apostolic writings, whether spoken of Christ by the saints or by him about himself, and attaches some to a man thought of separately from the Word of God, and others as befitting God to the Word of God the Father alone, let him be anathema.

5. If anyone dares to say that Christ was a God-bearing man, and not rather God in truth, being by nature one Son, inasmuch as the Word became flesh, and is made partaker of blood and flesh precisely like us,[19] let him be anathema.

6. If anyone says that the Word of God the Father was the God or Master of Christ, and does not rather confess the same both God and man, the Word having become flesh according to the Scriptures, let him be anathema.

18 John 2:2.
19 John 1:14; Heb. 2:14; Nestorius here comes closest to directly countering Cyril's position: "If anyone dares to say that after the taking of manhood (*post assumptionem hominis*), the Son of God is one by nature, when he is also Emmanuel, let him be anathema" (the counteranathemas are preserved in the Latin version of Marius Mercator; ed. in Loofs, *Nestoriana*, pp. 211–217; with comments in Bindley, *Oecumenical Documents*, pp. 125–137; translation in Percival, *Seven Ecumenical Councils*, pp. 205–218).

7. If anyone says that Jesus was energized as a man by the Word from God, and clothed with the glory of the Only-begotten, as being another besides him, let him be anathema.

8. If anyone dares to say that the man who was assumed ought to be worshiped with God the Word and glorified with him, and with him styled God, as being one [being] in a different one—for the constantly added "with" forces one to think this—and does not rather honor Emmanuel with one veneration, and send up to him one doxology, inasmuch as the Word has become flesh, let him be anathema.

9. If anyone says that the one Lord Jesus Christ was glorified by the Spirit, as making use of an alien power that worked through him, and received from him the power to prevail over unclean spirits and to accomplish divine wonders among men, and does not rather say that it was his own Spirit, through whom also he worked the divine wonders, let him be anathema.

10. The divine Scripture speaks of Christ as the High Priest and Apostle of our confession, and [says that] he offered himself for us for an odor of sweet savor to his God and Father.[20] If anyone says that the Word of God himself did not become our High Priest and Apostle, when he became flesh and man for us, but as it were another [who was] separately from him man of woman—or if anyone says that he offered the offering for himself, and not rather for us alone, for he who knew no sin had no need of offering,[21] let him be anathema.

11. If anyone does not confess that the flesh of the Lord is life-giving, and the own [flesh] of the Word of God the Father, but as of another besides him, associated with him in dignity, or having received merely a divine indwelling—and not rather life-giving, as we said, because it became the own [flesh] of the Word who is able to give life to all things, let him be anathema.

12. If anyone does not confess that the Word of God suffered in the flesh and was crucified in the flesh and tasted death in the flesh, and became the first-born of the dead, although he is as God Life and life-giving, let him be anathema.

[20] Heb. 3:1; Eph. 5:2.          [21] Heb. 7:26–28.

# VII. THE FORMULA OF UNION OF 433

## INTRODUCTION

At Ephesus in 431 the bishops of the Roman "Orient," headed[7] by John of Antioch, had arrived late and held a rival council which supported Nestorius and deposed Cyril. But when Cyril's Council and its decisions against Nestorius were accepted by the emperor and the other great sees, the Oriental bishops gradually came around to acknowledging its practical actions —subject to an explanation in favor of the Antiochene doctrine of the distinct human nature of Christ which Nestorius had maintained. Bishop Paul of Emesa went to Alexandria with a formula drawn up at Antioch; he was accepted as an orthodox bishop and preached in Cyril's presence on Christmas Day. Early in the next year Cyril confirmed the reconciliation by this letter to John of Antioch, in which he accepts the Antiochene statement, though not quite making it his own—Antioch would still prefer to speak of the unconfused, Alexandria of the undivided, union of God and man, and Antioch still suspected Cyril of Apollinarian tendencies. As an effort at reconciling the two points of view, the Formula of Union is an important step towards the combination of the two in the Chalcedonian Decree.

Cyril's letter to John begins dramatically: "Let the heavens rejoice and the earth be glad, for the middle wall of partition is broken down,"[1] and then takes note of the happy visit of Paul of Emesa. The main section is here translated as edited by Schwartz.[2]

---

1 Ps. 96 (95):11; Eph. 2:14.
2 *Acta conciliorum*, Vol. i, 4, Berlin and Leipzig, 1928, pp. 15–20; text and translation also in Bindley, *Oecumenical Documents*, pp. 138–148, 220–223; translation in Percival, *Seven Ecumenical Councils*, pp. 251–253.

## THE TEXT

. . . That the division which arose between the Churches was entirely superfluous and unjustified, we are now thoroughly convinced, since my lord the most God-beloved bishop Paul has produced a paper containing an unimpeachable confession of the faith, and assures us that this was drawn up by Your Holiness and the most devout bishops there. The document is as follows, and it is incorporated word for word in this letter of ours:

"We must necessarily state briefly what we are convinced of and profess about the God-bearing Virgin, and the manner of the incarnation of the unique Son of God—not by way of addition but in the manner of a full statement, adding nothing at all to the Creed of the holy Fathers put forth at Nicaea. For, as we have just said, it is sufficient both for the whole knowledge of godliness and for the repudiation of all heretical false teaching. We speak, then, not as daring things impossible, but by the confession of our own weakness shutting out those who wish to reproach us in that we look into things that are beyond man.[3]

"We confess, then, our Lord Jesus Christ, the unique Son of God, perfect God and perfect man, of a reasonable soul and body; begotten of the Father before [the] ages according to the Godhead, the same in the last days for us and for our salvation [born] of Mary the Virgin according to the manhood; the same consubstantial with the Father in Godhead, and consubstantial with us in manhood, for a union of two natures took place; therefore we confess one Christ, one Son, one Lord. According to this understanding of the unconfused union we confess the holy Virgin to be *theotokos*, because God the Word was made flesh and lived as man, and from the very conception united to himself the temple[4] taken from her. As to the evangelical and apostolic phrases about the Lord, we know that theologians treat some in common, as of one person, and distinguish others, as of two natures, and interpret the God-befitting ones in connection with the Godhead of Christ, and the humble ones of the manhood."

---

[3] The Antiochenes seem to write somewhat ironically, picking up Cyril's line of strict loyalty to the Creed of Nicaea, while gently disclaiming any effort to explain all mysteries.

[4] "The temple of his body," John 2:21, a text which Nestorius had rather overworked.

On reading these holy phrases, and finding that we ourselves
are also thus convinced—for [there is] one Lord, one faith, one
baptism [5]—we glorified God the Saviour of all, rejoicing together that both our Churches and yours have a creed agreeing
with the God-inspired Scriptures and the tradition of our holy
Fathers. But since I learned that some of those who are accustomed to be fond of finding fault were buzzing around like
fierce wasps, and were spitting out evil words against me, as if
I said that the holy body of Christ came down from heaven
and was not of the holy Virgin, I thought it necessary to address
a few words to them about this. O fools, who know only how
to slander! How did you pervert your thinking so far, and fall
sick with such folly? For you must surely clearly understand
that almost all our fight for the faith was connected with our
declaring that the holy Virgin is *theotokos*. But if we say that
the holy body of Christ the Saviour of us all was from heaven
and not of her, how could she be thought of as *theotokos*? [6] For
whom indeed did she bear, if it is not true that she bore
Emmanuel after the flesh? . . . [the true birth is supported by
texts from Isa., ch. 7; Luke, ch. 1; and Matt., ch. 1]. But since
God the Word, who descended from above and from heaven,
emptied himself, taking the form of a servant, and is styled
Son of Man, while remaining what he is, that is, God—for
he is unchangeable and unalterable by nature—now being
thought of as one with his own flesh, he is said to come down
from heaven, and is called [the] man from heaven,[7] being
perfect in Godhead, and the same perfect in manhood, and
thought of as in one person—for [there is] one Lord Jesus
Christ, although the difference of the natures is not ignored,
out of which we say that the ineffable union was effected.

As to those who say that there was a mixture or confusion
or blending of God the Word with the flesh, let Your Holiness
stop their mouths. For some probably report this about me, as
though I had thought or said so. But I am so far away from
thinking thus that I think they are out of their minds who can
at all suppose that a shadow of turning [8] could occur in connection with the divine nature of the Word. For he ever remains
the same, and is not altered; nor indeed could he ever be
altered or subject to variation. In addition we all confess that
the Word of God is impassible, though in his all-wise dispensation

[5] Eph. 4:5.
[6] Cf. Gregory of Nazianzus on the same point, Epistle 101, pp. 216, 217.
[7] I Cor. 15:47.                        [8] James 1:17.

of the mystery, he is seen to attribute to himself the sufferings undergone by his own flesh. So the all-wise Peter spoke of Christ suffering for us in the flesh, and not in the nature of the ineffable Godhead. [9]

[Finally Cyril declares that he holds fast to the teaching of Athanasius and of the Fathers of Nicaea, and sends John a correct copy of Athanasius' Letter to Epictetus, since corrupt versions are in circulation.]

[9] I Peter 4:1.

# VIII. THE TOME OF LEO

### INTRODUCTION

Eutyches was condemned by the "visiting synod" of bishops who happened to be at Constantinople—a curious but recognized piece of Byzantine ecclesiastical machinery—on November 22, 448. On this occasion the actual phrase "two natures" was first authoritatively insisted on, which later enabled Dioscorus of Alexandria to attack Flavian for an unauthorized addition to the Creed. As the meeting broke up, Eutyches spoke of appealing to the synods of Rome, Alexandria, and Jerusalem; one bystander heard him say Thessalonica as well.[1] On hearing from Eutyches, Leo realized that what the abbot called Nestorianism was orthodoxy at Rome; but Flavian did not send him the official minutes until May. Though somewhat irked at the delay, Leo gave Flavian his full support in the Tome, which would, he hoped, end the controversy. But Theodosius II had already summoned the council which was to go down in history as the Robber Council, *Latrocinium*, of Ephesus.

Suppressed at Ephesus, the Tome was approved at Chalcedon, and is thus the one representative of Western theology in the official documents of the Ecumenical Councils. It is a fine specimen of the straightforwardness and clarity of the Latin mind—as also of the Western approach to the mysteries of Christianity from the facts of faith rather than the speculations of philosophy. Basically, the pope tells the old monk that he should go back and read his Bible. In some ways, Leo's assertion of the gospel of God and man in Christ stopped short where Greek speculation on the subject began. But essentially he had stated the common faith. Not unnaturally, the doctrine here

[1] E. Schwartz, *Acta conciliorum*, Vol. ii, 1, Berlin and Leipzig, 1933, p. 175.

stated is further expounded in Leo's sermons for the Christmas feast, which has commonly been more central in Western piety than in Eastern. Leo could cheerfully have sung Charles Wesley's Christmas hymn, or joined in the words of a seventeenth century poet:

"Welcome, all wonders in one sight!
Eternity shut in a span!
Summer in Winter, Day in Night!
Heaven in Earth, and God in Man!
Great little one! whose all-embracing birth,
Lifts Earth to Heaven, stoops Heaven to Earth!"[2]

The Tome is preserved in collections of the Acts of Chalcedon as well as in those of the Letters of Leo, of which it is No. 28 in modern editions. The first critical edition of the works of Leo was that of the Jansenist Quesnel in 1675. This unorthodox association led the learned Pope Benedict XIV to encourage the improved, and still standard, edition of the brothers Ballerini in 1753–1757. There are several translations, of which that by William Bright[3] seems to come closest to reproducing in English the effect of Leo's solemn but compressed Latin; Leo was a master of a majestic style, both influenced by and influencing the then young tradition of the Roman Liturgy. Bright's version is here reprinted with some changes in capitals and punctuation.

## The Text

Leo to his beloved brother Flavian:

1. Having read Your Affection's letter, the late arrival of which is matter of surprise to us, and having gone through the record of the proceedings of the bishops, we have now, at last, gained a clear view of the scandal which has risen up among you, against the integrity of the faith; and what at first seemed obscure has now been elucidated and explained. By this means Eutyches, who seemed to be deserving of honor

---

[2] Richard Crashaw, "In the Holy Nativity of Our Lord God," in *Carmen deo nostro*, Paris, 1652.

[3] *Select Sermons of St. Leo the Great on the Incarnation, with His Twenty-eighth Epistle, Called the Tome*, 2d ed., London, 1886, pp. 109–123; cf. also text in Schwartz, *Acta*, Vol. ii, 2, 1, pp. 24–33; translation by C. L. Feltoe in Nicene and Post-Nicene Fathers, Series II, Vol. xii, New York, 1895, pp. 38–43; text and translation in Bindley, *Oecumenical Documents*, pp. 159–180, 223–231.

under the title of presbyter,[4] is now known to be exceedingly
thoughtless and sadly inexperienced, so that to him may apply
what the prophet said, "He refused to understand that he
might act well; he meditated unrighteousness on his bed."[5]
What, indeed, is more unrighteous than to entertain ungodly
thoughts, and not to yield to persons wiser and more learned?
But into this folly do they fall who, when hindered by some
obscurity from knowing the truth, have recourse, not to the
words of the prophets, not to the letters of the apostles, nor to
the authority of the Gospels, but to themselves; and become
teachers of error, just because they have not been disciples of
the truth. For what learning has he received from the sacred
pages of the New and Old Testaments, who does not so much
as understand the very beginning of the Creed? And that which,
all the world over, is uttered by the voices of all applicants for
regeneration is still not apprehended by the mind of this aged
man.

2. If, then, he knew not what he ought to think about the
incarnation of the Word of God, and was not willing, for the
sake of obtaining the light of intelligence, to make laborious
search through the whole extent of the Holy Scriptures, he
should at least have received with heedful attention that general
confession common to all, whereby the whole body of the
faithful profess that they "believe in God the Father Almighty,
and in Jesus Christ his only Son our Lord, Who was born of
the Holy Spirit and the Virgin Mary." By which three clauses
the engines of almost all heretics are shattered. For when God
is believed to be both "Almighty" and "Father," it is found
that the Son is everlasting together with himself, differing in
nothing from the Father, because he was born as "God from
God," Almighty from Almighty, Coeternal from Eternal; not
later in time, not unlike him in glory, not divided from him in
essence; and the same only-begotten and everlasting Son of an
eternal Parent was "born of the Holy Ghost and the Virgin
Mary."[6] This birth in time in no way detracted from, in no
way added to, that divine and everlasting birth; but expended
itself wholly in the work of restoring man, who had been

---

4 With reference perhaps to the etymology of "presbyter"—Eutyches does
not display the discretion one would expect in an elder.
5 Ps. 36 (35): 3, 4.
6 Leo has quoted from both the Roman Symbol (Apostles' Creed) and the
Nicene formula, apparently considering them, not as two different
documents, but as two statements of the same faith.

deceived, so that it might both overcome death, and by its power "destroy the devil who had the power of death." [7] For we could not have overcome the author of sin and of death, unless he who could neither be contaminated by sin nor detained by death had taken upon himself our nature and made it his own. For, in fact, he was "conceived of the Holy Ghost" within the womb of a virgin mother, who bare him, as she had conceived him, without loss of virginity.

But if he [Eutyches] was not able to obtain a true conception from this pure fountain of Christian faith, because by his own blindness he had darkened the brightness of a truth so clear, he should have submitted himself to the evangelical teaching; and after reading what Matthew says, "The book of the generation of Jesus Christ, the son of David, the son of Abraham," [8] he should also have sought instruction from the apostolical preaching; and after reading in the Epistle to the Romans, "Paul, a servant of God, called an apostle, separated unto the gospel of God, which he had promised before by the prophets in the Holy Scriptures, concerning his Son, who was made unto him of the seed of David according to the flesh," [9] he should have bestowed some devout study on the pages of the prophets; and, finding that God's promise said to Abraham, "In thy seed shall all nations be blessed," [10] in order to avoid all doubt as to the proper meaning of this "seed," he should have attended to the apostle's words, "To Abraham and to his seed were the promises made. He saith not, 'and to seeds,' as in the case of many, but, as in the case of one, 'and to thy seed,' which is Christ." [11] He should also have apprehended with his inward ear the declaration of Isaiah, "Behold, a virgin shall conceive, and bear a son, and they shall call his name Emmanuel, which is, being interpreted, God with us"; and should have read with faith the words of the same prophet, "Unto us a child has been born, unto us a son has been given, whose power is on his shoulder; and they shall call his name Angel of Great Counsel, Wonderful, Counselor, Strong God, Prince of Peace, Father of the Age to Come." [12] And he should not have spoken idly to the effect that the Word was in such a sense made flesh, that the Christ who was brought forth from the Virgin's womb had the form of a man, but had not a body really derived from his mother's body.

7 Heb. 2:14.  
9 Rom. 1:1–3.  
11 Gal. 3:16.  

8 Matt. 1:1.  
10 Gen. 22:18.  
12 Isa. 7:14 (Matt. 1:23); 9:6.

Possibly his reason for thinking that our Lord Jesus Christ was not of our nature was this: that the angel who was sent to the blessed and ever-virgin Mary said, "The Holy Ghost shall come upon thee, and the power of the Highest shall over-shadow thee, and therefore also that holy thing which shall be born of thee shall be called Son of God" [13]; as if, because the Virgin's conception was caused by a divine act, therefore the flesh of him whom she conceived was not of the nature of her who conceived him. But we are not to understand that "genera-tion," peerlessly wonderful, and wonderfully peerless, in such a sense as that the newness of the mode of production did away with the proper character of the kind. For it was the Holy Ghost who gave fecundity to the Virgin, but it was from a body that a real body was derived; and "when Wisdom was building herself a house," "the Word was made flesh, and dwelt among us," [14] that is, in that flesh which he assumed from a human being, and which he animated with the spirit of rational life.

3. Accordingly, while the distinctness of both natures and substances is preserved, and both meet in one Person, lowliness is assumed by majesty, weakness by power, mortality by eternity; and in order to pay the debt of our condition, the inviolable nature has been united to the passible, so that, as the appropriate remedy for our ills, one and the same "Mediator between God and men, the man Christ Jesus," [15] might from one element be capable of dying, and from the other be in-capable. Therefore [16] in the entire and perfect nature of very Man was born very God, whole in what was his, whole in what was ours. (By "ours" we mean what the Creator formed in us at the beginning, and what he assumed in order to restore); for of that which the deceiver brought in, and man, thus deceived, admitted, there was not a trace in the Saviour; and the fact that he took on himself a share in our infirmities did not make him a partaker in our transgressions. He took on him "the form of a servant" without the defilement of sins, augment-ing what was human, not diminishing what was divine; because that "emptying of himself," [17] whereby the Invisible made him-self visible, and the Creator and Lord of all things willed to be

---

[13] Luke 1:35.  [14] Prov. 9:1; John 1:14.
[15] I Tim. 2:5, a favorite text of Augustine's (e.g., *Confessions*, x, 43).
[16] With an economy that many preachers will understand, Leo used this and the following two sentences in one of his Christmas sermons (xxii, 1); and the previous sentence is almost reproduced in Sermon xxi, 2.
[17] Phil. 2:7.

one among mortals, was a stooping down of compassion, not a failure of power. Accordingly, [18] the same who, remaining in the form of God, made man, was made Man in the form of a servant. For each of the natures retains its proper character without defect; and as the form of God does not take away the form of a servant, so the form of a servant does not impair the form of God. For since the devil was glorying in the fact that man, deceived by his craft, was bereft of divine gifts, and, being stripped of this endowment of immortality, had come under the grievous sentence of death, and that he himself, amid his miseries, had found a sort of consolation in having a transgressor as his companion, and that God, according to the requirements of the principle of justice, had changed his own resolution in regard to man, whom he had created in so high a position of honor, there was need of a dispensation of secret counsel, in order that the unchangeable God, whose will could not be deprived of its own benignity, should fulfill by a more secret mystery his original plan of loving-kindness towards us, and that man, who had been led into fault by the wicked subtlety of the devil, should not perish contrary to God's purpose.

4. Accordingly, [19] the Son of God, descending from his seat in heaven, yet not departing from the glory of the Father, enters this lower world, born after a new order, by a new mode of birth. After a new order, because he who in his own sphere is invisible became visible in ours; he who could not be enclosed in space willed to be enclosed; continuing to be before times, he began to exist in time; the Lord of the universe allowed his infinite majesty to be overshadowed, and took upon him the form of a servant: the impassible God did not disdain to become passible, and the immortal one to be subject to the laws of death. And born by a new mode of birth, because inviolate virginity, while ignorant of concupiscence, supplied the matter of his flesh. What was assumed from the Lord's mother was nature, not fault; and the fact that the nativity of our Lord Jesus Christ is wonderful, in that he was born of a virgin's womb, does not imply that his nature is unlike ours. For the selfsame who is very God is also very Man: and there is no illusion in this union, while the lowliness of man and the loftiness of Godhead meet together. For as "God" is not changed

[18] This and the following sentence appear in Sermon xxiii, 2; Bright uses "accordingly" for several Latin connectives—*ergo, igitur, proinde*.
[19] This and the following sentence appear in Sermon xxii, 2.

by the compassion [exhibited], so "Man" is not consumed by the dignity [bestowed]. For each "form" does the acts which belong to it, in communion with the other; the Word, that is, performing what belongs to the Word, and the flesh carrying out what belongs to the flesh. The one of these shines out in miracles; the other succumbs to injuries.

And as the Word does not withdraw from equality with the Father in glory, so the flesh does not abandon the nature of our kind. For, as we must often be saying, he is one and the same, truly Son of God, and truly Son of Man: God, inasmuch as "in the beginning was the Word, and the Word was with God, and the Word was God"; Man, inasmuch as "the Word was made flesh, and dwelt among us." God, inasmuch as "all things were made by him, and without him nothing was made"; Man, inasmuch as he was "made of a woman, made under the law." 20 The nativity of the flesh is a manifestation of human nature: the Virgin's child-bearing is an indication of divine power. The infancy of the babe is exhibited by the humiliation of swaddling clothes; the greatness of the highest is declared by the voices of angels. He whom Herod impiously designs to slay is like humanity in its beginnings; but he whom the Magi rejoice to adore on their knees is Lord of all. Now when he came to the baptism of John his forerunner, lest the fact that the Godhead was covered with a veil of flesh should be concealed, the voice of the Father spoke in thunder from heaven, "This is my beloved son, in whom I am well pleased." 21 Accordingly, he who, as man, is tempted by the devil's subtlety is the same to whom, as God, angels pay duteous service.22 To hunger, to thirst, to be weary, and to sleep is evidently human. But to feed five thousand men with five loaves, and to bestow on the woman of Samaria that living water, to drink of which can secure one from thirsting again; to walk on the surface of the sea with feet that sink not, and by rebuking the storm to bring down the "uplifted waves," is unquestionably divine.23 As then—to pass by many points—it does not belong to the same nature to weep with feelings of pity over a dead friend and, after the mass of stone had been removed from the grave where he had lain four days, by a voice of command to raise him up to life again; or to hang on the wood and to make all the elements tremble after daylight had been turned into

20 John 1:1, 3, 14; Gal. 4:4.     21 Matt. 3:17.
22 Matt. 4:11; Mark 1:13.
23 Ps. 93 (92):3, 4; Matt. 8:26 (Mark 4:39; Luke 8:24, 25).

night; or to be transfixed with nails and to open the gates of paradise to the faith of the robber, so it does not belong to the same nature to say, "I and the Father are one," and to say, "The Father is greater than I." [24] For although in the Lord Jesus Christ there is one Person of God and man, yet that whereby contumely attaches to both is one thing, and that whereby glory attaches to both is another: for from what belongs to us he has that manhood which is inferior to the Father; while from the Father he has equal Godhead with the Father.

5. Accordingly, on account of this unity which is to be understood as existing in both the natures, we read, on the one hand, that "the Son of Man came down from heaven," [25] inasmuch as the Son of God took flesh from that Virgin of whom he was born; and, on the other hand, the Son of God is said to have been crucified and buried, inasmuch as he underwent this, not in his actual Godhead, wherein the Only-begotten is coeternal and consubstantial with the Father, but in the weakness of human nature. Wherefore we all, in the very Creed, confess that "the only-begotten Son of God was crucified and buried," according to that saying of the apostle, "For if they had known it, they would not have crucified the Lord of majesty." [26] And when our Lord and Saviour himself was by his questions instructing the faith of the disciples, he said, "Who do men say that I the Son of Man am?" And when they had mentioned various opinions held by others, he said, "But who say ye that I am?" that is, "I who am Son of Man, and whom you see in the form of a servant, and in reality of flesh, who say ye that I am?" Whereupon the blessed Peter, as inspired by God, and about to benefit all nations by his confession, said, "Thou art the Christ, the Son of the living God." [27] Not undeservedly, therefore, was he pronounced blessed by the Lord, and derived from the original Rock that solidity which belonged both to his virtue and to his name, who through revelation from the Father confessed the selfsame to be both the Son of God and the Christ; because one of these truths, accepted without the other, would not profit unto salvation, and it was equally dangerous to believe the Lord Jesus Christ to be merely God and not man or merely man and not God.

[24] John 10:30; 14:28; cf. the similar passage in Gregory of Nazianzus, Third Theological Oration, 17–20, pp. 171–175.
[25] John 3:13.                           [26] I Cor. 2:8.
[27] Matt. 16:13–19; Peter derives his solidity from Christ the original rock (*petra principalis*)—cf. I Cor. 10:4.

But after the resurrection of the Lord—which was in truth the resurrection of a real body, for no other person was raised again than he who had been crucified and had died—what else was accomplished during that interval of forty days than to make our faith entire and clear of all darkness? For a while he conversed with his disciples, and dwelt with them, and ate with them, and allowed himself to be handled with careful and inquisitive touch by those who were under the influence of doubt; and this was his purpose in entering in to them when the doors were shut, and by his breath giving them the Holy Ghost and opening the secrets of Holy Scripture after bestowing on them the light of intelligence, and again in his selfsame person showing to them the wound in the side, the prints of the nails, and all the fresh tokens of the Passion, saying, "Behold my hands and feet, that it is I myself; handle me and see, for a spirit hath not flesh and bones, as ye see me have" [28]; that the properties of the divine and the human nature might be acknowledged to remain in him without causing a division, and that we might in such sort know that the Word is not what the flesh is as to confess that the one Son of God is both Word and flesh.

On which mystery of the faith this Eutyches must be regarded as unhappily having no hold whatever; for he has not acknowledged our nature to exist in the only-begotten Son of God, by way either of the lowliness of mortality or of the glory of resurrection. Nor has he been overawed by the declaration of the blessed Apostle and Evangelist John, saying, "Every spirit that confesseth that Jesus Christ has come in the flesh is of God, and every spirit which dissolveth Jesus is not of God, and this is Antichrist." [29] Now what is to dissolve Jesus, but to separate the human nature from him, and to make void by shameless inventions that mystery by which alone we have been saved? Moreover, seeing he is blind as to the nature of Christ's body, he must needs be involved in the like senseless blindness with regard to his Passion also. For if he does not think the Lord's crucifixion to be unreal, and does not doubt that he really accepted suffering, even unto death, for the sake of the world's salvation; as he believes in his death, let him acknowledge his flesh also, and not doubt that he whom he recognizes as having been capable of suffering is also man with a body like ours; since to deny his true flesh is also to deny his bodily sufferings.

[28] Luke 24:39.     [29] I John 4:2, 3.

If, then, he accepts the Christian faith, and does not turn away his ear from the preaching of the gospel, let him see what nature it was that was transfixed with nails and hung on the wood of the cross; and let him understand whence it was that, after the side of the crucified had been pierced by the soldier's spear, blood and water flowed out, that the Church of God might be refreshed both with the Laver and with the Cup.[30] Let him listen also to the blessed apostle Peter when he declares that "sanctification by the Spirit" takes place through the "sprinkling of the blood of Christ": and let him not give a mere cursory reading to the words of the same apostle, "Knowing that ye were not redeemed with corruptible things, as silver and gold, from your vain way of life received by tradition from your fathers, but with the precious blood of Jesus Christ, as of a lamb without blemish and without spot."[31] Let him also not resist the testimony of blessed John the apostle, "And the blood of Jesus the Son of God cleanseth us from all sin." And again: "This is the victory which overcometh the world, even our faith"; and: "Who is he that overcometh the world, but he that believeth that Jesus is the Son of God? This is he that came by water and blood, even Jesus Christ; not by water only, but by water and blood; and it is the Spirit that beareth witness, because the Spirit is truth. . . . For there are three that bear witness, the spirit, the water, and the blood; and the three are one."[32] That is, the Spirit of sanctification, and the blood of redemption, and the water of baptism; which three things are one, and remain undivided, and not one of them is disjoined from connection with the others: because the Catholic Church lives and advances in this faith, that in Christ Jesus we must believe neither manhood to exist without true Godhead, nor Godhead without true manhood.

6. But when Eutyches, on being questioned in your examination of him, answered, "I confess that our Lord was of two natures before the union, but after the union I confess one nature," I am astonished that so absurd and perverse a profession as this of his was not rebuked by a censure on the part of any of his judges, and that an utterance extremely foolish and extremely blasphemous was passed over, just as if nothing had been heard which could give offense: seeing that it is as impious to say that the only-begotten Son of God was of two

[30] John 19:34, interpreted of the water of Baptism and the cup of the Eucharist, at least primarily.
[31] I Peter 1:2, 18, 19.          [32] I John 1:7; 5:5, 6, 8.

natures before the incarnation as it is shocking to affirm that, since the Word became flesh, there has been in him one nature only. But lest Eutyches should think that what he said was correct, or was tolerable, because it was not confuted by any assertion of yours, we exhort your earnest solicitude, dearly beloved brother, to see that, if by God's merciful inspiration the case should be brought to a satisfactory issue, this inconsiderate and inexperienced man be cleansed also from this pestilent notion of his; seeing that, as the record of the proceedings shows, he had fairly begun to abandon his own opinions, when, on being driven into a corner by authoritative words of yours, he professed himself ready to say what he had not said before, and to give his adhesion to that faith from which he had previously stood aloof. But when he would not consent to anathematize the impious dogma, you understood, brother, that he continued in his own misbelief, and deserved to receive sentence of condemnation.[33]

For which if he grieves sincerely and to good purpose, and understands, even though too late, how properly the episcopal authority has been put in motion, or if, in order to make full satisfaction, he shall condemn viva voce, and under his own hand, all that he has held amiss, no compassion, to whatever extent, which can be shown him, will be worthy of blame; for our Lord, the true and good Shepherd, who laid down his life for his sheep, and who came to save men's souls and not to destroy them,[34] wills us to imitate his own loving-kindness, so that justice should indeed constrain those who sin, but mercy should not reject those who are converted. For then indeed is true faith defended with the best results, when a false opinion is condemned even by those who have followed it. But in order that the whole matter may be piously and faithfully carried out, we have appointed our brethren, Julius, bishop, and Renatus, presbyter, and also my son Hilarus, deacon, to represent us[35];

---

[33] Eutyches admitted, contrary to his previous teaching, that Christ was, as man, consubstantial with us, but refused to abandon his confession of one nature after the union, and so was deposed (Acts of November 22, 448, in Schwartz, *Acta*, Vol. ii, 1, pp. 142–145). Leo seems first to blame Flavian for not having argued the point, and then admits it might have been useless.

[34] John 10:15; Luke 9:56.

[35] Of the legates thus appointed, Renatus died on his way to the East, and Julius, bishop of Puteoli, took no prominent part in the Robber Council. Hilary's Latin *contradicitur* stands out startlingly in the Greek of the record of the condemnation of Flavian on August 8. (Schwartz,

C.L.F.—24

and with them we have associated Dulcitius, our notary, of whose fidelity we have had good proof; trusting that the divine assistance will be with you, that he who has gone astray may be saved by condemning his own unsound opinion.

May God keep you in good health, dearly beloved brother. Given on the ides of June, in the consulate of the illustrious men Asturius and Protogenes.[36]

*Acta*, Vol. ii, 1, p. 191.) He escaped from Ephesus with some difficulty and years afterward when he had succeeded Leo as bishop erected a chapel in thanksgiving at the Lateran Basilica.

[36] June 13, 449.

# IX. THE CHALCEDONIAN DECREE

## INTRODUCTION

At its second session, on October 10, 451, the Council of Chalcedon approved a series of documents as statements of orthodox teaching—the Creeds of Nicaea and Constantinople; Cyril's Second Letter to Nestorius, which stated his position less combatively than the Third; his Letter to John of Antioch; and the Tome. In the fourth session, October 17, the Council discussed the Tome and approved it more thoroughly; at the fifth, on October 22, it produced its own definition. In spite of considerable Eastern reluctance at accepting the key phrase, "In two natures," it was finally included.[1]

The actual drafting was carried through by a committee, and the document thus produced shows some of the cumbersomeness likely to occur in committee work. It succeeds remarkably, however, in saying what its authors wanted to say and no more. It first reaffirms the Creeds of Nicaea[2] and Constantinople. The former is to "shine forth," the latter to be in force, which seems to describe the actual usage of the Church ever since—the Creed of Nicaea is honored, but that of Constantinople is the actual "Nicene Creed" of worship and teaching. The text here given is the first official text of the Creed of Constantinople, and is that still used in the Eastern Orthodox Church.

[1] Text in Schwartz, *Acta*, Vol. ii, 1, pp. 322–326; with translation in Bindley, *Oecumenical Documents*, pp. 183–199, 232–235; translation by Percival in Nicene and Post-Nicene Fathers, Series II, Vol. xiv, New York, 1905, pp. 262–265.

[2] Many manuscripts give the Nicene Creed here in an enlarged form, adding many but not all of the additional phrases of Constantinople; but Schwartz is probably correct in rejecting these additions from the text.

371

## THE TEXT

The Symbol of the One Hundred and Fifty at Constantinople:

We believe in one God, Father Almighty, maker of heaven and earth, and of all things visible and invisible,

And in one Lord Jesus Christ, the unique Son of God, begotten of the Father before all the ages, Light of Light, true God of true God, begotten, not made, of one substance with the Father, through whom all things came into being; who for us men and for our salvation came down from heaven, and was incarnate of [the] Holy Spirit and Mary the Virgin, and became man; he was crucified also for us under Pontius Pilate, and suffered, and was buried, and rose again on the third day according to the Scriptures; and ascended into heaven, and sits on the right hand of the Father, and is coming again with glory to judge living and dead; of whose Kingdom there will be no end.

And in the Holy Spirit, the Lord, and the Life-giver, who proceeds from the Father, who with the Father and the Son is worshiped and glorified, who spoke through the prophets—[and] in one Holy Catholic and Apostolic Church; we confess one Baptism for the remission of sins. We look for the resurrection of the dead, and the life of the age to come. Amen.[3]

[The Nicene Creed should have been enough, the decree continues, but the Fathers of Constantinople found it necessary to clarify the teaching on the Holy Spirit. Now that others either confuse or divide the Person of Christ, the Council has received as standards of orthodoxy the Synodical Letters of Cyril to Nestorius and the Easterns and the Letter of Leo to Flavian, that is, the Tome. Finally it proceeds to its own definition.]

For [the Council] opposes those who try to divide the mystery of the dispensation[4] into a dyad of Sons; and those

[3] The additions to the Creed in Western use may be noted here; both Latin and English versions retain the Nicene phrase "God of God" before "Light of Light"; the addition of the *filioque* ("and from the Son") after "proceeds from the Father" was made almost casually in Spain at the reconciliation of the Spanish Arians in 589, later spread, and since the ninth century has been considered in the East to mark an error in doctrine as well as an unauthorized addition. The omission of "Holy" before "Catholic" in *The Book of Common Prayer* seems to be a mistake of Cranmer's editing.

[4] A phrase suggested by Eph. 1:9, 10; the "dispensation" (*oikonomia*) is so often used with reference to the incarnation as practically to become a term for it.

who dare to say that the Godhead of the only-begotten is passible it expels away from the company of the priests; and it resists those who think of a mixture or confusion of the two natures of Christ; and it drives away those who fancy that the form of a servant[5] which he took of us was of a heavenly or some other substance; and those who imagine two natures of the Lord before the union but invent one after the union it anathematizes.[6]

Following therefore the holy Fathers, we confess one and the same our Lord Jesus Christ, and we all teach harmoniously [that he is] the same perfect in Godhead, the same perfect in manhood, truly God and truly man, the same of a reasonable soul and body; consubstantial with the Father in Godhead, and the same consubstantial with us in manhood, like us in all things except sin; begotten before ages of the Father in God-head, the same in the last days for us; and for our salvation [born] of Mary the virgin *theotokos* in manhood, one and the same Christ, Son, Lord, unique; acknowledged in two natures[7] without confusion, without change, without division, without separation—the difference of the natures being by no means taken away because of the union, but rather the distinctive character of each nature being preserved, and [each] combining in one Person and *hypostasis*—not divided or separated into two Persons, but one and the same Son and only-begotten God, Word, Lord Jesus Christ; as the prophets of old and the Lord Jesus Christ himself taught us about him, and the symbol of the Fathers has handed down to us.

Since we have determined these things with all possible accuracy and care, the holy and ecumenical Council has decreed that no one shall be allowed to bring forward another Creed,[8] nor to compose or produce or think out or teach [such] to others. But those who dare either to compose another Creed, or propound, or teach, or deliver another Symbol to those who

[5] Phil. 2:7.

[6] Strictly, "one nature" and "two natures" as dogmatic terms were both new in 448.

[7] The correct reading is "in," though older texts of the Acts often have "of" (*ek*); of the four following phrases, adverbs in Greek, the first two assert the permanence and the last two the inseparability of the two natures of Christ. In Greek, *monogenēs* still does not precisely mean "only-begotten," though it implies it and is recognized as equivalent to the Latin *unigenitus*; in the Greek version of the Tome of Leo, however, it also translates *unicus*.

[8] Different, that is, from the Creed of Nicaea as revised at Constantinople and interpreted at Chalcedon.

wish to turn to the knowledge of the truth from paganism or Judaism, or from any kind of heresy [9]—if they are bishops or clerics, the bishops shall be expelled from the episcopate, the clerics from the clergy; if they are monks or laymen, they shall be anathematized.

[9] In the ancient catechumenate the *traditio symboli,* or delivery of the Creed to converts, both as a sacred formula and as a scheme of instruction, was an important part of preparation for Baptism.

# X. EXTRACTS FROM LEONTIUS OF BYZANTIUM

## INTRODUCTION

The monk Leontius of Byzantium—*c*. 490–544—fell short of the highest distinction in his own day, though he was not without influence. He was probably one of the "Scythian monks" whose formula, "one of the Trinity suffered in the flesh," was rejected when Rome and Constantinople were reunited in 519, but afterwards approved by the Fifth Ecumenical Council. Later he emerged from his monastic retreat at Constantinople or Jerusalem to take part in several theological discussions of importance, including a formal conference between Chalcedonians and Monophysites in 533. He endeavors to balance the emphasis of Leo and Chalcedon on distinctness by a further exploration of the unity of Christ. His work left its mark on later Greek and so on Western theology, but his writings were long neglected or confused with those of others until modern studies re-established his importance.[1] His chief work, Three Books Against the Nestorians and Eutychians, was finally published by Cardinal Mai in 1844.[2]

The following extracts from it illustrate Leontius' handling of the problem of the kind of unity possible between God and man. Aristotelian terms and distinctions were coming back into use in the sixth century; on such a basis Monophysites advanced the argument that nothing can exist without a center of being, *hypostasis*—hence, if there is only one *hypostasis* in Christ, there

[1] Cf. Friedrich Loofs, *Leontius von Byzanz* (Texte und Untersuchungen, Vol. iii, 1–2), Leipzig, 1888; H. M. Relton, *A Study in Christology*, London, 1917, pp. 69–83; summary of studies in O. Bardenhewer, *Geschichte der altkirchlichen Literatur*, Vol. v, Freiburg, Herder, 1932, pp. 9–13.

[2] *Spicilegium Romanum*, Vol. x, 2, Rome, 1844, pp. 1–127, reprinted in Migne, *Patrologia Graeca*, Vol. 86, 1, Paris, 1865, cols. 1267–1394.

can be only one nature.[3] Leontius' reply is that the humanity of Christ is neither "uncentered," *anupostatos*—"impersonal" is a misleading translation—nor self-centered, but "encentered" *enupostatos*. in God. One might compare Paul Tillich's description of the Christian man as neither autonomous nor heteronomous but theonomous.[4] On the different kinds of unity Leontius comments:

## THE TEXT

Of those things which exist substantially and are united in substance,[5] some even in union preserve the proper character of their existence, while others are mixed together and injured so as to destroy the precise identity of the things united. The relation of things of the first kind, when observed with each other and in each other, produces one thing out of the two, and, as one might say, shows it to be one in number, still preserving the difference of being [existence] in the identity of the union. An example of this among living beings is our humanity, and among simple or natural objects the kind of relation to each other of things which have their own *hypostasis* and can exist by themselves. Such can be seen in the case of a torch; for the stock is one thing and the flamy nature of fire is another, but when they exist with each other and in each other, they make both into one torch. And as one might say, forcing it a little, fire is made wooden and wood fiery, the one sharing in the brightness of the fire, the other the earthy heaviness found in the firebrand, and each exchanges qualities with the other, while remaining in its own and unmixed identity.[6] . . .

Having distinguished these points, we must note that things which are exchanged with each other and transformed, being constituted out of different forms and substances, retain nothing unmixed after the composition of the things involved in the composition. But mixing and confusing the peculiar properties of all, all of them together, it has produced another mixed-up form, and there has been a jumbling and confusion

[3] And some of their more erratically consistent thinkers went further and agreed that three *hypostases* in the Trinity meant three divinities.
[4] Cf. Paul Tillich, *Systematic Theology* Chicago (University Press), 1951, pp. 85, 86, 147–150.    [5] Or, "According to essence," *kat' ousian*.
[6] Migne, *Patrologia Graeca*, Vol. 86, 1, col. 1304; the analogy is drawn out to parallel the "exchange of properties" (*communicatio idiomatum*) in Christ, by which one may say that God shed his own blood (Acts 20:28), or "the Son of Man came down from heaven" (John 3:13), etc.

in the mixture of many *hypostases* and natures, preserving neither the individuality of the *hypostasis* nor the common quality of the nature, but producing something else which has come into being out of these, yet is not the same as any of its constituent parts. So then if Godhead and manhood, when united in substance, do not retain even in the union the natural property of each, they are mixed together, and there remains neither Godhead nor manhood, but another kind of substance has been produced, formed out of them and yet not the same. What could be more impious or abominable than even to conceive of this, not to speak of affirming it and teaching it as a dogma? It remains, then, that from this examination of the character of substantial union, we should grasp the unmixed [respective] identity of deity and humanity, according to the previous examples, gathering a faint image from all these things of the truth which is above all things, which shows that one entity is produced out of these, of which I do not care whether you call it Person or *hypostasis* or indivisible being or substratum, or anything else you may prefer. For the argument has now beaten and put to flight those who separate [them] in their relationship [speaking] of dignity or authority or some other relation of divided things, showing that they divide the natures into separate *hypostases*, and [such natures] can have no real fellowship or share in an exchange [of qualities].[7] . . .

[A later passage comments significantly on the relation of nature to supernature, as of man to indwelling deity:]

And let us not pass it over unnoticed, that three causes may be observed from which every [kind of] energy is produced. One is from natural force, another from a corrupt state contrary to nature, and the other is observed to be a kind of advance or progress towards the better. These are and are called natural, unnatural, and supernatural respectively. The unnatural, as the name indicates, being a certain falling away of natural states and powers, injures the substance itself and its natural energies. The natural is produced from the unimpeded [natural] cause operating precisely according to nature. But the supernatural raises and elevates, and gives power for more perfect things, and such as could not be done while remaining in the natural [alone]. The supernatural does not destroy the natural [forces], but leads them on and impels them, so that they are both able to perform their own [functions], and also receive power for what is beyond them.[8]

[7] *Ibid.*, col. 1305.  [8] *Ibid.*, col. 1333.

# XI. THE ANATHEMAS OF THE SECOND COUNCIL OF CONSTANTINOPLE (FIFTH ECUMENICAL)

## INTRODUCTION

The Council of 553 was by no means such a simple victory for the imperial theologian as is often supposed. It does reflect the Cyrilline tradition in Eastern theology, for which the idea of God manifest in the flesh[1] was more congenial than the Leonine doctrine of two perfect natures. Monophysite ideas and even the favorite catchwords of the Monophysite party were thus given a place in the orthodox tradition; but even in the act of doing so, the Council of Constantinople protected the authority and the essential teaching of Chalcedon. Its decrees were thus ultimately acceptable to Rome and the West —and would not in any case have reconciled the Monophysites who at this stage did not want compromise but victory, and would have insisted on the repudiation of Chalcedon and the Tome of Leo.[2]

The ideas of the Council of Constantinople are most clearly stated in its anathemas, which are here translated from Mansi's great eighteenth century edition of the records of councils.[3] The plan of Schwartz's edition included this Council, but it has not been reached.

## THE TEXT

1. If anyone does not confess one nature or substance, one power and authority, of Father and Son and Holy Spirit, con-

1 I Tim. 3:16.
2 Cf. W. A. Wigram, *The Separation of the Monophysites*, London, 1923.
3 G. D. Mansi, *Sacrorum conciliorum nova et amplissima collectio*, Vol. ix, Florence, 1763, cols. 375–388. Text also in Bindley, *Oecumenical Documents*, pp. 153–156; translation in Percival, *Seven Ecumenical Councils*, pp. 312–316.

substantial Trinity, one Deity worshiped in three *hypostases* or persons, let him be anathema. For [there is] one God and Father, of whom are all things, and one Lord Jesus Christ, through whom are all things, and one Holy Spirit, in whom are all things.[4]

2. If anyone does not confess that there are the two generations of God the Word, one before ages of the Father, nontemporal and bodiless, the other at the last days when the same came down from heaven and was incarnate of the holy, glorious, *theotokos*, and ever-virgin Mary, and born of her, let him be anathema.

3. If anyone says that the Word of God who did wonders was one and Christ who suffered was another, or says that God the Word was together with Christ who came of woman, or was in him as one in another, but not [that he was] one and the same our Lord Jesus Christ, the Word of God incarnate and made man, and [that] the wonders and the sufferings, which he voluntarily endured in flesh, were of the same, let him be anathema.

4. If anyone says that the union of God the Word with man took place [merely] by grace or by energy, or by equality of honor, or by authority or ascription or relation or power, or by good pleasure—as of God the Word being pleased with the man, from his being well and truly satisfied with him, as Theodore insanely says [let him be anathema]—or [if he speaks of a union] by use of the same name, according to which the Nestorians, calling God the Word "Jesus" and "Christ," and naming the man separately "Christ" and "Son," and evidently speaking of two persons with one appellation and honor and dignity and worship, pretend to speak of one person and one Christ [5]—but does not confess that the union of God the Word with flesh ensouled with a reasonable and intellectual soul took place by composition, that is, by *hypostasis*,[6] as the holy Fathers taught—and because of this his *hypostasis* [is] one, namely, the Lord Jesus Christ, one of the holy Trinity—let him be anathema. For, thinking of the union in diverse ways,

4 Cf. Rom. 11:36.
5 On the ramifications of Nestorianism, which could in its own sense speak of either one *prosōpon* or two *prosōpa*, see L. Hodgson, "The Metaphysic of Nestorius," in *Nestorius, The Bazaar of Heracleides*, Oxford, 1925, pp. 411–420.
6 Or "according to synthesis" (*kata synthesin*) and "according to *hypostasis*" (*kath' hypostasin*); the actual phrase "hypostatic union" seems to be avoided in the ancient documents.

some, in accordance with the ungodliness of Apollinaris and Eutyches, assuming the disappearance of the components, affirm the union by confusion; while those who accept the ideas of Theodore and Nestorius, rejoicing in division, introduce the union of relation. But the holy Church of God, rejecting the impiety of each heresy, confesses the union of God the Word with the flesh by composition, that is by *hypostasis*. For the union by composition in the mystery about Christ not only preserves the components unconfused, but accepts no separation.

["5" reaffirms the ideas of "4," and "6" reasserts the propriety of the use of the term *theotokos*.]

7. If anyone who says "in two natures" does not confess that our one Lord Jesus Christ is made known in Godhead and manhood, in order that he may indicate the distinction of the natures, from which the ineffable union took place without confusion, neither the Word being changed into the nature of the flesh nor the flesh transferred into the nature of the Word —for each remains what it was by nature, even when the union by *hypostasis* has taken place—but takes the phrase with reference to division into parts in the mystery of Christ [let him be anathema]. Or .when [anyone] confessing the number of natures in the same our one Lord Jesus Christ, God the Word incarnate, does not take the distinction of the elements of which he was constituted, which was not taken away by the union, in contemplation only [7]—for [he is] one of both and both [are] through one—but uses the number as if he possessed separated natures with their own *hypostases*, let him be anathema.

8. If anyone who confesses that the union was effected out of two natures, deity and humanity, or speaks of one incarnate nature of God the Word,[8] does not so take these [terms], as the holy Fathers taught, that out of the divine nature and the human, when the union by *hypostasis* took place, one Christ was formed, but out of these phrases tries to introduce one nature or substance of the Godhead and flesh of Christ, let him

[7] Moderate Monophysites like Severus of Antioch were willing to admit that "in contemplation" (*theoria*) there were two natures in Christ, though opposed to describing him in any way by the number two (see J. Lebon, *Le Monophysisme Sévérien*, Louvain, 1909, pp. 345–369); this anathema admits the Severian proposition, but at once insists that, however "theoretical," the distinction of natures was real. This anathema, like no. 4, is complicated by the effort to do justice to both Alexandria and Antioch in one sentence.

[8] Similarly here the Monophysite phrases are admitted, but guarded by a Chalcedonian interpretation.

be anathema. For when saying that the unique [9] Word was united by *hypostasis*, we do not mean that there was any mixture of the natures with each other, but rather we think of the Word as united with flesh, each remaining what it is. Therefore Christ is one, God and man, the same consubstantial with the father in Godhead, and the same consubstantial with us in manhood. Equally therefore does the Church of God reject and anathematize those who divide into parts or cut up, and those who confuse the mystery of the divine dispensation of Christ.

9. If anyone says that Christ is to be worshiped in two natures, from which two adorations are introduced, one proper to God the Word and one to the man—or if anyone in terms of destruction of the flesh, or of confusion of the Godhead and the manhood, or strangely contriving one nature or substance of the components, so worships Christ—but does not with one adoration worship God the Word incarnate with his own flesh, as the Church of God has received from the beginning, let him be anathema.

10. If anyone does not confess that our Lord Jesus Christ who was crucified in flesh is true God and Lord of glory and one of the holy Trinity, [10] let him be anathema.

11. If anyone does not anathematize Arius, Eunomius, Macedonius, Apollinaris, Nestorius, Eutyches, and Origen, [11] with their godless writings, and all other heretics who were condemned and anathematized by the holy catholic and apostolic Church and the aforementioned holy four councils, [12] and those who have held or hold the like to the above-mentioned heretics, and remain till the end in their own impiety, let him be anathema.

[Finally "12" to "14" anathematize the "Three Chapters."]

---

9 *Monogenēs*.

10 The formula of the Scythian monks is thus recognized.

11 This casual and incidental condemnation of Origen is surprising and its authenticity has been doubted; however, Justinian was interested in securing a condemnation of Origen's more eccentric speculations, which reappeared from time to time in the more learned and sophisticated monastic circles, and probably did succeed in this incidental manner. Whether the specific anathemas against Origen ascribed to this Council are genuine is uncertain.

12 Referred to earlier in the Acts, and in the Council's formal statement condemning the "Three Chapters."

# XII. THE STATEMENT OF FAITH OF THE THIRD COUNCIL OF CONSTANTINOPLE (SIXTH ECUMENICAL)

## INTRODUCTION

Ancient Christology usually began from above, with the question, "How did the Son of God become man?" Modern Christology is more likely to begin from below, with the historical records, and ask, "How can we say that this man is God,[1] as Christian experience declares?" A sign of the coming shift to modern ways of thought is the interest of the Monothelete controversy in the concrete acting personality of Christ —his will and operation[2]—as well as in the more abstract categories of nature and substance. The doctrine it asserts is that in Christ as man everything is to be found that belongs to active humanity, perfected, not injured, by his perfect union with God. Historically it has a special interest for English-speaking Christians as the only ancient Ecumenical Council in which the English Church had some part. Pope Agatho's letter to the Council expresses regret that the Greek archbishop of Canterbury, Theodore of Tarsus, was unable to come as his representative. But Theodore had secured a statement from his provincial council on behalf of the doctrine of the two wills, and his unruly suffragan, Wilfrid, "humble bishop of the holy Church of York," took part in the preliminary council of Western bishops held at Rome in 680.[3] One may fairly list these actions as the first participation of English Christianity, led by the prelates of Canterbury and York, in ecumenical discussions.

[1] The phrase is used by Martin Luther, *De captivitate Babylonica*, section on the Lord's Supper.

[2] *Energeia*, or working—closer perhaps to our modern idea of specific human personality than any other term of this theological discussion.

[3] G. D. Mansi, *Sacrorum conciliorum . . . collectio*, Vol. xi, Florence, 1765, col. 305.

Whoever drafted the formal Statement of Faith adopted at Constantinople in 681 [4] emphasized in its very form that this Council wished to reassert the teaching of Chalcedon and develop its implications, as the Fifth Council had reaffirmed the teaching of Ephesus. It begins with a reassertion of the Creeds of Nicaea and Constantinople and the authority of the previous Ecumenical Councils, now five in number. The Creed should be enough, but the new error of one will and one operation has arisen, which must be met; against it Pope Agatho and his Council have written their letters, documents agreeing with the Council of Chalcedon and the Tome of Leo.[5]

## THE TEXT

Following the holy and ecumenical five councils, and the holy and approved Fathers, and unanimously defining that our Lord Jesus Christ, our true God, one of the holy and life-bestowing Trinity, is to be confessed perfect in Godhead and the same perfect in manhood . . . [the Chalcedonian definition is then repeated,[6] with the one additional phrase that Mary is called "genuinely and in truth *theotokos*"]. . . .

We also proclaim two natural willings or wills in him and two natural operations, without separation, without change, without partition, without confusion,[7] according to the teaching of the holy Fathers—and two natural wills not contrary [to each other], God forbid, as the impious heretics have said [they would be], but his human will following, and not resisting or opposing, but rather subject to his divine and all-powerful will. For it was proper for the will of the flesh to be moved [naturally], yet to be subject to the divine will, according to the all-wise Athanasius. For as his flesh is called and is the flesh of God the Word, so also the natural will of his flesh is called and is God the Word's own will, as he himself says: "I came down from heaven, not to do my own will, but the will of the Father who sent me," [8] calling the will of the flesh his own, as also the flesh had become his own. For in the same manner

4 *Ibid.*, cols. 631–640; on the Monothelete controversy generally, cf. George Every, *The Byzantine Patriarchate*, London (S.P.C.K.), 1947, Ch. v.
5 Mansi, Vol. xi, cols. 233–316; the letter of Agatho, though solid, is a heavy and ponderous document, scarcely worthy of being set beside the Tome.
6 See p. 373.
7 As at Chalcedon, there are four adverbs (one different) in the key statement, two stressing "the undivided" and two "the unconfused."
8 John 6:38.

that his all-holy and spotless ensouled flesh, though divinized, was not destroyed, but remained in its own law and principle, [9] so also his human will, divinized, was not destroyed, but rather preserved, as Gregory the divine says: "His will, as conceived of in his character as the Saviour, is not contrary to God, [being] wholly divinized." [10] We also glorify two natural operations in the same our Lord Jesus Christ, our true God, without separation, without change, without partition, without confusion, that is, a divine operation and a human operation, as the divine preacher Leo most clearly says: "For each form does what is proper to it, in communion with the other; the Word, that is, performing what belongs to the Word, and the flesh carrying out what belongs to the flesh." [11] We will not therefore grant [the existence of] one natural operation of God and the creature, lest we should either raise up into the divine nature what is created, or bring down the pre-eminence of the divine nature into the place suitable for things that are made. For we recognize the wonders and the sufferings as of one and the same [person], according to the difference [12] of the natures of which he is and in which he has his being, as the eloquent Cyril said. [13]

Preserving therefore in every way the unconfused and undivided, we set forth the whole [confession] in brief; believing our Lord Jesus Christ, our true God, to be one of the holy Trinity even after the taking of flesh, we declare that his two natures shine forth in his one *hypostasis*, in which he displayed both the wonders and the sufferings through the whole course of his dispensation, [14] not in phantasm but truly, [15] the difference of nature being recognized in the same one *hypostasis* by the fact that each nature wills and works what is proper to it, in communion with the other. On this principle we glorify two natural wills and operations combining with each other for the salvation of the human race.

---

[9] *Horos* and *logos*—boundary and rule.

[10] Fourth Theological Oration, 12, see p. 185; this is Gregory's general idea, though the quotation out of context is slightly confused.

[11] Tome, 4, see p. 365.

[12] *Kat' allo kai allo* (neuter)—a difference of two elements, but not of two persons, which would call for the masculine.

[13] Note the roll call of the theologians most conspicuously connected with each of the first four councils.

[14] I.e., his earthly life—literally, "His dispensatory conduct."

[15] A glance at the "phantasiasts" (see p. 34), whose ideas sometimes appeared even among Chalcedonians.

[The text now returns to that of Chalcedon and repeats the censure with which the Chalcedonian Decree closes, adding a condemnation of any who "introduce a new phraseology or turn of speech to overthrow what has now been defined by us."]

# INDEXES

## GENERAL INDEX

## Biblical References